Lives Illuminated

Book Two of *The Modern Salonnière* Series

Saxon Henry

SharktoothPress

Copyright © 2024 by Saxon Henry

All rights reserved worldwide.

No part of this book may be reproduced in any form or by any electronic or mechanical means, including information storage and retrieval systems, without written permission from the author, except for the use of brief quotations in a book review.

Lives Illuminated
Book Two in The Modern Salonnière Series
Published in the United States by Sharktooth Press
Kingston, New York USA
ISBN: 978-1-7353989-3-8

Library of Congress Control Number: 2024935723

www.sharktoothpress.com
Cover photo: Jean Goujon's sculpture the *Fountain of Diana* in the Louvre where Edith Wharton lured her lover at one o'clock one afternoon.
Image Copyright © Saxon Henry

10 9 8 7 6 5 4 3 2

ALSO BY SAXON HENRY

The Modern Salonnière

Stranded on the Road to Promise

Anywhere But Here

Four Florida Moderns

Collaborations: A Houston Penthouse

ACKNOWLEDGMENTS

This is my second ride with Lacey Howard as my editor and Gerard McLean of Sharktooth Press as my publisher: What a dream team these two collaborators are! I'd also like to thank my friends and family for listening to me blather on about these pieces I've been working on for well over three years now!

A NOTE TO MY READERS

Continuing in my quest to reinvigorate the stories of the past so that new audiences can discover them in a fresh light, I present you with this second book in *The Modern Salonnière* series. As I've written it, I've been reminded that if I ramble through the past long enough, famous personalities are inextricably woven together, and some associations are more surprising than others. In my reading for the essay about Johann Wolfgang von Goethe, his autobiography presented an event he attended that tied his story to Marie Antoinette's as he shared a detail about her handoff to the French that I'd never known, even after digesting so many books about the doomed queen. Marie Antoinette is also entwined with another Habsburg monarch's destiny as the great aunt of Marie Louise of Austria, Napoleon I's second wife. Following in the footsteps of her relative as she entered France, aspects of Marie Louise's story highlight what an ironic sense of humor the past can have.

Three seafaring events that served as the beginning of the end of her relationship with Napoleon bring this peculiarity

A NOTE TO MY READERS

into hyper focus, as you'll see in the essay "The Art of Capitulation." On April 20, 1814, Napoleon left Fontainebleau for his first exile, sailing in an English frigate named the HMS *Undaunted*, a designation that is so incredibly rich given he was once considered unbeatable. Less than a year later, the emperor escaped from the island of Elba with around five-hundred men aboard a ship emblazoned with the name the HMS *Inconstant*—a prophetic word given he sailed toward France for a stint in power that would be brief and would be his last gasp as an untrustworthy ruler. Then, on July 15, 1815, the emperor stepped onto the British ship the HMS *Bellerophon* to be ferried to his final exile. The epic name assigned to this frigate, which denotes the Greek hero who killed the Chimera monster, is a powerful omen in Napoleon's tale given the once-mythical brute was undertaking his final voyage to a tropical island in the South Atlantic Ocean. The conquered man would languish there for nearly six years before he died—the Emperor Chimera finally silenced by Bellerophon once and for all.

As you move around the U.S. and European maps with me, you'll see the warp and weft of other associations spring up: I'll leave them for you to discover as you go on a scavenger hunt that I hope will be an enjoyable adventure. I would also like to take a moment to thank those of you who reached out to me after reading the first book in *The Modern Salonnière* series because it means a great deal to know the pieces have value after I've labored for years to make each of them as whole as possible. My most romantic review came from renowned interior designer Michael Berman, who wrote from Africa, "I'm reading your book *The Modern Salonnière* as I sit on the veranda of our tent set up on the fringe of the Serengeti. I am only one-third through it and I greedily want to own every story for myself. Hildebrandt starlings are chirping, flies are buzz buzzing, the cool breeze is brushing my face and monkeys are playing on the canvas roof as I savor every word. Thank you so much. Your book is like a rich satisfying cup of rooibos tea and I just wanted to let you know." There are so many other heartening reactions for which I'm equally grateful. Now that *Illuminated Lives* is in your hands, I begin my first novel with a great deal of excitement (and a large dose of humility)! Thank you all for honoring my writing.

Saxon Henry

CONTENTS

1. Worthy of Applause *Giuditta Pasta in Lake Como*	1
2. A Force of Nature *Colette in Paris*	31
3. Where Serendipity Was Born *Horace Walpole at Strawberry Hill*	55
4. A River of Angst *Goethe in Frankfurt*	97
5. The House Where the Mind Ruled *Natalie Barney in Paris*	111
6. The Art of Capitulation *Marie-Louise of Austria in Parma*	137
7. How to Build a Better Husband *Edith Wharton in New Haven*	253
8. The Flower of Chivalry *King Charles V in Paris*	307
9. The Diminishing View of Madame Vitriol *Djuna Barnes on Patchin Place*	327
10. The Drawing-Room Diplomat *Consuelo Vanderbilt in Newport*	367
11. No One Gets off Scot-Free *The Fitzgeralds in Montgomery*	395
Notes	491
About Saxon Henry	517

1

WORTHY OF APPLAUSE

GIUDITTA PASTA IN LAKE COMO

As I stared across Lake Como to the hills that formed the opposite shore, I was absolutely captivated. The surface of the water mirrored the color of the slopes that plunge beneath its shallows, the apexes covered in wispy mists that echoed the raggedness of the clotted clouds. A long while passed before I could move away from the mesmerizing views framed by the windows in the tower of Villa Roccabruna. The eighteenth-century mansion, the most commanding building within the CastaDiva compound, once belonged to someone who was famous for a similar ability to fascinate. I had never heard Giuditta Pasta's name before being invited to the resort in 2010 so I knew nothing about her when I traveled to one of Italy's most gracious destinations. Having been so enthralled by the beauty that surrounded me while I was there, I vowed to change that. In getting to know the alluring woman, I learned that Giuditta was an Italian opera star popular during the early nineteenth century who had a way of infusing life with lyricism.

Now that I have learned so much about her, I will always

associate her life story with those conifer-covered peaks and the wind-ruffled water I admired for several days. Giuditta had achieved a significant level of success by the time she purchased the home, called Villa Ribier, in 1827. Once the property was hers, she set about refurbishing the mansion and renamed it Villa Roda. Her improvements included an entrance that resembled a colonnade at La Scala, as the Teatro alla Scala in Milan is widely known. The architectural addition paid homage to the famed theater in which she performed some of her most successful operas. Though my experience at the CastaDiva resort was not taking place in the same structure she enjoyed for many years—because in 1904 Villa Roccabruna replaced what had become a seriously run-down Villa Roda—my view of the water that laps the scalloped hem of the property was exactly the same. Equally as intriguing as the scene outside my window was a piece of local lore I learned from several Como natives soon after I arrived.

The story shared by my waiters one evening claims the lake brought Giuditta and composer Vincenzo Bellini together; that she became one of his muses when her voice drifted across the water to where he was staying in a beautiful mansion called Villa Passalacqua on the opposite shore. The fable claimed Bellini was so obsessed with finding the woman he heard singing, he rowed across the lake to find her; that once they were acquainted, she would light a candle and put it in a window facing the water to let him know when she had arrived. Looking at the photograph of the opposing hillside I'd taken during my visit, I marveled that her voice could have been powerful enough to reach the mansion in which Bellini was staying if the story was true. Villa Passalacqua is the most prominent building on the slope, its stucco-slathered stone exterior gleaming like a pale-yellow gem that day in spite of the muted light created by the dense cloud cover. Giuditta's home was on a point that juts out into the lake, narrowing the distance to the opposite shore. *Sound does carry over water,* I thought, *and the few recordings of her that exist demonstrate she had a commanding voice.*

It was then I realized proving whether the romantic tale was true or not was of little importance because the myth had already inspired me to take a deep dive into the entwined stories of a composer and his favorite soprano. How Bellini met Giuditta isn't explicitly fleshed out. In his biography of the composer, Herbert Weinstock claimed Bellini had possibly heard her sing at the Teatro San Carlo in Naples sometime between November 1826 and April 1827 as the opera season was in full swing, and he claimed they had become acquainted by the middle of 1828. In his thorough examination of Giuditta's life, Kenneth Stern agreed that Bellini first saw Giuditta on stage in Naples during her 1826-27 season, but he could only say that by November of 1828, their relationship was established. It was during the summer of 1830 when Bellini recorded proof that the lake had become a commanding character in their collaboration as he composed three operas—*La sonnambula, Norma,* and *Beatrice di Tenda*—as leading roles for Giuditta.

BEFORE WE JOIN them on Lake Como's facing shores, a backward glance is necessary to paint a fuller picture of the celebrities and their lives. Giuditta had been on the stage for twelve years by the time she purchased Villa Ribier. She entered the conservatory in Milan at the age of fifteen in 1812 and made her debut several years later. The soprano looked back on that time seventeen years after the fact during a conversation she had with Lady Sydney Morgan, a music lover and Italophile who would come to know the opera singer well. In her diaries, Morgan quoted Giuditta as saying, "I was a petite demoiselle, playing and singing in the amateur theater in Milan. [Giuseppe] Pasta and I played the Prince and Princess di Jovati, fell in love, and married."[1] Giuseppe was a fledgling tenor and an assistant *maestro* at La Scala at the time. He had studied under the same tutor as Giuditta and was given the task of taking her through her post-conservatory training. The couple's first joint appearance took place less than a month after their 1816 nuptials, and though it garnered them little notice, it provided the two singers with a number of important contacts, one of whom introduced them to the producers at the Théâtre-Italien in Paris.

The Pastas traveled to the French capital soon after their Italian premier with plans to perform together there, but Giuseppe developed a serious throat condition that prevented him from reaching his full vocal range. When it was determined it would be a while before he would be well enough to perform, Giuditta made her first Parisian appearance without him in a *dramma giocosa*, a popular genre of opera at the time that intermingled singing with flourishes of comedy. In the "playful drama," *Il Principe di Taranto*, composed by Ferdinando Paër, Giuditta was Rosina, a simple girl who impersonated a princess. "She appeared, at this point, ill at ease in comic roles, and obviously nervous," Stern wrote. He quoted the critic for the newspaper *Le Diable boiteux* as saying, "Madame Pasta had to prevail over detestable text, feeble music, and the inseparable tension of a debut; these obstacles have, no doubt, prevented the deployment of all her powers. Her voice was always unsteady; however, one could recognize that it was pleasing and expansive. Her technique appears good, and she was applauded for several passages executed with good taste."[2]

Other critics were not so kind about her voice control and her deportment, one writing that at least she was in Paris because it was the best place to learn the tricks of the trade. When she next appeared, Giuseppe was on the stage with her; the reviewers gave him a pass because of his throat problems, but they were not so benevolent with Giuditta. The *Journal de Débats* called her voice "weak and hoarse." Feeling empathy toward her, Paër stepped in to give her some intensive coaching. Though this helped Giuditta improve, a bigger problem was already evident in her career, and it would continue to hamper her progress for decades—composers at the time were not adept at creating operas tailored to her acting talents, which had they been, would have set her performances apart from the start. In his book *The Great Singers*, Henry Pleasants dubbed Giuditta a harbinger of the great dramatic sopranos who would follow, and pointed out that she was ahead of her time as a singing actress.[3]

He said the era she inhabited proved to be a challenge because, "During the age of bel canto, composers had always worked with certain singers in mind, tailoring their vocal requirements accordingly." He noted that these composers included Gioachino Rossini, Gaetano Donizetti, Bellini, and Giacomo Meyerbeer. He explained that Giuseppe Verdi and Richard Wagner were different because, "They wrote what they hoped to hear without reference to the talents of specific singers, and in some cases, they had to wait a generation for the ideal singer to materialize."[4] Since Giuditta was still an unknown, the parts that specifically suited her were non-existent, which meant disappointing performances continued for her entire first season. Only one role, that of Romeo in Niccolò Zingarelli's *Giulietta e Romeo*, brought her praise. At the end of the dismal run, a falling out with the management of the Théâtre-Italien propelled the Pastas to

London. They left Paris for the English capital in November of 1816, and by January of the next year, Giuditta was debuting at the King's Theatre, staring as Telemachus in Domenico Cimarosa's *Penelope*.

Leigh Hunt, an animated critic writing in his own publication *The Examiner*, called the production rather monotonous, though he did speak highly of Giuditta, saying there was a natural eloquence about her singing; that her dress and figure fit with the classical idea of the young Telemachus; and that her voice was good, her action was effective, and she had a handsome face and *very* handsome legs.[5] The fact that he complimented her legs is interesting given she was always the most nervous about her trouser roles—a theatrical term used to denote parts played by a performer of the opposite sex. Lady Morgan shared Giuditta's response to the predicament: "I was so ashamed at showing my legs! Instead of minding my singing, I was always trying to hide my legs. I failed!"[6] The remainder of Giuditta's 1817 season in London brought both good and bad reviews, the positive just enough to give her the incentive to continue. By the summer of that year, with no future engagements confirmed, she learned she was pregnant, and she and Giuseppe returned to Milan where Giuditta hired a voice coach so she could polish her techniques. She worked diligently as her pregnancy progressed; and, on March 27, 1818, she gave birth to a daughter named Clelia.

As she contemplated her future on the stage, she proved that her ambition would be one of her biggest assets throughout her career. She felt it was time to be more demanding and refuse *seconda donna* roles in lieu of productions where she would be billed as *prima donna assoluta*. Contracts were signed and five months after the birth of her daughter, Giuditta and her mother left for Venice, Padua, and Rome where she would appear as the top talent during each performance. One of the recurring themes for the soprano was her sadness when she had to be away from her daughter, whom she would leave with the child's great-grandmother in order to improve her career. Giuseppe decided not to travel with them, as he was determined to separate his engagements from hers in order to cement his own stardom. Unfortunately, his career sputtered when review after review claimed his voice was no longer powerful enough for operatic performances.

GIUDITTA'S STINT with a coach during her pregnancy, her experiences in Paris and London, and her excitement about being a mother coalesced to bring her increased confidence and to lend her voice greater tonal maturity. "In an age where multiple curtain calls were uncommon," Stern wrote, "Pasta was recalled to the stage at least twice, and often three times after each of her numbers."[7] The reviews for those first performances in Venice were positive, which inspired an array of successful heavyweights in the opera industry to help her improve her techniques and to introduce her to those who could further her ascendency. One of these was composer Giovanni Pacini, who revised the songs Giuditta sang in the Venice performances to better suit her voice. By this time, her roles throughout Italy were becoming more diverse, which elevated her reputation. Satisfied that she had made enough progress that she could afford to take a pause, she eagerly returned to her family in Milan, the months of being away from baby Clelia finally over.

She spent the waning weeks of 1819 strategizing her next moves, deciding to stay in smaller Italian theaters so she could continue to improve. This paid off as she took to the stage in both dramas and comedies during the 1819/1820 season. The French novelist Stendhal, who would eventually be a theater critic for publications in Paris, spotted her during this season of performances. He lavished praise on her techniques and her presence in his book *Memoirs of an Egotist*. As he and his friends flitted from one Italian theater to the next to take in the comic operas called *opera buffa*, they saw Giuditta in three leading roles: *Tancredi, Otello,* and *Giulietta e Romeo*. "In Italy, I adored the opera," Stendhal wrote. "The sweetest moments in my life, without compare, all occurred in the opera houses." He noted that Giuditta performed "in a way that not only has never been equaled, but had certainly never been foreseen by the composers of those operas." He declared that her sense of tragedy on the stage was pure, touching, and perfect. As Stendhal's friendship with Giuditta grew stronger, he described her as "without vices or failings, a simple, even-tempered, equitable, natural character."[8]

He said she "had the greatest tragic talent" he had ever known. Then, the twenty-year-old Frenchman confessed he had unwisely wanted something more than a platonic arrangement. "I would first of all have liked her to feel love for me, who so greatly admired her," he explained. "Today I can see that she was too cold, too reasonable, not wild enough, not caressing enough for our relationship, if there had been enough love in it, to continue. It would have been a mere passing fancy on my part; she would quite understandably have been indignant, and would have broken it off." He concluded it was best they had remained nothing more than close friends.[9] Stern took Stendhal's reviews of Giuditta's performances with a grain of salt because the writer was so enamored with her, but he deemed the man's criticism valuable because Stendhal's writing provides an eye-witness account of the spirit of their era. By the time Giuditta returned to Paris, performing at the Théâtre-Italien between

April and November in 1821, critics were acknowledging that she was beginning to fulfill her potential.

She sang Desdemona in Rossini's *Otello* and repeated one of her most popular roles by then in Zingarelli's *Giulietta e Romeo*. "Five years previously," Stern wrote, "Paris witnessed her initially awkward presence, but after steady growth as a vocal and dramatic artist in England and throughout Italy, the public and critics recognized Pasta as a significant and noteworthy artistic personality."[10] During this stint in Paris, Giuditta held salon evenings in her apartment in the Hôtel des Lillois, which became a gathering place for an array of European music lovers and upper-crust Italians flowing into the city from Milan. As a neighbor and one of her regular habitués, Stendhal knew Giuditta fairly well by then. "No matter what time my evenings out finished elsewhere, I would go to Mme Pasta's," Stendhal wrote. "I was staying a hundred yards or so away, at number 47 [rue de Richelieu]. Fed up with the angry porter, who was so vexed at often having to open up to me at three in the morning, I ended up staying in the same house as Mme Pasta."[11]

The writer said he spent an entire summer playing faro in her drawing room until daybreak each morning. This ended as fall approached and Giuditta prepared to return to Italy, signing contracts before she departed Paris that would bring her back to the French capital for two additional seasons for a sum larger than other artists of her time had ever been offered. After a four-month run in Turin, where she performed at the Theatro Regio to appreciative audiences, she made her way back to Paris with her husband and her daughter, and began a far more satisfying season in the city's theaters than she'd experienced before. As she participated in better orchestrations, her stardom grew and her enthusiastic fans gave her the nickname *Pastisti*. Her repeat performances included Desdemona and Romeo, and she landed one of the most celebrated roles of her early career, starring as

Medea in Giovanni Simone Mayr's *Medea in Corinto*. Stendhal wrote that she was making daily advances towards perfection. "In this manner, she is enabled to impart a new musical coloring to the sentiment, not by the accent of the words, and in quality of a great tragedian, but by the ever-varying shades of the voice, and in quality of a great singer," he explained.[12]

By now, Stendhal had signed on as an opera critic for *Le Journal de Paris*, and his reviews bore witness to the fact that Giuditta was participating in a transformative moment in opera because she and the other top singers were integrating acting into their performances. This is so common now, we take it for granted, but it was a revelation to audiences then. For the first time ever, the rows of fans facing the stage experienced vocalists modeling their expressions and movements to reflect the significance of the emotion the libretto was meant to convey. Illustrating the amount of pressure Giuditta carried as she sailed into these uncharted waters, Stendhal said she undulated between spending hours on her sofa weeping and having attacks of nerves after returning from performances to growing silent and impassive for hours on end. During this phase of her career, she was dealing with a string of illnesses and gave birth to a still-born child, the latter blamed on the fact she was performing too strenuously at a critical time in the pregnancy.

These physical challenges interrupted her stage appearances off and on beginning in the spring of 1823. Her salon was thriving in spite of her ill health, and celebrities like Rossini, who by then had reached his stardom in the major cities of Europe, began attending during visits to Paris. These intimate gatherings she hosted segued to private concerts when her health improved, the tally during the first three months of 1824 at thirty. The small performances for wealthy audiences brought her the lion's share of her income that year. Attendees included heads of state and members of the aristocracy, the latter group often paying homage by giving her expensive jewelry. An impressive invitation during this stint in Paris was a concert Giuditta performed with then adolescent composer Franz Liszt at his request. During their duet, the pianist astonished listeners with improvisations on Mozart's "Non più andrai," an aria from *The Marriage of Figaro*.

As the 1824 Paris season drew to a close, a crown was tossed onto the stage during Giuditta's final performance on April tenth. The praise she would receive in London, where she took the stage shortly after her Parisian triumph, was equally flattering. Her first performance at the King's Theatre that season astonished the press and the public, her progress so obvious the reviews raved that her voice and her expressiveness had an uncommon emotional power; that she had grown noble and dignified; and that she handled her roles with perfect intelligence. This level of praise marked a milestone in Giuditta's career, and critics noted that the soprano's rich middle voice had become the best part of her range and that her theatrical moves demonstrated taste and originality. She was also markedly more assured in her development as an actor. Giuditta's mother declared that the singer was finally experiencing a complete triumph, a distinction that catapulted Giuditta into the decade that would represent her zenith. Beyond operatic performances, she was offered other financially lucrative opportunities: Maria Malibran, a Spanish opera singer who was standing on the threshold of a luminous career at the time; Liszt; and Giuditta were asked by William Cavendish, the 6th Duke of

Devonshire, to perform in a concert for a well-heeled audience.

Soon after, Prince Leopold of Saxe-Coburg sponsored a concert at Marlborough House during which Giuditta and Malibran sang the duet *Ebben, a te ferisci* from Act 2 of Rossini's *Semiramide*. "Of all the selections that today one might fantasize about hearing," Stern wrote, "it would rank at the top of the list."[13] Though she was enjoying her notoriety and feeling a pleasant rush from the respect shown to her by her fans and intimates, Giuditta's successes were wearing on her unprosperous husband. This constituted a mid-life crisis for the despondent tenor, who hatched a plan to go to America where he would seek a new beginning in New York City. He was pressuring Giuditta to join him but she was adamantly against the idea. Being at the height of her career and singing for the titled gentry of Europe, she wasn't willing to risk the dangerous voyage to perform in what she deemed uncertain conditions before unsophisticated audiences. The letters between the couple reveal a desperate man who was in a pathetic state emotionally.

He fended off her pleas to reconsider the trip, saying that the thought of traveling to New York had revived him. She made one last attempt in a letter that urged him not to go but he ignored her and set sail on October 1, 1825, with a group of artists who would introduce Italian opera to America. With her husband away, Giuditta doubled down on her efforts to reach greater stardom. This included deciding there would be no lovers in her life because she didn't believe in adultery and she wanted to channel her sexual desire into her music. She was twenty-eight at the time and was mesmerizing audiences in the array of roles she continued to land—her portrayal of Medea in Mayr's *Medea in Corinto* was the hit of the London season in 1826. Meanwhile in America, things were not going so well for Giuseppe. His stay in New

York was a bust because he was sick during the entire eight months he was there.

Giusepe left the U.S. just as her run as Medea ended, and joined her in England. While he had no opportunities in sight, she was in high demand; and with the end of the London season, she prepared to travel to Naples to perform in her own country for the first time in four years. Initially, Giuditta's Italian reentry was bumpy, but Pacini once again came to the rescue and adjusted his arias to better suit her range. She appeared in his *Niobe* on more solid ground, though the other lesser-known composers in whose operas she appeared during this stint in Italy brought her a powerful realization: The dramatic works were so lacking, they were not contributing to her legacy. She decided these would be her last commitments in Italy for a while because she preferred to perform in cities where her style was appreciated and more money could be made, one of the most lucrative being London. Giuditta returned to Great Britain at the end of this string of Italian performances—touring Ireland and Scotland, and ending the trip with stage appearances in a number of English cities.

The intense travel schedule she maintained as she crisscrossed the British Isles left her seriously fatigued. In a letter to her husband, who was in Paris with their daughter, she told him she was struggling with bone-numbing tiredness. At times, the strain caught up with her on stage, which was understandable given the staggering number of performances she scheduled. "For Giuditta, 1827 had been an exhausting year of travel and performance," Stern wrote. "Her instrument seemed to gain in strength and staying power, though when fatigued her intonation wavered."[14] The weariness and the missteps she had been making on stage were signals that something had to give. For years, she had been saying that she would gladly give up the role of diva to be a country girl pottering in a garden, and she felt she was finally in a position to make this happen.

THE DESIRE TO escape the stage propelled her to Lake Como where she would find the property I visited, would set about updating the mansion, and would relax into a lifestyle she loved. Giuditta spent her first night in her newly refurbished Villa Roda on September 14, 1828, her reaction to the experience jotted down on a slip of paper Stern found among her belongings. She wrote that she had slept well, that she had strolled contentedly around the grounds, and that all of her thoughts were happy because she felt rewarded for her years of toil.[15] Giuditta stayed for several months, planting shrubs and flowers in the garden, and caring for a menagerie that included birds, dogs, and cats. Her respite ended when she began receiving offers she felt she couldn't, and shouldn't, refuse. Saying goodbye to her plants, animals, and the lake, she crisscrossed Europe during the high seasons for the next several years, not returning for any significant length of time to the blissful life at Villa Roda until the summer and autumn of 1830.

It was during those warm, lush months when she was presented with the higher-quality material she deserved after decades of trying to make unsuitable compositions work for her tonal range. Bellini, who would give her the superlative melodies, had composed seven operas by the time he was collaborating with Giuditta, the oeuvre he was building bringing him praise as one of the foremost Italian composers before he was thirty years old. He was a twenty-nine-year-old perfectionist by the time he was composing his first opera for Giuditta. Because he had watched her on stage in Naples during the 1826-27 season in a remarkably diverse number of roles, he felt he knew her strengths and her weaknesses. Bellini mentioned he was on Lake Como to see Giuditta in a letter to his former schoolmate Francesco Florimo, telling his friend he would be visiting her at Villa Roda with his favorite librettist Felice Romani in tow. They were eager to discuss with Giuditta the new opera that would be staged the following winter in Milan. After proposing several possible subjects, they agreed on Victor Hugo's *Hernani* but the idea was scrapped when they learned of the demonstrations the theatrical masterpiece had provoked in Paris and feared the same would be leveled at their production. They decided to compose *La Sonnambula* instead.

The delay as they scrapped one plan and began another caused Bellini great stress, which was a recurring refrain for him throughout his career because his personality demanded that his creations percolate for a while. "Whereas most of his contemporaries—Rossini, Donizetti, and Pacini included—were willing to rush out operas that could have been improved immeasurably by more thought, time, and effort, he [Bellini] was not," Weinstock explained. "Rossini composed (or, in some cases, substantially recomposed) thirty-nine operas in twenty years, Donizetti some seventy in twenty-eight years, Pacini about one hundred in forty-four years. In contrast, Bellini's creating operas at about the rate of one per year was looked upon as slow and finicking."[16] Given Rossini lived to be seventy-six, Donizetti to be fifty-one, Pacini to be seventy-one, and Bellini was only thirty-four when he died, it is understandable that his output would be much less—by the time he passed away, he had composed fewer than a dozen operas.

As he fleshed out his first composition for his new diva, he was suffering from the illness that would eventually kill him at such a young age—he had contracted amebiasis, an intestinal infection caused by parasites, while in Venice producing *Il Pirata* and *I Capuleti e i Montecchi*. Though the doctors recommended he stay put in the quieter atmosphere of Lake Como while working on *La Sonnambula*, he disregarded their advice and went to Milan to sign contracts for two more operas, one of which would be his greatest contribution to Giuditta's legacy. Bellini wrote *La Sonnambula* in nine weeks, and the debut at the Teatro Carcano in Milan took place on March, 6, 1831. "It was received with immediate, unrestrained enthusiasm," Weinstock wrote. "The next day Bellini wrote to [Alessandro] Lamperi: 'Here you have the happy news of the uproarious success of my opera last evening at the Carcano. I say nothing about the music; you will see that in the press. I only assure you that Rubini and Pasta are two angels who enraptured the whole audience to the verge of madness.'"[17]

Giovanni Battista Rubini would become a famous tenor who was known for his range at the highest register of his voice. During this premiere season of *La Sonnambula*, he appeared as the male lead Elvino opposite Giuditta as Amina, the female lead. They were also paired in another lauded performance that season—Donizetti's opera *Anna Bolen [Anne Boleyn]*. The Russian composer Mikhail Ivanovich Glinka was in the audience for the first performance of *Anna Bolen*: "To me, there seemed something somehow magical about it; Rubini, Pasta (who played Anne Boleyn with distinction, especially in the last scene), [Filippo] Galli, [Elisa] Orlandi, etc., all had parts. And since from our front box one could not miss the very softest *sotto voce*, [...] I was wallowing in rapture."[18] This season of 1830-31 in Milan was a triumphant one for Giuditta, and with the additions of Donizetti and Bellini to her repertoire, she had performed in operas by thirteen composers by this point in her career. Glinka also saw *La Sonnambula* during that run.

He said of the experience, "In the few performances given before the theaters closed, Pasta and Rubini sang with the most evident enthusiasm to support their favorite conductor; in the second act the singers themselves wept and carried their audience along with them, so that in the happy days of Carnival, tears were continually being wiped away in boxes and parquet alike. Embracing [Yevgeny] Shterich in the Ambassador's box, I, too, shed tears of emotion and ecstasy."[19] Italian critics were just as enthusiastic. The reviewer for *L'eco* wrote, "Bellini has sustained his reputation...After her [Giuditta's] duet with Rubini, it could truly be said, 'That is the way to sing.'"[20] Glinka's tears illustrate how the bridge joining singing with acting was being swiftly crossed by these vocalists during their careers. Weinstock said having his singers inspire emotion was a formula that had become a ruling belief for Bellini.

He shared an anecdote that proves this, one that took place between the composer and Rubini when Bellini was rehearsing the tenor for *Il Pirata* several years before the tenor appeared in the lauded performance of *La Sonnambula*. When Rubini could not live up to Bellini's desired degree of drama, the composer could no longer contain himself. "You are an animal!" he exclaimed. "You don't put into it half the spirit you have; where you should be driving the whole audience out of its mind, you are cold and languishing. Show your passion; haven't you ever been in love?" Softening his tone, Bellini added, "Dear Rubini... Don't you know that your voice is a gold mine that hasn't been discovered yet? Listen to me, and some day you'll be grateful to me. You are one of the best singers. No one equals you in bravura. But that isn't enough." As the exchange continued, Bellini urged the tenor to forget himself and throw himself into his character with all his soul.[21] Given how the composer praised Rubini in his letter to Lamperi, Bellini's depth of passion paid off for the opera star.

Following the success of *La Sonnambula*, Bellini and Romani began work on *Norma*, a role for Giuditta in which she would appear at La Scala. Once again Bellini felt great pressure in creating a masterpiece in a mere four months—far less time than he would have preferred. I was impressed at how inclusive he was in urging Giuditta to give him feedback on his music. He wrote to her in Paris, "By now you will have read it, [and] if any suggestion occurs to your mind, write it to me." He was once again lodging on the shores of Lake Como as he fretted over *Norma* and was having a harder time working than normal. His letters to his friends were riddled with fear over the cholera outbreak in July of 1831, which was spreading fast in Austria. Writing to Florimo, he said, "I am composing the opera without any zeal because I am almost certain that the Cholera will arrive in time to close the theaters..."[22] The pandemic didn't interrupt the debut, but the process leading to the stage hit a snag: Before rehearsals could begin, Giuditta was refusing to sing "Casta Diva" because she didn't feel her vocal abilities were worthy of it. Certain that he had to find a way to entice her to try it, Bellini came up with a plan.

"They made a pact," wrote Weinstock: "She would keep it for a week, going over it again each morning, and if at the end of seven days she still found performing it repugnant, Bellini promised that he would change it." The strategy worked, and not only did the soprano sing the aria, she sent the composer an ornate parchment lampshade, a bouquet of flowers, and a note just before the premiere. It read, "Allow me to offer you something that was some solace to me for the immense fear that persecuted me when I found myself little suited to performing your sublime harmonies; this lamp by night and these flowers by day witnessed my studies of *Norma* and the desire I cherish to be ever-more-worthy of your esteem. Giuditta P. your most affectionate friend." When the performance opened on December 26, 1831, it was received poorly by the first audience, so much so that Weinstock called the attitude of those in attendance a "chill indifference."[23]

Bellini wrote to Florimo, "I am writing to you under the shock of sorrow; of a sorrow that I cannot put into words for you, but that only you can understand. I have come from La Scala; first performance of Norma. Would you believe it?...Fiasco!!! Fiasco!!! Solemn fiasco!!!" By the end of that season, which spanned 1831-32, *Norma* had been performed thirty-nine times at La Scala to ever-growing appreciation.[24] As the opera traveled to other cities in Italy, it became a smashing success. This propelled Bellini and Giuditta into their next collaboration that followed fast on the heels of *Norma*. The composer had signed a contract with the organizers of the Carnaval à Vénise [Carnival of Venice] because its organizers had tapped Giuditta as the lead soprano and he was eager to write another opera in which she would appear in the starring role. Bellini penned a letter to Giuseppe that said he was traveling to Lake Como so he could discuss his ongoing progress with Giuditta as he composed the next piece.

By now, Bellini held her in such high esteem, he told her husband, "My *Norma*—having been portrayed by the Encyclopedic Angel [Giuditta]—could not have failed to have a good reception." Then, he stopped himself, saying, "Enough! For when I begin to speak of that divine donna, my mind doesn't give me terms adequate to express what I feel in my heart." Ecstatic as positive reviews for *Norma* continued to pour in, Bellini wrote to his friend Giacomo Barbò, "Norma has stunned all of Bergamo, and I myself have found it something different. Everything is more alive and spirited since the singers have mastered their roles. Pasta made me shed many tears."[25] Bellini once again tapped Romani as his librettist, but this collaboration was fraught from the start because the poet was feeling stymied. He ordered a cache of publications from Paris to see if anything sparked his imagination but he continued to waffle because Bellini wanted him to provide Giuditta with a role different from both Amina and Norma.

Bellini's request was that Romani put less emphasis on any of the secondary roles that might undermine Giuditta's greatness because he felt the capabilities of the supporting singers who had already been hired were inadequate. The composer's letters to his friends were filled with anxiety because Romani was not delivering; the more they pushed and pulled at each other, the worse the situation grew. After weeks of delay, Bellini wrote to Giuditta that they had finally settled on *Beatrice di Tenda*. But months would pass without any material from Romani, whom Weinstock described as overworked because he was popular with so many composers and he had accepted a staff position at La Scala. When Bellini reached the end of his patience, he told the governor of Venice about his concerns and the politician intervened, summoning Romani to town in January 1833. Realizing the seriousness of the situation, Romani sequestered there to concentrate on the work.

MEANWHILE, *Norma* was staged in Venice as a precursor to the new opera with the full ensemble who would bring *Beatrice di Tenda* to the stage. Bellini's initial worries that the lesser singers would not be able to support Giuditta were founded—he described them as mediocre. Giuditta held the opera together but the audience was indifferent to the other singers, which made her fear what was to come when they performed *Beatrice di Tenda*. A month later, Bellini wrote to Giovanni Ricordi that Romani had finally given him beautiful verses and he was putting his "usual devotion into composing." There was an intense undercurrent in the letter that illustrated how much strain he was under due to the fact he would have to create music that was beautiful enough to raise the inferior singers to a level at which they could support the opera. He then said, "I hope for everything from Pasta: a sure anchor in any shipwreck."[26] Considering his normally plodding process, Bellini created the melody to buoy Romani's phrases at lightning speed. He was left with only three pieces of the opera to finish after Romani's initial delivery of verses.

When nothing else came from the librettist, he was bashing Romani again, calling him "my sluggard of a poet." By then, Bellini was afraid he wouldn't be able to finish the opera, which was to open in two weeks' time. "I have the whole second act to do!!!" he wrote. "Oh, what a huge fiasco I foresee!" As I followed the story along, I felt the tension building as the debut met with delay after delay. It was finally presented at Theatro La Fenice on March 15, 1833, a month after it had been slated and only eight days prior to the scheduled season ending. Before the performance could take place, Romani made a stupid move. He published an advertisement asking that the audience be indulgent toward the presentation. Weinstock wrote, "That apology did nothing to reduce the fever in which that first Venetian audience, already in an unfriendly state of mind, received *Beatrice di Tenda*."[27] The debut was considered a disaster because the opera had been delayed for so long and Bellini told his friend

Filippo Santocanale that there were factions in the audience during that first evening who were out for revenge. Both Giuditta and Bellini were furious over the fiasco, to use one of the composer's favorite words. Opera critic Michele Scherillo declared that Giuditta, like the great artist she was, rose above the debacle by using her wits.

Explaining how clever she was, he wrote, "At that moment, Pasta conceived a cordial hatred of that stupid audience, which, while giving vent to its preconceived displeasure with the composer, did not respect her as the most skillful artist-singer of the time." Instead of turning toward the other vocalist during a duet, Giuditta faced the audience "and scornfully, energetically accented the phrase: *'se amar non puoi, rispettami!'* [if you cannot love me, respect me!]," Scherillo wrote. "It is said that the audience understood and responded with noisy applause. But that did not make it change its attitude toward Bellini's opera." Bellini told Santocanale the crowd made such a racket—shouting, whistling, and laughing—that he had the feeling he was "at a fair." The composer said the cacophony grew so intense, his Sicilian haughtiness came over him to the point that he grew stiff and emotionless, which silenced some and enraged others. "For the audience called out for me after four or five very effecting pieces," he explained, "but I remained in my seat as though nailed there." He then told his friend that he hoped, in time, Beatrice would "find her revenge" just as Norma had.[28]

After such a public feud with Romani over *Beatrice di Tenda*, Bellini decided to leave Italy with the Pastas; they traveled to London in order to produce *Norma* there. Giuditta's schedule in the British capital was as strenuous as ever—her performances included *Medea in Corinto, Anna Bolena, Il Pirata,* and *Norma*. Bellini wrote to Lamperi that he was alternating between feeling smothered by the

London season and having a marvelous time. "So you see I naturally find myself in the midst of a world of beautiful women, and truly of celestial beauties; but I indulge in nothing but sentiment," he explained, "and therefore I put more value upon friendship than upon love, so as not to run the risk of acquiring a wife." Culminating their 1833 season in London, *Norma* was staged at the King's Theater with Giuditta in the title role. Giuseppe Pasta wrote to the opera star's mother that the triumph of the evening surpassed Giuditta's desire and Bellini's hope. "The applause was extraordinary, and there were more than a few tears during the second act," he wrote. "Giuditta seemed possessed by the character, and displayed the strength of which her constitution is capable only when stirred by some extraordinary motivation. She accompanied Bellini onto the stage, and both of them were saluted with an expression of enthusiasm."[29]

Giuseppe reported which pieces had received the most response from the audiences, and said every move Giuditta made and every word she sang elicited sighs or surprise or affection or enthusiasm, each corresponding emotion appropriate to the experience she was dramatizing. The critics were so positive that Giuditta and Bellini realized they had finally achieved their dream of performing before intelligent audiences and being scrutinized by sophisticated reviewers. But there were a few critics who declared Giuditta's voice was showing evidence of "wear and tear." Weinstock noted that at thirty-five, from a strictly vocal standpoint, "her greatest days were beginning to draw in." As she went into and out of retirement over the next eight years, he noted she did so with varying results, "and with constantly increasing dependence upon her histrionic talent."[30] On March 4, 1835, she made her first serious attempt at leaving the stage. After singing the role of Norma at La Scala that season, she accepted no new engagements, declaring she was finished with her "slavery."

By then, Giuditta had bought additional property adjoining hers on Lake Como. The larger parcel that meandered up the rocky slopes toward Strada Procincale di Blevio was dotted with several buildings, which included a smaller house than Villa Roda, which she named Villa Trempo. As she settled created a new routine for herself, she was greatly missed by Bellini, whose popularity had solidified in London and in Paris, where he was living when he had news from the British capital that a performance of *Norma* by Giulietta Grisi, who had replaced Giuditta in the starring role, was panned by critics. He wrote to Florimo, "*Norma* was born and—let it be said between us—died, and let it remain buried in friendship's bosom. Our good friend Pasta had greater dignity, but though poor Giulietta did everything she could to do well, it was to no avail…" The composer then told his friend, "The journals say that she [Grisi] sang and acted less well than in any other opera, and they remember Pasta with great sorrow because she was not in this performance."[31] It was obvious by his laments to other friends that this upset him to no end, but he didn't have long to suffer. Within two and a half months, he was dead.

Giuditta learned of Bellini's passing from a letter written by her friend Lady Charlotte Hunloke, which didn't reach Villa Roda until several weeks after his death. In it, Hunloke told Giuditta of a gathering shortly before Bellini left for Paris, sharing that the composer glowingly praised "his favorite soprano" throughout the evening. She said he spoke of Giuditta with the greatest tenderness. Highlighting an odd custom of that era, Hunloke told Giuditta she had kept a lock of Bellini's hair and offered to send some strands to her. I found no record of Giuditta's feelings about Bellini's death but the fact that she already had a lock of his hair and an oval miniature of him by Frédéric Millet, both of which she carried with her during her travels for appearances, indicates she would likely have experienced some grief. Bellini's expression in the Millet painting is slightly quizzical, though serious and unsmiling. He has very curly dark hair and is wearing a black high-collared dinner jacket that rises above a white silk cravat. He was a very handsome man in his prime in the painting that captured him just five years before his death.

ALONG WITH THIS PORTRAIT, Stern included in his book an array of illustrations of Giuditta in different roles and paintings of her inner circle. There are also a number of photos of the Lake Como villas and their grounds. I studied the one taken of the view from Giuditta's bedroom window, which frames a misty Lake Como, and wondered if she had wistfully looked toward the other shore when she learned of Bellini's passing, remembering those days when he composed some of her greatest roles. By all accounts, his influence on her legacy was profound. In arias like "Casta Diva," he gave her the opportunity to explore her vocal gifts in a way that critics were finally able to celebrate, one noting that "the peculiar characteristic of this wonderful singer's voice is a moaning sound, which colors it throughout, deepening and intensifying its effect and beauty."[32] Stern declared that *Norma* was Bellini's masterpiece and said it catapulted Giuditta to the apex of her artistry. Given her primacy had since waned, I was surprised when I read that Giuditta brought her first retirement to an end in the spring of 1837, two years after she declared she was finished with her "slavery," and returned to London to perform in a concert.

Critics for the newspaper *Morning Herald* said she looked

largely unchanged since her last appearance, "except in her face, having a finer flush of health on it, as if the breezes of Como were still fresh upon it." But others were not so benevolent. Henry Chorley, writing for *Athenaeum,* declared, "Alas! Time has been at work upon her voice to a sad extent…her intonation was very false."[33] After taking the stage at the King's Theatre in a full opera, about which reviews were even less enthusiastic, she performed at Kensington Palace for Princess Victoria and the Duchess of Kent, and sang again for Victoria at Buckingham Palace after she had been crowned queen in June of 1837. Giuditta then traveled through southern England performing in a series of concerts. Though the less sophisticated critics in these towns praised her, Giuditta was feeling vulnerable, expressing deep gratitude when her mother wrote to her to try and shore up the soprano's confidence.

She spent most of 1838 making appearances in salon gatherings in Italy; and then launched into an international tour of Imperial Russia, Austria, Poland, and Germany, which ended in 1841. The final complete opera performance of her career took place in Berlin on August twenty-fourth. "Now an enormously wealthy woman, there appeared no economic incentive to remain on the stage," Stern wrote. "Her voice no longer equaled the rigors of opera performance, and further appearances could add nothing to her reputation."[34] With Giuditta's dream of seeing Russia ticked off the list, Italy beckoned, and she settled into her life there, splitting her time between Villa Roda, her residence in Milan, and a smaller home in the city of Como. She also spent a portion of her time coaching future opera singers. In "A Recollection of Pasta," an essay in the English soprano Adelaide Kemble's book *Past Hours,* the author described a spate of training she received at Villa Roda soon after Giuditta retired. "Many years ago, I had the happiness and supreme advantage of passing some days with her at her villa on Lake Como," Kemble explained. "On a lovely Sunday early in the autumn I arrived there." The younger soprano wandered into the villa on her own, greeted by a number of dogs when she entered through the front door—not a person in sight. "It was like a charmed palace in the 'Arabian Nights,' where, by some dire enchantment, all the human creatures have been transformed into beasts," Kemble wrote.[35]

When Giuditta finally appeared, she was coming in from the garden. "She was stout and under the average height, and, having one leg shorter than the other, waddled rather than walked," Kemble remembered; "but for all that she looked taller than everybody else." The Brit described Giuditta as filled with nobleness and sweetness. She then said she experienced a woman who was certain she had made the right decisions. "She never seemed to regret or miss the excitement of the old life," Kemble explained, "but appeared entirely absorbed in country pursuits and with the improvements she was making in the place."[36] Three different buildings on the property were receiving upgrades while Kemble was staying there—Villa Roda, where Giuditta lived; Villa Trempo, where her by-then married daughter Clelia Ferrante and her family lived; and a greenhouse Giuditta was in the process of building. Of all of the details Kemble shared, I was the most fascinated by her description of Giuditta's bedroom in which cages filled with birds were hanging over the door.

When I searched for an explanation as to why she would have wanted them there, I learned that Giuditta loved to hear their chirping because she envied their intonation. Another anecdote that Kemble shared, which involved Giuditta's pitch by this time, was rather cutting, though it also held a clue that could explain why the elder soprano's performances were lacking by the time she ultimately retired.

"Even at her best, she had always sung false upon three notes in the middle of her voice—the C of the third space, with the D and E which follow, were invariably considerably too flat," Kemble explained. Giuditta was coaching her on "Casta Diva" during this particular lesson and the older soprano told the younger vocalist she was singing sharp. After several more attempts, Kemble pressed the corresponding keys on the piano and looked at her mentor expecting her to give in, but she did not. Giuditta then sang the notes, which Kemble wrote were a full quarter of a tone too flat, and looked at her student "with an air of complacent triumph." The experience led Kemble to believe that Giuditta's challenges with intonation were due to hearing loss rather than a weakness in her voice.[37]

The younger soprano, who would become one of the well-known divas of the Victorian Era, didn't mince words about the fact that she believed Giuditta should have retired earlier than she did. As proof, Kemble shared the sentiments of "a well-known old dandy," who was sitting in front of her during one of Giuditta's performances when the prima donna returned to the stage after she ended her first retirement in 1835. He applauded Giuditta with a sort of good-natured condescension and said, "Oh, poor dear old thing! How stumpy she is! How old she had grown, to be sure! She oughtn't to have come back again!" Years after she heard the man make this comment, Kemble saw Giuditta perform for a charity event just before her last retirement in 1841, which left the young vocalist feeling much the same. She explained, "For the agony of her failure, I too could have found in my heart to cry, 'Why did she ever come again!' if afterwards I had not heard Viardot, who had seen her for the first time on this occasion, say of her, 'Yes, it is a ruin; but so is Leonardo's 'Last Supper.'"[38] Pauline Viardot was a French mezzo-soprano who would have a long and lustrous career as an opera star—judging from this comment, she also had a wicked sense of humor!

HAVING TRAVERSED the totality of Giuditta's career, I am happy that I went to Lake Como without knowing these details because my first experience of her voice was a fulsome one that I enjoyed without any preconceived notions. I will never forget how sumptuous it felt to walk into the lobby of the resort and hear "Casta Diva" wafting from the speakers. It flowed over me as I moved up the stairs of the tower and, just as I reached the door to my room, Giuditta's final mournful note faded away. When the door swung open, it was as if the lake and a pair of swans skimming along its surface were in the room. The water must have loomed just as large for Giuditta during the several decades she enjoyed the life she'd made for herself along these rocky ledges. She breathed her last breath beside the mesmerizing swath of water at the age of sixty-eight after battling a bronchial infection. Since returning home, I find myself listening to Giuditta's version of "Casta Diva" and wishing I could have seen how the feelings the music evoked played across her features.

A video of Maria Callas performing in the Palais Garnier in Paris in December 1958 provided me with a glimpse of the passion the song inspires. As Callas so convincingly expressed sadness as she reached the final crescendo that Bellini had determinedly composed over a century before, I couldn't help but wonder what he would have thought if he had seen her perform. Callas's expression was one of great emotion, and her stillness as she ended the piece, clutching herself with her demeanor unchanged as the audience applauded, was heart-rending. As she stood there, a pronounced exhale seemed to escape of its own volition and she finally allowed herself to fall out of character. A smile came, but her long, splayed fingers continued to clasp the wrap draped around her shoulders as if she needed to physically hold herself intact. It was just the level of emotion I feel Bellini would have loved. The one facet of this story I wish I had known as I'd walked up those stairs and approached the elegant suite with Giuditta's moving voice accompanying me was that the moving music had been composed in the captivating setting I had encountered. *Bravo!* I thought, and not just for the haunting pianissimo as the song ended, but for the slice of Lake Como's beautiful shore, Bellini's passion for music, Giuditta's charisma, and the romantic myth that sent me on this journey. Each of these was equally worthy of applause.

2

A FORCE OF NATURE

COLETTE IN PARIS

Can anything new be discovered about a renowned historical figure whose life has been plumbed in books and films? I asked this question with a bit of trepidation as I launched into my exploration of Sidonie-Gabrielle Colette because she has been depicted so vibrantly, particularly in the eponymous movie starring Keira Knightley that came out in 2018. The film illustrated with perfect pitch how the real Colette became a literary slave at twenty years old when her first husband, Henry Gauthier-Villars, known simply as Willy, forced her into a sweatshop-like routine as she wrote the *Claudine* books. The movie's script was masterful at presenting him as the cad he was, the ingrate going so far as to take full credit for the series of novels that looked back on Colette's school years in Burgundy. She proved her pluck by separating from him as she began a career as a mime. By then, she was a brazen thirty-three-year-old woman having a lesbian affair and crisscrossing France to appear on stage in a considerable number of cities night after night. I wondered, *Given Colette lived to cross the threshold of her eighties, what would I find by looking beyond the moment she ditched Willy in 1906 and finally divorced him in 1910?*

What I discovered was a life filled with plot twists, precarious decisions, and a genuineness that I had not expected to unearth. After the demise of the demoralizing marriage brought on by Willy's philandering and abusive behavior, Colette exhibited a disrespect for lovers that was just as cruel as Willy's had been. She tried to settle down with her second husband Henry de Jouvenel when she was thirty-nine years old, but she sabotaged the marriage by having an affair with her stepson Bertrand. Her husband's shock and subsequent push for a divorce in 1924 was understandable given his son was only sixteen at the time, more than three decades younger than Colette. By the following year, her story took a calmer turn and I began to see her through a different lens. The transformation came when she met a thirty-five-year-old Jewish bachelor named Maurice Goudeket when she was fifty-two. He would become her third and last husband, and a devoted partner for the rest of her life. Given the tenderness with which he describes her in his touching memoir *Close to Colette*, she finally made a wise decision when it came to affairs of the heart.

In his book, Maurice proved it is possible to see someone who was as well-known as Colette in a different light. In the narrative, he presents the woman he loved as a veritable force of nature in the primal sense of the term. He did so adoringly, following her with the utmost respect until the day she died. When he described the impact Colette's passing had on the people of Paris, who felt such a connection to her they placed bouquets on her grave, I was propelled to the Père Lachaise Cemetery on a cold January morning to see if she continued to inspire such attachment. I reached the tomb, which is honed from black-and-pink granite, to find homage was still being paid more than six decades later. It had been a while since fans had placed stems of cerise Astilbe in a matching urn affixed to the gleaming stone surface, the flowers faded to a very pale pink by the time I arrived. Clay pots holding spritzes of barely alive ivy and white Astilbe, in slightly better shape, were placed beside the urn, as was a plastic cup of purple pansies, still blooming brightly. On the opposite end of the imposing grave, a bouquet in a glassine sleeve and a lone rose had been placed at her feet, a gesture I knew Maurice would have loved.

Colette's first mention of Maurice was in a letter she wrote to one of her best friends, Marguerite Moreno, reporting that her new conquest had accompanied her on a theater tour along the Côte d'Azur. She told Moreno, "The sea and the sand have become my native elements. So is love. Am I not an abominable creature? (I need you to assure me otherwise.) Because it's three o'clock in the afternoon, my charming companion is sleeping but I don't need a siesta, I sleep so well at night. One always feels a little guilty writing next to someone who is asleep, even when it is only to acknowledge that he is charming and that one loves him. Tell me, wasn't it last winter that you warned me that during a voyage I would meet a man 'who would change my life'?"[1] Decades before they met, Maurice had a premonition that he would marry Colette. He explained his initial hunch and their clunky coming together in the beginning of his intimate memoir. "I was fifteen or sixteen years old when I discovered Colette, and received from that first reading of her a delicious shock," he remembered. "With the incredible pride and fanciful notions of that age, I said to my parents: 'I am going to marry that woman. She is the only one who will be able to understand me.'"[2]

He said he had not remained a bachelor because he honestly believed he would marry her; he merely wanted to save himself for a unique love. As he aged, he realized it was time to be honest with himself that he no longer believed this was possible. This was his state of mind when he met Colette in person and described her as "playing the part of herself" during a long and awkward dinner. As soon as she was seated at the table, she snatched an apple from a basket of fruit and bit heartily into it, which was seen as gauche; then, she took umbrage with so many conversations, it embarrassed the hostess. "I poured her out a drink and she looked astonished and shot me a look blue as night, ironical and quizzical but with an indefinable nostalgia in it too," Maurice explained. "Something countrified and healthy emanated from her. The rest of the evening dragged. She did not enjoy herself much. Neither did I."[3]

Several months later, after one other brief sighting of her at a theater, his feelings turned from distaste to fascination. "There is no doubt that the memory of my first meeting with Colette made me feel uncomfortable every time I thought of it," he said. "She had made a strong impression on me, and that was enough to put me on my guard." It was during a trip to Cap d'Ail in 1925 when he had his next interaction with her. He had offered Colette his chauffeured car so she could return to Paris in privacy, telling her he would take the train back. When he couldn't secure a seat, he asked her if she would be comfortable sharing his car for the trek back to town. He relished the experience of being her captive audience as they moved north through a series of landscapes. "Colette talked little but when she did she brought the whole countryside into the car," Maurice explained. "The very nature of the soil, the deep scent of all growing things, the invisible bird, the hidden water."[4]

He was able to see her spirit because her guard was down, which made her the polar opposite of the pretentious woman he had mocked after the uncomfortable dinner. "How clear and simple everything became when one was with her!" he proclaimed. "For the world which she restored to me was a real world, the world of everyday poetry, which was to become our dwelling-place." His realization that he had nearly missed the chance to experience this authenticity illustrates the thoughtfulness with which Maurice approached life. "I sometimes think how much the shaping of a destiny and the binding of a couple depend on successful meetings and the avoidance of snares," he explained. "A door which one thought was closed, a watch that is slow, a false step, a traffic jam, a sleeping car available…and your fate is settled."[5] He ended this chapter by pondering how many people, meant to be together, have passed each other in the fog, unaware that their soulmate was on the same patch of sidewalk, invisible to them.

He called Colette "French to her finger tips" and brought her earthiness to life by proclaiming, "She was provincial in her art of living, her household recipes, her tidy cupboards, her provisions, her punctuality, her proverbs, her boxwood and lily of the valley, her Twelfth-cake, her mulled wine, wood fires, chestnuts, and slow baking under the ashes." Maurice credited Colette's mother Sido for these predilections, as it was Colette's experiences in her childhood home and the love she felt for Sido's garden in Saint-Sauveur-en-Puisaye that made her so down-to-earth. He called that particular garden a lost paradise that had shaped Colette and her brother Léo forever afterwards. He then confirmed my suspicion that had Willy not locked Colette into a room until she produced a certain number of pages each day, she wouldn't likely have become a novelist. "She was sincere when she used to declare that if circumstances had not led her to write, she would never have done so all her life long," Maurice explained. "There may well never have been a writer with less of a vocation to write, and as soon as one knew her well one ceased to be astonished at this."[6]

He explained that her drive to put words on a page wasn't about being successful at writing; she simply always strove to accomplish every task with as much acumen as possible, and she was determined to perfect the craft forced upon her during her marriage to Willy. Maurice maintained that Colette lived so intensely, to be alive was in itself an occupation for her. "It was not a more novel activity to write than, for example, to make a pair of sabots," he explained. "Each needed to be performed as well as possible, with care and attention to detail."[7] He claimed she approached anything artistic with humility, patience, and self-exaction; and that pleasure was only possible once the task was completed, particularly when it was a well-finished article. He said she never let a page leave her hands if she had any doubts about whether it was as perfect as it could possibly be. Maurice wrote that 'inspiration' was a word she looked upon as suspect. While this falls in line with the pragmatic atmosphere in which she grew up, I wondered if her reticence to accept that her creative process benefitted from mysterious influences was a bit dishonest.

COLETTE MADE her mark in almost every literary genre known to man (and woman), writing not only novels and short stories, but plays, screenplays, and journalism—which included stints as a literary critic, a crime reporter, a social columnist, a war correspondent, and almost everything in between. For her to pump out so many words in a month's time, there must have been some sort of muse lurking in the corners of her beloved Palais-Royal apartment! Maurice described their attachment to this home they shared so lovingly, the flat became a character in their story. It was in 1938—thirteen years after Colette and Maurice met and ten years after they married—when they moved into the apartment where she spent the last sixteen years of her life. She snagged the spacious set of rooms after fruitlessly hoping for years that she could move into the larger apartment upstairs from the pied-à-terre in which she had lived a decade before. She had despised the low-ceilinged entresol that was wedged between the first floor and the shops beneath it because it was a cramped and gloomy place to call home.

She endured living there longer than she normally would have because she thought if she stayed, she would have a shot at renting the apartment above her. Sick of feeling so constrained, she finally gave up and moved away, residing in different locales around town until a serendipitous event made her wish to inhabit the first-floor spaces come true. During an interview with a reporter who said to her he understood she was about to move and that she liked nothing better than moving, she exclaimed, "What! Those who say that lie in their throats." She then told the reporter, "In the first place I've so far moved house only fourteen times, and each time it was because I was absolutely obliged to. The proof of that was ten years ago when I lived in the Palais-Royal. I went down on my hands and knees to try and rent the first floor of my house, and if I had been able to get it I should never have moved again." When the article appeared several days later, the owner of the apartment wrote Colette to say, "Madame: I read in *Paris-Midi* that you still hanker after the first floor of 9 rue de Beaujolais. I am living in this flat and I am quite ready to give it up to you."[8]

Maurice reported that their shock quickly turned to gratitude, though they saw the man's willingness to give up such an incredible apartment as sheer lunacy. It was January when they moved in, the same month I would traipse to their former address eight decades later. Colette wrote to her friends Charles and Lucie Saglio that she and Maurice were exhausted but she was finally settled in the apartment of her dreams. "Come and see my view!" she urged them.[9] I walked to the park to do just that, zigzagging my way along the graveled pathway between the rows of barren trees, my sights trained on the section of the building where the windows of her former flat were mirror-like in their brightness. A photo of her leaning on the balustrade, her gaze turned toward the garden, helped me imagine her there as I shielded my eyes from the sunlight reflecting off the gleaming stone façade. But there was no one leaning out a window on the frigid day I visited, one so cold I stayed only briefly in the quadrangle she had loved so much. Some of the most precocious anecdotes Maurice shared about Colette centered around gardens—the ones she created and the ones she explored during the nearly three decades they were together. He said her way of exploring the myriad elements in them was through the totality of her senses.

"It was not enough for her to look at them, she had to sniff and taste them," he explained. "When she went into a garden that she did not know, I would say to her, 'I suppose you are going to eat it, as usual.' And it was extraordinary to see her setting to work, full of haste and eagerness, as if there were no more urgent tasks than getting to know this garden." He described how she separated the sepals of flowers, examined them, smelled them for a long time, crumpled the leaves, chewed them, licked the poisonous berries and the deadly mushrooms, considering everything she had encountered with a rapt intensity. "Insects received almost the same treatment: they were felt and listened to and questioned," he remembered. "She attracted bees and wasps, letting them alight on her hands and scratching their backs. 'They like that,' she would claim."[10] His depictions of her were vivid as she left a garden with her nose and forehead covered in so much pollen, they were bright yellow. Her hair would be disheveled and filled with twigs; she didn't seem to feel the cuts on her skin; and her moist neck would gleam in the sunlight.

Only when she had exhausted her curiosity did she stumble along to exit the scene, out of breath. By then, he said, "She was like a bacchante after libations!"[11] During a summer stay in Saint-Tropez, she refused to believe a gardener that the great hornets would sting, a painful lesson she would not have to learn a second time. Despite this smarting from a marauding insect, discovering the natural beauty in the South of France brought Colette immense joy. It was Maurice's idea that they consider a second home there, and he said he was proud that he had introduced her to "new skies like a present to welcome her."[12] She was so enamored with the lifestyle they enjoyed along the Riviera, she agreed they should spend more time there, so they decided to buy a modest house in Saint-Tropez with four small rooms. It had no plumbing or electricity, but it had a small, north-facing terrace surrounded by a balustrade that was shaded by a thick wisteria vine. The retreat was set within two-and-a-half acres, half of which was planted with grapevines, the rest dedicated to a garden, a small copse of fir trees, and several fig trees.

Best of all was how close at hand the deserted beach and ocean were, accessed by ducking through a few of the vines and crossing a small road. Colette immediately began planning the garden, mentally cataloging the shrubs and flowers she would buy and where she would place them as she settled in. She felt the name the previous owners had given the property, Tamaris les Pins, was lacking, so she slowly walked around the perimeter of the house and noted attributes like the round well near the entrance to the garden and the ancient muscadine vine dripping with ripe grapes. "Good!" she declared; "we'll call it La Trielle Muscate."[13]

They set about improving the house, little-by-little, a process they continued year after year. As I read Maurice's reminiscences about their time there, I was incredibly jealous. He described the fullness and the savor of the days that unfolded with walks first thing in the morning; then gardening, bathing, and a siesta; and a light workload in the late afternoon when it was too hot to be out of doors. He adored the scented nights, murmurous with the songs of frogs and the chirping of crickets. As Colette worked her magic, the garden sprung to life.

"A great stretch of the wall was covered with a thick tapestry of morning glory of a luminous blue," he remembered. "The little crystal drinking troughs attached to the trees attracted the birds from all parts," the goldfinches particularly abundant, as Colette had planted sunflowers to entice them. She would invest a tremendous amount of energy in La Trielle Muscate during the thirteen years they owned it. They wouldn't have sold it when they did if the area hadn't become a tourist destination filling up with throngs of beachgoers lacking personal boundaries. "It was no longer possible to stay there," Maurice explained. "The little house was so accessible, so undefended, that Colette found journalists, intruders, visitors, and autograph-hunters hidden in the garden, waiting for her in the house, and coming up to her on the beach." Six years after they sold the property, Maurice decided to stop by as he was traveling through Saint-Tropez and the new owners allowed him access.[14]

"Alas!" he declared, "when the enchanter has gone, magic quits the scene. The 'park' had become a rather sad little garden, the 'forest' had lost its sacred-wood charm, and the 'countryside,' dotted with a few straggling peach trees, was reduced to a small vineyard rather badly kept." Colette memorialized the property in *La Naissance du Jour [Break of*

Day]. "If ever a novel appears to be autobiographical, that one does," Maurice claimed. "Everything is in it: 'La Trielle Muscate,' the garden, the vineyard, the terrace, the sea, the animals. Our friends are called by their real names. Colette puts herself into it, describing herself in minute detail. Never has she pushed self-analysis so far." He added that all of the allusions to her past in the book were authentic, including the letters her mother wrote to her, which Colette quoted verbatim.[15]

About her ability to capture the essence of their time in the South of France, he wrote, "The odors are those which still delight my nostrils. I have known those blue nights, I hear the wheezing of the cicadas, I feel the buffeting of the wind, my hand lingers on the warm wall. Everything is there, except that *La Naissance du Jour* evokes the peace of the senses and a renunciation of love at the moment when Colette and I were living passionate hours together, elated by the heat, the light, and the perfume of Provençal summers."[16] I was surprised he claimed it didn't bother him that she left their romance out of the story, and that he still deemed the narrative true and compelling in spite of this fact. He said she had not done so to spite him; it was because she was prone to self-denial and austerity. He illustrated this point by saying he never praised her without seriously considering what he would say and how he would say it because any flattery, even if it was true, made her uncomfortable. He deemed *La Naissance du Jour* his favorite of all of her books because it is "bathed in poetry and of unequalled destiny, richness, and eloquence."

MAURICE POINTED out that it was written midway in her long involvement with her craft at the height of her maturity.

After all this praise, he then admitted that he felt the storyline would have been better if she had included their love life! Colette would eventually mention Maurice in the memoirs she wrote later in life, but only identifying him as her best friend. In *The Evening Star,* which she began writing in 1943 when she was seventy, she declared, "Night, O night, sighs the Arab chant, O thou Night once more…When I embark on night in the name of rest and, if possible, sleep, she is already half-engaged in her course towards the limpidity of morning. We go to bed very late, my companion and I." She then shared this about their routine, which included her promise to call if she needed anything because they no longer shared a bedroom: "The door closed between us, I am free not to sleep, to wander around a little, to limp unconcealed, to go and eat what's left of the marmalade."[17]

She praised him the most in her letters. Again to Moreno, she wrote, "Last night Maurice and I had one of those talks that begin at ten minutes to midnight and goes on until four twenty-five in the morning. Would you believe it? How it satisfies me to fight with a certain finesse, and to find that my partner is on the right wavelength."[18] With Saint-Tropez behind them, they decided to buy a second home west of Paris in Montfort-l'Amaury tucked into the village of Méré. Maurice noted how it suited her taste for restrained horizons, quoting her as saying, "You must never allow a landscape to come into the house without your permission." He followed her around her new garden, the lawn, and the little copse of woods that descended abruptly toward the road, remembering her "diligent hand" in the "countryfied wilderness" that was "peppered with bulbs in the winter." He watched as she layered in new plants and tied artificial nests to the trunks of the trees.[19]

"For even before there was a piece of furniture in the house," he said, "the birds were provided for and a profusion of nuts was offered to hypothetical squirrels." He said to see Colette in the spring, eagerly on the hunt for hyacinths and lilies of the valley, was to know how profoundly she was connected to nature. "It was from Colette I learned that there is no true winter in our climates, but that a perpetual upthrust towards life goes on under the humus," he explained. "An old gardener with whom she used to exchange mysterious remarks knew this too."[20] Maurice would spy them as they examined plants, their faces "lit by the same conniving smile" as they made strange attempts at grafting. Maurice was fascinated to see the same small hands that wielded such a prolific pen grubbing in the dirt, the rake and trowel tossed aside because they were not as efficient. Once the new home's interior was furnished, they would spend weekends there, many times hiking in the Rambouillet Forest. Colette would carefully walk through the stands of trees with great caution, especially in the spring.

Maurice remembered how she would progress, "her ear suddenly alert, on the look-out for tracks, footprints, droppings." One day when he was walking behind her, he saw her wave away her bulldog Souci. When Maurice caught up to her, he found her on her knees, signaling to him that he should make no noise as he drew near. "Lying flat on the ground, among the pale green leaves of the lily of the valley, there was a nest on which sat a hen-pheasant hatching her eggs," he remembered. "In the face of that dog which she had seen approaching, and of her most redoubtable enemy, man, bending over her, she remained motionless, dominating her panic and resisting her instinct to flee, heroically awaiting death rather than abandon her eggs."[21] The hen's head as delicate and erect and Maurice could see that her breast was palpitating with anguish, and that her little body covered in tawny feathers was trembling.

He marveled at what he saw next. "Her hands apart,

Colette was whispering to her in a sort of cooing language, which for all we can know was perhaps her [the hen's] own, and trembling just as much as the bird," he explained. Maurice claimed he wanted to share this particular story to illustrate the depth of Colette's communion with the metaphysical world; to share "how she would quiver with pity and fervor, and be at one with everything that lived and breathed." Illustrating her complexity, he added, "But one must not confuse Colette's ardor for discovering the world, her passionate absorption in creatures and things with any kind of blind joy of living. Behind her enthusiasm, Colette was grave. There was no respect without gravity."[22] It was as if he realized at this moment in the book how intimately he was sharing the soulfulness he found in his wife, and needed to make it clear why he had decided to reveal so much.

"I was not master of Colette's hours of meditation as she sat at her tapestry and we respected long and trustful silences between ourselves," he explained. "The fact remains that I owe the public, in such measure as I am responsible to it, and in spite of the fragile nature of it, my testimony as to what lay at the root of Colette's behavior and was therefore the foundation of her work."[23] He accomplished this so beautifully, his forthrightness and sincerity often brought tears to my eyes. His first mention of the physical pain that would trouble Colette during her last decade enters the narrative in 1944 when arthritis from injuries suffered during her years on the stage, and from an accident during which she sprained her ankle and dislocated her hip set in. By this time, they were rarely apart, which made an unexpected separation a harrowing event for both of them—Maurice was imprisoned during the German Occupation of Paris for a torturous seven weeks during World War II. Colette's letters to her friends took on a desperate tone, as she was forced to sit in the uncertainty as to whether her husband would survive.

In her essay "The Colette I Knew," her friend Natalie Clifford Barney wrote about how desperate Colette felt: "She had to pull out all the stops in order to save him, and succeeded thanks to friends in high places both in France and abroad. But the anguish sapped her strength so much that when she caught sight of herself in the mirror she was unable to recognize herself in the distorted face reflected in the glass."[24] Maurice was equally shaken that their life together could have ended. Once they were reunited, he began a campaign to convince Colette it was time for her to turn her attention to arranging her complete oeuvres. The process was far from easy. "I had a great deal of difficulty in preventing her from using the scissors too briskly on her first writings," he said. More often than not, she acquiesced when he urged her to reconsider; and by the time they were finished, she had edited thousands of pages. "She would pause to say to me: 'Have I really written all that? Maurice, is it possible that I've written all that?'" Illustrating the austerity he spoke of earlier, he added, "Sometimes she would be sufficiently bold to say: 'It's not so badly done, this work, you know!' I knew."[25]

It is evident in her two memoirs written between 1943 and 1948 that she had a love/hate relationship with her writing life. "To unlearn how to write, that shouldn't take much time," she claimed in *The Evening Star*, published in 1946. "I can always try. I shall be able to say: 'I'm not concerned with anything here, except this rectangular forget-me-not, this rose shaped like a jam-puff, this silence when the sound of excavation produced by the search for a word has been suppressed.'" Then she busted herself by revealing it was not quite that simple. "Before reaching my goal, I continue to work. I don't know when I shall succeed in not writing; the obsession, the compulsion date back half a century," she explained. "The little finger of my right hand is somewhat bent because, when writing, the right hand supports itself on it like the kangaroo on its tail. Within me a tired mind continues with its gourmet's search, looks for a better word, and better than better."[26]

In *The Evening Star* she described how much she loved to cross-stich and how she struggled with all things literary, ending the book with this insightful analogy: "On a resonant road the trotting of two horses harnessed as a pair harmonizes, then falls out of rhythm to harmonize anew. Guided by the same hand, pen and needle, the habit of work and the commonsense desire to bring it to an end become friends, separate, come together again. Try to travel as a team, slow chargers of mind: from here I can see the end of the road."[27] The book also included a number of descriptions of the park that fanned out below her Palais-Royal windows, each of which had a meditative quality to them. This is how she pictures it during the winter: "It is usual to exclude the public from the garden when it snows. The snow is shut in. It becomes free to assume its snowy colors, to know that it is pink when the sun rises, blue along the zones of shadow, coppery beneath the setting sun."[28]

Here is how she presents it in the spring: "Changed…I finish writing this word and raise my eyes. Was it a magical word? Everything is new—the springtime arrives as I write. The Palais-Royal stirs at once under the influence of humidity, of light filtered through soft clouds, of warmth. The green mist hanging over the elms is no longer a mist, it is tomorrow's foliage. So soon! Yes, once again it is the sudden season. Let's continue to write; next time I lift my head it may be summer."[29] In her last memoir, *The Blue Lantern*, penned between 1946 and 1948, she described her debilitation as "a twisting pain, as if under the heavy screw of a winepress." By this time, she was battling insomnia and would write well into the middle of the night, the glow from her desk lamp visible to anyone passing through the section of the quadrangle her window overlooked. When she was able to doze and the weather was warm, she had figured out how to "sleep in the garden" by placing the head of her bed in the embrasure of the open window.

"From the garden, if it were not closed at night, you could see my bird's nest of hair through the balustrade," she wrote. "It's one of the attractions of this apartment: to be able to sleep outdoors."[30]

She declared that she had wanted her final two books to be journals but she hadn't conquered the knack of writing daily dispatches, which she described as "stringing together, bead by bead, day after day, a rosary whose value and intrinsic luster are relative to the writer's power of exact observation, of assessing his own importance and that of his time." She explained why it was impossible for her to do so: "The art of selection, of noting things of mark, retaining the unusual while discarding the commonplace, has never been mine, since most of the time I am stimulated and quickened by the ordinary." She returned to the subject of her ambiguity toward putting words on a page. "There I was, vowing never to write anything again after *L'Étoile Vesper* [*The Evening Star*], and now I have covered two hundred pages which are neither memoirs nor journal," she explained. "Let my reader resign himself to it: this lantern of mine, burning blue day and night between the pair of red curtains, pressed close to the window like one of the butterflies that fall asleep there on a summer morning, throws no light on events significant enough to astonish him."[31]

COLETTE WANTED to share for all posterity how one particular piece of furniture had been so important in her life. It was a writing desk given to her by the Princess de Polignac and rebuilt by Luc-Albert Moreau so that she wouldn't have to write sitting in a chair with her legs bent, which caused her tremendous discomfort. The desk was made to straddle her chaise lounge so that she could write while reclining. "I set great store by this piece of furniture," she explained. "Widened, made higher, reinforced, and stripped of most of its English eighteenth-century elegance, it bestrides my divan-bed and indeed, for a quarter of a century, had gladdened both my leisure and my working hours."[32] The blue light she referenced was also a constant in her life. "I ride at anchor beneath the blue lantern, which is quite simply a powerful commercial lamp at the end of a lengthy extensible arm, fitted with a blue bulb and a blue paper shade," she explained. Neighbors often commented to her about how they would spy it during all the darkened hours. "I tend to make less and less distinction between the hours of night and the hours of day," she said; "the hour for reading, for writing, for looking about me, all are equally good."[33]

Her neighbors gave her blue lamp a name, baptizing it *fanal*, the light that rakes the seas. "Madame Colette," one would say to her, "you can't imagine how pretty your lantern looked yesterday, shining through the fog." Another remarked, "Oh, but you can't tell me that you make sparing use of your blue lantern! It's on at all hours, in the early morning, at eight, sometimes at seven-thirty even!"[34] The nautical reference to her desk lamp was fitting, as Colette had long referred to her chaise lounge as a floating vessel. As Maurice described her nestled into it with her legs stretched out while reading, something occurred to me: He likely spent untold hours simply watching Colette. This is an example of an anecdote that must have been surreptitiously gleaned over a long period of time: "She read a great deal and with surprising rapidity, yet without ever skipping a line, and with attention too, as in everything that she did. From time to time she would unscrew her pen and correct a printer's error, out of habit and without being aware of it."[35] He said Balzac and Proust were her favorite authors; that she read their books time and again, stopping whatever she was doing when she received a new title by either novelist.

The twenty volumes of Balzac she owned, in the Houssiaux edition covered in red leather, were always close at hand, as was her famous unlined blue writing paper and her pen. Near the end of *The Blue Lantern*, she has her last say about the discipline that had enthralled, annoyed, and exhausted her for so much of her life. She said the stirring she felt was "an insurrection of the spirit," which "in the course of my long life I have often rejected, later outwitted, only to accept it in the end, for writing leads only to writing. I am still going to write; I say this in all humility. For me there is no other destiny. But when does writing have an end? What is the warning sign? A trembling of the hand?" She brought the book to a close with these insightful words about her craft: "I used to think that it was the same with the completed book as with other finished ploys, you down tools and raise the joyful cry 'Finished!', then you clap your hands only to find pouring from them grains of sand you believed to be precious. That is the moment when, in the figures inscribed by those grains of sand, you may read the words 'To be continued…'"[36]

Maurice described Colette's last years as ones of keen physical suffering because she was determined to retain some mobility. He had watched her transition from one cane to two; then a wheelchair whenever she went out of the apartment; and, near the end, a wheelchair for navigating inside. He said she never took sedatives because they made her gloomy. She told him, "I would rather suffer cheerfully."[37] It wasn't until she resigned herself to staying as still as possible that her pain lessened. Once she was able to admit she was no longer mobile enough to garden or to enjoy walks in nature, she decided it was time to sell the house in Méré. Save for rare excursions or trips to see her doctors, the Palais-Royal became her entire universe. As she grew progressively limited in her movements, she began to gather closer the treasures scattered around her, arranging them into what Maurice described as a captivating world. During my last evening in Paris, I walked along the dark shadowy exterior of the Palais-Royal as night deepened, looking up at the lit windows and the draperies that framed them, searching for a glimpse of red, a blue light, any signs of her world—but there were none.

The brightly lit French flag that waved above the Cour d'Honneur was snapping in the wind—so bright, it looked positively regal, just as it would have on some gusty evening when she and Maurice talked away the hours. He called the Palais-Royal Colette's true place, and then he prepared readers for the privilege of entering her inner sanctum, his words reverberating as I stood on the sidewalk in front of 9 rue de Beaujolais. "It is time that I took you into her room," he said. "Behind her there was a double door covered by a sliding curtain of thick red satin. In front of her, filling almost the whole panel between the window and the chimney-piece, which divides the room more or less in two, there is an arcaded niche hollowed out of the wall containing three shelves on which were crowded the books she most often read."[38] She loved travel books from the mid-nineteenth century most of all because the imagination and innocence of their authors appealed to her.

Maurice said her fascination stemmed from how naïvely

they left for "unknown parts of Africa in straw hats and button boots, accompanied by their dogs, which inevitably perished there."[39] In a letter to Moreno, Colette wrote, "Maurice has just given me a ten-volume series of travel books, dating from 1821, the best period. There is not a single detail which does not appeal to the purely extravagant mood, and the descriptions of South African wildlife...From the three-month-old sheep the size of a cow to the snake whose head is shaped like a human heart, to falling golden blocks—no, that's in Mexico—which destroy an entire village—one couldn't desire more. And when one stops to think that there is always a little bit of truth in these tales!"[40] As the number of unread pages in the book Maurice wrote about his beloved wife could be counted on one hand, he signaled he was transitioning readers into a graver period. By this time, Colette was always in a recumbent position so they asked permission to replace the chest-high panels at the bottom of the apartment's windows with glass so she could still see the garden below.

He explained the Palais-Royal and Colette were born to understand each other and there was a perfect communion between them so it was critical that she have the best possible view day and night. When she asked him to move her collection of earthly treasures closer, he realized her focus was narrowing: Bit-by-bit, books were hidden behind shadow-boxes of multi-colored butterflies, a smattering of seashells, and other "ornaments full of emblematic meanings." Maurice described her final weeks on her dependable vessel: "Everything was perfectly organized on the 'raft' for the thenceforward motionless voyage, in time and space, work on board, and soon, alas! the shipwreck."[41] He described her gaze as often fixed on the fireplace mantel, which was jammed with the colorful paperweights she had collected, and the beautiful butterflies that "bounded her immediate horizon." As he had done with so many other aspects of her life, Maurice brought these objects that Colette revered into a meaningful context. "A long life with its attachments, its infatuations, and its passion preferences had deposited there; its fetishes, its symbols, and its instruments, turning a bedroom somewhere in the world into a place enchanted above all others," he wrote.[42]

By the end of June 1954, her silences were more protracted, and Maurice noticed Colette's vitality was beginning to ebb. She no longer touched the newspapers brought to her each morning and rarely opened her letters. He said the exterior world was simply receding too far away. She kept a magnifying glass nearby so she could look more closely at things, particularly the butterflies. By late July, just a few weeks before she would pass away, she began sleeping deeply. "Colette only came out of her long torpors to give tender looks and angelic smiles," Maurice explained. "We sat her up and she asked for her butterflies, her illustrated books, raising in the air her little hands which mysteriously had become younger. Her face took on a strange beauty." Two days before she died, she awakened and asked for a large book of colored lithographs that Maurice had given her the week before, its pages filled with butterflies, insects, and birds. "We looked at the album together," he remembered. "I was sitting on the floor in the space between the bed and the window. It was a hot August day with a veiled sky. The swallows were passing level with the open window, with sharp whirrings. Colette bent toward me and I put my head against her side."[43]

She pointed to the boxes of butterflies on their shelf, the book, and the birds in the garden. 'Ah!' she said. So near to death and knowing it, everything appeared to her more beautiful and more wonderful than ever." He said her hands fluttered about her like wings. She leaned a bit closer to him and her arm made the shape of a spiral that encompassed the three representations of nature. "'Look!' she said to me, 'Maurice, look!' She spoke no more after that." On August third in the evening, with a heavy sky hanging over Paris and the Palais-Royal garden deserted, Colette let go. "Suddenly there was silence and Colette's head bent slowly to one side, with a movement of infinite grace," Maurice noted as he closed his narrative.[44] On the November day I was working on a draft of this essay, the first white-throated sparrows arrived for their over-wintering in Tennessee, as if Colette's spirit had summoned them. Their plaintive songs were so distinctive, it felt as if they had come to sing a dirge for the woman whose love of nature ran so deep. It was a mournful and fitting tribute that I will never forget.

3

WHERE SERENDIPITY WAS BORN

HORACE WALPOLE AT STRAWBERRY HILL

The magical mansion known as Strawberry Hill House, which sits majestically in the middle of a sizable lawn about twelve miles from Hyde Park Corner in London, remains one of my richest architectural experiences since I toured it in 2015. When I visited the newly refurbished building on a chilly Saturday morning in April, the white façade gleamed in the strong sunlight like a bastion to an earlier time. Approaching the entry to the neo-Gothic castle, I regretted that I knew so little about Horace Walpole, the home's creator, because the trip to Twickenham, where the mansion is located, was an impromptu decision. After touring the incredible architectural gem, my fascination with the atmosphere Horace concocted within it sent me on a journey to rectify this—an exploration that has now infused my encounter with the building with greater depth because I was lucky enough to have several expert guides. These did not exist within the building proper; they spoke to me from a distant and a not-so-distant past.

The first was Horace himself, who cataloged the artisans

he hired and the nearly four-thousand objects he collected to fill the home in his book *A Description of the Villa of Mr. Horace Walpole*. He also shared the ambiance he intended to convey within the fanciful country house in his many letters to friends. These writings have taken on greater import since 1842 because the treasures Horace brought together under the mansion's roof were scattered across the globe when one of his ancestors auctioned off the entirety of Strawberry Hill's contents during the "Great Sale" that year, four and a half decades after Horace died. That the restored shell of the building remains is a gift for architectural aficionados, the effort to preserve it requiring significant reconstruction because of neglect and the fact that Horace and his two collaborators who designed the villa—illustrator Richard Bentley and architect John Chute—were prone to experimenting with materials not meant to be used in the way they specified them.

The trio fancied themselves "The Committee of Taste," the name proving they were much more interested in aesthetics than engineering. The building was also bombed during World War II, which added to the challenges faced by the Strawberry Hill Trust, the organization established to oversee the building's restoration. My experiences within the mint-condition interiors they refurbished began when I stepped into the dimly lit entrance hall, which gave me a shock after such intense brightness outside. My reaction to the medieval mood was exactly what Horace intended, his name for the vestibule, the Great Hall, a bit deceiving because the room was quite small, though it was very tall given the vaulted ceiling with a sizable glassed dome culminated above a two-story stairwell. The shadowy space would have been even gloomier when he lived in the mansion because the quatrefoil-shaped windows set into the four sections of the dome would have been fitted with stained glass.

Horace claimed the most famous of the several suits of armor he had placed in the entry was worn by Francis I, the sixteenth-century king of France. Describing the arrangement of weaponry in his catalog, he said Francis's armor was made "of steel gilt, and covered with bas-reliefs in a fine taste"; the king's lance was fashioned from "ebony inlaid with silver"; and the steel sword was "beautifully inlaid with gold, probably the work of Benvenuto Cellini." Horace then noted the armor for the horse's head was also displayed in the same vignette and highlighted other suits in the room that were supposedly worn by other members of royalty.[1] I say "supposedly" because early on in my perusal of the catalog that held these assertions, I questioned whether he could have found such important antiquities outside of museums. Eventually, I realized it didn't matter because my doubt was taking all of the fun out of the exploration—if he could allow himself to be swept up in a jaunty enthusiasm for relics with outlandish provenances, so could I! Though Horace bemoaned the fact that he was outbid for Oliver Cromwell's nightcap, he was quite successful with other treasures that illustrate his desire to find relics previously owned by famous people.

Among the objects he said he acquired were an ornate, carved ivory comb made for the sixth-century queen Bertha of Kent; the red wide-brimmed hat worn by Cardinal Thomas Wolsey, Henry VIII's Lord Chancellor; and the spurs William of Orange sunk into the flank of his horse at the Battle of the Boyne. He then proved his penchant for creating alternative realities by telling his cousin Henry Conway he was going to claim all of the elements in his collection were from his great-great-grandmother's estate! In a letter to his friend Sir Horace Mann, a British diplomat based in Florence, Horace explained that he had achieved exactly what he had envisioned for the entry hall at Strawberry Hill and that it "succeeded to a miracle."[2] He went to great lengths to impress Mann in his letters when he was describing his home and its contents, growing frustrated when his friend didn't fully comprehend the imaginative power that made the spaces he decorated so dramatic. To get his point across about the Great Hall, he included a sketch by Bentley with the letter in which he highlighted the room.

"It is impossible to describe to you, as it is the most particular and chief beauty of the castle," Horace wrote. "Imagine the walls covered with (I call it paper, but it is really paper painted in perspective to represent) Gothic fretwork; lean windows fattened with rich saints in painted glass, and a vestibule open with three arches on the landing-place."[3] Mann, who corresponded with Strawberry Hill's creator for decades, would finally come to appreciate the depth of meaning his friend was determined to achieve, though he would never see it for himself. The letters between the two represent the largest in the glut of correspondence Horace and his acquaintances produced during his lifetime because they met only once. Stephen Clarke, who edited *Selected Letters of Horace Walpole*, noted why the number of missives they exchanged—more than seventeen hundred—was so robust. "Walpole did not see Mann after staying with him in Florence in 1741," he explained, "but they wrote to each other regularly until Mann's death forty-five years later."[4]

In a letter from Twickenham in April of 1753, Horace wrote a word portrait to describe to Mann the medieval weapons he had placed in the entry hall, noting that these included "trophies of old coats of mail, Indian shields made of rhinoceros's hides, broadswords, quivers, long bows, arrows, and spears." After confessing to his friend that when artifacts like these arrived by the cart-load, his servants thought he was nuts, he said each of the weapons were "supposed" to be taken by Sir Terry Robsart during the holy wars.[5] As he did with many others, Horace annotated this letter to indicate that Robsart had been knighted by the Most Noble Order of the Garter and was an ancestor of Horace's own father, Sir Robert Walpole, the 1st Earl of Orford and Great Britain's de-facto first prime minister. Horace highlighted the word "supposed" himself, whether the emphasis was because he was not certain or that he was making it up is not clear.

Though the regalia he collected was absent when I walked through the Great Hall, the space retained the haunting quality he had desired because the Strawberry Hill Collection Trust, a second entity that oversees retrieving or replicating the original contents of the mansion, had already begun to decorate the room with relics that would provide the same ambiance Horace achieved in the space. The armorial pieces the Collection Trust displayed in the entry were arranged in large niches, just as Horace's treasures would have been during his lifetime. Also omnipresent in the room were a number of beefy antelope finials perched inside metal cages atop posts at different points on the staircase, their blank stares and half-opened mouths quite disturbing as I moved through the space. The animal also shows up in other places in the home because it is one of the symbols adorning Horace's family crest. Though the depictions in their heraldry are lithe and graceful, those guarding the entry are muscular and downright creepy.

I was glad to leave them behind as I climbed to the second floor, called the primary floor because it is where Horace lived separated from the domestic activity that took place downstairs. Surrounding me as I ascended to a landing was the stone-colored trompe l'oeil tracery that Horace had described to Mann. The design of the delicate motifs was copied from the tomb of Prince Arthur Tudor, Henry VIII's older brother, in Worcester Cathedral, which Horace had seen in a book. The curving patterns that were ubiquitous during the Middle Ages were so delicately rendered, they created a winsome canvas on which was superimposed a chilling experience as I reached the top of the stairs. I'm not sure what brought on the strange sensations—it could have been the symbolism drawn from the crypt of such a doomed young man, the eerie-looking lantern made of dark metal and stained glass that lit the space with a flickering flame, the chivalric arms from barbaric wars that hung on the walls, or the antelopes gawking from their cages.

In truth, it was likely the sum of each of the effects Horace envisioned that manifested the medieval "gloomth" in the spaces, as he described the atmosphere. The Great Hall and the Armory, to which the stairs had led me, were the only rooms in Strawberry Hill I found to be depressing. Horace claimed one of the most important suits in the Armory had "the mark of a bullet" on it; and that it had likely belonged to Richard Neville, the Earl of Warwick—a powerful nobleman known as the Kingmaker because he was famous for elevating and dethroning monarchs. Horace believed the earl had worn it when he marched on Parliament during the reign of Henry VI. After leaving the Armory, I stepped into a brighter space that finally provided relief from the dreariness of the first two rooms. Horace named it the Green Closet after the emerald color on its walls, and said it is where he wrote his most famous novel *The Castle of Otranto*. Set like graceful chess pieces in the tiny space were a desk and a chair that date to Horace's time, each diminutive enough to have suited his frame.

WHERE SERENDIPITY WAS BORN

BY ALL ACCOUNTS, he was a peculiar looking dude. Horace described his own gait, which would eventually be hindered by intense gout, in one of his letters. He said he had been told he ran along like a pewit when he was young. The pewit is a bird in the northern lapwing family with big eyes and a flowing crest extending from the back of its head, its darting movements bringing to mind a young man with extremely thin legs who skittered along. It was also said that Horace had a high, pale forehead; a forced and uncouth laugh; and an unpleasing smile. In her *Anecdotes, Biographical Sketches, and Memoirs*, Laetitia Hawkins shared other physical attributes she remembered about a fifty-five-year-old Horace when she met him. She said his figure was "not merely tall, but more properly long and slender to excess; his complexion, and particularly his hands, of a most unhealthy paleness. His eyes were remarkably bright and penetrating, very dark and lively —his voice was not strong, but his tones were extremely pleasant, and, if I may say, highly gentlemanly."[6]

I laughed aloud when she shared his preferred manner of making an appearance, saying, "He always entered a room in that style of affected delicacy, which fashion had then made almost natural—*chapeau bras* [folding hat] between his hands as if he wished to compress it, or under his arm; knees bent, and feet on tip-toe, as if afraid of a wet floor." She said two of his favorite outfits when he would visit her during the summer were a lavender suit with a waistcoat embroidered in silver thread and a white silk suit worked in tambour embroidery. To complete these ensembles, he wore partridge silk stockings, had gold buckles on his shoes, and wore lace ruffles around his neck.[7] Hawkins referred to Strawberry Hill as Horace's "bauble-villa" and shared how he was derided by passersby, calling the home a "crazy bargain" and an "enormous folly" because he was constantly repairing the exterior. She said the "external decorations frequently provoked the wanton malice of the lower classes, who, almost as certainly as new pinnacles were put to a pretty Gothic entrance, broke them off." She added, "To do him justice, he bore it with great patience, almost confessing that he merited the punishment by the indulgence of his taste."[8]

In a book printed to celebrate the restoration of Strawberry Hill House, John Iddon claimed the spires were so easy to snap off because many of the exterior ornamentations were made of lath-and-plaster. In *The Gothic Revival: An Essay in the History of Taste*, Sir Kenneth Clark took Horace's construction processes to task for being inadequate. "Walpole's taste seems to have found satisfaction in just those things which were to bring about the collapse of architecture in the nineteenth century" because he was "an incompetent copyist," Clark wrote. He cites as one example the ceiling in one of the upstairs salons called the Holbein Chamber, which was originally made of papier-mâché. "Nothing in that house is simple, natural and solid," Clark added. "Instead of good workmanship he introduced the quaint—a word which covers everything silly and unnecessary in style. Walpole killed craftsmanship: it was reserved for later Gothic revivalists to resurrect it."[9]

Clark wrote this thesis long before the restoration by the Strawberry Hill Trust, the organization's efforts stabilizing the materials in the interior spaces. The outcome is stunning. As I walked through each of the rooms, the backdrop unfolded like a series of storybook illustrations. Adjacent to the Green Closet is the Breakfast Room where a fireplace mantle has a Saracen's head carved into it, the exotic profile another symbol from the Walpole family crest. Horace was not happy with the dark wood chimney-piece by architect William Robinson because it didn't meet his standards of prettiness. Clark pointed out that Horace was drawn to "a light and genteel" Gothic; and that, though features were copied from tombs and cathedrals built during the Middle Ages, once Horace adorned them with gold or slathered them with glossy paint, they would turn decidedly Rococo. The author said the elements would be "so far from the spirit of the original," they would outdistance Bentley's wildest designs.[10]

Once past the Breakfast Room, this premise was on glorious display. Gone were the macabre milieus, and the dreariness was replaced with vibrant spaces painted or papered in brilliantly rich or pretty pastel colors. These were complemented by crisp white and glossy ivory woodwork, some of the surfaces glinting with gilded ornamentation. Horace's ability to create folly-like atmospheres enthralled me, and the jeweled colors contrasting the pale or gleaming finery were triumphant! The Blue Bedchamber in a drenching hue of the color has a whimsical fireplace-surround in a pale cream, the spires rising above the mantle on each side extending above panels holding clusters of acanthus leaves. Moving along the hallway, I entered the most magical room, the Library. The idea for the shelves, fronted by Gothic arches that were adorned with intricately carved details, came from a side door to the choir in St. Paul's Cathedral, which Horace spotted in William Dugdale's book about the history of the church. The arches culminate in knobby spikes that form miniature flèches as they reach toward the ceiling.

Each shelf is surrounded by an identical section of fretwork that swings on hinges to make the books easier to access and is identified by a letter of the alphabet painted in blackletter script. The pieces of furniture Horace listed in the space, which were no longer in the room, were a Louis XIV writing table, six ebony chairs, five screens, and a clock that Henry VIII gave to Anne Boleyn. What I wouldn't give to see that! To maintain uniformity with the depth of the shelves, the door to the Library is a thick archway, which created the illusion I was entering an inner sanctum when I passed through it. There is a stunning chimney piece in the space—an imitation of the tomb of John of Eltham, the Earl of Cornwall, in Westminster Abbey. The story on the intricate ceiling, designed by Horace and painted by Jean-François Clermont, unfolded like a mythic fable that illustrated the themes of the crusades. Down the hall, the Holbein Chamber is another spectacular space. As my eyes slid across the lush purple walls and fanciful ceiling filled with medieval quatrefoil motifs in white, I was in awe of the intricacies Horace envisioned.

The design of the ceiling was taken from the queen's dressing room at Windsor and the magnificent chimney piece was inspired by the Canterbury tomb of William Warham, the archbishop of the cathedral during the sixteenth century. To the left of the fireplace is a screen with pierced arches, the profile of which is based upon the gates of the choir at the Cathédrale Notre-Dame de Rouen. These interior architectural details stood out so prominently because the rooms were either empty or almost bare of furnishings. One moment, I longed to see the many elements that would have made Horace's home an elaborate setting when his collection was in situ; the next, I was thankful those pieces were absent because there were no distractions to pry my attention away from how elegantly he melded his proclivity for ornate style and his desire to bring the medieval world to life. He claimed he had a head filled with Gothic story, which came to life when he described a number of objects he had placed in the last room on the tour of the mansion, the Great North Bedchamber.

Within the luscious red space with walls covered in a tone-on-tone brocade pattern, there would have been sculptures of the French King Francis II and paintings of his wife,

Mary Queen of Scots; King James I's gloves; a silver-gilt plate depicting Francis I of France meeting the Holy Roman Emperor Charles V; and those spurs he said William of Orange sunk into his horse's flank during the Battle of the Boyne. Though not of the era, there was also a 1770s bed that was reputedly made for Marie Antionette. Horace was able to spend so much time fixated on the vast array of objects, art, and furnishings he brought together because he was independently wealthy. As the third son of the powerful prime minister and eventually his heir as the 4th Earl of Orford, Horace was provided with several government sinecures when he was in his twenties, which gave him a lucrative income for the rest of his life. He wouldn't hold the title of earl until he was seventy-four because it passed to his brother Robert, the 2nd Earl of Orford, and then to Robert's son, Horace's nephew George.

When George died without any children, Horace stepped into the role in 1791. He had already completed Strawberry Hill by then, his plans for the building evolving as he began construction in 1749, several years after he bought the property that spreads along the banks of the River Thames. Horace made a clever design move as he envisioned his theatrical backdrop—rather than start from scratch, he took several existing cottages and combined them into one larger edifice because he liked the haphazard arrangement of the rooms and the sense of age the original buildings emanated. "One of his favorite words in relation to Strawberry Hill was 'sharawaggi,'" wrote Iddon, "a Chinese word for 'want of symmetry,' and a glance at the floor plan reveals how unsymmetrical it became."[11] The largest of the cottages was called 'Chopp'd Straw Hall' when Horace purchased it because it was owned by an earl's coachman who was able to buy the land with profits he made by selling off the hay the earl's servants planted and feeding his boss's horses inferior chopped straw.

Horace said he called the property Strawberry Hill because he saw the name on one of the deeds. His dream for the mansion was exactly what he achieved—a Gothic castle with pinnacles, battlements, and a round tower. Aided by "The Committee of Taste," he pulled out all the stops, decoratively eclipsing what had previously been off-the-charts ornate as they went along. "Together they were supposed to decide on alterations, to choose originals from which to copy, and to censor designs when made," wrote Clark. "But their aims were divided. Chute and Walpole fancied themselves as archaeologists, and liked to display their Gothicism by copying medieval shrines. Bentley employed Gothic because its name licensed any extravagant invention."[12]

ONCE THEY HAD WORKED their magic, Horace didn't have to wait long for the residence to create a stir because the artificiality of the made-up genre of architecture flew in the face of the classicism and Palladianism that were fashionable then. Though architectural aficionados criticized Horace's brand of exaggerated flair, dubbing it "Strawberry Hill Gothic," the mansion quickly became a tourist destination that eventually influenced others to copy aspects of the style. This was Horace's intention all along. Though his lineage reserved a place for him in posterity, his goal was always greater than this—he wanted to create an idiosyncratic reputation for himself that would be powerful enough to echo through the ages in a more dynamic way than it could have if he had remained merely one in thousands of names listed in the records of the peerage. The fact that I am able to imagine him traipsing through the rooms I toured brings his wish to fruition, which thrills me because it makes this essay a furtherance of his quest.

The more I learned about him, the more I wanted to know about his life and his habits, my digging bearing fruit when I found hints at his routines that concretize his movements within the mansion's rooms. In his preface to nine volumes of Horace's letters published in 1906, Peter Cunningham wrote, "For fifty years, the days and nights of Horace Walpole were very much the same."[13] He said Horace would return to Strawberry Hill from social occasions in London and write to his friends while sitting in the Library or the Blue Room until around two in the morning. "He wrote his letters as rapidly as his disabled fingers would allow him to form the characters of a remarkably legible hand," Cunningham said. "No rough drafts or sketches of familiar letters were found amongst his papers at Strawberry Hill, but he was in the habit of putting down on the backs of letters or on slips of paper, a note of facts, of news, of witticism, or of anything he wished not to forget, for the amusement of his correspondents."[14] The disability Cunningham mentioned was the gout that Horace cursed in many of the letters he wrote from those extraordinary rooms. My mind's eye can see him tiptoeing into the Library to take a book from the shelf and carry it back to the desk so he could carefully peruse it for a snippet he could insert into a letter to his pen pals.

I can hear his "forced and uncouth" laughter echoing from the room as he came up with a jesting insult or a piece of penetrating wit that he would record in his neat cursive. As I searched for clues as to what made the effete aristocrat tick, I was surprised that a number of the biographies written about him turned out to be a waste of time because their authors were myopic. One of them made me incredibly uncomfortable as he shouted to the heavens how gay Horace had been and how no one wanted to dish about it, using such derogatory terms to make his case I ditched the book soon after I started it. I put down others because I felt they presented Horace as one-dimensional in some way, one of them deeming him a frivolous dilatant and another focusing on what a spoiled brat the author thought he was. It wasn't until I found Horace as seen through the eyes of another collector, Wilmarth Sheldon Lewis, whose friends called him Lefty, that I knew I'd hit the Walpoliana lottery, as I had found my second guide. Lewis devoted his adult life to collecting belongings once owned by Horace and everything he could find written by or about him.

Once his cache of treasures was substantial enough, he staged the furnishings, art, and books in his home that would eventually become a research library. After ten years of gathering letters to and from Horace, the first of which he found in 1923, Lewis began publishing them in volumes, and continued annotating and publishing compendiums of them as he scored new ones, which showed up until he died in 1979. Lewis opened his 1951 book *Collector's Progress* with this quote by Horace written in 1784: "It will look, I fear, a little like arrogance in a private man to give a printed description of his villa and collection." The statement is an epigraph that appears before the preface to Horace's *A Description of the Villa of Mr. Horace Walpole*. "He was speaking for all collectors who write about their houses and collections," Lewis wrote. "The collector is afraid of being thought arrogant if he publishes an account of his collection; but he has a still stronger fear, the fear that the world will not know that he has a collection worth writing about."[15]

Lewis can illuminate this subject with the utmost authority, as he built what George E. Haggerty calls "the most astonishing collection ever amassed by a single individual" in his 2001 article titled "Walpoliana" in the journal *Eighteenth-*

Century Studies.[16] Among the relics and objects Lewis found were classical antiquities, paintings, drawings and prints, decorative arts objects, coins and medals, arms and armor, curiosities, furniture, and books. The thousands of extant letters Lewis would eventually publish had been dispersed so far and wide, he had to diligently hunt them down during trips to Europe or by corresponding with publishers and other collectors who were spread around the globe. Illustrating how passionately Lewis felt about preserving Horace's legacy, the Walpoliana expert bequeathed the entirety of his collection to Yale University along with his home and his fourteen-acre property in Farmington, Connecticut.

Set within the lawns fanning out around it, the eighteenth-century residence is now known as the Lewis Walpole Library. In *Collector's Progress*, Lewis leads readers through the front door of the Colonial home, the oldest portion of the house built in 1784, serendipitously the same year Horace wrote his semi-apologetic epigraph above. Lewis sets the scene of his written tour by describing the hallway leading into the house, saying the entire expanse was hung with colored drawings and prints of Strawberry Hill. Lewis 'got to know' Horace by pouring over the six-thousand letters he collected, the most he could amass of the more than seven-thousand Horace wrote to or received from friends. Lewis's motivation for publishing *Collector's Progress* was to answer an inevitable question posed to him—everyone was keen to know how he became interested in Horace Walpole.

LEWIS'S descriptive powers in *Collector's Progress* makes the book such a fun read, particularly when he describes his encounters with the idiosyncratic booksellers and auctioneers he met in Great Britain, his mantra as he was navigating through their shops: "One must be on one's guard against non-collectors."[17] His first excursion in the summer of 1922 took place in a draper's shop in Newbury, England, that was owned by the widow of a book collector. He climbed the narrow stairs to the upper floor with several friends and came upon a treasure-trove of volumes stacked on the floor. "Sinbad in the cave of diamonds was not more dazzled," he said of the experience. "The summer sun filtered through the windows of the attic; motes rose in the shafts of light, dust from the great books that were passing into our possession." He bought two hundred fifty books that day for about forty dollars. "I still regard those intoxicating hours at Newbury as one of the greatest moments of my collecting life," Lewis noted.[18]

During the same trip, he visited a bookstore in Plymouth where he found an avant-garde shopkeeper who was so savvy at selling, he said the great authors galloped through his store. Also during this excursion to Great Britain, Lewis was persuaded by the proprietor of Godfrey's bookshop in York to buy a copy of John Heneage Jesse's *George Selwyn and His Contemporaries*, published in 1843. The book about the eccentric man-about-town would turn out to be pivotal in the collecting journey Lewis took because it cemented his desire to dedicate his efforts to the eighteenth century. I was surprised when Lewis revealed he was a twenty-eight-year-old bachelor living in Greenwich Village at the time because this seemed like a young age for someone outside of the dealer profession to have the wherewithal to track down rare books. He had the luxury to do so because his mother had died the year before—nine years after his father had passed—and left him financially set for life. Though he could have afforded far more, the budget he established for collecting books and other paraphernalia when he began was five thousand dollars per year.

Lewis was a newly published novelist when he took the trip to England, describing himself as his own master and a "born collector," the latter taking precedence because the hunting-and-gathering bug was quashing his enthusiasm for the second novel he was writing. Though he had zeroed in on the eighteenth-century as his focus, it took him a while to center his efforts around a coherent subject. He wrote about his frustration just before the event that would change everything. "Here is all English literature spread out before me and I am not really interested in any of it," he explained. "Now, if I could only get going on someone—and there drifted across my mind 'outstanding collection,' 'delightful life.'"[19] Several months after his return from England, the evening that steered him in the direction he would take unfolded when a group of friends came over for dinner. As they were browsing through his purchases, they came upon the Selwyn book, into which was tucked thirty-three pages of notes and anecdotes by Lady Louisa Stuart, the granddaughter of the English aristocrat, writer, and poet Lady Mary Wortley Montagu.

When one of Lewis's friends read Stuart's notes aloud, the burgeoning collector's imagination was sparked. *Now, the true adventure begins!* I thought as he honed in on Selwyn, Stuart, and Montagu. Scouring books about them, his excitement grew because their stories confirmed his instincts to focus on the eighteenth-century was perfect. Before long he came across a description that sent him off to the races, a portrayal of Stuart that declared her prose sparkled with "eighteenth-century anecdote of the most brilliant character." The author of the book added, "It is not too much to say that, in some respects, Lady Louisa could give points even to the inimitable gossip Horace Walpole himself."[20] With the words "inimitable gossip Horace Walpole" lingering in his mind, Lewis drove to New Haven to confer with several professors he knew could tell him more about Horace. The fact that Lewis was a Yale graduate helped him greatly because he could turn to former teachers and university librarians for advice as to what he should read next.

As he followed their leads, Horace began to come into sharper focus and Lewis was able to widen the circle of characters who had orbited in Walpolian circles, such as the two sisters Mary and Agnes Berry. They were important because Horace had introduced them when they entered high society and they became so close to him, he moved them into a cottage he owned that was close to the mansion so he could spend more time with them. Lewis's adventure deepened when he bought his first Walpolian artifacts during his next trip to London. He was wandering down Chancery Lane when he decided to duck into the auction house Hodgson & Co. where he spotted a set of Horace's *Anecdotes of Painting in England* and six of his letters to the Scottish antiquary John Pinkerton. These were to be sold the next day and Lewis returned, successfully bidding on the items only to learn that buying the books was the first in a number of missteps he would take as a neophyte. He shared each of his blunders in *Collector's Progress* to serve as caveats for those who were considering building a collection.

He said he paid what he felt was a high price for the books because he believed the marginalia was in Horace's hand, which turned out to be wrong. Disappointed at first, Lewis came to realize over time that the books would be a valuable addition to his collection because they were printed on the private press Horace had set up at Strawberry Hill. Statements Horace made to Mann prove he was proud of his publishing efforts, which inspired Lewis to collect as many books as he could find that were printed on the Strawberry

Hill Press. The efforts Horace mentioned were volumes he published about heraldry and antiquities, sets of Madame de Sévigné's letters he printed, and a number of other books that related to the French socialite and her acquaintances. The more I read by Lewis, the more I trusted him because he never assumed anything. I followed him along like a lacky tracking a brilliant detective as he struggled with the fact that accounts of Horace varied so much, he couldn't decide which could possibly be true.

Lewis also felt it was important that Horace be a good person if he was going to dedicate himself to proving the aristocrat was deserving of a larger legacy than he had earned, the concern about Horace's reputation brought on by rumors that the Brit was nasty to and quarreled with all of his friends. Lewis also felt it was imperative to find out whether Horace had been responsible for the suicide of the poet Thomas Chatterton, as had been claimed by several magazine editors and was repeated by the editor of Chatterton's collected works in the preface to the book published after the poet's death. Lewis began his quest to decode the truth about Horace with this question: "What kind of man was he?" The answer would be a long time coming, as this list of opinions he shared highlights the varying takes on the complex man's stature and personality.

Lewis quotes Lord David Cecil, a renowned British biographer, historian, and scholar, as saying, "Countless writers have discussed him, but at the end all have confessed themselves baffled." While Lord David said Horace was "more like a sprite than a man" with "his dragonfly elegance," Lewis said Virginia Woolf found him "the strangest mixture of ape and cupid that ever was," and Thomas Babington Macaulay deemed him "a pâté-de-foie-gras made of livers preternaturally swollen." Lewis lists a slew of contradictions in the following quote that illustrates why anyone writing about

Horace had every right to be baffled, saying, "As a boy Horace was so sickly he was not expected to live, yet he lived into his eightieth year; though a petit-maître [dandy], he hardened himself by walking out of hot rooms into the cold without putting on a coat. When the monument to his mother [that he funded] was put up at Westminster Abbey, he was afraid to go alone among the schoolboys there to see it; yet when his friend Lord Lincoln was threatened by two drunken officers at the opera, he clambered over the intervening boxes and chairs to go to his aid."[21] Lewis called Horace a good businessman whose head was filled with romantic notions and a strident champion for underdogs the world over.

By the time the collector had digested a fair amount of anecdotal evidence about Horace's life through the aristocrat's exchanges with his family and friends, Lewis was growing more convinced Horace needed a champion of his own. He was able to confidently declare that the Englishman's interactions with the people who were closest to him were most often noncombative and that Horace actually had a gift for friendship, his relationships spanning young and old, manly and effeminate, and cynical and pious personalities. Lewis also felt Walpole's reply to the accusations against him regarding Chatterton, which Horace printed at Strawberry Hill and had published, was convincing. "His capacity for lasting friendship was one of his most endearing qualities," Lewis wrote.[22] Relieved that Horace was not an uncaring person, Lewis felt he needed to disprove several other pieces of gossip before he could commit to being the champion he sensed the Englishman deserved.

The first involved Marie Anne de Vichy-Chamrond, the Marquise du Deffand, to whom Horace's detractors said he was undeservedly cruel. In order to appreciate Lewis's defense of Horace in this matter, it's important to understand the awkward relationship that developed between the Brit and the woman he described as "an old debauchee of wit."[23] Horace met Deffand when he went to Paris for an extended stay in September of 1766, the introduction orchestrated by Selwyn, who was one of Horace's most fashionable and eccentric friends. Deffand, who was blind, was well known for presiding over one of the most brilliant salons in the French capital, which Horace clamored to get into but would find he had mixed feelings about even before he realized he had inspired romantic feelings in its hostess. His discomfort stemmed from the fact he was perpetually on guard around the intellectuals who attended because they maintained rigorous debates and philosophical discussions that caused him to fear he would make a blunder.

He grew even more uneasy when he realized the marquise was harboring an attraction for him because Deffand was in her late sixties by the time Horace met her and he was forty-nine at the time. Knowing how cruel courtiers could be, Horace felt any hint of attachment between them put him at risk of being ridiculed. In his letters to his friends during his first stay in Paris, Horace relates how much he respected Deffand, descriptions that show his feelings stopped at fondness and didn't come close to the romantic notions some biographers have claimed. He told his pal Thomas Gray she "was for a short time mistress of the Regent, is now very old and stone-blind, but retains all her vivacity, wit, memory, judgment, passions, and agreeableness." He added, "She goes to operas, plays, suppers, and Versailles; gives suppers twice a week; has everything new read to her; makes new songs and epigrams, admirably, and remembers every one [of them] that has been made these fourscore years." He shared aspects of her personality he admired when he said, "She is all love and hatred, passionate for her friends to enthusiasm, still anxious to be loved, I don't mean by lovers, and a vehement enemy, but openly."[24]

Though he continued to attend Deffand's gatherings out of respect even after he feared she would embarrass him, Horace preferred to spend time in the salon held by Marie Thérèse Rodet Geoffrin. In spite of the fact that Geoffrin was also in her late sixties, he gravitated toward her drawing rooms because he could cruise through them in a relaxed way knowing that wit, his preferred mode of sparring, rather than ideology ruled the day; and she didn't put him in an awkward situation by harboring an attraction toward him. In her biography *Madame du Deffand and Her World*, Benedetta Craveri devoted an entire chapter to Horace's relationship with Deffand. She said that within several months of Horace's arrival in Paris, the Brit grew certain the marquise's "vain illusions were becoming dangerously concentrated on him." She described Deffand's hopes as futile because Horace had always sublimated his emotional life to concentrate his energies on social engagements that didn't involve romantic dust-ups.[25]

"Erudition, the delights of society, the cataloguing of antiques, the pleasures of the table, a British love of dogs, the contemplation of a painting, the writing of a letter—these were all equally essential parts of his elaborate daily existence," she explained.[26] Craveri didn't believe this made Horace superficial, as she agreed with how Lytton Strachey saw Horace in a portrait he wrote about the aristocrat in his book *Biographical Essays*. In the piece, Strachey claimed Horace's shortcomings were caused by excessive sensitivity rather than a lack of genuine feeling or a coldness of heart. He said, "The masks he wore were imposed upon him by caste, by his breeding, and by his own intimate sense of the decencies and proprieties of life."[27] Craveri believed these disguises were necessary, "not only to present an image of himself which accorded with the code of behavior Strachey describes, but also to prevent others, and perhaps himself, from an awareness of a certain vulnerability which filled him with insecurity."[28]

She said Horace suffered from a constant, unrelenting fear of mockery that "poisoned even the simplest facts of existence," which would have made him especially wary of looking like a fool if the elderly marquise's attachment was made known. "Social life, which was so necessary to him, was also a dangerous game full of pitfalls and risks, taking place under the supervision of malevolent eyes ready to notice the slightest weakness or the least alteration in tone," Craveri added. The author claimed she was shocked that Deffand, who was suspicious of pretense and obsessed with naturalness, wasn't irritated by Horace's affected behavior. "She may have been distracted by the difference of language, education and culture," Craveri surmised, "or deceived by the brusque, cutting, even disagreeable manner which Walpole occasionally loved to display; or perhaps she simply sensed that he was a fundamentally insecure and vulnerable man." Craveri said the marquise's blindness likely contributed to the "exclusive, violent, and passionate attention" she lavished on Horace because she couldn't see how effete he was. The chapter of Craveri's book that presents the struggle Horace experienced as he pushed back against the desire the marquise felt for him ends with letters the two exchanged, the last few from her growing bitter in tone.[29]

Lewis defended Horace's attempts to navigate the tricky situation with Deffand, citing their age difference and the one-sided story that remains because all but seven of Horace's more than eight-hundred letters to her were destroyed. While Horace demanded that Deffand return the letters he wrote to her over the years so he could preserve and annotate them (and she complied); he had Mary Berry, his literary executrix, do away with his because he claimed they were in "very bad French" and he feared they would offend other society figures he had dissed in them. The fact that most of her letters to him and so few of his to her have survived skew the perspective that historians have always taken, which includes the stance that Horace was unkind to the demanding woman.[30] "Horace was undoubtedly aware of the comic aspect of their situation (which was platonic, much to her annoyance)," Lewis explained, "and since he knew that their letters were opened at the post and copied, I did not blame him for being embarrassed by her infatuation for him or for dreading the consequences of its being disclosed to a society that throve on ridicule."[31]

Horace's letters sent to Paris and those in answer to his were opened and sometimes transcribed because he was the English prime minister's son. "Any letter addressed to him, therefore, was liable to attract attention when passing through foreign post offices," wrote Warren Hunting Smith in "Cipher and Code in Horace Walpole's Correspondence," an article published in *The Yale University Library Gazette*. He said this fact is known because transcripts still exist.[32] Given Deffand's desires were never satisfied made me curious as to why she so obstinately tried to reel Horace in. Craveri said the marquise "had simply reached a stage of life when she no longer had the energy or the will to control herself." The author felt Horace's unwillingness to disengage was because he had reason to be intrigued with her.[33]

"Madame du Deffand must have seemed almost mythological to him," she explained, calling the marquise "an old sibyl retired in the corner of a convent" who "could describe half a century of French history." Craveri felt this was significant for someone like Horace because Deffand made it possible for him to relive the lauded decades the marquise had witnessed "as a privileged guest in the last act of a long uninterrupted charade now mostly populated by ghosts."[34] This lines up with Horace's dedication to chronicling history, or at least his version of it given he was selective in deciding which of the letters would survive in Deffand's correspondence. Lewis said each letter Horace knew he would be preserving was written with future readers in mind, his goal to cement the self-image he wanted to project into posterity, which is why he would destroy ones that didn't present a favorable impression of himself.

ONCE LEWIS'S research convinced him the rumors about Deffand were overblown, he set out to dispel one last myth: that Horace was a snob. He cites three situations he felt disprove this claim—that Horace's household staff adored him; that the aristocrat took one of his father's illegitimate children into his home and looked after her until she died; and that he often provided shelter to those considered derelicts of society, like the writer, critic, and lexicographer Samuel Johnson, who suffered from Tourette's Syndrome—then seen as a serious enough mental illness that anyone afflicted by it should be hidden away in an asylum. With all of his questions about Horace's character satisfied, Lewis decided he would put in the time and energy to rehabilitate Horace's reputation and to give him a more dynamic place in history. The collector actually felt buoyed by the decision because he had grown to respect Horace, not only as a person but as the "chief social historian" of his time.

Lewis said there wasn't a subject about which Horace hadn't shared his opinion in some written form. "As I read volume after volume of Walpole's letters, he became a companion who led me about the great world with wit and wisdom," he wrote. "I shared his love of friends, books, pictures, the theater, and collecting. I delighted in what he called the 'touches of nature' that he discovered in people and in his reading." Lewis found that the all-encompassing subject of "Giant Posterity" was a lifelong concern of Horace's, which the collector wanted to help him achieve.[35] I could feel Lewis's intensity as he began to fully embrace the cause. "Could I fill the eighteenth century with its people and see them moving about in it as they had lived?" he mused. "Doubtless I could not, but I knew I was more interested in the people of the eighteenth century than in what they wrote, Walpole, [Thomas] Gray, [James] Boswell, and [Frances] Sheridan apart."[36]

Lewis also respected Horace for the things he accomplished. "He made the Gothic revival popular by building Strawberry Hill and by writing *The Castle of Otranto*," he explained. "He gave great impetus to the study of English antiquities and fine arts, and his major accomplishment was writing the history of the eighteenth century in his memoirs and letters."[37] In the latter, Horace shared tens of thousands of accounts of his day-by-day life and the tenor of the collective mindset of his time. Lewis marveled at the number of subjects Horace covered—he once joked in a speech that the letters contain everything except bee-keeping. "The next unpublished letter I got was entirely on that subject," he said.[38] Horace was brilliantly systematic in preserving his correspondence by choosing his pen pals carefully, insisting they agree to keep his letters and to return them to him at intervals when asked to do so. As they sailed back to him in an ongoing flow, Horace spent decades annotating them so that the true gist of each of his exchanges was clear.

Given this resulted in a voluminous array of written material, Lewis admitted he was naïve about the effort his plan would require at first. "I was completely unaware of the vastness of the subject and the difficulties that lay in the way of attaining supremacy in it," he explained. "This was fortunate, for had I known, I should not have had the temerity to make the attempt."[39] The word vastness is spot-on because the letters represented a massive undertaking, not only due to the volume but to the complexity of Lewis's plan to present them. Initially, he collected only Horace's letters and further annotated them so that the modern reader would understand the current events during Horace's time that were being discussed.

As he began the process of organizing them chronologically to present the history Horace told as it unfolded, he realized he also needed to collect and collate the answers from Horace's pen pals in the order they were received to present a fuller picture. "To print only one side of a correspondence is like listening to one side of a telephone conversation where the invisible partner to it is a stranger," he explained. "Walpole's letters cannot be thoroughly studied or appreciated without the letters to which they are in answer, whether his correspondents were informative, entertaining, or dull. The letters to Walpole put his letters back into their original context."[40] To illustrate the span of time this represents, Horace wrote his first letter to his mother when he was eight years old and his last to Lady Anne FitzPatrick Ossory when he was eighty.

The Yale Edition of Horace Walpole's Correspondence that holds around six-thousand letters published in forty-eight volumes, the last several of which are indexes of the letters contained in the other books, was the result of Lewis's labors. After being so intimately involved with these exchanges between Horace and his friends, Lewis realized he had a quest on his hands: He wanted to be able to confidently present the Englishman as a living, breathing human being. Fortunately, he had an enthusiastic collaborator by the time he felt so strongly about the effort, as he had married Annie Burr Auchincloss in 1928. Annie became a true partner in a number of ways, her most impactful contribution the extensive catalog of the collection she created before she died in 1959, twenty years before her husband passed. She also became a partner in his collecting escapades, frequently traveling with Lewis as he chased down items he was hearing about because his reputation as a collector was growing.

Lewis's stories about many of the situations in which he and Annie found themselves are hilarious. At the height of one of his collecting boons in England, they took an excursion to Worcestershire when they visited the collector R.M. Holland-Martin. The home was filled with Walpolian artifacts, and they unearthed one of the elements of the Great Hall I had found so depressing—it turns out, I wasn't the only one! "Our host showed me a list of the Strawberry relics," Lewis explained. "As I copied it off I came to 'Gothic lanthorn.' 'Is that the famous Gothic lantern?' I asked." Holland-Martin answered that he wasn't sure whether it was famous or not but it was "the ugliest blasted lantern that ever was"! When Lewis told Holland-Martin he would rather see the light fixture than anything else in England, the collector said it was too late. He told Lewis his wife had thrown it out because she could not bear looking at it! "Threw it out!" Lewis shouted, which prompted Holland-Martin to jump up from his chair and loudly declare, "It just may not have gone." [41]

Holland-Martin rushed Lewis through the house, past the cloisters to a space he called "the lumber room." Lewis remembered, "There on a bench next to the door and oblivion stood the lantern, the epitome of Strawberry Hill and the neo-Gothic movement, a flimsy thing with a tin cross, ugly and original, a story connected with each of its bits of painted glass." When the fixture arrived in Connecticut, Annie was equally resistant to having to look at the fixture on a daily basis. Lewis explained, "The lantern is now at Farmington where, alas, it is also in disfavor with its chatelaine; but relics should be reserved for the faithful, and it is fitting that the lantern should cast its newly electrified beam only upon those who are willing to seek it out, well removed from the ordinary life of the house, in the book stacks."[42] Images of the East Library in Farmington today show the lantern emitting an orangey glow above row upon row of card-catalog drawers.

The fact that Lewis had rescued it enabled the Strawberry Hill Collection Trust to create a replica of the "lanthorn," the one that brought the Great Hall such a spooky atmosphere when I walked through it. I think Horace would have approved that the original fixture survived to illuminate the orderly records of the artifacts he had collected, and the index cards cataloging the writings he valued and his own works. Another trip the couple took to the home of Richard R. Bentley involved an entire afternoon as Lewis was kept in suspense as to what treasures he might find. Bentley was the grandson of a former publisher of Walpoliana with whom Lewis had corresponded (and not the Richard Bentley cited on "The Committee of Taste" above). As such, he was by then the archivist of everything published by Richard Bentley and Son, which had ceased to be in business. Lewis was so knowledgeable about the volumes of correspondence the firm had published, he suspected the original letters he sought—especially those William Mason wrote to Horace—were still in Bentley's possession.

In spite of his excitement, the collector also knew a certain British decorum demanded that he be patient during the long afternoon. Just after the Lewises entered Bentley's home, The Mere, which Lewis described as a large pseudo-Elizabethan house set in ample grounds, they were led into the home's library that had a long table in the middle of the room. "At the end of the table were sherry and biscuits," Lewis remembered. "We sat ceremoniously, and our host launched into the story of Queen Victoria's wedding. At the climax when the organ stalled, he dropped into dialogue and acted out the consternation of Sir Somebody Something who was responsible for the failure." Bentley's wife came in and sat down beside him as he went on with his tale. "Our host was in no hurry to reach Walpole, and that being clear, importunity was to be avoided," Lewis added. "Nothing could have been less like the Venetian palace where the Aspern Papers were hidden than The Mere, but on that day there was the same hope of discovery on the part of the visitor and the same reticence on the part of the owner to gratify it."[43] When Lewis and Annie were eventually led into the neighboring drawing room, they immediately spotted a set of miniature portraits by G. P. Harding that Horace had hung in Strawberry Hill House.

"Not to have noticed or commented on them would have been a mistake," Lewis wrote. "The comment having been made without ill effect, I went on to observe that owners of books and manuscripts may not know they own them. 'There might be,' I said, 'letters from or to Walpole right here in the house.' Mr. Bentley's stare suggested I had been precipitate and I did not bring up the Walpole-Mason correspondence until a second opening occurred at lunch." As the meal progressed, Lewis said he began to feel bolder, pressing his host by asking, "The Walpole-Mason letters were published by Bentley's; could the originals be here?" Bentley countered, "I have a book that will answer that question." When no further encouragement was uttered as the dishes kept being served, Lewis felt his courage had been brushed aside "as if it were a crumb." More time passed and the gardener came in, reporting the temperature as if it was an important state secret that had to be shared with great urgency.[44]

Soon after, when a maid appeared and declared the thermometer had just crossed the eighty-degree mark, Lewis said "pleased astonishment went around the table" and Bentley exclaimed heartily that it was a *very* warm day! "Lunch was of eight courses and lasted until 3:30," Lewis wrote. "With the disappearance of the strawberries, I ventured to ask our host: 'And now the book?' Mr. Bentley looked at me stonily. 'You must see the house first.'" The tour included instances of bizarre surprises and elaborate explanations of each space. When the Lewises thought they had reached the end of the prolonged torture, Bentley exclaimed, "But you haven't seen Windsor!" Climbing the stairs to a cupola with a view of the castle, they paused just long enough to satisfy their host, then made their way back into the hallway where he was waiting. Bentley pointed to a wall and said, "You would say, Mr. Lewis, that this is the end of the house?" When Lewis answered he would, Bentley said, "Let us see," and pressed a button that made a door slide back to reveal another wing.[45]

Finally, after an exhaustive presentation of the rooms in it, Bentley said, "Now, the book!" The wily man led his guests back to the dining room where a sizable ledger was hidden in a cupboard. "Mr. Bentley got it out and sat with it on the arm of a large stuffed chair," Lewis remembered. "'What year did you say the Mason letters were published?' Bentley asked." Lewis responded, "1851," feeling a bit alarmed as he watched Bentley struggle with the very heavy book that was hard to handle from his precarious position. Realizing he was about to teeter to the floor, Bentley finally said, "Here; you take it." Lewis was beside himself to finally be holding *the book*. When he found the entry that proved the letters had been in Bentley's possession at one time, he asked his host if he had given them away or sold them, to which Bentley replied he had not. "Then they must still be here!" Lewis exclaimed. "There was a pause. 'Time for tea,' said Mr. Bentley firmly, struggling up from the chair and taking the book away from me."[46]

Lewis would not leave with any of the letters that day but after an involved correspondence with Bentley that took place over the next several years, Lewis scored what he considered to be a coup: not only Mason's letters but Mann's letters to Horace, and Horace's "Short Notes of My Life."[47] Lewis called the seven-thousand-word document weighed down by three-hundred-and-sixty-one footnotes the most important Walpole manuscript he had come across at the time and placed it at the center of an enticing story he shared in his book *Rescuing Horace Walpole*. Titled "The Fantasy," the reverie begins, "Two years ago the Almighty called me into His office and said, 'I am going to destroy every object in your house except one, and you have twenty minutes to choose it.'" Without hesitation, Lewis told the deity the one object would be Horace's "Short Notes." As the exchange evolved, Lewis was told he could save twenty-six objects, which led him to ask for a year to report back. "I think, Sir, I can make the choices fairly quickly," he explained, "but I would like to write them up as I go along."[48]

This narrative was such a clever way to begin the book because the twenty-six chapters in it were essentially the explanations he wanted to write about the objects he deemed important, including "Short Notes." The entries in this Walpolian manuscript are a mix of Horace's most important life events, his writing credits, printing-press activities, notes about his travels, descriptions of his political views, and relational skirmishes that prove he was a pretty scrappy fellow. A notation on September 9, 1766, said, "Set out for Paris." Soon after he arrived, Horace mentioned a battle with a literary luminary that came about because he hatched a misguided plot to best the fellow author. He recorded his vain act in the manuscript only briefly, noting, "Wrote the 'Letter from the King of Prussia to Rousseau.'"[49] Though he does not go into detail, Craveri does, pointing out that the period in which this happened was just after Jean-Jacques Rousseau was sent into exile for claims he made about religion in his novel *Emile*. Rousseau, who had been living in Switzerland and Germany, stopped over in Paris on his way to England while Horace was in town.

"The fugitive writer's brief stay in the capital was an exciting event for high Parisian Society," Craveri wrote. "Madame du Deffand did not participate for reasons of personal dislike and probably out of loyalty to Voltaire who had openly split with Rousseau." Craveri said the marquise was not the only one to have some reservations about being seen with the rebel. "Rousseau's extravagances were an inexhaustible source of humor and presented a perfect opportunity for wit," she explained, "a temptation which Horace Walpole, after only three months in Paris but having been introduced into the heart of society, could not resist." An evening at Geoffrin's salon, during which Rousseau was the sole topic of conversation, inspired Horace to write to the exiled author in the guise of Frederick II, King of Prussia, to invite Rousseau to take shelter in Geneva. One of Horace's miscalculations—that he thought the jabs in the letter would draw admiration from Paris's intellectual elite—was a grave mistake; instead of praise, the insults drew ire. In closing, Horace (as Frederick II) wrote, "If you persist in racking your brains in search of new misfortunes, choose whichever ones you want; I am a king, I can obtain for you what you wish; and as will certainly not be the case with your enemies, I will stop persecuting you when you stop glorifying in persecution." Horace signed the letter, "Your good friend Frederick."[50]

Rousseau was offended and Horace's disrespect threw the upper-crust of society in Paris into an uproar. "Walpole had certainly not wanted his joke to cause such a furor, nor foreseen that it would," Craveri said. To illustrate how badly the slight was taken, she quoted a letter the Scottish philosopher David Hume wrote to the society maven Marie-Charlotte de Boufflers. "It is a strange inclination we have to be wits in preference to anything else," Hume wrote. "He [Horace] is a very worthy man; he esteems and even admires Rousseau; yet he could not forbear, for the sake of a very indifferent joke, the turning him into ridicule, and saying harsh things against him. I am a little angry with him; and I hear you are a great deal: but the matter ought to be treated only as a piece of levity."[51] Another battle Horace fought with his pen sprang up in reaction to his book *Historic Doubts on the Life and Reign of King Richard the Third*, which he wrote while visiting Paris.

His entry in "Short Notes" for June 20, 1768, includes this anecdote: "Received a letter from Voltaire desiring my 'Historic Doubts.' I sent them, and 'The Castle of Otranto,' that he might see the preface, of which I had told him. He did not like it, but returned a very civil answer, defending his opinion. I replied with more civility, but dropping the subject, not caring to enter into a controversy; especially on a matter of opinion, on which whether we were right or wrong, all France would be on his side, and all England on mine." Voltaire then published the private letter he had written to Horace in the literary magazine *Mercure*, which Horace decided to ignore. When Louise-Honorine de Choiseul sent Horace a copy of the magazine with the letter published in it, he felt he could no longer steer clear of the controversy. He said the fact that Voltaire was circulating negativity about him instilled in him such contempt for the man's disingenuousness, he dropped all correspondence with his combatant.[52]

The interactions Horace had with the French elite that were so briefly cataloged in "Short Notes" fascinated Lewis so much, he was determined to hunt down a journal Horace had kept that chronicled his five visits to Paris. The entries in it show how determined the aristocrat was to leave evidence he traveled in exalted circles while in France, each one listing the roster of nobles and socialites with whom he hob-knobbed. The diary was owned by Percival Merritt, a Bostonian who was the most active Walpolian collector when Lewis began his own efforts. Merritt loaned Lewis the journal that recounted evenings when Horace rubbed elbows with courtiers during an ongoing series of fêtes. After he launched into the effort, Lewis called it a near-impossible project. "In the middle of 1932, I set myself to a formidable task, that of making an index to Walpole's journal of his five visits to Paris in 1765-75," he explained.[53] As Lewis began this sleuthing, he struggled greatly when he tried to identify the madames, mademoiselles, messieurs, princes, lords, and ladies because Horace gave no first names. Lewis cited one particular entry about a banquette in December 1765 that included eighteen people.

"Identifying the members of such a supper party took me hours in the beginning," he wrote. "The Boufflers ladies were a considerable problem in themselves: There were seven of them." As Lewis clawed his way through Horace's interactions with Parisian society, the Boufflers would turn out to be easy—there were twenty-eight Montmorencys, thirty-three Bourbons, and thirty-five Choiseuls to identify! "In the beginning, only my belief that this was a life-and-death test of my character and endurance kept me at it," Lewis quipped. "My struggle with the ancien-régime proved to be the most salutary exercise I have ever undergone."[54] I was shocked that Lewis would say this about the effort because his desire to tell a fuller story with both sides of Horace's correspondence seemed to me to be a much heavier lift. The full conversation Lewis was witnessing by thoroughly cataloging Horace's exchanges with others made the diligent work a powerful experience for him.

He said until he had delved into Walpole's life, the eighteenth century was represented by the portrait of George Washington by Gilbert Stuart, "The Spirit of '76," a revival of *She Stoops to Conquer* at prep school in which he played the part of Miss Constance Neville to considerable applause, and "a fancy-dress affair with everyone giggling in wigs and tights." He said reading Horace's letters changed that for him. "Thanks to him and Lady Louisa Stuart, the men and women in [Joshua] Reynolds' and [Thomas] Gainsborough's pictures stepped out of their frames and became real people," he explained. "This sense of flesh-and-blood reality was, I think, the first thing that struck me in Walpole's letters. At school and college the people of other ages had only been people in books, pressed between leaves, mythical creatures about whom I would presently be examined by instructors who (with a few notable exceptions) did not believe in their existence, either."[55]

THE REALNESS HAD SHOWN up early and had only increased as Lewis perused everything he could find about Horace. "The young man who made the eighteenth century come alive for me was, at the end of Volume I of his collected letters, just my age, twenty-eight," Lewis explained. "He made me feel that I was at his elbow. It is a short step from being at the elbow of a character in history or fiction to being the man himself."[56] By the time Lewis had spent several decades inside Horace's head, he came to know the nobleman so well, he was able to pinpoint the very essence of Horace's quest in life. Lewis illustrated this by highlighting a statement Horace made to the antiquary and clergyman Rev. William Cole: "You will laugh at my earnestness, but if I have amused you, by retracing with any fidelity the manners of ancient days, I am content, and give you leave to think me as idle as you please." Lewis explained why he felt this statement was so powerful, "Posterity might think him [Horace] frivolous and gossipy (it has thought him so), but that did not bother him much so long as posterity also believed that his history was accurate. If it did, he would gain the only immortality he believed in."[57]

Horace's *Historic Doubts on the Life and Reign of King Richard the Third* is evidence of this because it refuted the smear campaign the Tudors had carried out against the Plantagenet dynasty, which was not a widely accepted truth at the time as it is now. Lewis said the fact that Horace made the declaration to the reverend was significant because Cole was a conduit between the past and the future as an antiquarian. "Stating his purpose in life to Cole was stating it to the twentieth century," Lewis explained. I see Horace's determination to build his Gothic mansion as his desire to make his immortality extend even further into the future, which is now the case since the property has been so beautifully refurbished. Lewis visited Strawberry Hill several times, his first trip to Twickenham in April of 1925. When he arrived, Strawberry Hill was transitioning to a training college for teachers run by the Society of St. Vincent de Paul. He and two of his friends went unannounced, which he sheepishly deemed "a crass piece of intrusion."[58]

He explained, "As the Fathers had not yet taken up residence, it was not open to the public, but an army with banners is not more terrible than a collector who wants to see something." After strolling through its rooms, he said, "Gradually one is able to enter into the spirit of the place and to see what Walpole wanted visitors to feel, 'the romantic cast of the mansion.' Strawberry's pastiche is pioneer and amateurish, not professional and stale."[59] Lewis lamented the disbursement of the myriad fascinations the mansion once held, which took place during the "Great Sale" in 1842. He noted how quietly the hundredth-anniversary of it, April 25, 1942, passed because World War II was casting its evil shadow over civilization, calling the date one of the saddest for Walpolians. "One hundred years earlier began the sale that shredded out and undid the labor of a lifetime," he explained, "and, incidentally, gave posterity the delightful job of trying to do it all over again."[60]

Lewis quoted the sale catalog as saying, "The valuable contents of Strawberry Hill, it may fearlessly be proclaimed, formed the most distinguished gem that has ever adorned the annals of auctions."[61] Highlighting how crucial he saw the mansion in Horace's story, Lewis declared, "If I could keep only one book, it would be the scrapbook into which Walpole pasted Richard Bentley's drawings for the remodeling of Strawberry Hill. The whole Walpolian structure rests upon this book, for Strawberry Hill is a projection of Walpole himself."[62] Though Kenneth Clark had a lengthy list of negative things to say about the original mansion's flimsy construction, he did agree that the building holds significant importance because Strawberry Hill is an historical document of great importance since more is known about the mansion than about any other building of its age because of Walpole's detailed description of it, the innumerable descriptions of visitors, the volumes of his letters, his account-book with 170 folio pages of notes, a scrap-book containing the original drawings for it, and Strawberry Hill itself.[63]

Clark quoted Horace near the end of his life as saying, "Every true Goth must perceive that they [my rooms] are more the works of fancy than imitation." By the time he penned the words, Clark said the taste for Gothic had spread "from a few eccentrics to the mass of fashionable country gentlemen." For this reason, he deemed Horace an instrument of romanticism that popularized what he called "aristocratic Gothic." Clark concluded, "Walpole gave Gothic social standing. It was perhaps his greatest contribution to the revival."[64] A number of authors who have written about Horace and his fascination with the earlier era his home embodies say he lacked authenticity because he randomly chose what was then such an outmoded style, which they saw as pretentious. I have a different take on his fascination with Gothic style—I feel it is deeply authentic because Horace would have absorbed the built medieval world naturally through a constant exposure to it during his aristocratic life.

It would have confronted him within the educational institutions he attended, and during his political and social activities. The grandiosity of the style that became Horace's artform is much flirtier than the architecture that sprung up during the Middle Ages, but the forms he consistently repeated were extremely familiar to him. Consider his surroundings as he studied at Eton and Cambridge, both complexes perfect examples of a less fanciful Gothic style. As Horace said in his memoirs, he had passed some of his happiest hours in Eton; and in a letter he wrote to Reverend Cole on May 22, 1777, when he was sixty years old, Horace described his reaction to a piece of Gothic architecture he would have entered countless times while attending university at Cambridge. "The beauty of King's College Chapel, now that it is restored, penetrated me with a visionary longing to be a monk in it; though my life has been passed in turbulent scenes, in pleasures—or rather pastimes, and in much fashionable dissipation," he said.[65]

Gothicism would also have enveloped him during any number of occasions after he graduated: from going to church in Westminster Abbey to going to work in the palace next door when he was a member of the Parliament from 1741 until 1754. As I was working on this piece, I watched King Charles III being crowned in the cathedral and I reveled in being able to study the interior ornamentations of the storied building from so many angles, particularly the mighty columns that arc as they rise to the ceiling because they have delicate, miniature replicas in the Strawberry Hill House. In the Tribune, a pale violet-hued room nearing the end of the tour of the mansion, the columns culminate in a filigree pattern in shimmering gold as they intertwine with thinner quatrefoil shapes that were so popular in the Middle Ages. Not only were these visual echoes serendipitous, the Gold State Coach awaiting Charles as he exited the cathedral was as well.

The incredibly ornate carriage was first used by King George III, Horace's monarch beginning in 1760, for the State Opening of Parliament on November 25, 1762. This is an event Horace recorded in his *Memoirs of the Reign of King George the Third*, a recounting of the political skirmishes that took place during the sovereign's rule. That there was magic at work as I watched the coverage is no surprise, as Horace was the one who coined the word 'serendipity' in 1754, the meaning inspired by the ancient Persian fairy tale the "Three Princes of Serendip," which recounts the exploits of a trio of boys who succeeded in finding a lost camel by twists of happenstance. The good luck they experience inspired the definition of Horace's new term: "being able to make delightful discoveries purely by accident."

Though I can say there were a number of instances

during this journey I've taken toward knowing more about Horace that were fortuitous, the one I value the most is finding Lewis's name in the source notes in each of the biographies I tried to read. Having him as my second guide as I tried to bring Horace to life has been a great privilege I will always tresure. Lewis made the journey so exuberant that I now have a deep affection for both of these men who have since grounded my pleasurable experience in Twickenham, and I marvel that falling in love with a building can lead to such a rich tapestry of captivation. As Lewis said, Strawberry Hill whispers from its towers "the last enchantments of the Middle Ages."[66] I couldn't have said it better myself.

*I would like to thank Pippa Roberts for arranging the tour of Strawberry Hill during my trip to England in 2015.

4

A RIVER OF ANGST

GOETHE IN FRANKFURT

Though the modern aspects of Frankfurt, Germany, have now eclipsed its time-honored characteristics for those who flock to its massive tradeshow complex, an intimately scaled neighborhood that has always been at its center gives history buffs a reason to explore the city. Known as New Old Town, the district sits so quaintly at the edge of the River Main, it feels like ancient spirits still lurk there. Beneath the pavers of the rebuilt plazas are earthen pathways over which emperors trod when the town was a speck on the vast map depicting the Holy Roman Empire, and stones that witnessed the comings and goings of the Carolingian kings beginning in the eighth century have been unearthed to map out the footings of a formidable castle. Known as the Free City of Frankfurt by 1372, it remained self-governing for nearly five centuries until the hopscotch of history situated it in the Kingdom of Prussia, which eventually became a unified Germany. For the long stretch of time between the medieval era and the brutal bombings that destroyed most of the city during World War

II, the antiquities that told the town's story quietly rested within their anointed places.

Fortunately for Johann Wolfgang von Goethe, who was born in 1749, the city's relics were still on display when the precocious boy scampered around town looking for evidence of the heralded nobility he admired. Goethe's lively account of his childhood in his memoir *Autobiography: Truth and Fiction Relating to My Life* includes details that were still fresh in his mind decades after he experienced them when he began the book in 1811 at the age of sixty-two. In the narrative, which recounts the first twenty-three years of his life, he shares the joy he felt each time he crossed the river on his favorite bridge and spied a gilded weathervane glittering in the sunlight. A sense of pride swelled in him when he passed the Saalhof, which served as the customs house for several centuries; and the Stadthaus, near which the remains of the imperial palace of the Frankish sovereigns were uncovered. Goethe and his friends knew by heart the legends attributed to Charlemagne, who first mentioned the castle, then called Kaiserpfalz Franconofurd, in a document inviting foreign dignitaries to the Council of Frankfurt in 794 AD.

Other heroes Goethe admired were Rudolph I, the first Habsburg monarch who ruled during the thirteenth century; and Günther XXI, a disputed fourteenth-century king. The boy and his friends were so fascinated by the latter, they devised a plan to wrangle their way into the room in the Imperial Cathedral of Saint Bartholomew that held his tomb. When they made it in, Goethe declared their visit to the isolated chamber where the sepulcher was placed was disappointing. "The door leading into the conclave remained long shut against us until we at last managed, through the higher authorities, to gain access to this celebrated place," he explained. "But we should have done better had we continued as before to picture it merely in our imagination;

for we found this room, which is so remarkable in German history, where the most powerful princes were accustomed to meet for acts so momentous, in no respect worthily adorned."[1] Their dismay stemmed from the fact that the chamber was being used to store construction materials at the time.

This adventure was followed by escapades with his pals in and around Römerberg, or Roman Hill, a plaza that fans out around Frankfurt's city hall, the Römer. This is one of many buildings that had to be reconstructed after the war, as did the home in which Goethe grew up—the ample residence, which was restored between 1947 and 1951, is now a museum known as Goethe House. His memories of his youth in his memoir propelled me to this replica of his childhood home that stands on the footprint where the original building was situated before it was destroyed. 'Hearing' Goethe speak about his life when he was a little boy made the rooms he described come to life as I entered them. He presented two versions of the house in his autobiography—the first when it was owned by his paternal grandmother Cornelia, who lived there until she died; the second after a renovation his father Johann Caspar oversaw once Cornelia had passed away.

Goethe's memories of watching each of them make their marks on the home are surprisingly vivid given his grandmother was gone by the time he was five years old. The escapades he shared that unfolded there crystalized as I walked up the curving staircase that led to the rooms on the top two floors. His favorite place to spend time was a large wooden lattice box that extended from the street-side of the house where he and his sister would perch to have an unobstructed view of the narrow lane on which they lived. It's no longer there but I could imagine the terrace-like appendage as I looked out the window of one of the second-floor salons.

"A bird-cage of this sort, with which many houses were provided, was called a *Geräms* [frame]," he explained. "The women sat in it to sew and knit; the cook picked her salad there; female neighbors chatted with each other."[2] He told a funny story about his father's cunning in renovating the house when he gutted the interiors while the family lived there.

They'd move from floor to floor as walls were removed and reconfigured, and windows were ripped out and replaced with ones holding larger panes of glass. This went on until very late in the construction when the dust and danger got the best of them. The elder Goethe, an imperial councilor who knew how to get around the laws, had taken this tack because he could keep the *Geräms*, which added more square footage to the home. He had to be secretive because the architectural treatment had been outlawed on any new construction, as the authorities felt the protrusions darkened the streets over which the buildings rose. "While comparatively none of the old structure remained, the new one merely passed for a repair," Goethe said of his father's adroitness.[3] Goethe's delight that the updated home was filled with light and was cheerful holds true today, as does the beauty of the broad central staircase he described and the abundance of agreeable parlors he said were situated in the home.

After the construction was complete and the residence was cleaned, the first thing his father organized was his collection of books, the finest of which, in calf and half-calf binding, filled the glass-encased shelves in Johann Caspar's study. Goethe admired his father's curatorial prowess as he bought beautiful Dutch editions of the Latin classics, and volumes about Roman antiquities and jurisprudence. "The most eminent Italian poets were not wanting, and for Tasso he showed a great predilection," Goethe remembered.[4] The titles the councilor acquired also included travel literature and dictionaries in various languages, as well as encyclopedias about science and art. There were so many volumes, at least half of his collection had to be placed in an attic area. "The acquisition of new books, as well as their binding and arrangement, he pursued with great composure and love of order," Goethe explained. The organizers of the museum had once again filled the shelves with books from Johann Caspar's time, and had arranged the displays of art just as Goethe described them in his memoir.

"The pictures, which in the old house had hung about promiscuously, were now collected, and symmetrically hung on the walls of a cheerful room near the study," he wrote, "all in black frames set off with gilt moldings."[5] Because his father didn't believe in paying premium prices for old paintings, he employed a battalion of local artists to create likenesses of the classics, telling the nay-sayers who pointed out the works should look aged in order to be fashionable that the compositions would certainly turn brown over time! One artistic display in the museum that came to life in front of me was a series of etchings depicting Roman views. These had piqued Goethe's imagination as powerfully as his father's books. "They were engravings by some of the accomplished predecessors of [Giovanni Battista] Piranesi, who well understood perspective and architecture, and whose touches were clear and excellent," he explained. "There I saw every day the Piazza del Popolo; the Colosseum; the Piazza of St. Peter's; St. Peter's Church, within and without; the castle of St. Angelo; and many other places. These images impressed themselves deeply upon me, and my otherwise very laconic father was often so kind as to furnish descriptions of the objects."[6]

ONCE GOETHE MOVED into his teen and young adult years in the memoir, he exposed his vulnerable side as he laid bare his hopes and dreams, and revealed his fears and failings. He didn't shy away from writing about how he and his sister had serious issues with their strict father, the taciturn man causing each of them a great deal of grief when they were growing up. The young man's torments included an education in law he was forced into when his preference would have been to spend his life steeped in *belles-lettres*. There was also a serious lack of empathy from his father when Goethe became quite ill with a tumor on his neck that forced him to leave his undergraduate studies at a university in Leipzig without a degree in 1768. He returned to Frankfurt to convalesce and had to bear the burden of his father's frustration over his condition. "He concealed as well as he could his vexation at finding, instead of a vigorous, active son, who ought now to take his degree and run through the prescribed course of life, an invalid who seemed to suffer still more in soul than in body," Goethe said. "He did not conceal his wish that they would be expeditious with my cure." His father's severity cut so deep, it made him question whether he had become overly preoccupied with his own health. "One was forced to be specially on one's guard in his presence against hypochondriacal expressions because he could then become passionate and bitter," he remembered.[7]

By the time Goethe was convalescing in his childhood home, he had become a voracious reader who consumed volumes on philosophy, art, and alchemy; and study religious manuscripts and treatises on science while he quietly submitted to surgery and caustic treatments for the tumor and several other illnesses that kept him from thriving for nearly two years. He also decided to read the letters he'd written his father and sister from Leipzig, which his father had stitched together into what I can imagine would have looked like a quilt-top of correspondence. As he continued to be "occupied with his solitude," Goethe was in a reflective state of mind. "Time is infinitely long," he wrote; "and each day is a vessel into which a great deal may be poured, if one would actually fill it up."[8] In 1770, Goethe left Frankfurt behind to study for his doctorate at a university in Strasbourg. An event that took place in the town brought me to a dramatic moment in his story and reminded me that if I ramble through history long enough, famous personalities from the past are inextricably woven together, and some associations are more surprising than others.

The anecdote Goethe shared recounts his reaction to some of the most notable textiles that exist today just before they would be seen by one of history's most maligned women. The sensitive man became upset when he went to the spot where Marie Antoinette would enter France and become the dauphine. The future queen had made her way to Kehl where she would leave her homeland and take her first steps into France as she walked into Strasbourg through a building erected above the Rhine River, which marked the border between her past and future domains. A pavilion was constructed to serve as the backdrop for her transition from the Holy Roman Empire into France—anyone who has seen Sofia Coppola's film *Marie Antoinette* will be familiar with this event in the soon-to-be dauphine's life. Goethe set the scene, "Especially remarkable to me was the building which stood on an island in the Rhine between the two bridges, erected for her reception and for surrendering her into the hands of her husband's ambassadors."[9]

He described it as slightly raised above the ground with a grand salon in the center flanked by smaller ones, which were followed by other chambers that extended to the banks on each side of the river. "In short, had it been more durably built," he added, "it might have answered very well as a pleasure-house for persons of rank." As he walked from one of the smaller chambers into the larger central room, Goethe was unsettled by a series of tapestries hanging on the walls because he felt the subject matter of the aesthetically vibrant depictions on them was inappropriate for the occasion. "I went and came, and came and went, and could not satiate myself with looking, but the larger, more brilliant and richer hangings in the main salon troubled me," he explained.[10] He was overwrought because he saw the mythological themes that had been chosen as "excessively revolting," as they depicted the love triangle that had ensnared Jason, Medea, and Creusa in Ovid's *Metamorphosis*. He said the remarkably unhappy marriage illustrated in them should not have been chosen to greet a young bride-to-be. His description of how gruesome the scenes were flow like a river of angst in his memoir.

"To the left of the throne was seen the bride struggling with the most horrible death, surrounded by persons full of sympathizing woe," he explained; "to the right was the father, horrified at the murdered babes before his feet; whilst the Fury, in her dragon-car, drove along into the air." He railed against the atrocious magic bull and the fire-spitting beast, and felt empathy for Jason who was fighting them—his reaction was so strong, he did not go quietly on his way. "A blunder like that in the grand salon put me altogether out of my self-possession, and with animation and vehemence I called on my comrades to witness such a crime against taste and feeling," he said. Goethe was so incensed, he raised his voice so that no one could ignore him. "'What!' cried I, without regarding the by-standers, 'Is it permitted so thoughtlessly to place before the eyes of a young queen, at her first setting foot in her dominions, the representation of the most horrible marriage that perhaps ever was consummated?'" he scolded.[11]

"'Is there among the French architects, decorators, upholsterers, not a single man who understands that pictures represent something, that pictures work upon the mind and feelings, that they make impressions, that they excite forebodings?'" he implored. "'It is just the same as if they had sent the most ghastly specter to meet this beauteous and pleasure-loving lady at the very frontiers!'" The staff readying the pavilion for Marie Antoinette's transition tried to silence him, edging him out of the room to keep him from disturbing everyone else visiting the venue. "They then assured me that it was not everybody's concern to look for significance in pictures," he said; "that the whole population of Strasbourg and the vicinity, which was to throng thither, would no more take such crotchets into their heads than the queen and her court."[12] The fact that a tragic death and a dire mythic legacy would be this particular young woman's fate makes the twenty-one-year-old man's first-hand account a powerful one, though I had to wonder whether his memoires were infused with more agony given he was writing them over a decade after the queen's execution.

WHEN THE DAY came for Marie Antoinette's transition to her future country, Goethe returned to the riverfront to witness her hand-off. He described the fifteen-year-old bride-to-be's demeanor as she rode past him in her coach. "I yet remember well the beauteous and lofty mien, as cheerful as it was imposing, of this youthful lady," he explained. "Perfectly visible to us all in her glass carriage, she seemed to be jesting with her female attendants, in familiar conversation, about the throng that poured forth to meet her train."[13] The haunting anecdote that Goethe shared, now etched into Marie Antoinette's story for me, is one I'd never come across, even after reading dozens of books about her—it is a treasure Frankfurt gave me, as I wouldn't have found it had I not visited Goethe's hometown. Continuing on his path to being a frustrated student, Goethe left Strasbourg without graduating for a second time and bounced around a bit during the next four years. He returned to Frankfurt to practice law before traveling to Wetzlar to acquire the highest level of legal experience he had yet to gain in the supreme court of the Holy Roman Empire. After about a year, he returned to Frankfurt and had a burst of creative energy that resulted in a number of works for which he would become known—one of them his most famous novel *The Sorrows of Young Werther*.

I was awed to learn the book, which cemented his fame as a novelist when it was published in 1774, was written at a desk I came upon in a bedroom on the top floor of Goethe House. Given the building had been so badly damaged during the war, it was a miracle the desk had survived. The wood was splotched with ink drippings deposited by those who had written on its surface, and I had a tough time obeying the sign that ordered "Do Not Touch!" Though the storyline of the novel he wrote while sitting at that very desk is quite dark—Werther is a young man who was caught in a love triangle that caused him to commit suicide—it gained immediate popularity throughout Europe when it was released in multiple languages. As his literary star rose, Goethe developed feelings for a Frankfurt banker's daughter named Lili Schönemann. After a sensual summer romance in 1774, he proposed to her in April of the following year with almost immediate misgivings that he'd done the right thing. Before long, he was so desperate to escape from the "girl who seemed to paralyze his will," he broke off the engagement and skipped town.[14]

Goethe was able to make such a speedy exit because he leapt at the opportunity to join the court of Karl August, the

Grand Duke of Saxe-Weimer-Eisenach. The duke respected Goethe so much, he made him a member of his privy council even though Goethe lacked a level of governmental experience many felt he should have had. The duke pushed aside the criticisms because "people of discernment" were congratulating him on landing such a genius to be a member of his "most important collegium."[15] As one of the duke's esteemed officials, Goethe gained great respect for his legal and political prowess, which would keep him so busy for the next decade, he would finish no major literary projects during that time. After the ten years he'd put in, Goethe was seized by such a pressing desire to escape the suffocating atmosphere of the court, he left for Italy without telling the duke or any of his friends. He stole away in the middle of the night on September 3, 1786, with almost no luggage and traveled under a pseudonym in order to fly under the radar during his time away.

His book of essays that recount his grand tour of the country titled *Italian Journey* greeted me in my last stop in Goethe's home, the giftshop where I bought an edition of the book with my favorite painting of him, *Goethe in the Roman Campagna* by Johann Heinrich Wilhelm Tischbein, on the cover. The narratives he wrote about each of the cities he explored reveal a perceptive man who is processing a lifetime of dreaming about the country his father had inspired him to choose for the involved adventure he was having. His meditation on Venice is an example. "It was written, then, on my page in the Book of Fate that at five in the afternoon on the twenty-eighth day of September in the year 1789, I should see Venice for the first time as I entered this beautiful island-city, this beaver-republic," he wrote. "So now, thank God, Venice is no longer a mere word to me, an empty name."[16] He said when the first gondola pulled alongside the boat in which he was riding, it called to mind a toy he'd loved as a child, one he hadn't thought about in twenty years.

"My father had brought back from his journey to Italy a beautiful model of a gondola," he explained; "he was very fond of it and, as a special treat, he sometimes allowed me to play with it. When the gondolas appeared, their shining steel-sheeted prows and black cages greeted me like old friends."[17] As the incognito traveler visited other cities, John Zilcosky said Goethe's goal was to lose himself, though not in a physical sense—he wanted to escape from the man he had become.[18] Several affairs he had in Italy proved shrugging off the person that kept getting him into trouble was an impossible task. These liaisons and the transformative experiences he had in Italy made him reluctant to return to Weimar but the duke put his foot down in June of 1788 after granting him a second year's delay. Not long after his return, his doppelganger took control again as he began one of the most criticized and passionate love affairs he would ever have. Weimar courtiers rejected Goethe's romance with Christiane Vulpius because they felt having her as his mistress was beneath him. They were particularly disparaging when their illegitimate son Julius August Walther von Goethe was born in late 1789.

Goethe was in his forties when his first child came into the world, and the next decade was a trying time for the couple because three other babies they conceived died soon after they were born. Goethe finally married Vulpius in 1806 and he would remain intensely attached to her until she died. In spite of his devotion to his wife, Goethe was emotionally unfaithful to her at least once. Two years before Christiane passed in 1816, her husband spent his sixty-sixth birthday in a spot along the shores of the river in Frankfurt that lured me to it during the evening after I had toured his childhood home, the two experiences bookending much of his life in a single day. I was dining in a restaurant called Gerbermühle, a building significant in Goethe's life because it was the former residence of his friend Johann von Willemer. While staying with Willemer for nearly a year beginning in 1814, Goethe developed an infatuation for the man's foster daughter Marianne.

After spending time with her, Goethe grew to adore the young musician and dancer who had a passion for translation. When he learned Willemer had other plans for Marianne (he intended to marry her himself), Goethe sent her two gingko leaves and a poem he had written that symbolized his deep feelings for her and acknowledged he had put aside his hopes for a romance. Titled "Ginkgo Biloba," the poem is included in one of Goethe's last great works *West-Eastern Divan*, which he began in 1814 and published in 1819. In it, he extols a "secret sense" for them to savor and asks, "Are there two which choose to mingle / So that each as one now hides?"[19] Because Goethe had studied botany for years, he knew the Ginkgo is dioecious, which means there are separate male and female trees but they can't survive unless they pollinate each other. The mystic in Goethe saw this as symbolic of his relationship with Marianne, whom he loved but would never be able to physically possess. Many experts claim Marianne inspired the verses in *West-Eastern Divan* and some say she helped Goethe compose them.

A number of scholars believe their love endured throughout their lives. They cite a secret code running through *West-Eastern Divan* and clues they left in their letters as hints, the correspondence between them spanning eighteen years. Marianne would not be Goethe's last infatuation: He developed romantic feelings once again when he was in his seventies. While visiting the spa town of Marienbad in 1823, he fell for a teenage girl who refused his proposal, which inspired him to write "To Werther," a set of poems that documented his heartbreak. The closing of the "trilogy of passion" as they were deemed, is bereft in tone. Goethe leads the reader on a journey through "passion's labyrinthine ways" during which there is "anguish with each breath" because the parting of two lovers is a death. He then inserts himself into the poem as its creator, saying he's entangled in the torments while being "half to blame."[20]

Before I'd taken the time to get to know Goethe in advance of my trip, I'd seen him as a stiff, distant figure in the *Sturm und Drang* literary movement and a participant in what I vaguely knew to be German Romanticism. The man who obliterated this automaton was a sentient being whose heart was repeatedly broken because he couldn't help but give in to his lusty nature. In his poem "Restless Love," he laments, "Oh hearts that to one / And another are drawn, / How keen is the pain, / How the soul is torn!"[21] It was this love-sick Goethe who bathed my evening in the restaurant in a palpable poignancy. That I was seated in a room I was certain he had entered during his time in Willemer's home was extraordinary.

As I tried to intuit how different the building would have been when he strolled through a nearby door, the elemental music of the river flowing beyond the windows eclipsed the tinkling of utensils striking china and the lively chatter filling the restaurant. Suddenly, the room was quiet and he was the only one there. After staring out at the opposite shore for a long while, he returned to a table in a corner of the room where a sheaf of papers was stacked on its surface. Without hesitation, he bent over the pages and did what he was driven to do throughout his life—explore the vagaries of the human condition with his pen.

5

THE HOUSE WHERE THE MIND RULED

NATALIE BARNEY IN PARIS

erspective is one of life's ubiquitous buzz kills, I thought as I stood in front of the black double doors to the Paris apartment Natalie Clifford Barney once called home. Given its sad appearance, you'd never guess a jaw-dropping array of rebellious creatives sauntered through the entrance to the building at 20 rue Jacob for more than sixty years. Though many of them were from stateside, British and French non-conformists also paid courtly favor to the American expat who in 1909 moved to the address she would make famous. As I tried to find a redeeming angle for a photograph a little more than a century later, the effort was hopeless—the granite surrounding the doors on the six-story building was badly scared, an ugly PVC pipe angled down the façade from the guttering just below the mansard roof, and the carriage doors themselves were scuffed where they met the threshold. Just then, a painful truth hit me: Daily wear-and-tear has its own say about whether the built world lives up to a legendary figure's exploits, and I felt certain the state of the façade would have insulted this infamous salonnière's sense of self-importance.

"I didn't create a salon," Natalie declared. "A salon was created round me."[1] This may have been the case early on as La Belle Époque was interrupted by the First World War and the Jazz Age blasted off, but she would eventually produce insightful events that gave some of history's greatest writers the chance to expose their work to a much wider audience. Given her reputation as a literary lioness would take time to build, the fascination she inspired in her early acolytes had more to do with drama than with literature. I am not speaking of personal drama, though there was plenty of that to go around—for Natalie, performance art was a religion. Before she moved to the Left Bank and took up residence in the building I attempted to photograph, the twenty-year-old had rented a home in Neuilly-sur-Seine, a neighborhood in a nearby suburb. Here, she was famous for staging her own plays and *tableaux vivants* in the garden. In her book *Wild Girls,* Diana Souhami reported that Natalie was evicted from the property after less than a year because her landlord read an article in *Comoedia* about nude women cavorting in her shady garden in the spirit of Bilitis and Sappho.[2]

During one production, Colette described the scene when a naked Mata Hari, wearing only turquoise jewelry and a tinsel crown atop her loose black hair, rode a horse bareback onto the lawn. Murmurs erupted when the exotic dancer exited the bushes and they saw "the long thigh against the white flank of the Arab stallion."[3] The sans-clothing frolicking was such a regular occurrence, it is said the neighbors breathed a sigh of relief when Natalie was forced out, though there must have been a voyeur among them who was sad to see her go! She chose each of her Paris homes because they provided her with easy access to the Bois de Boulogne where she could gallop on horseback to her heart's content. Neuilly was situated near the north end of the park and rue Jacob was not far from its southern tip. There are a number of images of her dressed in riding habits with bowler hats capping her curls and riding crops held confidently in both hands.

Imagine how shocked I was to see that this diehard rebel dared to conform by riding side-saddle like the respectable women of her era! While Natalie was seen as disreputable in Neuilly, her relocation to the Left Bank proved to be the right move because avant-garde behavior was not frowned upon in the 6th arrondissement. The proximity to the Latin Quarter, a veritable playground for eccentrics at that time, also suited her attention-seeking pals to a tee. Karla Jay wrote in her introduction to *Adventures of the Mind,* one of the few books of Natalie's collected essays that have been published in English, "Her house is ironically situated on the block between the rue des Saints Pères (the street of the Holy Fathers) and the rue Bonaparte. We would hardly expect to find a hotbed of lesbianism or feminist rebellion here."[4]

But that's exactly what any unsuspecting visitor would discover when they made their way into the apartment during the six decades Natalie held her Friday gatherings. During these events, attendees entered the Victorianesque interiors through a series of rooms with walls either painted in gray or covered in faded maroon velvet wallpaper that had become a dull red by the time she moved in. The reflections of these pleasure-seekers would have shadowed them in a succession of large mirrors as they strolled toward the heart of the apartment and helped themselves to refreshments that varied depending upon Natalie's mood—one day it might be the chocolate and vanilla cake the painter Romaine Brooks preferred; on another, author Djuna Barnes's favorite fruit tarts would have been served. Natalie, who often wrote about herself in the third-person, described seeing herself glide through her inner sanctum, "She liked to look at the mirrors on her walls, the only self-portraits she had."[5]

Novelist Radclyffe Hall provided moody impressions of the apartment in her semi-autobiographical book *The Well of Loneliness*. In it, the character Stephen, a gay woman who has been brought to meet Valérie Seymour (the character Hall created around Natalie's persona) described the room in which the salon was held as large and as having "a rather splendid disorder." She said there was "something blissfully unkempt about it, as though its mistress were too much engrossed in other affairs to control its behavior."[6] The rooms were dusty and the residue of someone's Oriental scent was mingling with the aroma of tuberoses in a sixteenth-century chalice. Papers and books were strewn about, the piles accumulating as the interests of the salon's hostess and her favorite guests broadened. Stephen said, "On a divan, whose truly regal proportions occupied the best part of a shadowy alcove, lay a box of Fuller's peppermint creams and a lute, but the strings of the lute were broken."[7]

Like the other expats who had flocked to Paris during this explosive literary era, Natalie felt more at home in France than she had in America because she craved the freedom to be herself. She certainly fulfilled this yearning, a resolve that created an incredible amount of chaos among the gal pals vying for a romantic commitment from her. I laughed when I read she was born on Halloween Day in 1876, the date famous for its melodrama likely marking her from the beginning. Her hometown was Dayton, Ohio; though she grew up in Cincinnati when she was not at boarding school in France, lived in Washington D.C. during her teen years and early twenties, and spent summers when she was a girl in Bar Harbor. Growing up with a French governess and attending Les Ruches in Fontainebleau, a tony boarding school for girls with a roster of famous American alumnae that includes Eleanor Roosevelt, Natalie was comfortable in Parisian society because she knew the customs and she was fluent in

French, though by all accounts her manner of speaking had a dated eighteenth-century formality to it.

NATALIE HAD female lovers as early as her teens and she had such a seductive way about her, she captivated one of La Belle Époque's most famous French courtesans, Liane de Pougy, for a time. In his book *Americans in Paris*, Tony Allan called her tryst with the paramour Natalie's first significant love affair. De Pougy nicknamed her Flossie and recorded reminiscences about Natalie in her memoir *My Blue Notebooks*. She also penned a novel about their liaison titled *A Woman's Affair*. These two anecdotes from her *Notebooks*, both of which include Natalie's mother Alice Barney, illustrate from whom Natalie likely inherited her unconventional side. In the first, de Pougy described Alice, a well-known painter, as "an eccentric old woman who can't be less than sixty-five and looks eighty, was reckless enough to marry—two years ago, I think—a young man of twenty-five. It didn't last. She has returned to filial love which will, no doubt, be kinder to her."[8] De Pougy's memoirs are written diary-style, each entry dated.

Several years later, in a kinder mood, she wrote, "My Flossie! What a matchless creature she is, what a rare wit! When someone said that her house was very dusty, she answered: 'But dust is pretty, it's furniture's face powder.' We saw her little old mother, frisky, alert, sparkly…An incredible youthfulness runs in her veins, shines in her eyes, curls her white hair and vibrates the feather on her hat. Long ago, in our wild young days, she disapproved of my relationship with her daughter. I can hardly blame her."[9] The courtesan was one of many women Natalie would seduce and be seduced by over her long life, the notorious Bohemian behavior continuing as she added literary maven to her repertoire and welcomed a very long list of creatives into her apartment, or the "petite pavilion" as she called it. Among the celebrities who attended at least once—and many of them became regulars—were Auguste Rodin, Paul Valéry, T. S. Eliot, Ezra Pound, Colette, Gertrude Stein, Djuna Barnes, André Gide, Anatole France, Ford Madox Ford, W. Somerset Maugham, Zelda and F. Scott Fitzgerald, Sinclair Lewis, Sherwood Anderson, Thornton Wilder, William Carlos Williams, Rainer Maria Rilke, Peggy Guggenheim, and Sylvia Beach.

In 1932, Edna St. Vincent Millay drew a standing-room-only crowd to the salon. There are so many Yanks on the roster because Natalie saw herself as a literary ambassador between French, English, and American writers. Her aim was to have them translate the others' works into their non-native languages in order to open each voice to other cultures. As a former debutant in the States who intended to be an expat for the rest of her life, Natalie was perfect for the job. She also had one other card up her sleeve that made her and her cerebral existence a stellar match: she had financial independence, which came when her father died in December of 1920 and left her more than four million U.S. dollars (which would be equivalent to several billion in 2023). She was twenty-six at the time, and, since money talks, her roster of habitués also included some of the wealthiest people in the world. De Pougy bragged about captivating one of them. "Robert de Rothschild came to meet me at the first of Natalie's Fridays," she remembered. "He was charmed by this amusing and ill-assorted gathering, and enchanted to see me again and find me still so beautiful."[10]

We know so much about these events because Natalie and quite a few of her regulars, like de Pougy, were eager to describe the activities in which they were involved—some thinly veiled fictionalized accounts and others unvarnished portrayals of real events. The ever-evolving cadre of aesthetes showed up on Fridays from May through early July and mid-October through mid-December, the soirées kicking off at four-thirty in the afternoon and ending at around eight in the evening. There was an open-house feel to them with habitués coming and going, though her inner circle came early and stayed later. During the most serious evenings, the main focus of the discussions was literature, which sometimes involved critiquing works-in-progress by attendees or holding readings to celebrate the publication of books or poems by the salon's notables. Over time, Natalie's home became a petri dish of inspiration for fiction: Djuna Barnes, who was a regular at the Friday salons when she was in Paris, drew inspiration for her characters in *Ladies Almanack* from Natalie and her coterie, portrayals that the literary hostess encouraged her to write. In the outrageous satire, Natalie is Dame Evangeline Musset.

In Hall's *The Well of Loneliness*, which was banned in England for obscenity, the character based upon Natalie is its main protagonist. Representations of her in books like these cemented her fame with a charismatic set of lesbians, but this wasn't enough for Natalie. Unlike many salonniéres who were content to enjoy their popularity and leave the writing to others, she felt she deserved to be published. This was in spite of the fact that she was so indifferent to even the slightest whiff of discipline. She would use notebooks as filing cabinets, jotting down scattered thoughts, the opening lines of stories, a draft of a difficult letter, or snatches of dialogue. When she felt she had something even slightly cohesive, she moved the material onto sheets of full-sized paper and then hired a secretary to transform her handwritten pages into a typed manuscript. The lightness of her editing, which was extremely minimal, led Ezra Pound to call her a lazy writer. Ford Madox Ford, the editor of the *Transatlantic Review*, said her output was nothing more than "distracted volumes of stray thoughts."[11]

In the opening essay of *Adventures of the Mind*, "Forewarning," Natalie illustrated how lackadaisical she was about her process. She began the essay with a question that people often posed: "What are you preparing?" She then admitted, "I'm always a little startled when someone asks me this question, because I'm not preparing anything. Things prepare themselves slowly within me. I have no more desire to read than to write, but I allow this little bit of writing to trace, on bare skin, a unique tattoo." She said she had to force herself to empty her notebooks and the drawers of her writing desk about every ten years, and that the material these contained became books, almost without her knowing. In spite of this, she considered herself a "born writer" merely because she had a compulsion to scribble.[12] Though she did garner attention as a published poet, it was not because of her literary merits; it was her ample connections. She managed to get her work into the hands of the famous semi-recluse Remy de Gourmont. By this point in his life-story, he was known for isolating himself after being disfigured by lupus.

As one of the founding members of the literary journal *Mercure de France*, he would introduce her poetry to French readers when he tapped four of her poems for inclusion in the publication. Natalie had strategized his exposure to her work by having a neighbor and friend of hers, the publisher Edouard Champion, take her newly self-published book of poems to de Gourmont, a move she made because the serious critics of the day would not have considered reviewing the book. Janet Flanner, who covered the Paris scene for *The New Yorker* during the early- and mid-1920s, was interviewed by George Wickes, who wrote the biography *The Amazon of Letters: The Life and Loves of Natalie Barney*. Flanner made it clear she did not believe Natalie deserved the publicity. "Her association with the old victim of lupus—what was his name?" she asked. Wickes answered, "Remy de Gourmont." Flanner said, "Yes. Well, that was not a very valid qualification for her literary reputation, was it?"[13]

It was de Gourmont who gave Natalie her famous nickname, The Amazon. When she burst into his apartment on her way home from horseback riding one day, wearing a bowler hat and a black bow tie with a riding crop in her hands, de Gourmont declared her *"l'Amazone"* and Natalie loved it. He knew it was the perfect nickname for her because of her equestrian skill; her reputation for romantic conquests; and her fearlessness, which he saw as a kinship with the legendary female warriors of ancient times. De Gourmont, who was no intellectual slouch, would say to her, "You are the only person to whom I have ever submitted intellectually."[14] Natalie's essay on de Gourmont in *A Perilous Advantage: The Best of Natalie Clifford Barney* reveals a strange element to her personality, a maddening trait that would also show up in other relationships: She was prone to running extremely hot and cold at the drop of a hat.

Initially, she asked herself how she could persuade him to join the living once again, saying she had hardly noticed his scarred face and swollen lips when she first shook his hand. When she invited him to go for a car-ride in the Bois de Boulogne and he tried to refuse, she pushed back by saying, "Sometimes one needs to rebel against one's habits; even if only to return to them with renewed pleasure." She eventually won him over on this matter and others, and after declaring that the conquest of a person's mind is a long and difficult affair, she said "his was worth all my patience and all my prudence."[15] She would swing from this determination to liberate de Gourmont from his solitude to seeing the effort as a burden she no longer relished. "What a responsibility it is to become part of someone's life!" she declared. "Did I have the right? Should I run the risk of disturbing my new friend with hope and expectations? Had he not recently replied to a woman who was infatuated with his writing and who had asked to meet him, that: 'There was not even room in his life for a hairpin?'"[16]

By the time Natalie had worked her charm on him, she was the only woman de Gourmont allowed into his apartment. He wrote so many letters to her, they fill two books: *Letters to the Amazon* and *Intimate Letters to the Amazon*. In one of these missives, he told her, "Perhaps you will make me rediscover a lost interest in life: if it can be done, it will come from you because you are a true friend and because I love you." He told her plainly how his feelings about her shifted after their initial meeting. "Since then I have felt that not only were you a woman friend, but a man too," he declared, saying he would call this male version of her "Natalis" because the merging of the opposing aspects of Natalie's personality deserved a flowering name.[17] While de Gourmont was writing seductive letters, Natalie was questioning whether she could handle the depth of his feelings. In the end, the relationship was more heartfelt for de Gourmont than it ever was for Natalie, who was in America when de Gourmont died in 1915.

She said of his passing in her essay about him, "I did not go to his funeral; I hardly know where his grave is. Each of us is devout in their own fashion, each of us lives with our dead and keeps them alive in ourselves." Natalie ended the piece by describing a visit to his apartment after he was gone. As she took a stroll around his study, she pointed out his reed pen, his ink well, the pages pocked with burns from cigarette sparks, each contributor to his former writing life sentenced to stillness after the exit of this man with whom

THE HOUSE WHERE THE MIND RULED

she had grappled.[18] This piece on de Gourmont began the chapter profiling her "Friends from the Left Bank," which ends with a narrative titled "When Poets Meet," which is so enjoyable because it humanizes the great literary figures in it. The event Natalie recounted in the essay was an evening when Sylvia Beach and Adrienne Monnier hosted Edith Sitwell at the Shakespeare & Company bookstore.

Sitwell had agreed to present a lecture on the work of Gertrude Stein, who was also in attendance. Instead of following the program, Sitwell decided to read from her own book and Natalie said not one person in the audience dared return Sitwell's smile as she recited her poetry because Stein's expression was "forbidding." She then shared the atmosphere after a select few of the attendees had moved upstairs to Beach's apartment in which the bookstore owner was hosting an intimate supper. "The glass of sherry I proffered Edith Sitwell made her question: 'Won't it go to my head?'" Natalie wrote. "I smilingly reassured her and refrained from murmuring, 'No spirits but Miss Sitwell's own could accomplish that!'" When Natalie turned to hand a glass to Stein, whom she had seen behind her before approaching Sitwell, she was told the offended woman had abruptly left.[19] Each remembrance she penned about the famous people she knew is infused with the confidence that comes with familiarity.

IN THE first essay in *Adventures of the Mind*, Natalie presents an intimate glimpse of Oscar Wilde, whom she met in 1882 when she was five. Wilde was crisscrossing America lecturing on art history and aesthetics; she was running away from several boys who were pelting her with preserved cherries that had become stuck in her hair. Titled "First

Adventure: Oscar Wilde in the United States," the less-than-one-page piece is tender in tone. She said Oscar, who was the only one in the room at the time because the event during which he would speak had not yet begun, lifted her up when she ran through the door. "I was reassured by his eyes, which had sympathetically witnessed my flight; by his hair, which was as long as mine; and especially by his voice which swept me into a story," she remembered. "As the two of us sat together on a raised throne facing the arriving public, he never stopped astonishing me…" Her mother came to take her from his lap when she found Natalie there, bringing the tale to an end as he complimented Natalie on her lace dress and her "precious attention."

Natalie was seventeen when Wilde was imprisoned for gross indecency. "When I learned, as an adolescent, that my friend had just been imprisoned in England, I wrote to him at Reading Gaol, hoping to comfort him as he had comforted me, reminding him of his marvelous protection of me against the pursuits of other little people," she said. "But did he ever receive my letter?"[20] I honestly question whether she never learned if her message reached him because she would eventually have relationships with two consequential people in Wilde's life. When she was twenty-five, she was briefly engaged to Lord Alfred Douglas, Wilde's former lover and the person who was responsible for his being jailed. Then, in her fifties, Natalie had an affair with Dorothy (Dolly) Wilde, who strikingly resembled her uncle Oscar. These two relationships, which were riddled with controversy, illustrate how remarkably brazen she was, her promiscuousness displaying a callous arrogance and a sexual indiscrimination she was driven to maintain.

Disproportionately, the treatment she meted out toward women was much more brutal than it was toward men. Wickes noted that Natalie had an untold number of affairs during the 1920s and 1930s, and that one of the most unsettling to her coterie was with Dolly. It's no surprise Natalie was attracted to her, as Dolly was capricious, was well-read, and was already an insider in the Parisian clique of foreign and French writers by the time they were introduced. Dolly would meet many more luminaries while attending Natalie's salon, which she told her friends she particularly enjoyed. Wickes quoted Bettina Bergery, another American who attended the salon regularly during the early 1930s, as saying Dolly shone her brightest when she flitted from conversation to conversation in Natalie's apartment.[21] Like she did with de Gourmont, Natalie would attempt to save Dolly, not from reclusiveness but from her ingrained destructive behavior. She failed miserably with Dolly, which made the relationship a very troubled one until Dolly died in 1941 at the age of forty-six. "Natalie had been lucky in love all her life, for everyone fell in love with her and she had had a thousand liaisons," said Renée Lang, whom Wickes quoted in his book.[22]

A Swiss scholar, Lang had intended to write a biography of Natalie but couldn't pen the narrative she felt would have been truthful because Natalie was so strong-willed she was determined to direct what would be written. While she may not have wanted her liaisons to be exposed in a biography, Natalie didn't hesitate to admit she had betrayed many of her lovers in her own writing, defending herself by saying, "One is unfaithful to those one loves so that their charm will not become mere habit."[23] The smugness in a statement like this infuses her epigrams in *A Perilous Advantage*. Highlighting her sense of self-importance, she asked, "Might I be the one I am looking for?"[24] This level of self-love exasperated her paramours, and though she charmed more than she offended, a number of the rejected girlfriends and other contemporaries presented Natalie in an unflattering light.

Antoinette Gabrielle Mortier de Faucamberge, who wrote under the pseudonym Aurel, ended a published portrait of Natalie that appeared in *Le Monde Nouveau* in 1925, with: "No, Natalie doesn't bring anything 'new' because that is not the kind of life she advises. And the new exists only in the direction of life. She brings a visage amused with dying; she brings a form bewitched by shipwreck."[25] In an interesting move that illustrates how Natalie never shied away from criticism, she published Aurel's entire profile in *Adventures of the Mind* in a section of the book that began with a foreword titled "An Academy of Women" because she was introducing the female writers she profiled in the book.[26] Author Tony Allan called the cadre of women a "bohemian entourage," and said they attracted a great deal of interest. He said society seekers and foreigners wanted to witness the eccentric nature of the salon's habitués for themselves at least once because the gossip they would be able to share when back in their own societies was akin to a souvenir from Paris![27]

He quoted an anecdote that Sylvia Beach shared with him about "an ungrateful guest at the salon who, hurrying into her bookshop with a letter of introduction from Miss Natalie, hissed eagerly, 'Have you anything more about *those unfortunate creatures?*'"[28] Of course, the woman meant they were unfortunate because the "creatures" had chosen to live alternative lifestyles. They certainly were an unconventional group, as can be seen in the collection of avant-garde portraits Romaine Brooks painted of them. One of Natalie's closest confidants with whom she had a protracted love affair, Brooks depicted a number of the privileged women in the male dress they preferred, as is the case with Lady Una Troubridge wearing a man's suit and a monocle. The odd assortment of characters often had forlorn looks in their eyes, which might say more about Brooks than her subjects, as she was extremely paranoid and hypochondriacal, and Natalie was continuously being unfaithful to her. Djuna Barnes, who made studying Brooks during the salon evenings an artform, told one of her biographers the painter was so woefully unhappy over Natalie's infidelities, she would sit around and sulk.[29]

Brooks painted several self-portraits, one of which depicted her sporting a man's suit. This painting and those of women like Troubridge drew criticism from Natalie, who thought it was ridiculous that her lesbian confidants chose to don masculine clothes. In *Women of the Left Bank: Paris, 1900-1940*, Shari Benstock said it was because Natalie disapproved of dressing like or behaving as though homosexual women were really men trapped in women's bodies. Not only did Natalie object to cross-dressing, Benstock explained, she rejected "the anger, self-indulgence, and self-pity" that marked the behavior of many of her friends.[30] Unlike her pals who preferred suits and trousers, Natalie chose to dress in women's clothes, a rather contradictory aspect of her story since there were facets of her character that were far from ladylike. The staunch feminism that flowed through her writing was so tough, it proved she loathed the idea of entrapment with the opposite sex.

"How many men want to be our lovers who are not worthy to be our valets?" she asked. In her treatise titled "Breasts," she claimed she dedicated the piece to the male sex because "man" is "never fully weaned."[31] And this meditation in "Brute!" is cutting: "She: 'You want inexpressible joy, you will have it, more exquisite than you can imagine. You will unwind not only the veils from my body but also the veils from my soul; you will watch not only the rhythmic swaying of my hips but all the subtle shifts of my mind. You will possess me in every way except that in which others have possessed me…No, don't come near…No, not that…I want to stay fresh for you and forever virgin like an untapped spring...Do you want that?' He: 'I want your body.'"[32] Karla Jay claimed the ellipses that appear in narratives like the above are "little clitoral dots that omit the unspoken/unspeakable words of women's desire"; that they were used as "a subversive tool of lesbian writers" at the turn of the century because obscenity laws brought serious consequences if the writing published by a woman was considered too risqué.[33]

Because of this Natalie kept her independent streak in her writing from ever approaching the level of what was then considered indecent, concentrating mainly on her avowed freedom to be herself. "If life is to be the expression, and not the suppression, of self, have I not roundly fulfilled and succeeded in mine?" she asked. "What's more, does it not require deep concentration to catch hold of the messages of our interior being, and thus experience the mysteries of self-initiation?" At times, she was remarkably obstinate. "I love my life," she boasted. "Principally because I have been able to keep it free, in order to freely give it. Guided by love—the kind which forces us to surpass ourselves—I have loved my fellow man, and particularly my fellow woman, with passion. That such feelings and dispositions may be seen as blameworthy or too intense, has never bothered me."[34] She then swaggered, "Living in the eye of love is an adventure for which few are suited. It's a very trying environment; most of those who attempt it are in danger of burning up with fever or of starvation. Few constitutions survive. As for me, the striving, the pain and the mystery are more than just my native land. It is only there that I feel I am in my element. My life is truly my own, without pretense, and so, consequently, is my work: my writing is simply the accompaniment." She was absolutely defiant about her unfaithfulness: "My love affairs? Many. My friendships? Loyal and faithful."[35]

I believe she could so easily move from lover to lover without guilt because she cared so much more about herself than about anyone else, which made her attitudes about the sexual superficiality she saw in men rather disingenuous to me. "I am the most curious about myself," she wrote. "I judge people's charm by the ease with which I express myself in their presence."[36] One of the most fascinating aspects of her narcissistic personality is that she was able to intermittently escape her selfishness to prove she cared a great deal about her inner circle, which added up to around twenty women at its fullest. Among the array of gestures that helped many of them were financial support and introductions to important figures who furthered their careers. Proof of her effect on those closest to her is that they remained Natalie's most ardent friends as long as they were alive. Dolly Wilde dubbed the loyal group "the Knights of Natalie's Round Table," as they were so often gathered around her circular dining room table as she asked them about their latest creative projects.[37]

Suzanne Rodriguez, who wrote the biography *Wild Heart: A Life*, described Natalie as queenlike as she aged. "No longer did she sail from group to group, lightly touching one or whispering to another," she explained. "These days she observed the goings-on from her armchair. Guests were led to her, one by one, and allowed to sit by her side for a tête-à-tête."[38] One of the women who vied for an intimate moment with her was Elizabeth Eyre de Lanux, a young American woman who lived in a third-floor apartment at 20 rue Jacob and who sometimes attended Natalie's salon. In her unpublished memoir, she described Natalie as "robed (one cannot say dressed) in white, a white not too cruel for the ancient walls, her hair hanging loose like cornsilk, the clear eyes of ice." De Lanux situated the regular attendees in this vivid memory: "Gertrude Stein was the permanent occupant of right wall center. With her stout tweeds and her sensible shoes, she seemed like a game warden scrutinizing the exotic birds."[39]

De Lanux described the intensity of the experience of being on the scene, "I found myself or rather lost myself like an invisible fish in exotic waters. The famous and beautiful women sat in file against the wall…perhaps a certain ferocity lay underneath their exoticism." De Lanux also described a number of parties she attended, including a masked ball in Natalie's garden into which was set a small Doric temple with the words *"Temple d'Amitie"* [Temple of Friendship], carved into its pediment. Natalie saw this inscription as the perfect representation of her ability to remain "loyal and faithful" in her platonic relationships with her friends—some of whom had never been her lovers and a number of whom remained confidants after their affairs with her had ended. While De Lanux also described how cruel her behavior could be—particularly to her cooks and her chauffeur, Joseph, whom she would whack on the shoulder with a riding crop if he drove too fast—many of her inner circle and acquaintances steered clear of discussing any less-than-stellar conduct.[40] Those who chose not to degrade her concentrated instead on Natalie's beauty. Bettina Bergery described her eyes as extraordinary: "very sparkling, with stars in them: the irises had a delicate marking like the little round petals of pompom dahlias."[41]

Natalie herself wrote about her eyes in *A Perilous Advantage*, saying, "The fine veins of her temples, little blue streams under her transparent skin, seemed to have poured their color into the irises of her eyes."[42] Though Natalie seemed always at the ready to repel anyone who tried to change her mind about her romantic freedoms, her argumentative nature didn't apply to artistic subjects, as Bergery shared that Natalie always agreed with each of her habitués about their aesthetic beliefs, even when they had opposing views. When Bergery asked her, "What are your real opinions?" Natalie answered, "I have none. I gave them up long ago. An opinion is a limit to understanding. There are two and sometimes two hundred sides to every question. Why limit yourself?"[43] Her school of thought about artistic endeavors was so vague, she paid no attention to diction, and said, "To mis-quote is the very foundation of original style."[44] Karla Jay noted that this lack of seriousness stymied Natalie's literary reputation because any writer who received journalistic attention during her time had to stay within the traditions and standards of style and context that were acceptable to male literary critics.

Because she dared to rebel against this idea, she received less acclaim from the establishment she lavishly entertained in her home. Miffed by their disregard, Natalie derided the journalists and academics as "fraudulent usurpers of fame, mind-pickers, and culture snobs."[45] That's quite a statement given the long list of the intellectually elite who darkened her door at 20 rue Jacob and made her home a centerpiece for so much artistic advancement. Late in life, she told a reporter for *France-Soir*, "My salon is a monument to contemporary literature. No one has the right to alter it. I have sworn to defend to my last breath this house where the mind has ruled."[46] Given how determined this declaration was, it astounds me that Natalie never purchased the apartment, particularly because she could have easily afforded it. This would be one of her great regrets, as a little more than two years before she died, she was forced to leave it—and this was after she had endured nearly four years of interior construction the new owner was undertaking in the apartments surrounding hers as he improved the building and tried to force her out.

Her statement to the reporter was made when she first began the fight to keep the apartment, a battle she would lose in the end because she waited too late to try and buy it, and didn't push hard enough when she did. In a video that was taped in 1966 in the garden surrounding the Temple of Friendship, the year the new landlord served her notice that she would have to move within four years, she was ninety and still spry. It illustrates why she is seen as one of the powerhouses of the modern movement, as she shared anecdotes about meeting the fabled writers she knew and talked about her views on a number of issues, including idleness. The interviewer asked her about the subject because she had devoted an entire essay to it, and her answer is so on message given her financial means. "I think one must be idle in order to become oneself," she wrote. "If you have a profession, you become part of that profession and it seems to me that that's the idlest thing of all because you become a function instead of a free-thinking individual finding out who you are and what you are, and what other people are."[47]

In *Wild Girls*, Diana Souhami makes the point that for both Natalie and her mother Alice, "Money gave them confidence and freedom: to travel, to express themselves in poetry or painting, to pay for publication, to live for art and love."[48] Natalie saw her Friday gatherings as her most valuable form of self-expression, her naturalness as a hostess leading Suzanne Rodriguez to declare she was "a marvel as a literary salonist."[49] Benstock concurred, saying, "Natalie never allowed herself to be consigned to the shadows of literary Paris. Indeed, her own writing may have suffered because of the prominent social role she played within the community, and commentaries on Natalie have tended to focus on her life to the exclusion of her art." Benstock believes it's a misstep that Natalie's place among women in the artistic community has been viewed almost entirely as a function of her sexual orientation.[50]

"In the gossipy biographies and memoirs of her life, Natalie's lesbianism is the crucial factor," she explained, saying it was time for this to change. Benstock was writing in 2010 during a moment when feminist critics had just begun to reexamine Natalie's work in order to place her at the center of a group of women committed to producing serious art. "Natalie Barney never used her salon to further her own career as a writer, nor did she set herself up as the center of the salon," Benstock continued. "Her purpose was to bring people together, to foster the work of other artists (many of whom were women), and to embrace the cultural life of the Left Bank Community."[51] Natalie's role as one of the main players in an electric time in literary development is what made me so excited about trying to capture the essence of her apartment building on rue Jacob. Though my photographs of the façade will always disappoint, the fact that I was able to place my hands on the doors of the entrance to a domain where "the life of the mind" had ruled is compensation enough.

As Natalie's story drew to a close, the address was suddenly hers no longer, as the stress of the construction surrounding her apartment proved too great. Giving up, she moved into a suite at the Hôtel Le Meurice with a view of the Tuileries Gardens where she lived out the rest of her days. Wickes, who managed to see her in 1971, the year before she died at the age of ninety-five, described Natalie as having very fine white hair and wearing a powdery blue dressing gown that matched her pale blue eyes. He said she looked like "a carefully wrapped doll in that expensive hotel drawing room with its vases of tall expensive flowers—not at all the setting in which she had lived her life—but there was still a spark of animation behind the vague look in her eyes." Wickes said she kept repeating, "Oh, why didn't you come sooner?" He felt the statement meant she wanted to be remembered because Natalie knew he had written a book about Americans in Paris and she must have wished she could have been more prominently featured in it.[52] This sentiment has strong echoes to this day given the words Natalie insisted be chiseled on her headstone.

Below the epitaph stating she was Remy de Gourmont's Amazon is the phrase, "I am this legendary being in which I will live again." Rodriguez explained that the sentiment has often been misinterpreted because Natalie used the ancient, obscure adverb *où* in the declaration.[53] The real meaning was explained by Françoise Chapon, whom both Rodriguez and Wickes interviewed. He had been a habitué of Natalie's salon for the last twelve years she held it and was her literary executor. He knew what Natalie intended to convey because she told him what she meant—she would have a second life as a legend.[54] Given her role in one of the earliest overt gay-rights movements in France, she must have had a premonition that the fables she encouraged would inscribe her name in lesbian lore for the ages. She must have also known her own descriptions of the greats with whom she rubbed elbows would cement her celebrity someday.

When Natalie died, Berthe Cleyrergue, who had been her house manager for more than forty-five years, counted twenty-three in attendance at her funeral. "As the service ended and they were all about to leave," Wickes wrote, "Berthe suddenly realized it was a Friday and this was the last gathering of Natalie Barney's salon."[55] Cleyrergue was one of the many people Wickes interviewed when he was preparing to write his biography. He ran into one frustrating setback after another because there were so many conflicting opinions about Natalie, it was difficult to establish "biographical fact." He published the interviews with people who had known Natalie so he could let readers decide for themselves which versions of the same story were the most believable.[56] Among these in-person exchanges were Natalie herself, twice; Cleyrergue, a number of times; Janine Lahovary, Natalie's last lover; and Chapon, who allowed Wickes to see some of Natalie's papers and journals.

Wickes also spoke with Cheryl Hughes, an American student who took a deep dive into Natalie's life, though she had not known the salonnière personally. Hughes was a graduate student in political science at Stanford University when she dropped everything to travel to Paris and plumb the archives that Natalie had bequeathed to the Bibliothèque Nationale. Hughes gave Wickes insight into several of Natalie's most important lesbian relationships, telling him that Natalie was incredibly advanced for her time. "And yet… and yet…at the end of our conversation Cheryl said she kept changing her mind about Natalie," he explained. This is because Hughes had begun to see Natalie as sexist after realizing she regarded men as her equals and women as her inferiors. Hughes also felt Natalie was someone who was very cynical about love. "This sort of thing left Cheryl Hughes wondering if she would have liked Natalie after all," Wickes added.[57] Elyse Blankley, whom Benstock quotes, agreed with Hughes that Natalie was a pioneer when it came to thumbing her nose at convention but she saw her sexism as a form of pluck: "Few lesbian women were able to live as bravely as Natalie Barney," she said.[58]

Natalie addressed her fortitude by challenging readers with a number of questions, including these two astute ones: "Does it not take more courage to dare to be oneself than to conform to contemporary morality?" and, "Which of all our pasts will be *the* Past?"[59] The question was one of my favorites among her "scatterings," as she called her epigrams in *A Perilous Advantage*, which I was reading in the elegant Bar 228 tucked into the corner of the historic Hôtel Le Meurice. I was there to salute Natalie, whose last stop before she died was a posh suite upstairs. Sitting at the end of the counter with the faint washes of light reflecting on the quartz stone surface, I studied the chocolate-colored paneled wall behind the bar, which was inset with a large mirror that reflected the drifts of clouds painted on the ceiling.

The moment felt otherworldly because the characters about whom I had been reading had drifted beyond earth's billowing firmament and exited time itself. In front of me was a glass of pink champagne; I raised it to pay homage to those unconventional rebels, realizing as I made the toast that Natalie was one of the rare characters I've come across whom I envy. It isn't just because she had the financial means to be exactly who she wanted to be; she also had the temperament to stay the course of defending personal freedoms that were unheard of in America at the time. Someone once asked her, "What did you see in the Salon?" She answered, "I saw—that I was seen."[60] Within the luxurious atmosphere of the bar, the effervescing liquid I was sipping was such a fitting tribute to Natalie given I was doing so in her chosen hometown.

"In France, thought, food, and love have remained a matter of individual choice where each person follows their own inclination, instead of that of their neighbors, which is probably why the country is so difficult to govern, and so easy to live in," she wrote. "I was predestined for free choice, for, contrary to the warnings given back home in the United States of 'what is and is not done,' I have always done as I've pleased."[61] She was fortunate that her situation provided her

THE HOUSE WHERE THE MIND RULED

with everything she required to live in a city where the open-mindedness of its inhabitants allowed her to flaunt her darkly frivolous behavior. She certainly wasted no time in rushing headlong into the mysteries of self-initiation, which she continued to explore for more than nine decades as she created an epic existence for herself and turned herself into a lasting legend that remains alive to this day.

6

THE ART OF CAPITULATION
MARIE-LOUISE OF AUSTRIA IN PARMA

ave I somehow left Italy and been plunked down on French soil? I asked myself as I turned to take in the beauty of the boiserie-clad Rococo room. The illumination from the glass chandeliers overhead effervesced on the fanciful paneling and penetrated two large glass cases holding distinguished regalia. In one was an iridescent gown, the front of the skirt heavily embroidered and the tiny waist cinched by a turquoise band that held a silk and tulle train in place. The luxurious cloth that unfurled behind the dress was ornamented with a glimmering pattern that flowed along its outer edges. Inside the second case was a grandly-scaled vessel called a *corbeille de mariage*, or wedding basket, that was mythic in its stature. The monumental metal sculpture, which balanced a massive oval lidded bowl atop the arcing wings of kneeling angels, stood over five-feet-tall and measured nearly five-feet in circumference.

It would have held a treasure trove of jewelry and accoutrements when it was given to the woman whose epic portrait was hanging nearby. The painting depicts her as a symbol of wealth when she was young, her jewels sparkling and the sumptuous setting in which she is shown the epitome of opulence. I lingered there, gaze-to-gaze with Marie Louise of Austria, Emperor Napoleon I's second wife, and marveled at the splendor her husband was a master at demanding. The 1812 painting by portraitist Robert Lefèvre is one of the finest examples of Napoleonic vainglory I've ever seen. The emperor's bedecked wife is wearing a white empire-waist gown embroidered with platinum thread and silver beads, her right hand gently clasping a jeweled crown sitting atop a plump beaded pillow. Adorned with fleurs-de-lis, the cushion rests on a table covered in red velvet cloth dripping with shimmering gold fringe.

The diamond-encrusted diadem placed snugly over her curls sparkles as brilliantly as her jewelry and the gilded accents placed around her. Ensuring he was not left out of the allegory, a throne-like chair behind her declares her husband's domination, its back emblazoned with a prominent N from which a filigree starburst radiates. *How apropos that atop the chair's arms, warring swans hiss angrily!* I thought. *Such a perfect stand-in for Napoleon whose conquering ways were repeatedly unleashed on other countries when he was in power.* Also in the room were two smaller portraits, one of the emperor that depicts him as a young man in his military uniform and one of the couple's sleeping son. Glass-topped tables filled with an array of Marie Louise's personal effects lined the walls of the elaborate space that is today the most magnificent room situated within the Museo Glauco Lombardi in the heart of Parma.

The atmosphere was so noiseless and serene, I was startled when I opened the door to leave—the scooters zipping along a busy Strada Garibaldi dashing the ruse that I had been transported to nineteenth-century France. I made my way along the porphyry-paved lane thinking about how important it is to physically stand in front of historical arti-

THE ART OF CAPITULATION

facts because seeing them in person lends the past a forcefulness that is difficult to grasp when coming across objects in books or viewing them on a computer screen. I took a seat on a bench beside the towering façade of the Palazzo della Pilotta, a brute conglomerate of buildings near the museum, so I could record my impressions of the mementos I'd seen and jot down the questions that puzzled me. First on the list: "Why was such a formal display of splendor containing important French masterpieces permanently on view in the Italian city?" As I searched for answers to that question, I found myself bouncing like a ping-pong ball between Italy, Austria, and France.

The Parma duchy has a long history of French occupation beginning with the House of Bourbon-Parma in 1748. French troops controlled it during Napoleon's rule; and after Marie Louise reigned from 1816 to 1847, the Bourbons returned. The seat of power until the Duke of Parma became a titular designation, as it is today, was the Parma Ducal Palace, now called the Palazzo di Riserva. The ornate room in the museum in which I had time-traveled with the duchess as my guide was formerly the grand ballroom of the palace. Dating back to 1764, the salon was designed by French architect Ennemond-Alexandre Petitot and painstakingly realized by Benigno Bossi—a renowned Italian engraver, painter, and plaster and stucco artist. I imagined Marie Louise's existence as carefree when I pictured her floating across the terrazzo floor in the extravagant gown during one of the evenings she would have been holding court but the narratives I scoured tell a very different tale.

I learned that the princess-turned-empress in the painting, depicted about midway through her four-year reign, was treated like a trinket her entire life. After nearly two decades of being seen by her father, Holy Roman Emperor Francis II, as a shiny jewel to attract a powerful alliance, Napoleon considered her a cherished bauble to be protected, quite literally, at all cost to his freedom and his empire. Once Marie Louise was wrested from Napoleon's grasp by her father's allies, the man Francis inserted into her life to ensure she would betray her husband saw her as an arm-charm and a gateway to an easier existence. As these relationships unfolded in the first-hand accounts of her life I read, the relics in the museum were infused with greater meaning—not only were they once her belongings, they became talismans that led me deeper into her life story. An emblem of her first reign is the wedding basket that represents the ostentation enveloping her when she nervously debuted as the Empress of France.

The portraits of her and her son depict them during a time when treachery was bubbling up around them because Napoleon was so determined to keep expanding his empire, he ignored warning signs that he was headed for ruin. The gala gown Marie Louise ordered from Paris in 1838 is a symbol of her reign as the Duchess of Parma living a still privileged, though tainted, life. By the time she wore the ensemble, she had given birth to several illegitimate children with her second husband before they entered into a morganatic marriage, as a union between a royal and a non-royal is called. The lower-born Austrian general who precipitated these lapses in judgement was dead, and the French diplomat who stepped in to accompany her to the theater was lured into a second morganatic marriage at her bidding. One of the most ironic asides to this list of husbands given his temperament is that Napoleon truly seemed to care about her while the others merely saw her as a chance to elevate their standing. The intensity of the emperor's allegiance to his wife would bring about one of history's greatest reversals of fortune, as it reduced the once-proud usurper of European countries to a powerless whiner who complained about

Marie Louise's disregard for him to the rulers he had previously conquered!

During his first of two abdications, Napoleon signed a decree known as the Treaty of Fontainebleau in 1814 that ensured Marie Louise's reign in Italy in order to give their son a territory to rule when he came of age. The prince never took over the duchy so the Bonaparte regime in Parma ended with Marie Louise, who took physical possession of her kingdom in March of 1816, nearly a year after her husband had been sent into his final exile on the island of Saint Helena. When I happened upon the museum in Parma, I knew much less about her than I did about Napoleon's first wife Josephine, whom he regretted having to divorce in order to shore up his power. Because Josephine was thirty-two when they met and wasn't able to give him children, he was forced to go baby-momma shopping in the hopes of landing himself a younger wife of child-bearing age who could give him an heir.

ON THE SPECTRUM OF PERSONALITIES, the two empresses couldn't have been farther apart. Claude-François Méneval, Napoleon's private secretary until 1813 and Marie Louise's secretary for several years after, recorded his impressions of both of the emperor's wives in his massive memoir about Napoleon's rise and fall. His remembrances of his time in the emperor's inner circle are so remarkable because he leaves eyewitness accounts of both of Napoleon's marriages. In the three volumes he penned, he quoted the poet Jean de La Fontaine as saying Josephine "had that grace which is more beautiful than beauty's self," and described Napoleon's first wife as having a charm and delicacy that won all of the hearts around her.[1] Méneval depicted Marie Louise as an innocent who swung from passive and obedient to spoiled and petulant—her subservience and childishness so pronounced, the twin behaviors drove the plot of her marionette-like tale from beginning to end.

"Having been brought up in the habit of severe discipline and passive obedience, she belonged to a family in which the Austrian princesses are regarded as the docile instruments of the greatness of the Habsburgs," wrote Arthur Léon Imbert de Saint-Amand in his book *The Happy Days of the Empress Marie Louise*. "Consequently, she resigned herself to following her father's wishes without a murmur, but not without sadness."[2] Francis approached Napoleon about a potential match with his daughter when Marie Louise was eighteen years old. The plan was to prevent the French emperor from marrying the Russian grand-duchess Anna on whom Napoleon had set his sights because Francis feared an alliance between Napoleon and Czar Alexander I would be dangerous to his throne. Still undecided as to which affiliation would be more advantageous for his empire, Napoleon gathered a council of his ministers at the Tuileries Palace on January 21, 1810, to discuss whether marrying a Russian, a Saxon, or an Austrian would be the most favorable choice. This was the very date that Louis XVI had been slaughtered seventeen years before; his wife, Marie Antoinette, who was Marie Louise's great-aunt, followed him to the guillotine nearly nine months later.

Marie Antoinette's beheading had been a cautionary tale for Marie Louise as long as she could remember. "She had been taught from the moment she left the cradle that France was the hereditary enemy, the savage and implacable foe of her country," Saint-Amand explained.[3] That was, of course, until her father's craving for power turned the caveat into a footnote and a cloying web began spinning around her. As rumors of her betrothal were spreading, she wrote to her life-long friend Victoire de Poutet about her feelings. "I know that they at Vienna are already marrying me with the great Napoleon, and I hope it will go no further than talk," she said. "I am making counter-wishes that it may not come to pass, and if it had to be, I think I should be the only one who would not rejoice at it."[4] Marie Louise would learn the hard way that wishing was a fruitless endeavor when major players like Napoleon and Francis were at the negotiating table. She later confessed to Napoleon that she couldn't help but feel a kind of terror when her marriage with him was first proposed because she had heard so many horror stories about him from family members.

She had every reason to be frightened: As she waited to learn her fate, Napoleon was having his ministers draft their marriage contract almost word-for-word after the one joining Louise XVI and Marie Antoinette forty years earlier. One of Francis's diplomats involved in the negotiations that would codify their marriage, Karl Philipp, the Prince of Schwarzenberg, declared, "I pity the princess, it is true, but let her nevertheless not forget that it is very noble to give peace to such worthy nations, and to establish herself as the guarantee of tranquility and general repose."[5] While the unhappy young woman fretted, Austrian society buzzed in disbelief and the French courtiers marveled at their emperor's aristocratic coup. "Napoleon, learning the Vienna waltz and sending for his tailor to 'fit him properly,' imagined that he had never gained such a triumph, and Paris was delighted with the news," Edith Cuthell wrote in her biography of Marie Louise titled *An Imperial Victim*. "In Vienna, however, it burst like a bombshell."

This is because Austrians had assumed France would never be considered a friend to their country given the warring past between the two nations. *Could it possibly be true that Marie Louise would marry Napoleon?* the princess's countrymen and women questioned as the gossip spread. The leaders of Austria's neighboring countries, Russia and Prussia, were stunned that the French emperor was once again favored by Francis, as they had considered him an ally in despising Napoleon. Prince Klemens von Metternich, who brokered the deal for Austria, wrote to his wife, "The new empress will be popular at Paris, and should please by her great sweetness and simplicity. Rather plain than pretty in the face, she has a very fine figure, and when she is dressed up a little she will do very well. I have begged her to have a dancing-master directly when she arrives, and not to dance before she can dance well. She has the greatest wish to please, and with such a wish one does please."[6] Determined to have a magnificent wedding in Paris that would outshine any to have taken place in the city before, Napoleon ordered his staff to comb the official archives for details about the marriages of the great Bourbon kings and to meet with the royalists of the old regime who were still alive so they could make his ceremony even grander.

Back in Vienna, witnessing her father's delight over the match he'd made, Marie Louise did what she had been taught to do: she acquiesced. The French ambassador to Vienna, Louis-Alexandre Berthier, who was styled the Prince of Neuchâtel, was given the assignment of puffing her up to her soon-to-be-husband. He told Napoleon that she had a very sweet disposition, common sense, and talent; and that she spoke well in several languages and was dignified. He then described the qualities her husband would value the most— she was an innocent who had been so protected, she didn't have the slightest blemish to her reputation; and she would enter Napoleon's court clueless about the lapses in morality that corrupted its members. Metternich wrote to the French officials involved in the negotiations that they shouldn't have any doubts the union would take place because Marie Louise was bound by duty; that she dared not refuse her beloved parent "her most absolute devotion."[7]

He said she felt the full extent of the sacrifice, "but her filial affection overpowers all other considerations," a declaration that was nothing short of an ominous bellwether given her fidelity to her father would plunge her into the most sacrificial moments in her life. All of this was being said behind Marie Louise's back until her father sent Neuchâtel to ask if she wanted to marry Napoleon, deciding not to go himself because he claimed he didn't want to sway her decision. Neuchâtel relayed to Francis that Marie Louise said her father's command should match his duty as a sovereign and not his personal feelings for her. This is an important moment in her story because it shows how profoundly she had been molded into who she was by a demanding etiquette and a sequestered existence. Onlookers like Robert Stewart, Viscount Castlereagh, who would eventually help finance and organize the alliance that would bring Napoleon's rule to an end, recognized how the union relegated Marie Louise to victim status. "The Minotaur demanded a sacrifice of an Austrian maiden," he succinctly declared.[8]

Before the princess could be devoured, Napoleon had to clean up a substantial mess resulting from his penchant for gobbling up territory others did not see as his. The French emperor, who had been slowly annexing the Papal States to France since 1808, wrote to several advisors in 1809 that Pope Pius VII should be locked up because he was mad, an insult that he only meant metaphorically. When General Étienne Radet, who was in charge of Napoleon's forces in Rome at the time, was given one of the letters, he interpreted his leader's words literally and imprisoned the pontiff in Savona, Italy. This was problematic for Napoleon when it came time to wed because the head of the Catholic Church was the only official who could pronounce the divorce between him and Josephine legal—by locking up the pope, Radet had seriously hamstrung Napoleon's efforts to remarry because Pius refused to do the emperor's bidding. As the drama played out, a volley of dispatches sailed to Vienna that left the Austrian emperor ringing his hands over Napoleon's sloppiness.

Francis need not have worried that his counterpart wouldn't wriggle out of the tight spot. In his usual brash way, Napoleon declared he did not need the pope's blessing and, preferring to keep the pontiff as his prisoner, circumvented Pius by ordering his French clerics to form tribunals that would result in the ratification of a marriage contract. When it was announced that the document, which Rome deemed counterfeit, had been signed by Napoleon and Francis, spectacular fêtes got underway in the capitals of France and Austria. During the initial nuptials in Vienna on March 11, 1810, which took place during a proxy wedding because the two royals hailed from different countries, Napoleon's stand-in was Marie Louise's uncle, the Archduke Charles. After exchanging rings, Marie Louise took back the one intended for Napoleon so she could give it to him during the final ceremony in Paris. Flaming torches were waved, cannons boomed, and bells clanged to announce to the Viennese that the marriage was accomplished. Neuchâtel told the absent emperor that all eyes had been on Marie Louise.

"Her modesty, the dignity of her presence, the ease with which she replied to the speeches made to her, delighted everyone," he wrote. "She replied to my address that she would do all in her power to please His Majesty the Emperor Napoleon, and to contribute to the happiness of the French nation, which was from this moment her own." The ambassador then quoted her father's words to his daughter's soon-to-be husband: "I give your master my beloved daughter. She

THE ART OF CAPITULATION

deserves to be happy. Cannot you see the joy expressed on all the faces? Our nations need repose, they approve the line we have taken."[9] Two days after the Viennese wedding, Marie Louise began her journey to France with a large retinue. "At eight o'clock in the morning the whole court was assembled in the reception-rooms," Saint-Amand explained. "About nine, the Austrian empress appeared, leading her stepdaughter by the right hand."[10] The empress was Maria Ludovika of Austria-Este, and, though she was only four years older than Marie Louise, she had been the young woman's stepmother for two years.

ONCE HER GOODBYES to her family were said, Marie Louise's progress toward the Bavarian border where she would be handed off to French officials began. Braunau am Inn had been chosen as an advantageous spot for the transfer because the town was just over the Austrian border in the Confederation of the Rhine, which was under Napoleon's protection. "The scene was a close imitation of what had taken place forty years before, on the occasion of the marriage of Marie Antoinette," Saint-Amand wrote. "On the frontier line between Austria and Bavaria three pavilions were set up, opening from one to the other: the first of these was regarded as Austrian; the second as neutral; and the third as French. These three connected buildings formed a wooden edifice in three compartments, and was placed between Altheim and Braunau."[11] Saint-Amand said the pavilions were beautifully furnished, the fireplaces were blazing, and an armchair covered in luxurious gold cloth in the middle of the neutral room served as a throne.

Saint-Amand listed all the major French players in attendance and described the hand-off. "Towards two o'clock

Marie Louise entered the Austrian room, and after resting a moment, she was ushered into the middle room, the neutral one, by the Austrian master of ceremonies where a throne had been set and the formal ceremony was to take place," he explained; "Marie Louise seated herself on the throne."[12] *The naïve princess's fate was now sealed*, I thought. In his *Private Memoirs of the Court of Napoleon*, Baron de Bausset-Roquefort —the Prefect of the Imperial Palace and Napoleon's principal attendant during peace-time progresses and military expeditions when France was a war—set the scene as the French courtiers waited for Marie Louise to be ushered into the French room. "An eagerness easy enough to be explained made me desirous of seeing the empress as soon as she should arrive and enter the middle apartment to take her seat on the throne," he wrote, explaining he had brought a small, corkscrew-like drill with him and made several holes in the door to the chamber so everyone could see Marie Louise before she was presented to them.[13]

He then described Marie Louise. "The empress was standing upright before her throne; her tall figure was perfectly symmetrical, her hair was fair and beautiful, her mild blue eyes bespoke the candor and innocence of her soul, and her countenance beamed with freshness and goodness," he remembered. "She wore a dress of gold brocade, worked with large flowers in their natural colors, the weight of which must have fatigued her very much. Round her neck she wore the miniature of Napoleon, enriched with sixteen magnificent diamonds."[14] The baron went into excruciating detail about the ceremony. Once it was over, as the dowry was being counted (five-hundred-thousand francs, all in new golden ducats, along with diamonds and other jewels), it was time for Marie Louise to say goodbye to the courtiers from her home country who had traveled with her.

She described the feelings that welled in her during these

THE ART OF CAPITULATION

farewells in a letter to her father, the first she wrote as the Empress of France. "All my people came up to kiss my hand, and I could hardly control myself," she told him. "I shuddered, and I was so much moved that the Prince of Neuchâtel had tears in his eyes." She related how shocked she felt when one of her new courtiers spontaneously hugged her, then admitted to her father that her transition to one of them had begun: "I assure you that now I am already as much perfumed as the Frenchwomen."[15] She was upset that Napoleon had not yet written to her. "Now that I have had to leave you, I had rather be with him than travel longer with these ladies," she wrote. "Heavens! How I miss the happy moments I spent with you! Now, alone, I value them at their true worth. I assure you, dear papa, that I am sad and inconsolable. I hope you have got over your cold. Every day I pray for you. Excuse my scrawl. I have so little time. I kiss your hands a thousand times, and have the honor to be, dear papa, your obedient, humble daughter."[16]

That evening Marie Louise would be introduced to more members of her new French court during a party. These included Sophie-Henriette Cohendet, known as Madame La Générale Durand, whom Napoleon had assigned the position of first lady to Marie Louise. Her years serving in this capacity meant she had carte-blanche access to the life Marie Louise led while she was on the French throne. She recorded her experiences as one of the empress's closest attendants in *Napoleon and Marie-Louise, 1810-1814: A Memoir*. In it, she wrote, "Among the number of persons awaiting the new empress, there were several who had known Marie Antoinette. All these pictured to themselves what must be the feelings of Marie Louise on coming to seat herself upon the throne which had brought such misfortune to her grand-aunt."[17]

Though a less docile woman would have felt qualms,

Durand claimed Marie Louise seemed unaffected by this parallel because her only concern was to please everyone she met, a task she would find difficult to achieve with the jaded members of the French court. After leaving Braunau, the next stop for the entourage was Munich, which was as far as Marie Louise's Austrian servants would accompany her. As Durand watched the young empress say goodbye to the people who had attended her, some of them since she was born, she said one of the most moving scenes was the reaction of the sixty-five-year-old grand master of her household. "He raised his clasped hands to Heaven, as if imploring Providence on behalf of his young mistress," she explained. "His eyes revealed a soul full of great thoughts and sad recollections; his tears drew answering tears from the witnesses of this touching scene."[18]

Though Marie Louise imagined she had all of the emotional goodbyes behind her, the political backstabbing for which the French courtiers throughout history are famous sent another Austrian rushing back to Vienna just before the carriages moved away from Munich. Napoleon's youngest sister began a campaign to expel the only attendant Marie Louise had been allowed to bring with her to France. After barely any back-and-forth, Durand said Marie Louise conceded to say goodbye to her former mistress of the robes because she "sincerely desired to gain the affection of the persons with whom she would have to live." Not only did she relinquish the attendant, she handed her a small dog she had brought with her. Durand said, "She was required to deprive herself of this dumb friend on the pretext that the emperor had frequently complained of Josephine's dogs."[19] Given Marie Louise was being jealously targeted before she was even on French soil, it was fortunate that her husband would protect her from the members of the court, even if it meant she would essentially be his captive. Closing in on the borderline of her future country, Marie Louise began receiving a letter from Napoleon each morning, some of them in his own handwriting, which Méneval described as illegible and another secretary said resembled hieroglyphics.

She would answer each letter that arrived before she resumed her journey the following morning, which involved a grinding fifteen days of clattering over rutty roads, with the help of Louise Antoinette Lannes, her new mistress of the robes. Known as the Duchess of Montebello, she could decode the emperor's longhand because she had a knack for deciphering and had often been asked by her husband, Jean Lannes, to read the emperor's personal dispatches to him—as one of Napoleon's marshals before he died on the battlefield, Jean had received hand-written notes from Napoleon over the span of his military career.[20] This early intimacy with Montebello and the confidence that resulted from it created a strong bond between the empress and her lady-in-waiting. On those days when Napoleon's letters were delayed, Marie Louise would ask again and again why they had not arrived, revealing how uncomfortable she felt without an authority figure around. Fortunately for her, her husband couldn't wait to fill the position.

"Napoleon, on his part, was extremely eager to behold his young bride," Durand remembered; "this marriage was more flattering to his vanity than the conquest of an empire would have been."[21] She explained this hyperbole by saying Napoleon thought Marie Louise had consented to becoming his wife without hesitation or regret, which meant a member of one of the greatest dynasties of Europe held him in such high esteem. Though Marie Louise would share several contented years with her husband, she would not remember her betrothal as a personal choice. Near the end of her life, when a friend asked her about her marriage to Napoleon, she said, "I was sacrificed."[22] As his bride's day's-long journey continued, Napoleon cursed the distance that stretched out between them and the ceremonial niceties that would drag on once she arrived. In his voluminous memoirs that recount his time as Napoleon's minister of police, Anne-Jean-Marie-René Savary, 1st Duke of Rovigo, believed the emperor was "love-stricken" before he even met the young woman, a claim that Napoleon's behavior seems to corroborate.[23]

Waiting in a camp that had been set up at Soissons, where their formal meeting was to take place, Napoleon learned Marie Louise was within ten leagues. Exercising the aspect of his personality that would bring him great victories and crushing defeats in war, he dumped all decorum and raced off to meet her. "The two carriages encountered each other at four leagues distance from Soissons; the emperor got out of his, opened the door of the empress's, and rather flung himself into than entered it," Durand wrote. "The Prince of Neuchâtel had given Marie Louise a portrait of Napoleon, and she had so often looked at it that his features were familiar to her."[24] Marie Louise must have been pleased by what she saw because she remarked that the painting had not done him justice. "Napoleon was charmed with her; indeed, such was his enthusiasm that he stopped at Soissons, where they were to have remained until the next day, for a few minutes only, and then went on at once to Compiégne," Durand wrote.[25] She described Marie Louise as so caught up in his excitement, she gave in to Napoleon's urgings so that her all-too-eager bridegroom could enjoy the privileges of a husband before the two Parisian ceremonies, one civil and one religious, would take place. The day after the civil ceremony was held at the Château de Saint-Cloud, their final nuptials were exchanged in the Louvre on April 2, 1810.

THE ART OF CAPITULATION

As Napoleon was being outfitted for the occasion, the courtiers witnessed an embarrassing situation as he arrayed himself in his finery for his performance. "The emperor was a long time before he could settle himself comfortably into his gorgeous Spanish costume of white satin, embroidered in gold, with a mantle of the same covered with golden bees," Durand explained. "He found his black velvet cap adorned with eight rows of diamonds and three white plumes fastened by a knot—with the regent blazing in the center of it—particularly troublesome." She described a number of tries before they were successful at placing it on his head.[26] After the Parisian ceremony, Napoleon led Marie Louise onto the balcony at the Tuileries so the crowds gathered below it could salute her "as a pledge of lasting peace and alliance." According to Laure Junot, the Duchess d'Abrantès, this concept looked terrific on paper but would not hold in reality.[27] D'Abrantès, who was extremely critical of the young empress in her memoir *At the Court of Napoleon*, exemplifies how contentious the courtiers could be.

"As for Marie Louise herself, who had sobbed bitterly when she was told she was to marry the Corsican ogre, she found Napoleon an almost ideal husband," she wrote. "He was devoted to her, allowed her to indulge in almost every whim (as long as it did not break the now sacrosanct etiquette), and, best of all, introduced her to what eventually became her favorite pastime, sex." No wonder Durand claimed the forty-one-year-old Napoleon was so smitten, he barely left his bride's side for months! She and other courtiers marveled that the once irritable man who was prone to fidgeting was suddenly happy in his private life. Napoleon was so pleased with his new bride, he ushered her in from the balcony on their wedding day and said, "Well, Louise, I must give you some little reward for the happiness you have conferred on me." He took her hand and led her along a dark corridor of the Tuileries, stopping at a closed door behind which a dog was barking. Once inside, d'Abrantès said, "She found herself in a room magnificently lighted; the glare of the lamps prevented her for some moments from distinguishing any object; imagine her surprise when she found her favorite dog from Vienna was there to greet her."[28]

This same dog she'd had to relinquish when she was traveling to France was ensconced in an identical apartment to the one she had inhabited in Vienna, the rooms copied so closely, she was once again surrounded by the luxury she had enjoyed growing up. "In short every object was there, and placed in the room in the same manner as she had left them on quitting her paternal roof," D'Abrantès explained. This infamous courtier, who was renowned for intrigue, was not in Paris at the time; letters sent to her from others filled her in about the tenor of life in the French capital and the attention Napoleon lavished on his new bride. One of these was from Jean-Sifrein Maury, who told her, "I will not attempt to describe how much the emperor is attached to our charming empress. This time he may be said to be really in love; more truly in love than he ever was with Josephine."[29] Durand agreed. "I have seen him, when present at the empress's toilet, tease and plague her, pinching her neck and cheek," she said. "If he was vexed he took her in his arms, kissed her, called her *grosse bête* [big beast], and peace was made."[30] Durand went into meticulous detail about the tactics Napoleon employed to ensure Marie Louise would not fall victim to the loose morals of his court.

He allowed only a handful of women the right to attend to his wife in private: these were the ladies-in-waiting; the lady of the bedchamber; the mistress of the robes; and the lady ushers, also known as the *Dames d'Annonces* because their duty was to announce anyone requesting entry. To avoid petty jealousies he had been forced to endure when Josephine was empress, he ordered a woman he trusted to choose daughters or widows of generals and former generals to be placed in service, which is how Montebello ended up in her position as the mistress of the robes. These women, who made up the largest contingent of Marie Louise's attendants, were either from the Parisian suburb of Saint-Denis or from Écouen, a village about eighteen kilometers north of the capital. They were chosen because they didn't have relationships with anyone at court. At least two members of the group of guardians was always at the empress's side, circulating through her rooms when she rose and retiring only when she was in bed.

All doors to Marie Louise's apartment except one were locked, and the unbolted one connected her suite to the chamber where the women slept. Even Napoleon had to enter Marie Louise's inner sanctum through this door when he wanted to visit his wife, including at night. There were only a handful of men—doctors, a secretary, and her music and dancing teachers—allowed to enter Marie Louise's chambers during the day, and the lengths Napoleon took to make sure none of them were alone with her was extreme. While scolding one of the ladies for not being in the room when a man was present one afternoon, he made it clear he wouldn't tolerate any male, regardless of his rank, being alone with the empress for two seconds. "Napoleon had established in the empress's household an order of service by which she was so fenced in, one might have thought him jealous," Méneval wrote.[31] His theory seems spot-on given Marie Louise's tailor was banned for remarking she had beautiful shoulders as he was fitting her for a new gown! From that moment on, her dresses were made on a mannequin the tailor was given. Once they were assembled, her maids would fetch the dresses, try them on her, pin them, and take them back to him for alterations.

The same strictures were applied to any other males who were involved in fashioning her wardrobe. To make sure Marie Louise was not exposed to the most jaded women of the court, any female other than her attendants had to have the emperor's permission to enter her rooms, a rolling list he approved on any given day as Marie Louise studied music, drawing, and dancing. At this point, I thought about what a school-girl vibe I was getting from the descriptions of the life she was leading. The empress, in essence, had gone from being treated as a cosseted child in Austria to a pampered teenager in France. Her husband's control extended to all of the events she attended at court because Marie Louise was so awkward in public. "When she received on certain grand occasions, her timidity was noticeable and the efforts which she made to surmount this shyness gave her an embarrassed bearing," Méneval wrote. This did not occur at her private receptions held in the evenings because her husband saw to it that only people who put her at ease were invited.[32]

ONCE HE WAS certain his wife was sufficiently surveilled, Napoleon thought his work was done but he was mistaken—his plan of choosing outsiders to attend to Marie Louise so he wouldn't have to be bothered by grievances didn't solve the problem. Two of the women who surrounded his wife day-in and day-out, Madame Jeanne Charlotte Luçay, the lady of the bedchamber, and Montebello became hostile opponents. Rather than put a stop to the infighting, Marie Louise chose to take one of them as her favorite and from that point on Montebello was her greatest confidant. Durand claimed the empress chose Montebello because she appreciated her frankness, which was so novel at court in France but was the norm in Austrian high society. This, of course, put a bullseye on her lady-in-waiting's back due to the jealousy Montebello's influence caused. Given Durand's description of Montebello, the thirty-year-old duchess likely thought nothing of being a target because Durand described her as cold, hard, abrupt, and harsh.

The one positive description Durand shared about her was that she was one of the best-looking women at court when in full dress. Montebello was likely uncivil because she was independently wealthy and she had not wanted the position in Marie Louise's household. She couldn't refuse because Napoleon demanded she accept the post to fulfill a promise he made to her dying husband, whose last words to the emperor when he was killed while fighting in Austria were meant to guilt Napoleon into taking care of his family. "Your glory makes it your duty to protect them, and in addressing you these final criticisms I do not fear that I shall change your disposition towards them," Jean said. "You have just committed a grave error, one which has deprived you of your best friend, but this will not change you." As his life ebbed away, he scolded, "Your insatiable ambition will finish you. You sacrifice, without need, without attention, without regret, the men who serve you best."[33]

Not only must Montebello have agreed with her husband's rebuke and resented the fact that he died on Austrian soil, she was furious that Napoleon had denied her request to award her father a vacant senator-ship. There was no love lost on the French emperor's side either, as he made it clear in his memoirs that he regretted choosing Montebello over someone who would have helped Marie Louise be less aloof to the courtiers surrounding her. By the time he realized Montebello was manipulating the young empress into becoming more dependent on her, his wife was too attached to the duchess for Napoleon to get rid of her. Durand watched as Montebello "listened with sympathy to the outpourings of her royal mistress's heart, bemoaned her, pitied her, consoled her, and insinuated herself so cleverly into her confidence and good graces that the empress could not do without her. Marie Louise loved the duchess like a sister, and sought to prove this to her by the kindest attentions both to herself and her children. She was happy to find a present which could please the duchess, and to offer it to her in a frank and graceful manner, which was very charming."[34]

Driven by immaturity and a lack of finesse as a courtier, Marie Louise liked those whom Montebello liked and disliked those the duchess found repugnant—cliquish behavior that would reach a crescendo with the birth of a Bonaparte baby. One year and nine days after the first nuptials took place in Austria, Marie Louise went into labor and would experience the trauma of a breach birth. At seven o'clock in the evening on March 19, 1811, she felt her first labor pains, which lasted through the night. The mild contractions had completely subsided by five o'clock in the morning so Marie Louise took an hour's-long nap from which she was awakened by violent pains that continued to increase in intensity. Knowing he was facing a difficult birth, the surgeon, Baron Antoine Dubois, went to Napoleon, who was bathing, and told him he felt the emperor should be at his wife's bedside. "M. Dubois did not conceal from him that he feared it would be impossible to save both mother and child," Durand noted. "'Think only of the mother!' cried Napoleon, 'and do all you can for her.' He would hardly let himself be dried; and went to the empress's room."[35]

Durand said as the pains increased, Napoleon begged his wife to persevere but he couldn't stand to be in the room for more than a few minutes so he would come in and briefly hold his wife's hand only to hastily retreat to the dressing-room next door. "He was as pale as death, and seemed to be beside himself," Durand remembered. Miraculously, Marie Louise delivered the child, feet-first, after a twenty-four-hour ordeal. Napoleon rushed back into the room when he was told the baby had been born and heard nothing—the newborn's silence lasted for seven minutes. "Napoleon cast his eyes upon it for an instant, thought it was dead, did not utter a single word, but occupied himself solely with the empress," Durand said. "A few drops of brandy were put into the child's mouth, its whole body was slapped with the flat of the hand, and it was wrapped in hot cloths. At length it uttered a cry, and the emperor turned to embrace the son, whose birth was the crowning point of his happiness, and the last gift of that fortune which was so soon to forsake him."[36]

By sharing the story of the birth, which she witnessed first-hand, Durand was dispelling a rumor that had been circulating throughout the court. It claimed Marie Louise had delivered a still-born daughter and another child had been substituted for the dead baby. "These reports, as ridiculous as they were improbable, were without the very slightest foundation," she explained. She named the other twenty-two people who had attended the birth and said each of them was in a position to refute the gossip, herself included. The birth of the French heir, who was named Napoleon François Charles Joseph and styled the King of Rome, was marked by a one-hundred-and-one-gun salute that echoed throughout the streets of Paris.[37] Méneval noted how the eager Parisians held a collective breath as the first twenty-one shots were fired because the guns would have stopped there if the child was a female. "When the twenty-second boomed forth," he wrote, "an explosion of applause and of cheering burst out which was re-echoed from every corner of Paris."[38]

Durand said Napoleon, standing at a window in Marie

Louise's room, was deeply affected by the uproar. "Tears rolled down his cheeks without his feeling them flow," she said, "and it was in this state that he came to embrace his son anew."[39] Making the rounds at the palace as he told members of his household he had a baby boy, Méneval said Napoleon admitted to one of his servants he would rather have been present at a bloody battle than to have watched the painful sight of his wife giving birth to his child.[40] As Marie Louise recovered from such a harrowing experience, the emperor began assigning some of the most exceptional people he knew to his son's service. Determined that the prince would have the finest French education, Napoleon appointed the Countess of Montesquiou as the baby's governess, which did not sit well with Montebello because Montesquiou was a member of the nobility. Within days, a feud between them erupted in the nursery.

Montebello told Marie Louise that the governess didn't care a whit for her son; that she was only feigning affection in order to satisfy her own ambitions. Montesquiou approached Marie Louise about the slander and the empress once again took sides with her lady-in-waiting over the perceived adversary. Durand claimed Marie Louise would eventually recognize she hadn't been fair to Montesquiou, though it would be too late to remedy the damage by the time she did. Méneval regretted that Marie Louise treated Montesquiou so poorly because he said the forty-six-year-old governess was a woman with "a great simplicity of manners, a firm character, and solid principles" who deserved the highest respect.[41] While Marie Louise was bungling her interpersonal skirmishes, Napoleon was brushing his aside. Soon after his son was born, he learned that Pius VII, whom he had kept under lock and key since Radet had arrested him, excommunicated the emperor a second time for going forward with his marriage to Marie

Louise in spite of the fact that the pontiff had never recognized his divorce from Josephine.

Napoleon decided to ignore the entire affair because he felt his position was unshakable with an heir apparent in place, and he was determined not to let the pontiff spoil his good mood as a doting father and a happy husband. Durand said Napoleon was so content after the birth of his son, he seemed transformed. In her narrative to this point, the memoirist had been remarkably complimentary about Napoleon, which made me wonder whether she was hesitant to be completely honest about his notoriously edgy personality because she published the memoir while he was still alive and living in exile. She was probably smart to hedge her bets in case the emperor came back into power in France, which he had a habit of doing. I also wondered if Napoleon had read the memoir and was floored to confirm he had. Lady Elizabeth Holland, an English Baroness and an admirer of Napoleon's, had sent him both volumes of Durand's memoir during his exile on Saint Helena.

When Christie's put these particular books up for auction in 2015, they were deemed extremely valuable because so many of the pages were peppered with fiery marginalia Napoleon added to tell his side of the story. Would I love to know what portions of Durand's chronicle of his marriage upset him! The fact Durand agreed with Napoleon about his wife's victimization at the hands of the Austrian emperor and his allies meant he must have been annoyed that the author painted him as helplessly smitten with Marie Louise; exposed his numerous weaknesses, including his military blunders; and put in writing his naïveté regarding his father-in-law's treachery. Napoleon also likely detested how clear Durand made two critical points: that the confluence of these three circumstances hastened his downfall and that many of the French courtiers blamed his ouster solely on his wife, though Durand was not one of these. Her memoir also claimed that Marie Louise's immaturity bothered Napoleon because he wanted her to charm her subjects as beguilingly as Josephine had, which Durand saw as unrealistic because Marie Louise had been born a royal and had been treated with deference since she was a baby.

The young empress was also clueless about French attitudes, which were much more effusive than those in her home country. Méneval felt Napoleon's desire for the empress to bewitch was a case of wanting it both ways because his wife's timidity kept her from participating in courtly seductiveness, which meant she wouldn't be lured into liaisons that would have angered the emperor. The bashfulness that made her aloof was just one of Marie Louise's challenges as she struggled through the indoctrination forced upon her as a figurehead—she was so lacking in all of the social graces, she developed the habit of adopting every attitude Montebello held. This intensified Marie Louise's cold, impassive behavior in public. "She was constantly told that one ought to be natural, and to appear just as one is; an excellent principle in private life, no doubt, but it does not work in the case of sovereigns," Durand explained.[42] In private, the author said Marie Louise exhibited qualities that could have endeared her to the French people but the empress retreated into her shell in public.

Durand shared an anecdote that took place during an evening at the Théâtre-Français to describe the influence she saw. When a courtier ventured to tell Marie Louise that the audience had been upset because she had remained at the back of her box, depriving them of the privilege of seeing her, Montebello stepped in. The lady-in-waiting asked the woman why it mattered so much that the empress should trouble herself. Durand, who identified the courtier as Madame D, said the woman told Montebello that a large number of people in attendance had gone to the theater solely to see Marie Louise and they had been very disappointed when they could not; that the empress should consider their desire as a sign of affection that should always to be welcomed by a sovereign. Montebello argued that when someone is frank and sincere, they should put how they truly feel above any considerations for other people.

Durand said about how Marie Louise's lady-in-waiting was fueling the unfriendliness, "With such advice as this always at hand, it is not surprising that the young empress allowed her face and demeanor to betray to the public the weariness and distaste the duties and etiquette imposed upon her. Back again in her private life, she was kindly, gentle, merry, affable, and beloved by all."[43] When d'Abrantès was presented to Marie Louise in 1811, the courtier described the empress's disdain as she stared "bovinely ahead, unable to think of anything to say." The courtier felt contempt for Marie Louise's interactions with others, saying the standing questions she lobbed at anyone new who approached were insultingly trite. "And how many children do you have, Madame?" Marie Louise would ask.[44] The gossiping members of the court like d'Abrantès spread a rumor that the disregard the empress showed to them was extended to her son. The jaded duchess said Marie Louise suffered from an apathy of the soul, which she illustrated by pointing out that she stayed only fifteen minutes when she visited the prince and embroidered the entire time she was there.

D'Abrantès claimed Marie Louise was able to slip away so quickly because she timed her visits just before she knew her drawing or dancing teachers would come for her. "It would have been as well had she remained longer every day with her child to take a lesson in maternal feeling from the woman who so admirably took her place," D'Abrantès wrote, speaking of Montesquiou. "But it would have been of little use—feeling is not to be taught."[45] Durand did not agree that the empress's standoffishness was caused by a lack of caring. She said the chilliness they noticed toward her child was due to the fact that, because she had little experience with children, she was afraid to take the baby in her arms for fear of hurting him. Méneval backed up Durand's claim, saying, "The empress had so little trust in herself in taking the child from the nurse that Napoleon would hasten to take his son into his arms and carry him away, covering him with kisses."[46]

It was as if Méneval couldn't take his eyes off the emperor as he played with his son because he effusively recorded how delighted Napoleon was with the little boy. When the emperor teased the child one day at lunch by holding a piece of food near his mouth and pulling it away twice, the young prince turned his head aside and refused to open his mouth again. When Napoleon was surprised by this, Montesquiou, whom the prince called "Maman 'Quiou," said the child did not like for people to play tricks on him. "He is proud and sensitive," she added, which prompted Napoleon to declare, "It is a very good thing; it is because he is like that that I love him!" Méneval said the baby was often brought to his father's office and Napoleon would drop whatever he was doing to lie down on the floor "at the side of his darling son" to play with him as if he was a child himself.[47] D'Abrantès shared a similar level of devotion she saw when she walked into the little boy's nursery one day to find Napoleon there, "playing with him in the way he did with everyone he loved—that is to say, teasing him."[48]

She then described how touching she found the interactions between the father and son. "The emperor had been riding and had a whip in his hand, which the child wanted," she wrote. "When his little hand had succeeded at last in seizing it, he shrieked with laughter and then kissed his father." She said Napoleon's moist eyes revealed how happy he was as he turned toward her and asked, "Isn't my son beautiful, Madame Junot? Agree with me that he is beautiful." The duchess said she didn't hesitate to say the boy was angelic and resembled "one of those figures of Cupid which have been discovered in the ruins of Herculaneum."[49] Durand also described Napoleon's effusiveness with the child, saying he couldn't pass a mirror without stopping to make grimacing faces at the boy. "At breakfast, he would keep the child in his lap, and, having dipped a finger in the sauce, make him suck it, or smear his face with it," she remembered. "The governess scolded, the emperor laughed, and the child, who was almost always good-humored, seemed to take pleasure in the rough play of his father."[50]

AS THEY IMMORTALIZED the early months of Napoleon's marriage to Marie Louise, the memoirists had steered clear of military matters, which changed as war loomed. The first hint of discord Durand records took place in 1811 when a dashing Russian envoy known for his battlefield victories, his chivalrous language, and his fine manners came on the Parisian scene. Rumors were circulating that the czar sent the military attaché Prince Alexander Chernyshev to spy on the Russian ambassador Alexander Kurakin because the czar feared Kurakin was sharing too many confidences with Napoleon. It would soon become clear that Chernyshev, who appeared at the most dazzling parties thrown by members of high society and was sought after by glamorous women, had an assignment that was much more sinister. Rovigo grew suspicious of Chernyshev after finding out he was meeting regularly with the Duke of Feltre, France's minister of war, not buying the claim being offered that their "intimacy was founded wholly and solely upon their common taste for music."[51]

When Rovigo brought up his suspicions, Napoleon brushed them aside. Things changed when Chernyshev disappeared in the middle of the night, and it was discovered the plans for a military campaign in Russia, documents describing the state of France's forces, and other war material were missing from Feltre's residence. Though Napoleon had been able to resist the czar's attempts to lure him into battle for some time, this betrayal felt like an overt declaration of war he couldn't ignore. He told his ambassadors to keep trying to diffuse the Russian ruler's opposition to him and ordered his generals to begin organizing a campaign to march on Moscow in case diplomacy failed. Méneval said he had watched Napoleon hesitate to go to war with Russia a number of times and he believed this stemmed from a bit of hero-worship the emperor felt for the czar. Others agreed.

In his introduction to d'Abrantès' memoirs, Olivier Bernier described the chemistry between the czar and the emperor. "In many ways, the relationship between Napoleon and Alexander I of Russia was one of reluctant and disappointed love," he wrote. "There is no doubt the young Russian czar was deeply impressed by the strength and genius of his French counterpart; this much was evident when the two emperors met. As for Napoleon, he was unquestionably fascinated by Alexander. Even more important, it seemed clear that the two monarchs, together, could rule Europe, and that they had agreed to do exactly that." This unity would be fleeting, wrote Bernier, who pointed out that history is littered with examples of gentlemen's agreements being left behind when the needs of their realms grew more important. "From 1809 on," he added, "whether Alexander and Napoleon liked it or not, France and Russia were on a collision course."[52]

Sensing he was about to have to finance a massive military campaign, Napoleon told his staff to plan the most magnificent social season ever experienced during his rule because he had to impress the upper crust of French society whose help he would need to fund the offensive. Durand's tone was dripping with sarcasm as she described the ritzy array of festivities and explained how Napoleon's actions were about to launch France into a dangerous era. "It was during fêtes and entertainments of every kind that Napoleon planned the conquest of Russia," she wrote. "The spoilt child of fortune, intoxicated with adulation, never contemplating the possibility of a reverse, seemed to be celebrating his future victories in anticipation, and to have called on all the pleasures to aid the preparations for war. Not a day passed but there was a play, a concert, or a masked ball at court. Nothing could exceed the brilliancy of these entertainments; the theatre especially was a dazzling spectacle."[53]

She said the masquerades were particularly lavish because they were Napoleon's favorite amusements—he loved taunting courtiers when they thought themselves hidden enough that he wouldn't recognize them. He could identify them because he made sure he knew in advance the costumes worn by each of the party-goers he wanted to goad. "As he was acquainted with all the scandalous stories, secret intrigues, and general gossip of his court, he took a spiteful pleasure in tormenting the ladies, disturbing the husbands, and alarming the lovers," Durand explained.[54] When the resplendent season came to an end in May of 1812, she was among the courtiers who traveled with the emperor and empress to Dresden where Napoleon would meet with a number of rulers to discuss his Continental System, a plan he had devised to paralyze Great Britain's ability to carry out commerce on the continent. If his ambassadors couldn't convince the czar to stop baiting him,

Napoleon would begin his Russian advance as soon as these conferences were over.

Though the other European leaders were there solely to discuss the trade policies Napoleon had drafted, the French emperor knew he also had to ensure the emperors, princes, and kings who had joined him in Dresden would support his Russian campaign if his hand was forced. To remind the royals he had been welcomed into one of the most distinguished sovereign families himself, Napoleon decided to parade a lavishly attired Marie Louise around to put himself on equal footing, a tactic that worked fabulously at first. "What a moment for Marie Louise!" declared Durand. "Once more to find herself in the arms of her father, and to reappear before the dazzled eyes of her family as the happiest of wives and the consort of the greatest of sovereigns!" The author said Marie Louise's father was emotional as he "tenderly embraced his son-in-law" in public. In private, he assured Napoleon that he could count on Austria's support if France decided to attack Russia.[55]

By the end of the conference, the list of rulers who were willing to back Napoleon was a dignified one, many of them eager to strengthen their alliances with the French emperor. King Frederic William III of Prussia met with Napoleon to inform him, "Sire, my brother, I repeat to you my assurance of inviolable attachment to the Continental System which unites us."[56] The king then said his son would be an excellent choice to act as Napoleon's aide-de-camp during the Russian campaign. Being a major player in these Dresden negotiations brought Napoleon such a heightened feeling of triumph, Méneval described the trip as the apogee of his power. When dictating his memoirs years later, Napoleon said his time in Dresden was his happiest. "Surrounded by a bevy of sovereigns, his court surpassed them all in magnificence," Cuthell claimed. "The other leaders hastened to do him service, as vassals of a chief. The oldest names and the most illustrious families bowed before the conqueror's beck and call. As Napoleon said at Saint Helena: 'The reign of Marie Louise had been a very short one, but she must have enjoyed it, for she had the world at her feet.'"[57]

Witnessing the splendor surrounding his daughter and her husband, Francis regretted that he had not brought his court to Dresden because he felt small surrounded by the excessive display of wealth Napoleon had on view. As the days passed, the Austrian emperor struggled between being delighted over his favorite daughter's exalted position and feeling a wounded sense of self-worth because he believed he had allowed his country to be humiliated. Francis wasn't the only member of Marie Louise's family who was offended. Napoleon had arranged for an array of the crown jewels to be taken to Dresden, and the empress was literally weighed down by them. This brought rancor from her stepmother, who had done her very best to make a splash only to find she was completely eclipsed by her stepdaughter. "At Dresden, Marie Louise must have noticed the great change that had come over her stepmother with regard to herself," Cuthell wrote. "The Empress of Austria was jealous of the Empress of France, though Emperor Francis II shut his eyes to it. The victim, whom she had been instrumental in sacrificing to the Minotaur, instead of returning to them a martyr, reappeared not only as a magnificent sovereign, but also as an indulged, beloved, and contented wife, and a happy mother."[58]

The mention of motherhood is especially important here because Maria Ludovika had not been able to have children, a fact that made her further resent her stepdaughter. To soothe her bruised ego, she would go into Marie Louise's rooms in Dresden while her stepdaughter was dressing and riffle through her laces, ribbons, shawls, and jewelry; and she reportedly never went away empty-handed. Either Napoleon didn't pick up on the ill-will or didn't care because he grew ever-more ostentatious as the days passed, each act of flamboyance making the Austrian empress detest him more. Cuthell believed that Marie Louise was so young and cheerful, she took pleasure in eclipsing her stepmother without realizing the consequences. Once Napoleon came out of his supremacy stupor and saw how the richness on display was upsetting his wife's parents, he asked Marie Louise to tone it down. Each time he admonished her she cried so he dropped his efforts to get his wife to refrain from outshining every other woman in town.

Because she had come off as an innocent in other ways so far, I found it interesting that Marie Louise had at least mastered the art of emotional manipulation by the time she had married Napoleon. Seeing crying as a way to get what she wanted, she later boasted to her closest confidants, "Whenever I desired anything, no matter how difficult, I had only to weep." One day, as he was recording the remembrances Napoleon was dictating to him on Saint Helena, Count Emmanuel de Las Cases shared this with Napoleon, who laughed and said he would have expected it of Josephine but not of Marie Louise.[59] As the glittering parties in Dresden came to an end, Napoleon had exhausted all diplomatic efforts to achieve peace with Alexander. Méneval, who was there to handle the correspondence between the negotiators, said once it became clear to Napoleon that he had to attack, he set out to strike such a great blow on the enemy it would forever be known as one of his most renowned conquests.

IT WAS in late May of 1812 when Napoleon left the Saxon capital to lead a multi-nation army that included French,

THE ART OF CAPITULATION

Austrian, Italian, German, and Prussian forces. Durand said this moment could have remained a source of French national pride had things gone differently because Napoleon "marched at the head of the finest army that France had ever raised, reinforced by auxiliary troops, and provided with formidable parks of artillery and immense stores."[60] While Marie Louise's husband and his army were dragging such prodigious provisions closer to the battlefield, she was being celebrated in Prague where she had traveled with her father and stepmother. The Austrian emperor was waxing poetic about her and patting himself on the back because he'd made such an illustrious match for his "dear Louise." Balls and other soirées were held in her honor, which inspired Neuchâtel to remark she was not only being used as a political pawn by her husband, but by her father as well. Cuthell agreed. "For all the pomp and splendor with which she was surrounded at Prague. Marie Louise really was regarded by each side as a kind of hostage," she wrote.[61]

There were clear-cut explanations for why she was being exploited by the two countries she had called home—in Austria, she represented a sense of security that Francis knew played well with the feudal lords he would need to back him when it came time to marshal his own forces; for France, Napoleon believed she was his guarantee of neutrality in case he suffered defeat in Russia, which at the time no one felt was likely. When Marie Louise returned to Paris, booming cannons saluted her retinue as it entered the city gates, a festive atmosphere that drastically contrasted the experience her husband was having as he and his troops slogged over muddy roads to inch their way toward Moscow. Marie Louise wrote to her father that she was sad and lonely. "God grant that my husband may soon come back, for the separation is very painful, and I am not brave enough not to complain," she whined.[62]

Without Napoleon to accompany her to parties, the empress attended as few as possible, escaping to the Château de Saint-Cloud as often as she could because she preferred fresh air and riding horses to being trapped in court formalities. When she learned that Bausset-Roquefort was about to leave Paris to join Napoleon and his army, she asked him to take a newly painted François Gérard portrait of their son to her husband. "Traveling night and day across Europe, Bausset-Roquefort reached Napoleon's camp on the heights above the Borodino," Cuthell wrote. "The emperor's delight at the picture was touching. He sent for all his staff to admire it, and then had it placed on a chair outside his tent that his *braves* might share his pleasure and admiration. 'Messieurs,' he said to his generals, 'if my son were but fifteen years older, he would be here in person, and not in portrait.'"[63]

By this time Napoleon had advanced to within eighty-four miles of Moscow and it's a good thing his heir was safe in Paris because soon after the emperor entered the Russian capital, an explosive fire broke out. The flames spread so rapidly, they devoured three-quarters of the city in three days. "The town was one mighty furnace from which sheaves of fire burst heavenwards lighting up the horizon with the glaring flames and spreading a burning heat," Méneval remembered. "These masses of flame, mingling together, were rapidly caught up by a strong wind which spread them in every direction." He said the scene was so shocking, Napoleon was stunned. "Motionless and in the silence of stupor, we looked on at this horrible and magnificent spectacle with a feeling of absolute helplessness," he explained.[64] The czar had ordered the governor of Moscow to set the city on fire after removing everything that might have helped enemy troops put out the flames. Napoleon retreated a safe distance and returned to Moscow when the fires had burned themselves out, setting up his command center in the Grand

THE ART OF CAPITULATION

Kremlin Palace, which had been spared, to bide his time for several weeks as he attempted to reestablish communications with the czar.

"Now, Napoleon, installing himself in the Kremlin, waited for what he felt sure must come," D'Abrantès wrote; "but instead of peace overtures, there was nothing but an ominous silence."[65] Once news of Moscow's burning reached Paris, a dark mood took over the capital. "In every drawing room hung a war-map into which anxious women stuck pins as they followed the movements of their nearest and dearest," wrote Cuthell. "By the beginning of October, bad news was beginning to circulate."[66] With the fears of defeat growing, other worries were cropping up in France as the fall season of 1812 progressed, including a new tax that had been ordered by the councilors of the empire. When the unrest over the tariffs escalated into an attempt to overthrow Napoleon's government, Marie Louise was not in town; she was still hiding out in Saint-Cloud. "It must be said, to her honor, that she showed coolness and courage on the occasion," Durand said. "She commanded the few troops at the palace to place themselves under arms; but this was barely done when she learned the conspirators had been arrested."[67]

A rumor was spreading throughout Paris that Napoleon had been killed and the reaction from his citizens was chilly at best. Durand said it was as if the capital was filled with spectators watching a game of dominos—rather than being invested in who the victor would be, the onlookers had merely resigned themselves to following along until the back-and-forth ended. This did not bode well for the emperor whose stubborn nature was inching him toward catastrophe. Alexander finally resumed negotiations with Napoleon and hinted that proposals of peace would soon be coming but this was a trick; the czar was keeping the emperor in a waiting game while he drew auxiliary forces to his aid because he knew the combined armies would be much more fatal to Napoleon's troops than Russian forces alone could be. The wise men among his advisers told him they suspected something was up but the emperor wouldn't listen.

Napoleon's mantra by then was that he couldn't retrace his steps back to France without having struck a single decisive blow because it would make him look weak. "Napoleon's star was already waning," Méneval wrote. "The burning of Moscow seemed to show that Russia had decided to resist our armies to the death. In spite of this, so great was Napoleon's partiality for Alexander that the emperor still flattered himself with the hope that he could convince the czar to be friendlier to France."[68] The secretary described the disastrous cold weather they endured as winter came on. "In one night the thermometer went down to twelve degrees below zero and two days later to eighteen degrees below," he wrote.[69] He said the soldiers scoured Russia for sustenance, but no provisions were found in the towns they raided so they were forced to eat their horses. The situation was so dire, Prussian troops defected, leaving France in a deplorable situation as its soldiers were butchered. Out of the 600,000 troops Napoleon had led to Moscow, only 30,000 limped back to France. "This was Napoleon's first great defeat," D'Abrantès wrote; "and it proved so severe that he never recovered from it."[70] Rovigo said the army's reversal was a harbinger of Napoleon's future defeats.

"The disastrous Russian campaign was the first fatal event with which France had been visited during the emperor's reign," he added.[71] The loss sent Napoleon racing back to France in such haste, Durand called his retreat "a precipitate flight."[72] Given the size of the forces Napoleon had commanded, there were a stunning number of European families mourning someone as he unexpectedly arrived in

Paris. Disguised under layers of heavy furred cloaks, he burst into Marie Louise's quarters where her frightened attendant threw herself in front of the bedroom door. Hearing the lady-in-waiting's shriek, the empress was getting out of bed to find out what was going on when Napoleon came into the room. Marie Louise wrote to her best friend Victoire, "I am sure you will share with me the joy which I experienced in seeing him again after an absence of more than seven months. The New Year could not begin under happier auspices for me."[73] She would soon find that she was the only one who was cheerful—Napoleon, who came home gloomy and absent minded, refused to resume courtly entertainments because he was in such a bad mood.

WITH PUBLIC SENTIMENT toward him on the ebb, Napoleon wrote a letter to the French senate to defend his loss in Russia, which was published in *Le Moniteur Universel* on December 21, 1812: "I could have armed a great part of the population (in Russia) against itself by proclaiming the freedom of the serfs. I was asked to do so in a large number of villages, but when I saw the degraded state of this large class of the Russian population I refused to take a measure which would have condemned many families to death and to the most horrible tortures."[74] As he was assessing his position in the world order, he learned that his battle-fatigued country was going to have to arm itself again. The dispatches he was receiving from his ambassadors in Austria and Prussia alerted him that France would likely be attacked by a coalition of armies that would include his father-in-law's. Napoleon didn't share his doubts about Francis's loyalty with his wife, who couldn't bear the thought of her husband and her father being at odds.

She was prone to profusely thanking Napoleon for continuing to have confidence in her father, which signaled to her husband it was best to keep her in the dark. Though this worked for his naïve wife, the savvy courtiers could not be so easily deceived. "In vain did the emperor endeavor to conceal the real state of affairs by pretending confidence," D'Abrantès noted. "Meanwhile the clouds gathered more and more thickly, and the storm seemed ready to break."[75] As if sensing the disasters that were to come, Montesquiou taught Napoleon's twenty-month-old son an addendum to his prayers each morning and evening: "Inspire, O Lord God, my papa with the desire to make peace, for the welfare of France and of us all."[76] When Napoleon happened to be in the room one night as the boy knelt beside his bed, he smiled when he heard the words but said nothing, as he was already aware his skirmishes were far from over. In early 1813, Napoleon began to strategize his next moves to fend off his foes while his wife returned to the carefree life of a wealthy and privileged young woman of twenty-one.

Courtiers like d'Abrantès found her lighthearted behavior insulting. "At this critical moment, how was Marie Louise employed—she who, of all others, might be supposed to tremble when the Austrian cannons were about to roar on the heights of Montmartre?" the duchess sneered. "The empress occupied herself in working embroidery and playing the piano."[77] Durand was amazed at how quickly Napoleon built an impressive army and collected all the necessities the soldiers would need to wage war. "New arms seemed to fall from the sky; immense magazines of provisions, forage, and munitions were gathered; and men rose apparently from the earth to fill up the roster of the former regiments or to form new ones, which passed in succession before the emperor," she wrote. "One day, as he was looking at a newly formed regiment of chasseurs defiling under the windows of the Tuileries, he cried, 'What a fine regiment! With that, one may be sure of conquering everyone and everywhere.'"[78]

Napoleon knew the expense of building up resources after the devastating losses in Russia would draw rancor from the old nobles and the wealthy bourgeois who had already paid considerable sums to keep their sons off the battlefields a number of times. The resentment they would feel and the uprising over taxes that had taken place when he was at war with Russia convinced him he had to be more strategic to protect his empire and his family, so he put the wheels in motion to have Marie Louise appointed Regent of the Empire and his brother Joseph President of the Council of the Regency. He assigned Méneval, who had been recuperating since the Russian campaign during which he nearly froze to death, to the post of Marie Louise's secretary. When the documents were completed that would legitimize his wife's power, Napoleon hesitated to make it official because Marie Louise was so inexperienced and unsophisticated when it came to politics (precisely because he had made sure she knew nothing about anything related to state affairs).

In the end, he decided his wife would be the perfect figure-head for the job because she would be fortified by politicians he trusted. While he finalized the governmental tasks that would clear the way for him to be gone, his generals planned a campaign against Prussia. Napoleon had chosen the country as his target because the emperor wanted to punish King Frederic William, whose relationship with him had soured since their Dresden meeting, for trying to take back territory Napoleon had previously annexed to France, and he wanted to punish Prussia for the defection of its army during the Russian debacle. "Austria had not yet declared herself against us but she signified that the contingent she had supplied to our army during the last campaign should take no part in the hostilities," Rovigo said. "Thus she deprived us of resources so that our enemy could combine a force as great, or even greater, against us."[79] Also predicting that Austria's behavior would be fatal to Napoleon's rule was a friend of his from childhood named Louis Antoine Fauvelet de Bourrienne. Though the two of them had a falling out early in the establishment of the First Consulate, the government that preceded the First French Empire, Bourrienne knew Napoleon so well, his biography about the emperor is filled with rich details about his friend's personality.

He described the ruler's frame of mind as he prepared to join his troops. "Napoleon now saw clearly that since Austria had abandoned him and refused her contingent, he should soon have all Europe arrayed against him but this did not intimidate him," he wrote.[80] Méneval, who took his post as Marie Louise's secretary several days before the emperor left Paris, also described the confidence Napoleon exuded as he was preparing to march, saying the emperor had arranged his activities so thoroughly, he rarely had any reason to speak to Marie Louise about anything political. "She was in reserve for extraordinary circumstances, such as the death of the emperor, which fortunately did not occur," Méneval explained. "My chief employment was my correspondence with the emperor when he was away."[81] Before his departure, Napoleon put in writing the sums of money and properties Marie Louise would inherit if he died on the battlefield—two-hundred-and-forty-thousand francs, the Élysée Palace, and the Trianon estate were to be hers.

During the ceremony in which she was made regent, she swore to carry out her duties "as good wife, good mother, and good Frenchwoman." When the police reports were about to be read, Napoleon stopped the arch-chancellor, telling him, "One must not soil a young woman's mind by certain details."[82] These two anecdotal fragments are perfect examples of how he continued to coddle her, why she was so unprepared for the responsibilities she would eventually bear, and why she would feel so helpless during a number of critical moments. Given how awkward she was in public, it's a miracle she did as well as she did. When Napoleon won his first battle, a resplendent celebration was held during which Marie Louise made her first appearance as regent. Méneval described her as noble and affable when she presided over the ceremony. Marie Louise reported to her father that the affection her husband inspired during the fête was touching. "Never have the French so cheered his name," she told him. "He is both conqueror and peacemaker."[83]

Francis, who definitely didn't see his son-in-law as a peacemaker, told the Prince of Schwarzenberg, who was negotiating with the other allies on behalf of the Austrian emperor, to begin to lure Napoleon toward his annihilation. Schwarzenberg was far from subtle about the fact that the French emperor was about to lose what his ego deemed his most distinguished prize. "Politics made the marriage, politics can unmake it," he told Napoleon's minister of foreign affairs, who was in talks with Austrian and allied diplomats to try and diffuse the situation.[84] To remind Francis that he was a member of his family, Napoleon wrote to his father-in-law from the battlefield, "I have news of the empress, with whom I am extremely satisfied. She is today my chief minister, and acquits herself to my great satisfaction. I cannot let you be ignorant of this, knowing how it will please your paternal heart." Napoleon also pressed him for an answer as to whether he had Francis's support for his Prussian campaign. Marie Louise's father replied that he was proud to know this about his daughter but he left Napoleon's question as to whether Austria would stand behind him in battle unanswered because he was renewing his relationships with the leaders of Russia and the country Napoleon was fighting. "I will get myself fit for the saddle," Francis told Metternich; "but first of all, get me my alliance back."[85]

Early on, Napoleon's army performed superbly but the victories came at a high price. After winning several battles, Napoleon lost one of his top marshals when his abdomen was torn open by a cannon ball. Rovigo said the death of the general, who survived for an incredibly painful thirty hours while refusing any surgical treatment, was "an irreparable loss." He explained, "Fate thus deprived the emperor of a man whose zeal, spirit of order, and strict integrity were at that time most necessary to him."[86] The emperor was so shaken by the brutal way his loyal friend died and by what the death might portend, he told his doctor if he was ever severely wounded and unconscious, he was to give him the dose of poison from the sachet he wore around his neck. Soon after this scare, Francis showed his hand, sending Metternich to Dresden where Napoleon was occupying the palace to tell him his father-in-law and the other rulers with whom Austria was aligning were expecting the French to return wide swaths of territory to their countries and revert to France's borders as they were before Napoleon began his numerous campaigns to expand the French empire.

Napoleon scoffed at the idea, which inspired Metternich to say to Neuchâtel as he left the meeting, "Upon my oath, your master has gone out of his mind."[87] The French emperor would later say had he known a secret treaty was being signed in which Austria joined Great Britain, Russia, Sweden, and Prussia to carry out the War of the Sixth Coalition against France, he would have acted differently. When he was dictating his memoirs to Las Cases, he said his assassination during the early weeks of his Prussian advance would have been less fatal to his empire than his union with an Austrian princess. "I loved Marie Louise well; she did not mix herself up with intrigues," he added. "My marriage with her ruined me because it is not in my nature to be able to believe in the treachery of my relatives, and the day of my marriage with Marie Louise her father became, according to my bourgeois customs, a member of my family."[88] Napoleon said he could never have fathomed that the Emperor of Austria would have the audacity to turn his arms against him, nor that Francis would ultimately dethrone his daughter and grandson in favor of the return of the Bourbons.

When French forces pulled off a victory at Lützen, coalition leaders declared a ceasefire and asked Napoleon to resume negotiations with them. Napoleon took advantage of the break and summoned his wife to the French army's command center in Mayence to remind the allied leaders he had married the favorite daughter of one of their compatriots. To celebrate her arrival, he conducted a review of the troops and held an opulent banquet, neither of which succeeded in the minds of the courtiers who accompanied her there because the couple seemed anything but festive. An attendee at the dinner described Napoleon as monosyllabic and the empress as "timidly putting in a few words." After six days, the "happy little holiday," as Cuthell sarcastically deemed it, ended, and Marie Louise wept as her husband lifted her into her carriage.[89] The wheel ruts made by the French retinue were barely dry when Napoleon saw the negotiations requested by the other leaders were turning out to be a joke. Suspecting Francis was about to put country before family, Napoleon repositioned his troops.

"The empress returned to Paris about the time the emperor reentered Dresden and the armistice was broken,"

Rovigo wrote. "Fate had decreed that nothing should avert the events which speedily completed our destruction. The crisis was approaching, and there were no means of escaping from the impending storm."[90] On August 15, 1813, Napoleon's soldiers celebrated his birthday, which would be the last respite the army would have before Francis and his allies declared war on France. Méneval said her father's fatal betrayal deeply affected Marie Louise. "She feared that it might result in a diminution of the emperor's affection for her," he explained, "but Napoleon did not cease to give her proofs of his confidence."[91] As Méneval watched the young woman try to act as peace-maker between her father and her husband, an effort that would be an epic failure, he felt sorry for her. One of his duties as her secretary was to read her the dispatches coming from the battlefield, which he said nearly overwhelmed her.

Several early ones related victories like the one the French army pulled off in Dresden but these were followed by a succession of heavy losses, the last of which was a crushing defeat at Leipzig in October of 1813 that caused Napoleon's few remaining allies to desert him. He raced away from Prussia just as quickly as he had left Russia. Durand said he was only able to reach safety because he was surrounded by noble guards who were cut to pieces covering his retreat. When he arrived at Saint-Cloud in a disheveled, incognito carriage, Marie Louise was informed that her husband had returned. She ran to meet him as he was crossing the courtyard leading to the palace and, as Durand witnessed, "threw herself into his arms in a flood of tears." She said Napoleon, who was deeply moved, "clasped her to his heart with the utmost tenderness." Because Marie Louise had learned of her father's betrayal, she had dreaded her husband's return as much as she had longed for it because she feared his feelings for her may have changed. She was relieved to find that he did not blame her, and that he was calm and resigned while he assessed his situation. "He did not show the slightest disposition to hold his wife responsible for the faithlessness of her father," Durand said.[92]

In an imploring letter to Francis, Marie Louise wrote, "You cannot imagine how much I am troubled by the thought that you and my husband are enemies."[93] While she hounded her father, Rovigo pled with Napoleon. "I perceived the danger on all sides so pressing that I determined to speak on the subject to the emperor," he explained. "He asked my opinion on the state of affairs. I answered that they could not be worse; and what was more, that the intentions of the allies were evident, that they could not be misunderstood, and that they had resolved upon his ruin." Napoleon countered, "You believe so?" Rovigo assured him he did and told Napoleon he could lose no time in preventing Francis from allying against him.[94] Even if the emperor had heeded his advice (and he did not) it was too late: The coalition generals were already finalizing their plans to invade France. Marie Louise continued to lob letters at her father to remind him that he had always assured her he would never sacrifice her or his grandson.

Méneval said Francis might have upheld his promises if the coalition had not overrode his desire to keep the members of his family on the French throne. He called Francis's involvement with these major players as they gathered in Châtillon-sur-Seine to draft the documents holding the demands they wanted to impose upon Napoleon "shameful." The tradition of agreeing to an armistice as all sides negotiated was honored per usual but, as had been the case during the past several skirmishes, the promises made during the delay were empty ones—the allies had secretly agreed they would accept nothing less than Napoleon's complete overthrow. The stipulations they put in writing, which they knew he would never accept, included that the

French emperor would restore the borders of France to what they were during the ancient regime. Napoleon pretended he would be amenable to the idea and employed a number of other delay tactics to buy more time.

"It was his established principle never to sign a disadvantageous peace: To him, a tarnished crown was no longer a crown," Bourrienne wrote. He said the fact that Napoleon was acting more like a conqueror dictating to his enemies than a man overwhelmed by misfortune was so ingrained in the emperor's nature, he couldn't help himself. "Napoleon never intended to make peace at Châtillon on the terms proposed," Bourrienne went on to say. "He always hoped that some fortunate event would enable him to obtain more favorable conditions."[95] He said the emperor would never back down; that he would sacrifice everything, even his own glory, to try and keep his empire intact. "He fell from a great height," Bourrienne added, "but he never, by his signature, consented to any dismemberment of France." The author then pointed out the biggest miscalculation Napoleon made, which would hasten his downfall: The emperor believed France would once again rally around him as it had in the past.

"With the aid of his veteran troops, Napoleon and his genius might have again turned the scale of fortune," Bourrienne explained. "But Napoleon reckoned on the nation, and he was wrong, for the nation was tired of him. His cause had ceased to be the cause of France."[96] While Napoleon continued to fiddle around with the paperwork holding the terms everyone knew he would reject, the allied rulers lost patience and ended the pretend negotiations. Marie Louise was appointed regent for a second time as her husband prepared to defend France from forces that were already approaching its borders. It amazed me that he could still inspire fervor. Before he left Paris, he delivered a speech to around eight-hundred members of the Paris National Guard who were gathered in the Salle des Maréchaux at the Tuileries Palace. Shouts of "Vive l'Empereur!" resounded when he walked into the room accompanied by Marie Louise and Montesquiou, who held the two-year-old King of Rome in her arms.

With his wife and son by his side, he addressed the guards in a loud voice: "Gentlemen, a part of the territory of France is invaded; I am about to place myself at the head of my army, and, with the help of God and the valor of my troops, I hope to drive the enemy back beyond the frontiers." Napoleon then took the empress and their son by their hands and added with great emotion, "If the enemy approaches the capital, I confide the empress and the King of Rome, my wife and my son, to the devotion of the National Guard." Durand said Marie Louise nearly fainted and the simple address stirred everyone in the room. "Several of the officers stepped out of their ranks and kissed the emperor's hand; the greater number shed tears," she said. "Among the latter were many who were by no means partial to the imperial regime, but the scene had affected them."[97]

Bourrienne also attended the rally that day. "I have rarely witnessed such profound silence in so numerous an assembly," he remembered, describing Napoleon's voice as being as firm and sonorous as when he had cajoled his troops in Italy or in Egypt, but without the air of confidence he had then. "Napoleon had become master of Europe, and was now on the point of sinking beneath the efforts of his enemies" Bourrienne added. "I confess that my feelings were deeply moved when he uttered the words, 'I leave you my wife and my son.' At that moment my eyes were fixed on the young prince, and the interest he inspired in me had nothing to do with the splendor which surrounded him or the misfortunes which threatened him." This is because he was not looking at the King of Rome, but at the adored son of his old friend.[98] Bourrienne, who had not seen Napoleon in a while, didn't paint a flattering picture of his friend's physique or his state of mind.

He said the emperor was heavyset and pale; that his expression held a mix of sadness and irritability; and that the muscles that had always twitched on the back of his neck moved more frequently. Bourrienne's concerns for the emperor's son were warranted—that evening, Napoleon held his child for the last time. The little boy went to sleep in his father's arms, his head on Napoleon's chest and his arms around his father's neck. When the boy's nurse approached, Napoleon made a sign not to awaken the child, preferring to place his son carefully on the cot himself. The emperor left Paris on January 25, 1814, at three o'clock in the morning at the head of a hastily formed army. They didn't have a chance in hell against the number of soldiers pouring into France. "Once more he believed that the star which had guided him so long had reappeared above the horizon," Durand wrote; "and he declared that he would not think of peace until he had forced the enemy to re-cross the Rhine."[99]

Napoleon executed a skillful maneuver which should have brought him success but his fate was sealed when one of his generals betrayed him and allowed Alexander's army to enter the country through an unexpected route. The foreign troops were lying in wait as Napoleon was confidently planning to cut them off before they could reach French soil. Durand quoted a number of Napoleon's marshals as saying if he had not been duped, the campaign would have been one of his most brilliant. History reminds us it was not and, as Napoleon's grasp on power lessened, the army of Marie Louise's father was among the forces marching against him. Foreseeing the disaster they faced, Joseph urged his brother to give in. "If you can make peace, make it at any price," he implored him. "If you cannot, you must perish like the last Emperor of Constantinople—there is a splendid end for you!"[100]

WORRYING about her husband's survival and knowing her father was going to be partially responsible for the danger he was facing, Marie Louise descended into an intense confusion. With two powerful men in her life standing firmly on opposite sides, she didn't know which one to trust, and the self-doubt that dogged her was the reason her husband would never see her or their son again. As Napoleon faced the fierce fighting unleashed by a much larger army than his, he must have realized victory was far from guaranteed because he wrote to Joseph, "In no case must you let the empress and the King of Rome fall into the enemy's hands. Do not abandon my son, and remember that I had rather see them both in the Seine than in the hands of the enemies of France."[101] Joseph tried to be a stabilizing influence on Marie Louise, who couldn't make up her mind whether to flee or to stay in Paris, but his advice wouldn't hold because she had fallen into the habit of agreeing with the last person with whom she had spoken. Given she was surrounded by people who were rooting for both sides, she was in a grand state of uncertainty.

On March 28, 1814, as the troops of the Sixth Coalition drew near Paris, the officers of the National Guard urged her to stay, saying they would defend her; that same night, the minister of war came to her at eleven and declared there was not a moment to lose if she was serious about leaving, as he felt she should. Frustrated at being bombarded by so many different opinions, she was overheard murmuring, "My God, let them make up their minds and put an end to this agony."

[102] As she paced in her rooms, she had a rare moment of clarity as the only person who could have protected her son's monarchy: When it occurred to her that her father would ensure that she and his grandson would not be physically harmed, she realized she didn't have to race away. "What do I risk by remaining?" she asked. "I am the daughter of one of the rulers who have formed a confederacy against France so I can be certain of being treated with respect by the allied troops if they should enter Paris. And, supposing Napoleon were to lose the crown, was it not possible that I might preserve it for his son?" She astutely added, "By leaving Paris, don't I dash every hope and open the door for the Bourbon dynasty to return?"[103]

This self-confidence held for a few hours until Marie Louise was visited by Montebello, who was determined to undermine the empress's position of power. Due to the trust she placed in her attendant, Marie Louise was confused anew —sitting in her apartment frozen while those who had the means to flee were packing their most precious possessions so they could race off to the provinces before the allies entered the city. By the time the wealthy Parisians were loading their trunks onto their carriages, throngs of people from the neighborhoods, villages, and farms surrounding Paris were pouring into town, clogging the thoroughfares with their livestock and their carts heaped with what they had been able to gather in the hopes they would be protected by the Paris National Guard. Looking back on the situation from so far removed, it seems like Marie Louise was expected to play a fool's game—as she made her last appearance as the Empress of France, she was directed to extoll the genius of her husband after one of his messengers presented her with fourteen flags his army had captured from enemy forces.

Bausset-Roquefort spelled out her dilemma compellingly:

"She had all the weakness of kindliness and never made up her mind about anything, and really, in the affairs of government, had no other opinion than that which was inspired by people in whom she knew the emperor placed confidence." The baron then described the second regency as very different from her first stab at holding the reins because it was no longer a mere figurehead that was required; it was "a bold and clever brain, and it was lamentably lacking."[104] A letter she wrote to her father the evening after the flag celebration, reveals how frightened she was. "Only think, my dear father, in what a situation I should find myself. I implore you therefore, my dear father, to remember me and my son," she begged. She then ended her plea in a surprise bout of bravado: "You know how much I love you, and I believe that I possess your paternal affection…It rests with you to put an end to my anxiety, does it not? You will do it!"[105] This was a profound declaration of blind faith given Francis had already caved to the position of his allies and said he would support the return of the Bourbon monarchy.

As Marie Louise searched for a savior, she found that her husband was no help, either. "I am really to be pitied," she told Rovigo. "Some tell me to go, others to remain. I write to Napoleon and he does not reply to my request. He tells me to write to my father. Alas! What can my father tell me after the injuries which he allows to be inflicted upon me? I am deserted, and must now trust entirely to Divine Providence! It had once suggested to me the wisest course when it inspired me with the idea of becoming a canoness. I should have done much better in yielding to that inspiration than in coming to this country!" She told Rovigo she could not take the advice of those who urged her to travel to where Napoleon was encamped because she could not leave without their son, whose protector she was, and she could not take him with her because it was too dangerous. She also made the point that if she did go, she would be a hindrance if Napoleon found he was about to be captured and needed to quickly escape. "I don't know what to decide!" she said. "I only live in tears."[106]

She shared with Rovigo how incredibly cruel her father's behavior felt to her and how perplexing it was that Francis had married her to Napoleon only to come after the French ruler. Rovigo told her he could understand her anguish but said she had to pull herself together and convene a meeting so the Council of the Regency could agree to the conditions the allies demanded to save the city from being destroyed by their armies. Marie Louise and Joseph were signing the Allies' demands as Napoleon was blundering through a series of wins and losses that infuriated his brother. Joseph wrote a barrage of letters to Napoleon, urging him to allow his wife to intercede with her father but the emperor refused because he was too proud to be helped by a woman. He responded to Joseph's letters, "I am annoyed that you have been speaking to my wife of the Bourbons and of the opposition which the Emperor of Austria might bring to bear against me." Napoleon cautioned Joseph to limit his conversations to things that would not "trouble her tranquility and spoil her excellent nature."[107]

With this continued refusal to expose his wife to the vagaries of politics, Napoleon was responsible for the quagmire into which he and Marie Louise were sinking—the longer he tried to protect her, the more vulnerable he left his family and his throne. He didn't let up on his overprotective behavior until he learned the English had slipped through the gates of Bordeaux. Far too late in the game, he asked his wife to intervene but it was no use. Marie Louise said she would reach out to Francis but she warned her husband, "My father never listens to me about business."[108] She then told Napoleon she was enjoying the spring because it was warm

THE ART OF CAPITULATION

enough for her to go riding. Talk about fiddling while Rome burns! This letter to Napoleon was intercepted, the address it was meant to reach alerting Alexander that the coast was clear to march into Paris because Napoleon was encamped near Lorraine. With very few letters from the French capital reaching him, Napoleon realized his communications were being commandeered. Against the advice of his generals, he told them to keep fighting and raced toward the capital with a small contingent of troops.

By this point, Parisians were filled with terror at the thought of the allies approaching because they were worried coalition leaders would seek revenge on them for the many invasions Napoleon had conducted in their territories. "There was no spurt of courage, no national leader, no patriotic movement," Cuthell wrote. "Marie Louise did not seize the situation and her courage in both hands" at a time when "Joseph was shaking in his shoes, the garrison was weak and ill-armed, and the Russian Czar and King of Prussia were fourteen leagues off!"[109] With chaos swirling around her, Marie Louise called what would be her last council meeting to try and decide whether she and the King of Rome should leave Paris. There was disagreement as the ministers debated, each of those gathered around her arguing their points of view. To try and bring clarity to the situation, Joseph decided to read aloud two letters Napoleon had sent him—the one stating he'd rather see them both tossed into the Seine than let them fall into enemy hands and another declaring Napoleon preferred to have his son's throat cut than to have him brought up in Vienna as an Austrian prince.

I had to wonder if Marie Louise wasn't horrified by her husband's attitude about her and the prince given how he had always tried to shield her from such ideas, but none of the memoirists shared her reaction to the words Napoleon wrote to his brother. It was only noted how embarrassed she was that she couldn't make up her mind about leaving Paris. Certain members of the council whom she trusted for advice refused to tell her what to do because they felt either side had the chance of winning and their opinions could result in the appearance of disloyalty to one or the other. There were also councilmen who wanted her to stay for their own political ambitions—the thought of an inexperienced woman for a regent was very appealing to certain diplomats who were already scheming to become prime minister because they believed Napoleon was going down in flames. Seeing the disfunction of the council, Joseph was convinced the solution was to move Marie Louise and the King of Rome to a safe distance outside Paris so they could continue the regency if the allies managed to kill his brother.

He derailed the discussion by saying anyone who was disregarding his brother's orders that the allies be prevented from gaining control of his wife and child were rebelling against the empire and would be treated as traitors when his brother returned. Not willing to risk any further charges of treason, the members agreed to suspend the meeting. Several of the councilmen escorted Marie Louise to her apartment and urged her to stay because her presence would foil the plots of the allies who expected to march into a city with no one at the head of its government. They told her a retreat would be disastrous for her personally and begged her to take a stand of her own. "Marie Louise was torn all ways at once," Cuthell wrote. "At one moment, she was determined to go to the Hôtel de Ville [the town hall] and show herself [to the officials there]; the next she lacked the courage to take the responsibility [to declare the throne wasn't empty]."[110] In the end she told the men she would not disobey her husband and if they found her and the prince in the Seine, they could consider it had been an order.

The next day, she gave in to those who wanted her to

leave Paris. As her entourage was preparing to depart, Méneval witnessed an upsetting incident when the King of Rome pitched a tantrum as he was being escorted from his apartment. "The poor child seemed to guess what the future reserved for him," he wrote. "'Don't go to Rambouillet,' he cried out to his mother, 'it's a nasty palace; let us stop here!' He struggled in the arms of the equerry who was carrying him, saying: 'I don't want to leave my house; I don't want to go away; since papa is absent, it is I who am the master.'" Méneval said the boy clung to door handles and to the balustrade on the staircase. After such a heart-rending scene, he said the mood as the carriages rolled slowly away from the heart of town resembled a funeral procession. "Marie Louise had tears in her eyes and death in her soul," he wrote. "On arriving at the Champs-Élysées, she saluted the imperial city which she was leaving behind for a last time and bade it farewell forever."[111]

Durand, who had stayed in Paris to gather more of Marie Louise's belongings she'd been forced to leave behind because there wasn't enough time, was at the Tuileries on March 30, 1814, the day before the allies marched on Paris. Prince Paul of Württemberg arrived and asked where he could find the empress. "On learning she had left Paris, he seemed greatly disturbed," she wrote. "He added that he had been charged to provide a guard for her, and to take command of it."[112] The prince asked her what Marie Louise would have had to fear—as the daughter of the Emperor of Austria, she certainly had their respect. Durand gave no answer, which likely meant she put little faith in that word in that particular moment when cannon-fire could be heard in the distance. The fighting was so fierce, Joseph abandoned his forces at Montmartre hoping to catch up with Marie Louise, who was on her way to the town of Blois. "The precipitate flight of Joseph astonished only those who did not know him," Bourrienne wrote. "I know for a fact that several officers attached to his staff were much dissatisfied at his swiftness on this occasion."[113]

As Napoleon's brother, wife, and little boy were leaving town, he was hurrying toward it. "He was only five leagues away when he learned that Paris had capitulated," Durand wrote.[114] Knowing this did not bode well for him, he changed course and headed toward Fontainebleau with the troops he had in tow. The soldiers shouted they should be marching on the capital to conquer the enemy or be buried under the ruins but Napoleon ordered them to calm down, saying they would encamp at the palace while he met with a number of his top marshals. For the next several days, the military strategists told their leader his stubborn determination to stay in the fight would tip France into a frightful abyss and the country might never recover, which put the emperor in a volatile mood. Bourrienne said the generals made the case to Napoleon that his army was in shambles, which meant he didn't have the resources to win. The besieged ruler was livid as they continued to argue with him and was practically apoplectic when he learned the senate had made the bold move of publishing a declaration claiming he had forfeited the throne. The decree stated Napoleon's right of succession was abolished so the troops were no longer under his command. They were ordered to leave Fontainebleau, a directive they could not disobey.

When the advisors around the French emperor finally convinced him to consider the survival of his country above his own ambition, he agreed to dictate the terms he would accept if he abdicated, but Bourrienne claimed the document was useless because of the cunning way Napoleon had worded it.[115] Distracted by his attempts to stay in power, the emperor didn't realize the strings controlling Marie Louise had quietly and adroitly changed hands—the puppeteers who made every decision for her were now her father's cronies. Francis felt no qualms about allowing them to repress her—not only did he lust after territory he could win if France's borders were reconfigured, he knew he was no match for Alexander, who was dead set on preventing a regency from being formed because he knew that as long as one of Napoleon's family members sat on the French throne, the tiger crouching behind the figurehead would take every opportunity to pounce. The visual was an apt one as Napoleon stubbornly argued with his few loyal generals remaining at Fontainebleau, each of them urging him to capitulate.

Napoleon's fury was a stark contrast to Marie Louise's state of mind—she had arrived at the Royal Château at Blois in a state of near collapse. Unaware she was in such dire shape, Napoleon began firing off dispatches to inquire as to her whereabouts because he felt if she and their son were by his side, his chances of avoiding abdication were much improved. The contingent of people who had accompanied her was large enough that there were a fair number of them who were determined this would never happen. Among the ranks who wanted her gone were several councilmen, a handful of courtiers, and a number of attendants. The most deceitful of them decided they would ensure she remained clueless about the information that would have made her want to return to Paris—they accomplished this by forbidding anyone to show her a newspaper. Durand, who smuggled several Parisian dailies into Marie Louise's rooms once she rejoined the court at Blois, wrote, "The empress had been kept in such complete ignorance of events, she hardly believed what she read."[116] Durand was among the small number of loyalists who urged her to travel back to town before the Bourbons could arrive.

As the allies had suspected they would, these insiders assured her they would help her set up a regency to protect the throne for her and Napoleon's son. Those who were encouraging her to return to the city pointed out how easy it had been for Durand to travel without once having to use her passport. This convinced Marie Louise to return to Paris, a determination which held until that evening when Montebello and Dr. Jean-Nicolas Corvisart, Napoleon's former principal physician, set about changing her mind. Durand said a few "cowards" on the Council of the Regency supported the "evil advisers" and they won in the end. "The unfortunate princess was deceived anew, and lost the opportunity of recovering what her flight had forfeited," she added.[117] During this chaotic time, Marie Louise's mood alternated so frequently between fear and hope, she found herself trapped in a merry-go-round-like dizziness. Writing to Francis from Blois to try and find out what his plans were, she said, "My dear father: Our situation is so sad and alarming that my son and I have no refuge except with you. I am sure that, at this moment, you alone can come to my help, and that you will not sacrifice my tranquility and the interests of your grandson to England and Russia. I know that the Duke of Vicenza has gone to Paris to negotiate and that Czar Alexander has refused to see him."[118]

She then pointed out to him why he owed it to her to treat her with respect. "Paris would have made a better defense had it not thought it was being attacked by you and that you would never abandon your daughter and grandson," she wrote. "It is, therefore, into your hands that I commit myself, dear father: I am convinced that you will save us from this awful situation. My health is suffering from all these misfortunes. I am sure that you would not wish me to remain in this cruel anxiety long. Once more, have pity on me. I place in you the safety of what is dearest to me in this world—a son too young to understand misfortune and grief. I hope soon to have to thank you for the happiness and repose which we shall owe to you. I kiss your hand and am your obedient daughter."[119] These pleas would eventually be answered by her father but not out of consideration for her—he would only 'rescue' her and his grandson because he knew he had to imprison them to keep them away from Napoleon, who was finally giving in and signing his abdication. The way he had the document worded made it clear he didn't see himself as the stumbling block to harmony in Europe that the coalition rulers were claiming he was.

It reads, "The allied powers having proclaimed that the Emperor Napoleon was the sole obstacle to the re-establishment of peace in Europe, the Emperor Napoleon, faithful to his oath, declares that he is ready to descend from the throne, to leave France and even to lay down his life for the welfare of the fatherland, which cannot lie separated from the rights of his son, those of the regency of the empress, and the laws of the Empire." Though Rovigo believed Napoleon knew having his son on the throne was a pipe dream, the minister pointed out he had no choice but to abdicate to his offspring because the laws of the French Empire stipulated it was the only way Napoleon could step down, which is why it had been so critical that he have an heir. "Perpetually trembling at the mere name of the father, the allies had refused to acknowledge the son, and demanded the absolute forfeiture of his dynasty," Rovigo explained. "The emperor was outraged at so bold a pretension."[120]

Méneval, who was bereft about all that was happening, would have stayed by the emperor's side until the bitter end but Napoleon had one more assignment for him—he asked the loyalist to stay on as Marie Louise's private secretary.

This was likely a strategic move since Napoleon had agreed to be exiled on the island of Elba, off the coast of Tuscany, and Méneval's proximity to his wife and son would increase the chance he would receive regular news about them. Méneval left Fontainebleau for Blois and described the pitiful state he found Marie Louise in when he arrived. "Her anxiety had reached its highest pitch," he remembered; "the violent emotions which she had undergone, the tears which she was constantly shedding, her painful sleeplessness had cast her into a state of nervousness which nearly approached a convulsive state." No longer deceived because Durand and Méneval didn't hesitate to share with Marie Louise the news that was coming out of Paris, she still couldn't wrap her head around the fact that her father would sacrifice her husband and their son. "She was confounded," Méneval explained; "but like a drowning woman she clung to the parental affection which seemed to her to be her only means of safety."[121]

Rovigo was equally pained by her distress, saying that during the week they spent at Blois, her face was continually bathed in tears. "Had the empress, a young woman of less than two and twenty, been of an age and experience which gains self-confidence, and allowed her to avail herself of the advice of those in whom she could trust, events would probably have taken a different turn," he wrote. This was impossible, of course, because the ministers she was told to obey had conflicting opinions and there was no way she could have embraced a level of boldness that could have kept her husband in power because she was raised to be a model of complete submission. Rovigo said the time he spent alone with her during the "painful moments" at Blois confirmed to him that she was still devoted to Napoleon because she told him, "Those who were of the opinion that I should stay in Paris were right, and my father's troops would perhaps not have driven me out. What can I think when I see that he allows all this?"[122]

Feeling quite certain Napoleon would not be able to recover the throne, his brothers Joseph and Jérôme were determined to see a regency set up in their nephew's name. The two rode toward Orléans in the wee hours of April 4, 1814, to see if the town was occupied by enemy troops so they could decide if it was a good choice for establishing a regency government, but they never made it. Allied soldiers had flooded into the surrounding countryside and the brothers were almost cut off by the troops so they hurried back to Blois. Napoleon, unaware of his brothers' plans because they were also unable to circumnavigate the opposing armies to confer with him at Fontainebleau, sent Colonel Nicolas Galbois to Marie Louise to announce his abdication. The colonel had a hell of a time trying to reach her because he had to evade coalition forces. Galbois said when he arrived, she saw him immediately and told him Napoleon's abdication shocked her.

She then declared, "Even though it should be the intention of the allied sovereigns to dethrone the Emperor Napoleon, my father will not suffer it. When he placed me on the throne of France, he repeated to me twenty times his determination to uphold me on it; and my father is an honest man." Galbois said she wished to be left alone to reread the emperor's letter. "I then went to see Joseph and Jérôme—the former was very much upset; the latter was very angry with Napoleon," he wrote. "The empress then sent for me again. She told me that she wished to rejoin the emperor. I informed her this was impossible. Her majesty replied eagerly: 'But why? You are going to him, are you not, M. le Colonel? My place is with the emperor at a time when he must be very unhappy. I want to rejoin him, and I shall be allright provided I am with him.'" Galbois told her it was too dangerous to travel, describing how difficult it had been for him to reach her, which made her realize the best she could do was to write to her beleaguered husband. "I returned safely to the emperor," Galbois remembered. "Napoleon read the empress's letter with avidity; he seemed much struck with the affectionate interest that Marie Louise showed him.[123]

The empress spoke of the possibility of collecting 150,000 men; the emperor read that part of the letter out to me, and then uttered these remarkable words, 'Yes, doubtless I could hold my own, and perhaps with success; but I should bring about civil war in France, and that I will not do. Besides, I have signed my abdication, and I will not go back on what I have signed.'"[124] Joseph and Jérôme were confounded by the resignation Napoleon displayed and by the fact that Marie Louise, who had previously been the empress of half of Europe, had been reduced to such a helpless creature. With allied troops fast approaching, the brothers knew the situation was growing dangerous for the fugitive court at Blois and they had to act fast. They implored Marie Louise to let them escort her and the prince beyond the Loire where they would raise the Napoleonic flag on her son's behalf. Given the brothers had been prevented from navigating around enemy forces the day before, I'm not certain how they thought they'd pull this off. Marie Louise asked them if the plan was Napoleon's and they said no so she told them she would not allow it.

Their argument grew so heated, the guards of her household demanded Joseph and Jérôme leave—they had only been gone three hours when a Russian commissioner and a squadron of Cossacks brandishing long lances arrived to take over the security detail for Marie Louise and the prince. The soldiers, under the command of Count Peter Ivan Shuvalov, were sent by Schwarzenberg, who had become the commander-in-chief of the coalition's armies. Shuvalov told Marie Louise's attendants they were there to ensure the empress's safety, which meant she would remain the prisoner of her husband's enemies as the final events she would experience in France played out. Schwarzenberg had made it clear to Shuvalov that his soldiers were to guarantee that Marie Louise would never see Napoleon again—a direct order from Francis. Other allied leaders gave Schwarzenberg instructions to be absolutely certain Marie Louise would not be able to reconcile her husband and her father, which proved other coalition leaders didn't trust Francis not to succumb to his daughter's histrionics.

Méneval, who had set to work burning documents Napoleon would not have wanted his enemies to see, was starkly aware of how irrefutable Marie Louise's captivity was. "From that moment forward, it was put out of the empress's power to join the emperor," he said. "Whatever illusion she may have wished to retain on this point, the separation of the two spouses was decided." Marie Louise's next stopover in her choreographed exit from France was the bishop's palace in Orléans. The evening they arrived, Méneval received a letter from Napoleon, in a secret code, which he said caused him great concern. "It had been written in a moment of discouragement and bore the impress of deep sorrow," the secretary explained. In the letter, Napoleon revealed he was considering suicide. He told Méneval to burn the letter after reading it, which he did. "I then waited for news from Fontainebleau in terrible anxiety," the secretary added.[125] His concern was warranted because just after Napoleon wrote the letter, he took the poison from the sachet he had worn around his neck in case he was wounded in battle and was about to ingest it when his doctor came into the room.

The physician saw what Napoleon was up to, grabbed his

hand, and managed to toss half of the substance into the fire. The next morning, Napoleon took what was left and diluted it in liquid before swallowing it only to find it was not enough to kill him; just enough to make him seriously uncomfortable. "Death will have nothing to do with me," the defeated emperor lamented.[126] Méneval's fears were lifted several days later when a steady stream of letters from Napoleon began showing up in Orléans, proving his suicidal thoughts had been fleeting. In answer to his repetitive inquiries about his wife's plans, the secretary told Napoleon that Marie Louise was no longer at liberty to join him; that she wanted to do so but she was helpless to defy the coalition. Curious as to Napoleon's true state of mind, Méneval wrote the man who had replaced him as Napoleon's secretary, Baron Agathon-Jean-François Fain, to see if the emperor was still thinking of self-harm.

Fain said Napoleon's survival instincts had kicked in and he had chosen fantasy as his coping mechanism—he told Méneval the emperor was at that moment so fixated on his reunion with his wife and son, he was fleshing out their travel plans. Napoleon described the trip to Fain in detail, saying he would escort his wife and the prince to Parma where Marie Louise could rest while he prepared rooms for them on Elba. "He was particularly anxious as to who would have charge of the King of Rome," Fain told Méneval, "suggesting that Madame de Bombers be asked to undertake the post if the Comtesse de Montesquiou wished to return to Paris."[127] Napoleon was also dictating elaborate instructions as to how the empress's household would be set up and how her ceremonious arrival on Elba would be arranged, which Méneval related to Marie Louise. Rovigo noticed how she suffered when news like this was shared with her because it illustrated how much her husband still cared for her.

He said she was also reeling from having to be the one to

dismiss people who had been loyal to her and her husband while they were on the throne. As she said farewell to the ministers and officers of the crown who had traveled to Orléans with her, Rovigo said the pain on her face "would have melted a heart of stone." As each one of them bowed before her, she held out her hand for them to kiss and ceremoniously ended their service to the empire. Within a few days, Marie Louise's French servants lined up to say goodbye—a painful process that unfolded as the dethroned empress sat in limbo because her father had stopped communicating with her. Rovigo said there were now just a handful of attendants in her service, including Montebello, whom Rovigo criticized because she had turned against Marie Louise. Rather than have integrity and leave her service as "the storm burst over their heads," she stayed on to ensure the empress's downfall was irrevocable. The lady-in-waiting was so crass, she made fun of Napoleon's suicide attempt, sharing snide anecdotes she had heard with Marie Louise, which upset the former empress so much her insomnia became chronic. When Montesquiou's son Anatole, who was in Napoleon's service, came from Fontainebleau with a letter for Marie Louise, he requested an audience with Montebello so he could hand it off.[128]

After he gave it to her, the duchess drolly asked, "Well, is it all over? Is he dead?" When he asked her who she meant, she said, "Why, the emperor; we have been told here that he has destroyed himself." Anatole told her the rumor was not true. Rovigo seemed to feel it was his duty to describe how complicit Montebello had been in Marie Louise's humiliation and why the empress should not be blamed that she didn't go to Elba. "Madame de Montebello, who possessed a very large fortune, was not at all disposed to bury herself alive on the island of Elba," he explained. "Her inclinations led her back to Paris, where she could live in a state of independence." Rovigo said Montebello knew if Marie Louise was reunited with Napoleon, she would stay with him through thick and thin, which would mean the duchess would be forced to live on the island with them. The lady-in-waiting urged Marie Louise to follow her father's demands because she knew she would be rid of the forlorn young woman once Francis had full control of her again.[129]

Voices like Montebello's were easily amplified while Marie Louise was held captive because she had noticed a change in the tone of her husband's letters. Though he still wrote to her almost every day, he no longer urged her to join him at Fontainebleau because he felt she was better off distancing herself from him until they could travel to Elba. Montebello took advantage of the fear this fostered in Marie Louise by launching a smear campaign, telling her that her husband had never loved her; that he had "enjoyed the favors of several mistresses during their marriage"; and that he had only married her as a political move.[130] With claims like these being spoken with such vehemence, it's no wonder Marie Louise would later say her marriage had been nothing more than a political one. The combination of emotional assaults and disorienting relocations continued as Marie Louise's small circle was on the move again. She was ordered to travel to Rambouillet where Francis claimed he would immediately grant his daughter an audience.

JUST BEFORE HER entourage headed north, Russian troops replaced the French Imperial Guards who had been escorting her up until then, the latter dismissed to return to Paris. By this point, the only high-ranking French attendants left in Marie Louise's retinue besides Montebello were Méneval, Bausset-Roquefort, and Corvisart—each allowed to stay because the allies saw them as useful in some way. Montesquiou and several nurses still accompanied the King of Rome. When the carriages pulled up to the entrance of the castle at Rambouillet, Marie Louise noticed the entire building was surrounded by Russian sentries. She learned that Francis was nowhere to be found, the promise that she could make her case to rejoin her husband a sham. His disrespect left her feeling a feverish impatience as she paced the floors in her rooms one minute, and sitting motionless and crushed the next. When her father arrived three days later, she rushed to greet him, launching into her complaints about how she had been treated and telling him she believed it was her right to stay with Napoleon.

Francis claimed he sympathized with her but he could not help her because her situation was out of his hands. He then told her the bald-faced lie that every decision about her and his grandson had been made without his consent because he had been unable to communicate with any of the other allied sovereigns. Méneval noted how cowardly this was because Francis had purposefully stayed away from Paris so he could tell her he'd had nothing to do with removing her and the prince from power. Rovigo agreed, saying it was shocking to everyone that the Emperor of Austria would have consented to dethroning his daughter but the only explanation for his absence from Paris was his complicity. Rovigo then claimed Alexander's determination to ruin Napoleon forced Francis to play a humiliating role, as the czar had "assigned to him no other share in the triumph than the disgrace of dethroning his daughter."[131] Rovigo added, "The least unfavorable opinion that can be formed of the Emperor of Austria's conduct is that in order not to appear to participate in the act of being involved, he had prolonged his absence and left it to his allies to sacrifice his daughter."[132]

Adding insult to injury, soon after he arrived at Rambouillet, Francis insisted that Marie Louise receive Alexander. She agreed to do so but she wasn't happy about the meeting. "She did not carry her deference so far as to give a favorable reception to him whom she regarded as the author of all her misfortunes," Bourrienne wrote. He said she listened with considerable coldness to the czar's claims that her plight was unavoidable.[133] When Alexander left Rambouillet, the Russians who had stood guard at the castle went with him, the sentries replaced by two battalions of Austrian infantry and two squadrons of cavalry. Francis then insulted his daughter further by declaring he intended to be the sole guardian of the King of Rome, whom he had just met. This began the weakening of her influence over her son, which would continue to dwindle as the prince aged. It was also the moment the child became his grandfather's prisoner for the rest of the prince's life.

While Francis was charmed by his grandson, the little boy did not find his grandfather's long, pale, solemn face to his liking. "I've now seen the Emperor of Austria," he remarked to Maman 'Quiou, "and he is not handsome." Napoleon, who refused to believe he had lost control of his wife and son, was sending such a constant flow of letters to Francis to ask when he could be reunited with them, the emperor decided to put a stop to them. Francis wrote to Napoleon that Marie Louise was not feeling well and would "spend some months in the bosom of her family." He said when she recovered, she would travel to Parma and her rule of her new territories would begin. He ended the missive, "It is superfluous to say that her son will form part of my family, and that I will share his mother's care of him while with me."[134]

Francis's reference to the prince as "her son" rather than their son was certainly meant as a slap in the face. Napoleon finally got the memo, writing to his closest friends that

Marie Louise was "no longer a free agent"; that she was the "victim, not the accomplice, of the coalition."[135] On April 20, 1814, Napoleon left Fontainebleau for his first exile, traveling to Fréjus where he would board an English frigate named the HMS *Undaunted*. Three days later, Marie Louise left Rambouillet for her journey back to Austria. As she traveled those final miles through France, she followed the same route that had been packed with revelers during her initial arrival in the country four years earlier. She also followed the same roads along which the allies had marched toward Paris, leaving a war-torn countryside in their wake. The scenes she witnessed as her carriage swayed along were distressing, as many of the towns and villages had been so battered, not one house was left standing—only brick chimneys rose toward the sky like lost appendages.

When she crossed the border into Switzerland, she received a letter from Napoleon written on the day he departed for Elba. Méneval noticed it caused her remorse, though he said she hid it fairly well. Her distress didn't dissipate until she entered Austrian territory—suddenly, she was not the wife of a dethroned emperor fleeing a conquered country; she was the proud daughter of a great ruler returning to her homeland. One of the people in her entourage said the Austrians saw Marie Louise's journey as the triumphant return of a beloved daughter who had facilitated a conquest. Enjoying the attention the Austrians showered on him, the prince's spirits also lifted as he rode in the carriage with his governess and his nurses. He stood at the window and saluted the throngs of people lining the roads, his proud demeanor the stance of an adorable little soldier. One day, the child asked Montesquiou why he couldn't kiss his papa anymore, which made everyone in the coach terribly sad.

He also told his attendants that he hated King Louis XVIII

because he had taken the place of his father, he had made him leave his home, and he had stolen his toys. He then declared the king would forever be his greatest enemy. As the little boy was calling out his foe, Marie Louise came face-to-face with one of her biggest adversaries. When the entourage was twelve miles from Vienna, the line of carriages suddenly halted and one of her stepmother's footmen opened the door of Marie Louise's coach. The Empress of Austria appeared and told Montebello to ride in her carriage the rest of the way. Maria Ludovika then seated herself across from Marie Louise in the imperial coach, her haughtiness and disregard for what her stepdaughter might have wanted a sign of things to come. When the cortège trundled into the courtyard at the entrance to Schönbrunn Palace, Marie Louise returned to Vienna the victim Castlereagh had predicted she would be. "How the scheming, malicious Kaiserinn [Maria Ludovika] must have chuckled inwardly, triumphant over her enemy's downfall!" Cuthell so aptly declared.[136]

WITH HIS DAUGHTER safely in Vienna and Napoleon in exile, Francis headed straight to Paris to see to it that Austria was not denied its share of the spoils being syphoned from his daughter's life and his grandson's inheritance. So wisely, Méneval described the treatment to which the now empress-turned-princess had been subjected. "When she had been destined to become Napoleon's wife, her father, the emperor, had said, in taking leave of her: 'Be a good wife, a good mother, and render yourself agreeable in everything to your husband,'" he explained. "Austrian politics had mentally added: 'as long as he is powerful, happy, and useful to our house.'" Marie Louise's return to her childhood home

THE ART OF CAPITULATION

launched a concerted effort to transform her from a foreign monarch back into the Austrian archduchess she had been when she left. "As my daughter, all that I have is yours, even my blood and my life," her father told her; "as a sovereign, I do not know you."[137]

Méneval said the best she could do was bow her head to the brutal force of such an argument and condone it by her silence. Soon after she arrived in her home country, several of the French attendants who had been responsible for her humiliation exited stage left. First to get the boot was Montebello, who happily returned to France with Corvisart. The allies felt the duchess and the doctor could be dismissed because they had played their parts in weaning Marie Louise from her husband, and they were no longer needed given their charge was under guard in a Viennese palace. Maria Brignole-Sale Ferrari took Montebello's place, a perfect fit since she was Italian nobility and Marie Louise would eventually rule in that country. The other campaign that was launched in earnest was a covert one: Metternich enlisted Marie Louise's stepmother to ensure that the letters Napoleon was writing to his wife were intercepted. Sequestered once again, a familiar pattern reemerged for the now archduchess Marie Louise: She returned to her beloved pastimes of horseback riding, playing the piano, and drawing.

Three months after she arrived in Vienna, she asked her father if she could travel to Aix-les-Bains, a spa town located in far-eastern France near the borders with Italy and Switzerland. She told him she believed if she could bathe and relax there, the treatments would help steady her nerves. After Francis agreed, Metternich warned him that his wife had been masterful at stopping the flow of letters from Napoleon. He also cautioned Francis that the Bourbons may not be open to having the former empress back on French soil. Stipulations were put in place that Marie Louise had to accept if she was allowed to go: The prince would be left behind in Vienna so as not to alarm the Bourbons that Napoleon's heir was back in France, and she would have to agree to be accompanied by a security guard. The subtext of the latter demand, of course, was that she would be overseen by a man who would be tasked with keeping her from communicating with her husband. She agreed to these conditions and left for France accompanied by Méneval and Ferrari on July 29, 1814.

This trip would bring a sea-change to Marie Louise's life, one that would eventually obliterate her desire to return to her husband. When her carriage rolled into Carouge, Switzerland, it was met by a general on horseback named Count Adam Albert von Neipperg. He was wearing a Hungarian Hussars uniform and had a black patch over his right eye, which had been gouged out in battle. "At first sign of him, Marie Louise received an unpleasant impression," wrote Méneval. "Was it the instinct of a loyal heart but little confident in itself, which pointed out this man as an evil genius, and warned her secretly of the danger of abandoning herself to his advice?"[138] He had every reason to speak negatively about Neipperg because the general had a ghastly reputation for womanizing. The secretary shared these details he heard from one of the general's contemporaries to prove it: When Neipperg received notice he had been selected to guard the future Duchess of Parma, the general was in Milan ensconced in the house of a mistress who tried in vain to keep him with her.[139]

Méneval said the general didn't hesitate to cast her aside because his ambition was much stronger than any feelings he had for any woman; when the mistress asked Neipperg what his intentions were toward Marie Louise, he answered, "I hope to be on the most intimate terms with her before six months are out, and soon to be her husband." He then told the mistress, whom he obviously did not see as a worthy choice for matrimony, that he was meant only for extraordinary marriages. Neipperg's wife at the time was a countess from a noble Italian family so she certainly lived up to his aggrandized ideals, though he obviously felt a Habsburg archduchess and former empress was an even better prize. Copping his most exalted manners to impress his target, Neipperg turned on the charm and Marie Louise found herself being drawn in. "The general's manners were polite, insinuating, and flattering," Méneval wrote. "He possessed agreeable talents, and was a good musician. Active, clever, possessed of little scruple, he knew how to conceal his acuteness under an exterior of simplicity."[140]

The secretary said the general was a fine conversationalist, that he expressed himself with grace, and that he knew how to listen with studied attention—qualities that proved to be catnip for Marie Louise. It was easier for Neipperg to make inroads with her in Aix because there was no one around who disagreed with his behavior—soon after Méneval escorted her to the spa town, he took seven weeks off to be with his wife in Paris. Either Ferrari had been instructed not to get in the way or she had no interest in policing the impressionable young woman, who became less devoted to Napoleon the longer Neipperg guarded her. Still riding in a carriage emblazoned with the imperial arms and attended by footmen in the green imperial livery of France, Marie Louise had been given leeway by the Bourbons to show such audaciousness because Metternich had assured them of Neipperg's loyalty to Austria. When their time in Aix was winding down, a colonel who was posted to Napoleon's regiment on Elba visited the archduchess. He was carrying a letter from her husband that said the soldier was to escort her and their son to the island. Needless to say, his mission did not succeed and the colonel was ordered to leave without Napoleon's wife and son.

Méneval arrived the next day and was surprised to find a completely different Marie Louise than he had experienced when he left her several months before. At first blush, he said it was a refreshing change. "I had occasion to congratulate her on the happy state of mind in which she seemed to be," he explained.[141] It wasn't until he noticed how she lit up when the general walked into a room that he realized why Marie Louise was in such a good mood: he felt sure she was having a romantic relationship with Neipperg, which appalled him. "You know my affectionate devotion to her," he wrote to his wife; "it has redoubled since I see her entering on a road which will lead her to ruin. Whatever happens to her, one must respect her for her rank, her valuable good qualities, the gratitude which I owe for her kindnesses. She is full of good feelings, but she is surrounded by shoals. Her youth and inexperience need a guide and a protector so much!"[142] Méneval immediately made an excuse to take a trip to Prangins, Switzerland, so he didn't have to witness the couple's breaches in etiquette.

His summation just before he left was blunt: "Extraordinary circumstances had united her destiny to that of a great man. These bonds had been violently severed by the selfish and cold policy which had formed them on the day when Napoleon was no longer to be feared. The faults into which Marie Louise fell must be imputed to those in whose hands she had been an instrument of hatred and revenge."[143] Henry Vassall-Fox, 3rd Baron Holland, was much more pointed about the fact that it was Marie Louise's father who was responsible for her plight when he said, "As for his daughter's marriage, one must admit the alternative, either that he consented to sacrifice his child to a cowardly policy, or that he cravenly abandoned her, and dethroned a prince he had chosen for his son-in-law. He separated his daughter from the husband he had given her, and helped to disinherit his grandson. To obliterate from the mind of the daughter the memory of her exiled and dethroned husband, whose conduct to her had been irreproachable, they say he encouraged, and even himself connived, at making her unfaithful."[144]

At this point, Francis was still in the early stages of ensuring his daughter's disgrace, his scheming obvious as soon as Marie Louise and Neipperg returned from Aix. After Francis greeted them, he met with the general to inform him he was appointing him to the position of chamberlain to the Duchess of Parma, which gave Neipperg the right to reside with Marie Louise as long as he held that post. Word began to spread that Neipperg was officially her jailer and that his job was to keep her from ever rejoining her husband. With the general taking on greater responsibility in her life, Marie Louise was yet again being managed by a strong, selfish man. Cuthell compared her to a helpless prey who was being stupefied by a python before it squeezed her to death. Neipperg's aim was a opportunistic one, his cards revealed when he scolded Marie Louise for not pushing harder when Francis delayed her possession of her Italian territories. The general was seventeen years older than Marie Louise, and Parma was his ulterior motive for aligning with her because he wanted a better life for himself.

Cuthell wrote, "He was no longer young; he had had enough of fighting; and the position of a prince-consort in a snug little independent kingdom with an attractive young ruler was a prospect not unpleasing to the wily diplomatist." [145] Priscilla Anne Fane, Countess of Westmorland, who was a close friend of Marie Louise's, said it was hardly surprising that Neipperg could so quickly seduce Marie Louise because she was frightened, lonely, and mystified at what was happening to her. Fane said Marie Louise was "only too ready to fall under the influence of a clever man, who, on his side, pitied her, and was genuinely devoted to her."[146] Realizing Neipperg wouldn't be happy until they were on Italian soil, Marie Louise implored her father to let her take over her duchies. He put her off time and again during the next several years because there was political upheaval in the region, the government in her territory was nearly bankrupted, and her rule was still in question because a number of the allied leaders were not keen on having her in power.

There was so much disagreement about Marie Louise's Italian rule, the subject became the hot topic of conversation when the Congress of Vienna commenced in September of 1814. The series of international diplomatic meetings was focused on dismantling the empire Napoleon had created, which kept the allied sovereigns in town for months. It was clear early on that many of the leaders wanted the Treaty of Fontainebleau to vanish into thin air. "Marie Louise, once so lofty, had fallen so low that she and her son could be disposed of without consulting her," Méneval noted.[147] One of the loudest voices demanding that Marie Louise not be allowed to rule was her stepmother, who was also against the prince ever sitting on a throne. She was floating the idea that the child should take holy orders until Francis told her to knock it off.

THE POLITICS at play during the congress could fill a poly-sci text book and would only bog down this story so I leave the machinations of Europe's leaders behind to focus on Marie Louise's behavior and the effect it would have on her son. A statesman from Belgium who visited the little boy while he was in Vienna attending the congress said Napoleon's child had only one thought in his head, which was reuniting with his father. I find the fact that Napoleon and his son were longing for each other to be one of the saddest aspects of this twisted story. Believing the prince must have forgotten him, Napoleon sent a letter to Ferdinand III, Grand Duke of Tuscany, who was Marie Louise's uncle and their son's godfather, asking why he'd had no news of his wife and child for months. The duke ignored him and gave the letter to Francis, who read it aloud during the congress. Napoleon was then informed that his dispatches to his wife were being intercepted and that his pleas to other family members were being shared with his enemies so he stopped writing for a while.

Sitting in the vacuum created by her husband's absence, Marie Louise gave in to her emotional attachment to Neipperg and would do all in her power to avoid returning to Napoleon from that point on. The only courtesy she would show the latter as manipulations to keep her from him increased in intensity: She refused to divorce him and would not remarry until he was dead. To avoid bumping into the politicians who had plotted her separation from her husband, Marie Louise essentially went into hiding in her suite of rooms in the palace, "living in absolute retirement," as Méneval called her lifestyle. "The empress remained shut up in her apartments all day long, not daring to go out for fear of meeting faces whose triumphant expressions would have contrasted too strongly with the obscurity of the position which had been forced upon her," Méneval added. "She nevertheless had curiosity enough to enjoy the sight of the court ball incognito, watching it through a window in the attic. Four years earlier, she had been the queen of a brilliant fête given in this same hall on the occasion of her marriage." [148]

Marie Louise soon made a decision that gave those who

accused her of being an uncaring mother plenty of ammunition: She agreed to Neipperg's plan to relinquish any future claims over her son because she would not be given her Italian territories if she did not. The boy had become the sticking point to her rule because the coalition leaders attending the congress couldn't stomach the idea that a child of Napoleon's would have an ounce of power. During a meeting with Metternich and Francis, Méneval surmised Marie Louise had told them she would let go of any power over the prince and grant Francis full guardianship because rumors began circulating that she had saved her duchies. She later told Méneval that it was at that moment when she was forced to give up any attachments to her husband and child, a preposterous claim given she had already emotionally abandoned Napoleon and her interest in their son had taken a back seat to her fascination for Neipperg.

As she hid away in her rooms, singing to the melodies the general played on the piano during the evenings, the politicians and leaders attending the congress paraded their riches around town as they attended parties. Méneval claimed that these entertainments glossed over the darker forces of human nature they displayed during the day. "A curious book might be written on the secret history of the Vienna congress," he explained. "Passions, abuses of power, jealousies, grudges, and fear covered themselves with the brilliant varnish of the festivities."[149] The mention of grudges is so apropos at this moment in history because the leaders gathered in Vienna would soon learn Napoleon had his own agenda. As his enemies were whittling away different aspects of his former power, including his son's sovereignty, and toasting their conquest of the exiled emperor during splendid banquets, the dethroned ruler threw his wife and the entire political machine in Europe into chaos by escaping from Elba. "It is impossible to describe the sensation which was produced by this news," Méneval remembered.[150] Napoleon had around five-hundred men with him aboard a ship emblazoned with the name HMS *Inconstant* as he sailed toward France.

Suddenly, the theater performances, balls, and sumptuous dinners that had been distracting the leaders in Vienna ceased as the rulers pontificated how they would respond. "When the first intelligence of Bonaparte's escape was received at Vienna, it must be confessed that very little had been done at the congress," Bourrienne noted, blaming the snail's pace at which things had moved on the socializing and the magnitude of the task at hand, which amounted to drawing a completely new European map.[151] With this monumental effort put on hold, Méneval watched a tortured Marie Louise try to cope with the fact that her husband was a free man. "The empress was so agitated by the rapid succession of events, by the continual alternations of the emperor's success and failure, she lost her peace of mind altogether," he wrote.[152] To settle her nerves, Neipperg had Marie Louise sign a letter written to the allies that stated she no longer had any dealings with Napoleon.

The Viennese police commissioner declared that Neipperg's influence had reached an ascendency and that he was in lockstep with Francis because, "The character of the count is a guarantee that he will never give advice not in keeping with the intentions of her august father." Méneval said after a few days, Marie Louise grew stoic but he knew she was just pretending that Napoleon's escape meant nothing to her. To her closest confident Victoire, she told the truth: "You can imagine how anxious I am; I am quite crushed, and, if God does not help me, I shall never have the moral or physical strength to bear it all."[153] Méneval said Marie Louise admitted how horrible it was to feel so persecuted. He sympathized with her, telling her no one knew better than he did that she had wanted to join Napoleon early on and had been prevented from doing so by the spies surrounding her.

In a rare moment during which he put honesty above rank, he said her declaration in the letter stating she was free from Napoleon's actions made him sad. He urged her not to sign anything else that would align her with her husband's enemies. Marie Louise told Méneval she regretted the letter but she was no longer the "mistress of her actions"; that she had promised her father she would place herself entirely in his hands; and that she would "conduct herself only in accordance with his advice." She then reminded Méneval that to go against her father would be devastating to her son's future. "I was born under a fatal star and am doomed never to be happy," she added, a sentiment that would remain true until Neipperg achieved his *Coup de Coeur*.[154] The hibernation Marie Louise had managed since returning from Aix came to an end when the powerful rulers who had ensured her husband's downfall began showing up to ask after her intentions given they suspected Napoleon would likely return to power.

When Alexander visited and asked her about her plans, she told him she would decline any regency for her son and would refuse to go to France if her husband ordered her to his side. Soon after the czar came to call, as if on cue, a letter in her husband's own hand, written as he marched toward Paris, was smuggled into her rooms in a courier's boot. As she had suspected he would, Napoleon told her to join him in Paris and bring him his son. "I hope to embrace you before the end of March," he wrote.[155] With so many powerful men around her telling her to stand firm, Marie Louise ignored him, but the reminder that her husband still hoped she would come back to him unraveled her nerves. Napoleon's march toward Paris was so triumphant, the allies were fran-

THE ART OF CAPITULATION

tic. The major players participating in the congress informed Marie Louise she would have Parma if she pledged not to return to her husband. Not only did she agree to reject him for good, she put it in a formal letter requesting that the allies place her and the prince under the coalition's protection. On March 19, 1815, the day before Napoleon returned to Paris, Louis XVIII fled the capital and went into exile.

As the king slipped out of harm's way, Marie Louise was informing Montesquiou that the prince was to be moved to The Hofburg, a palace in the heart of the walled city of Vienna, giving no explanation except that Francis decreed it. By eight o'clock that evening, she escorted her son, his nurse, and his governess there, forcing the little boy to give up his sunny apartment overlooking the beautiful garden in which he loved pretending to be a soldier for a dark and dreary suite of rooms. The date Napoleon re-entered The Tuileries was March 20th, his son's fourth birthday. Rather than enjoying a celebration as he normally would have, the child was trapped in a bedroom outside which armed guards stood, his situation taking a sorrowful turn when Montesquiou, who was ordered to return to France, was removed from his household that day. The grieving governess was detained in a separate apartment while she awaited her papers and was never allowed to see the boy again.

Her absence caused the prince to weep incessantly for the woman whose presence had been a constant for him as long as he could remember and who was the only mother he had ever had. Immersed in the religious observances of Holy Week, Marie Louise was ignorant of the trauma she had allowed to be inflicted on her son. She was once again wrapped up in herself, complaining that she could barely keep calm as letters from Napoleon arrived. The allies allowed her to receive them because they wanted their spies

SAXON HENRY

to watch as she read them to see if she was as resolute in refusing her husband's commands as she claimed she was. "Ma Bonne Louise, I am master of all France," said one of Napoleon's letters. "All the nation and the army are most enthusiastic. The so-called king is crossing to England. I expect you here in the month of April, with my son. *Adieu, mon amie*."[156] The disgraced emperor also wrote Francis a letter ordering him to send him his wife and son, which the Austrian emperor passed around to all of the big-wigs at the congress and refused to answer. Marie Louise was equally silent.

Napoleon's insistence that his wife and son rejoin him was so intense for several reasons: not only did he truly want to see them, he needed them to maintain his power because he knew the French would not accept him as the country's leader if they felt there was any chance the allies would invade again. Having Marie Louise and the prince by his side would assure his countrymen he was still favored by Austria. To convince the French people he had control of the situation, Napoleon published an article that claimed the empress and his son would soon travel to Paris. He also announced he would be holding a convocation that would, among other things, assist with the planning of the coronation of Marie Louise. Bourrienne, who said this was a dangerous bluff, wrote, "Her presence, and that of her son, was spoken of as something that was certain, though Bonaparte knew there was little hope of their return from Vienna." One of the reasons the author cited for this unlikelihood was how resistant Marie Louise had grown to the idea of returning to her husband and how determined she was to prevent her son from "being spirited off to join his father." He added, "She herself was fast falling under the influence of the one-eyed Austrian General Neipperg and speaking of her life in France as 'a bad dream.'"[157]

THE ART OF CAPITULATION

The emperor had not yet learned of his wife's sordid downfall so he thought she would still want to join him. Believing it was solely her father who was preventing their reunion, he hatched a plot to kidnap her and their son. The few French attendants in Marie Louise's household who were still loyal to Napoleon secretly forged passports, set up relays of horses, and coordinated the steps that would return the pair to France. When one of her Austrian servants found out about it, Francis was informed about the plan, which would have placed him in a very awkward position had it been successful. He told his ministers to begin dismissing all the French people around his daughter, and told Marie Louise to stop riding in the imperial coach and to formally declare she relinquished the title of the Empress of France. Because Napoleon had published the fact that his wife and son would be returning, Francis had inflicted yet another blow that would hamper Napoleon's efforts to stay on the French throne.

Failing to get his family back wasn't Napoleon's only problem: As he attempted to pass new laws and pull together an army, it became clear the doubts his subjects had about him couldn't be stuffed back into Pandora's Box and he began to realize he wouldn't be able to achieve the absolute power he had held before his abdication. Not long after he was told by his ambassadors that his kidnapping plot had failed, Napoleon learned of Marie Louise's infidelity. "One evening I was summoned to the palace," Count Antoine Lavallette remembered. "I found the emperor in a dimly-lighted sitting room, warming himself in a corner by the fireplace." When Lavallette approached Napoleon, the emperor said, "Here is a letter, which the courier from Vienna says is meant for you—read it." Lavallette said he was familiar with the handwriting and that the letter took him quite a while to digest because it was so long. The gist of it was that Napoleon could no longer count on his wife's return because she had developed a distaste for her husband. The author of the letter said her behavior was causing him indignation because "she was 'wholly enamored of ——' and didn't even take pains to hide her ridiculous partiality for him."[158]

Napoleon and Lavallette would have known who the letter referenced because the person would have been named; the dashes were substituted for names in many memoirs of that era to maintain the privacy of others when remembrances were recorded. Though the person who wrote the letter was also never named, I believe it must have been Méneval. "The handwriting of the letter was disguised, yet not so much that I couldn't discover whose it was, though I found it expressed a warmth of zeal and a picturesque style that did not belong to the author of the letter," Lavallette said. "While reading it, I all of a sudden suspected it was a counterfeit intended to mislead the emperor. I communicated this idea to him, and the danger I perceived in this fraud." Pouring over the letter a second time, the count was more convinced it was forged, though Napoleon remained skeptical. "How is it possible," Lavallette asked Napoleon, "that —— should have been imprudent enough to write such things to me, who is not his friend, and who has had so little connection with him?"[159]

Napoleon answered the count, "—— is attached to me; and though he is not your friend, the postscript sufficiently explains the motive of the confidence he places in you." Napoleon was referencing this sentence that was written at the bottom of the letter: "I do not think you ought to mention the truth to the emperor, but make whatever use of it you think proper." Lavallette then asked the emperor, "How can one suppose that the empress should forget herself, in such circumstances, so far as to manifest aversion to you, and, still more, to cast herself away upon a man who undoubtedly still possesses some power to please, but who is no longer young, whose face is disfigured, and whose person, altogether, has nothing agreeable in it?" Napoleon told Lavallette to take the letter to the Duke of Vicenza, who had others by the same person, saying, "Let the comparison decide between your opinion and mine." The duke assured Lavallette the letter was authentic and told him to tell the emperor to forget Marie Louise. "So sad a discovery was very painful to the emperor," Lavallette wrote, "for he was sincerely attached to the empress, and still hoped again to see his son, whom he loved most tenderly."[160]

PROVING how correct the letter was, Marie Louise was pitching a tantrum because Francis had ordered Neipperg to lead a contingent of Austrian troops in Italy to shore up his interests there given Napoleon's escape could have ripple effects. When she learned Neipperg was to leave Vienna, Marie Louise begged her father not to send him away. She need not have worried that Neipperg would forsake his role as her puppet-master. Before he left, the general penned a long list of instructions for her because he knew she could no longer function without his guidance, and he maintained a heavy correspondence with the duchess to keep his interests top of mind. Méneval took advantage of Neipperg's absence to see if he could convince Marie Louise to return to her husband and to reconsider disinheriting her son. He felt he had nothing to lose given his days as her secretary were numbered because he would be returning to France as soon as he was given his passport. When Méneval pressed her, she told him she would not return to her husband and that her decision was irrevocable.

"This princess, deprived of all protection, surrounded by pitfalls, led astray by perfidious advice, had become the too docile instrument of unscrupulous politicians," he wrote. "I was painfully affected to see that Marie Louise abandoned the only line of conduct which any care for her own glory she ought to have kept steadfastly before her."[161] Marie Louise did not see returning to the French throne as upholding her legacy—by this point in time, her only aim was to rule in Parma with Neipperg by her side. On May 9, 1815, her loyalty to the allies and her commitment to ditch her husband were rewarded when the leaders of the congress told her she would have her Italian territories when the documents could be ratified, which took place during the final act of the Congress of Vienna on June 9, 1815. They had decided to move quickly because they feared Napoleon might try to take the duchies for himself.

The declaration that Marie Louise would rule in Italy shut the door on any hope Méneval had that she would consent to returning to France, which made him relieved his time with her was waning because he was saddened by how far from grace she had fallen. His discomfort climaxed one evening during dinner when she announced to everyone how excited she was about the fact that Countess Neipperg, her lover's wife, had died. The only pang Méneval felt about his eminent departure was sadness over leaving Napoleon's son behind. He visited the boy once he received his passport to see for himself how the prince was faring so he could report the truth to the emperor, and the news was not good. The child did not run to meet Méneval as he would have in the past; he did not chatter as he once did—instead, he backed into the recess of a bay window and stared at Méneval as if he was frightened. It wasn't until the secretary asked the child if he had any message for his father that he engaged. He took Méneval's hand, tugged him down to the level of his golden curls, and whispered, "M'sieur Me'va, you will tell him that I am still very fond of him."[162]

Méneval left the child's room feeling heartbroken because he saw an adored boy, who could have been thriving if he'd been with his father, reduced to a traumatized orphan. That evening, Méneval told the duchess goodbye. He said she seemed moved by his parting, asking him to ensure Napoleon that she wished him well and that she hoped he would understand her unhappy situation. "She repeated to me that she would never agree to a divorce; that she hoped he would consent to an amicable separation; and that he would not retain any resentment about it because their parting had become inevitable," he explained.[163] Marie Louise gave Méneval a snuff-box ornamented with her initials in diamonds and hurried out of the room. His journey to France began the next morning and he wasted no time in requesting an audience with Napoleon once he was back in Paris. Méneval was warmly greeted by the emperor when he arrived at the Élysée Palace where Napoleon had set up his offices. The emperor immediately began peppering the secretary with questions about his wife and child.

"Napoleon spoke to me of his son with great tenderness and listened with deep emotion to the most insignificant particulars about his darling child," explained Méneval, who then made a surprising statement given the revelations the letter to Lavallette had held about Marie Louise's indiscretions: "The things he said about the empress were full of respect and consideration for her."[164] Napoleon summoned Méneval to the Élysée for several days in a row and continued his questioning, which would likely have continued if war hadn't once again demanded the emperor's attention. Because the allies were ramping up their efforts to take him down for good, Napoleon decided his strategy would be to attack before their armies had time to draw together. Thinking he was going to be able to defeat the Prussian forces and convince his enemies they should think twice, he headed north. This may have panned out if the Duke of Wellington and British forces hadn't shown up, ensuring Napoleon's last defeat at Waterloo on June 18, 1815. When Méneval learned the beaten emperor had returned to Paris, he rushed to the Élysée.

"I found Napoleon there, overwhelmed with fatigue and yet mastering the grief with which he was devoured," he remembered. "He was in a bath into which he had plunged himself on his arrival to promptly restore his exhausted strength."[165] Napoleon told the secretary his last trouncing was so ruinous he felt little hope that he would be able to stabilize his government. He said the opposing factions on his council were so strong, the best thing he could do for France was to abdicate a second time. Rovigo also sought an audience with Napoleon when he learned the ruler was back in Paris. He asked the emperor how he was going to get himself out of his latest mess, and Napoleon shouted, "I will hear nothing more about myself. But poor France!"[166] The soon-to-be twice-deposed emperor's discussions with the politicians who filed into and out of his headquarters convinced him his only course of action was to abdicate. After he signed the papers, he made several statements that told those around him he would have considered death preferable.

As one of the stipulations of his removal, Napoleon tried once again to have his son named to the throne as Napoleon II but the forces in favor of the return of the Bourbons won out. The former emperor moved to the Château de Malmaison and sequestered there as he tried to decide what to do next. Walking in the garden with Méneval one afternoon, he told the secretary he wanted him to follow him wherever he went, telling his loyal attendant he had thought of going to America but he would likely end up in England. That evening, Méneval decided to return to his wife and children in Paris rather than stay with Napoleon, a decision he would regret because he would never see the emperor again. After the secretary left Malmaison, Napoleon sent Lavallette on a mission to bring back the provisional government's order that promised him safe passage to the U.S., the papers necessary to ensure he would not be arrested by the British navy for being a fugitive. The politicians Lavallette approached made it clear they had deceived the former emperor and that no such protection would be offered.

Knowing the danger Napoleon was in, Lavallette hurried back to Malmaison and tried to persuade the emperor to leave in the middle of the night, saying he didn't have an hour to lose. "It was two o'clock in the morning when I returned and the emperor was in bed," he remembered. "I was admitted to his chamber, where I gave him an account of the result of my mission, and renewed my entreaties. He listened to me, but made no answer. He got up, however, and spent a part of the night in walking up and down the room."[167] During this spate of pacing, Napoleon decided he would leave Malmaison the next day, beginning what would be the last odyssey in a remarkably mythic life. Accompanied by a number of attendants who had agreed to stay in his service, Napoleon made his way west toward Rochefort on the western coast of France. As he traveled, he hatched a plan to escape to America but when he reached the port city, he realized there was no way he'd make it because the entire western seaboard was being vigilantly patrolled by the British navy. I find it remarkable that this man, who had gained renown for using his wits, actually believed the British would allow him to live in exile in their country given all of the headaches he had caused its monarchs and the belligerence he continued to express toward them.

In this declaration he wrote to England's prince regent, the future George IV, a few days before he boarded one of the British navy's ships, he referred to the soon-to-be king as one of his greatest foes: "A victim to the factions which divide my country, and to the hostility of the greatest Powers of Europe, I have terminated my political career, and come, like Themistocles, to throw myself on the hospitality of the British people. I place myself under the protection of their laws; which I claim from your Royal Highness, as the most powerful, the most constant, and the most generous of my enemies." The reference to Themistocles is a marvelous morsel and a harbinger of things to come given the Athenian politician also died in exile. Bourrienne described Napoleon's arrival as he stepped onto the British ship the HMS *Bellerophon*, which was docked in Rochefort Harbor, "On entering the vessel he took off his hat, and addressing Captain Maitland, said, 'I am come to throw myself on the protection of the laws of England.'"[168]

And just like that, on July 15, 1815, at around six a.m., Napoleon gave up his freedom for good—by all accounts clueless that he would not be the one making decisions about his life from that point on. He wouldn't learn his true fate—that he would live the rest of his life on a rocky island in the South Atlantic Ocean—until he'd been on board the ship for thirteen days. "Napoleon complained bitterly on the subject of his destination," wrote Bourrienne. "'To banish me to an island within the tropics!' Napoleon proclaimed. 'They might as well have signed my death-warrant at once, for it is impossible that a man of my habit of body can live long in such a climate.'"[169] Napoleon would be aboard the ship for two more months, reaching Saint Helena in late September of 1815 at the age of forty-six. The conquered man would languish there for nearly six years before he died, the island so heavily fortified, there was no chance he could escape.

"Every platform, every aperture, the brow of every hill was planted with cannon," Bourrienne explained. Early on, Napoleon was given temporary quarters that were so confining he felt like a caged animal, which brought on the first signs of the decline in his health he had predicted. "The emperor did not possess that constitution of iron which was usually ascribed to him," Bourrienne said; "the strength was in his mind, not his body."[170] Once the authorities on the island had finished renovating a compound that could house Napoleon and his attendants, he was moved to Longwood House, as it is known, and began a painfully slow process of coming to terms with his humiliation. In his riveting foreword to his book *The Black Room at Longwood*, Jean-Paul Kauffmann said Napoleon battled against disintegration by using his imagination, which crushed and pulverized the past. "As the tropics rotted everything, he tried to pick up the pieces and put them together again," Kauffmann wrote, which he said would not be enough to save Napoleon's sanity because, "Confinement itself is a kind of erosion."[171]

The author, who visited Longwood before he wrote his book, called the group of huts on a windswept plateau "an island within an island" and "a haunted place." He said captivity made Napoleon a naked, vulnerable man, who, consumed with insecurity, tried to resist by replaying his former glory in his mind. "He certainly found consolation in reliving his exploits as well as his disasters," Kauffmann wrote. "For a prisoner, there is no worse suffering than remembering happier days."[172] As the ghostly existence of the defeated man wore on, Neipperg returned to Vienna a war hero to, as Méneval put it, "resume his role as supreme director of Marie Louise's sentiments and will."[173] He showed up in early 1816 with perfect timing, as the duchess would begin her reign in Parma in March. I was relieved to see she finally expressed some remorse over having to abandon her son just before she set off on her journey.

She wrote to Francis, whom she would see in Italy on her way to Parma, "At the first moment, I thought only of the pleasure of seeing you again, dearest papa. It was only after some minutes that there came over me the painful thought of the separation from my son. I could make no greater sacrifice to his welfare, or to your wishes, and I do not know how I shall find strength to bear it. It also costs me a dreadful pang to separate from all my family and from my fatherland, where I have been so kindly received after all my misfortunes. I can only find comfort with you, and in the hope that you will often allow me to see you and my son again. I need this consolation, and also the consciousness that I am fostering the future interests of my child by going to a country where few rosy days, but much unpleasantness, await me."[174] She repeated this anxiety over her impending situation to Victoire. "By the twentieth, I expect to be at Parma where life will not be very agreeable," she wrote; "only the feeling that I am doing my duty in sacrificing all for my son sustains me."[175]

If she really believed she was serving the best interests of her son, who was being held prisoner in Vienna, she must have been lying to herself or been so naïve she hadn't understood that giving up all control over her child meant he would never be allowed to rule in Italy. While her little boy languished in a dark, depressing castle in Austria, she took up residence in the luxurious palace in Parma. Soon after she moved in, a report was sent to Louis XVIII, who was back on the throne in Paris, which was meant to soothe his nervousness that Napoleon's wife was serving in a ruling capacity in a French territory. The brief claimed that Neipperg and several courtiers were such astute spies, Marie Louise never had a conversation they didn't overhear and she was not allowed to speak with anyone they saw as a threat. Neipperg kept such a tight grip on her, his apartment was separated from Marie Louise's by one small room in which a young *dame de compagnie* slept. Each night after the duchess retired, he locked the door to her bedroom and retired to his with the keys.

HAVING ALREADY MADE it clear that society bored her to tears, Marie Louise informed her courtiers in Parma that she did not intend to see them every day. During this first audience with them, she said she would send for them when she needed them. "Marie Louise did not find Parma the bed of roses her fancy had depicted," wrote Cuthell.[176] Not only did the return to the tedious decorum of royal duties upset her, she now had three royal residences to manage. Besides the palace in Parma, which was enormous, there was one in Colorno that was so grand, it was called "The Little Versailles." Though the third, named Sala, was deemed merely a country house, it had three large floors of living space, a chapel, a theater, and a long gallery flanked by colonnades. Once she was acclimated, she moved between the two palaces when duties demanded she hold court in one or the other, and tried to escape as often as she could to Sala where she gardened and galloped around the countryside. To Victoire, the spoiled duchess wrote she was frustrated because the simplest household tasks caused chaos and she was expected to deal with the drama, which she felt was beneath her.

Marie Louise was also offended that she was surrounded by poverty and disease as epidemics routinely ravaged Italian cities and beggars proliferated in her duchies. While she was finding Parma distasteful, Neipperg must have relished his life there because he had achieved a modicum of power and he was finally free from the prying eyes of the Viennese court, which had kept him from irrevocably ensnaring the duchess. His coup-de-grâce manifested in late 1816 when Marie Louise learned she was carrying his child, a girl named Albertine Maria born on May 1, 1817. They tried their best to keep the birth and baptism secret, but the Parmesan courtiers found out about the distasteful turn of events and had their fun at the couple's expense. Neipperg's response to the gossip when he learned of it? "His majesty, the Emperor of Austria, gave her to me and told me to do with her what I would," he declared.[177] The following month, Marie Louise was forced to accept what she had been too misguided and self-involved to see: The allies formally declared the title given to her son, the King of Rome, was no longer valid and her only outcry was that her sacrifices had been in vain!

Rather than fighting for the boy's eventual place in Parma, she resigned herself to his fate because she said she had no ambition herself—such an ironic statement given she was the only one of the three members of her immediate Bonaparte family who had managed to retain a royal territory! She then declared she was glad her son would not have to endure being a political pawn, though that's exactly what he would continue to be. On June 10, 1817, Francis put in motion the process of changing his grandson's title to the Duke of Reichstadt and his name to Prince Francis Charles Joseph. From that point on, he was known as 'Franz' by his Austrian relatives. "When they ceased calling him by the name of Napoleon, he was greatly displeased," Méneval wrote, "for he found the name Franz, which had been forced on him, both trivial and ugly."[178] Instead of the duchies in Italy, it was decreed he would inherit fiefs in Bohemia, a kingdom that has since been absorbed into the present-day Czech Republic.

The patent conferring his new title referred to him as the "son of our well-loved Archduchess Marie Louise," treating him as if he was illegitimate by not mentioning a father. The proclamation also stated that the name Napoleon would be dropped from all records relating to him. Try as Francis might to wipe all aspects of Bonaparte from his grandson's history, it would take more than decrees to eradicate his dad from the child's heart. "For his part, the boy did not forget his father," Saint-Amand wrote. "In vain they gave him an Austrian title and name but he knew very well that his title was the King of Rome and name was Napoleon II. He knew that in his veins there flowed the blood of the greatest warrior of modern times."[179] The efforts to turn Franz into an Austrian included removing the last of the French influences surrounding him—he was just six years old when Montesquiou's assistant, whom the governess had left to look after him, and her sixteen-year-old daughter, whom he adored as a playmate, were sent back to France.

Accompanying them was his nurse who had slept in his room every night since he was born. The loss of these caring attendants cruelly cut him off from the last three intimate relationships that extended back to his earliest days. The French servants were distraught because they knew how alone he would feel given the coldness of his Austrian relatives. This was not the first time the attendants taking care of him expressed their exasperation at his family's lack of compassion for the boy, particularly Marie Louise's. A letter Montesquiou had written to her husband while she was still his governess bears this out. "If this child had a mother, all very well, I would put him into her hands; but that is the last thing he has. She is a person more indifferent to his fate than the most recent stranger in his service," she wrote. "We are a company weeping round his cradle, not for what he has lost —for I think he will be happier than he would have been otherwise—but for what he misses."[180] She meant his father, of course.

Traveling through the phases of Marie Louise's life, I often wondered if the one-dimensional dilatant frittering her way through pastimes would ever embrace a more redeeming existence. The first glimmer that she had a shred of empathy showed itself as she began dedicating herself to making advancements that would improve the lives of the citizens of her duchies. Many of these highlighted an interest in the built world as she created or upgraded infrastructure, and restored important architectural gems and constructed new ones. She also enhanced cultural institutions that had been practically outlawed during Napoleon's reign and strengthened women's rights by decreeing that females would have the same laws of inheritance as males. Her projects included constructing La Villetta Cemetery in Parma, building a new hospital, and erecting a bridge over the Taro River to connect Parma, Piacenza, and Milan. The connector, which was under construction for three years, provided work for the beggars she found so distasteful and linked an agricultural district that had been cut off from trade to the markets that could sustain it. Orphanages, schools, and a maternity institution were planned; and she expanded the Parma library, which she renamed the Ducal Library during a ceremony on January 1, 1818.

The cemetery had hardly been finished when the first burials took place in March of that year during one of the typhus epidemics that broke out in the region. As I read through the list of developments, I thought about what a juxtaposition there was between Napoleon's and Marie Louise's realities. She was busy undertaking projects that would have formerly absorbed her husband's ambitions of creating architectural and engineering excellence at the same time his imprisonment in Longwood prevented him from accomplishing much of anything. This man who had peppered Europe with grand bridges, luxurious buildings, and lush parks was so sedentary, his doctor, François Carlo Antommarchi, said he needed exercise and told him he should plant a garden! "The idea was instantly seized upon by Napoleon with his characteristic ardor," Bourrienne wrote. "Noverraz, his chasseur, who had been formerly accustomed to rural occupations, was honored with the title of head gardener, and under his direction Napoleon proceeded to work with great vigor. He sent for Antommarchi to witness his newly acquired dexterity in the use of the spade."[181]

Napoleon asked him, "Well, doctor, are you satisfied with your patient—is he obedient enough? This is better than your pills, Dottoraccio; you shall not physic me anymore." Antommarchi said of Napoleon's project, "The Emperor urged us, excited us, and everything around us soon assumed a different aspect." Besides planting, they dug basins and planned roads. "We made alleys, grottoes, cascades; the appearance of the ground had now some life and diversity," the doctor said. "We planted willows, oaks, and peach trees, to give a little shade round the house. Having completed the ornamental part of our labors we turned to the useful. We divided the ground, we manured it, and sowed it with an abundance of beans, peas, and every vegetable that grows on the island."[182] These activities each afternoon took place after Napoleon dictated his memoirs to Las Cases for several hours every morning. His preferred place to recite his story was in his bedroom surrounded by mementos. Above the fireplace mantle in this room hung a portrait of Marie Louise along with several of his son, one of which Marie Louise had embroidered. There was also a small marble bust of the boy on the mantle. On the opposite side of the room from where he would sit and dictate or read was Isabey's portrait of Marie Louise holding their son in her arms.

"Not a day passed on Saint Helena without his introducing her into his private conversations," Las Cases wrote; "if they lasted any length of time, she was sure to come in for a share in them, or to become the exclusive subject of them. There is no circumstance, no minute particular relating to her, which he has not repeated to me a hundred times."[183] The author said Napoleon was so proud of his son, the boy drifted into their conversations often, which adds a mournful footnote to this story: The parent who wasn't allowed to see his son was the one who would have given anything to hold him again, while the one who could have comforted the child was either not interested enough or not brave enough to insist she had the right to do so. Marie Louise's first trip to Vienna after moving to Parma took place in 1818 when Franz was about to turn eight. For several reasons, she would not see him after that for more than a decade: She was pregnant with her second child with Neipperg, a son named William Albert who was born on August 8, 1819; and there was such unrest in Italy, she didn't dare leave Parma for fear her absence would cause an overthrow of her government.

During the dozen years she avoided returning to Austria and seeing her son, Marie Louise put a significant amount of energy into improving infrastructure. When the bridge over the Taro was finished, a grand celebration took place in September of 1819. She wrote to Méneval that she was satisfied with her developments in her kingdom because she was leaving enhancements that helped her people rather than merely erecting palaces that were expensive for them to maintain and gave them little in return. In her hyperbolic (and difficult to believe) New Year note to the secretary in 1820, she wrote that Franz was prospering and was developing "to his great advantage, under the eye of his grandfather, who cherishes him tenderly, and in the hands of his excellent tutor, who is attached to him as if he were his own son."[184] As she monitored her first child from afar, his father grieved for him until his dying days, which were upon him in the spring of 1821.

Knowing he was nearing the end, Napoleon finalized his will, telling Antommarchi he wanted his heart to be taken to Parma to his "dear Marie Louise." He said, "You will tell her how tenderly I have loved her; that I have never ceased to love her; and you will report to her all that you have witnessed, all that relates to my situation and my death."[185] Proving how authentically he must have cared for her in spite of the fact that she had betrayed him, he told a friend several days before he passed, "Be sure that if Marie Louise makes no efforts to relieve my distress, it is because she is kept surrounded by spies, who hinder her from knowing all that they have made me suffer, for Marie Louise is virtue itself." Napoleon made his wife his executrix, declaring in his will, "I have every reason to be pleased with my dearest wife, Marie Louise. I retain for her, to my last moment, the most tender sentiments." On May 2nd, Napoleon developed a high fever and lay in his camp bed mumbling to himself about France, his son, and a number of his old companions-in-arms. The last intelligible words he spoke before he died of the stomach cancer that had spread to his colon were "tete d'armee [head of the army]."[186]

Marie Louise, who learned of Napoleon's death from a newspaper article, scolded her uncle in Florence because no one in her family had bothered to inform her of her husband's passing. "I confess that I expected more interest and affection on that side, and it gave me a cruel blow by showing me how little one can count on one's own people," she wrote. Marie Louise told Victoire, "I was extremely startled at his death, though I have never had any deep feelings of *any kind* for him. I cannot forget that he is the father of my son, and that, far from behaving badly to me, as everyone believes, he always showed me every consideration—the only thing one can look for in a political marriage. I was therefore very grieved at it, and, though one should be glad that he has ended his unhappy life in a Christian manner, I could still have wished him many more years of happiness and life—provided that it was far away from me." Franz, who was ten years old, was not told of his father's death until July 20th. His tutor Jean-Baptiste Foresti, who broke the news, said the boy was devastated. "It was noticed, a few days later, that he walked about hanging his head and looking sad," Foresti wrote. "I saw him yesterday, and he is in deep mourning with all his household."[187]

While Napoleon's son grieved in private, Neipperg arranged the memorial services in Parma during which Marie Louise put on a public show. "Her majesty insisted upon being present in her pew at these mournful ceremonies," Neipperg wrote to Metternich. "The emotion of her majesty was very great, and very natural, when she recalled the father of her child and his unhappy end."[188] One of Napoleon's last wishes—that his heart be sent to his wife—was ignored because the English government refused to let it leave the island. The allies wouldn't allow it because they didn't want any further associations between Napoleon and his wife, and Marie Louise declined to take it because she wasn't keen on dealing with the malcontents who would have made pilgrimages to Parma to pay homage to the organ! Not knowing the allies would refuse the transfer, Antommarchi removed the heart from Napoleon's body and placed it in a silver vase filled with wine. Once he learned it would remain on the island, the organ was hermetically sealed in alcohol and placed in the corner of the coffin holding Bonaparte's body.

Napoleon had given his doctor the assignment of hand-delivering his last letter to Marie Louise. It took Antommarchi until October 15th to reach Parma due to bad weather conditions and delays at the hands of the authorities keeping Bonapartists at bay. Neipperg prevented the physician from having an audience with Marie Louise, saying he would give her the letter. The doctor caught sight of her at the theater that evening and said she lacked the brilliant freshness about which Napoleon had so often spoken to him. "Thin, crushed, worn, she bore traces of the sorrows through which she had passed," he said. Antommarchi then claimed the glimpse proved she had paid a price for her betrayals, just as her husband had, and he was satisfied that Napoleon had not been the only one to suffer.[189] The following day the doctor went to Rome to find Napoleon's family to tell them all that had transpired on the "remote and miserable rock," as his patient called it. He ordered the doctor to, "Tell them that the great Napoleon expired in the most deplorable state, wanting everything, abandoned to himself and his glory."[190]

IN HIS WILL, Napoleon left only a few personal effects to "his well-beloved wife," which included a bracelet made of his hair fastened with a gold clasp. He bequeathed Franz sixty-million francs, which was vehemently contested in Paris. When the money was seized by the French government, Marie Louise tried to have the decision revoked, saying it was her son's rightful inheritance, but she was no match for the greedy politicians who had stolen it so she gave up the quest. It's not clear whether the boy ever knew about the money or whether he received the substantial list of items

Napoleon left to him in the hopes that each of the possessions he had hand-picked for him "would be dear to him," but the emperor's death gave his son an intangible inheritance—it made Franz a cult hero.[191] Seeing the fervor of the Bonapartists organizing secret societies in France, Austria, Italy, and Spain, Francis tightened his grip on his grandson to thwart their plans to have Napoleon II placed on the French throne with Marie Louise as regent.

Illustrating how ridiculous it would have been to have the duchess back in power in France, regardless how many able ministers would back her up, is an anecdote from the autumn of 1821. The absurd episode was shared by Alexandrine du Montet, who knew Marie Louise because her own family had been exiled from France to Vienna when she was a girl. She wrote in her memoirs that a Count Scarampi, who was the husband of Marie Louise's mistress of the robes at the time, abruptly retired from his position as the archduchess's private secretary because the frivolousness with which she treated her responsibilities had caused him to have a mental breakdown. "Poor Scarampi persuaded himself that Vienna would hold him responsible for the weaknesses of Marie Louise, and for her governmental negligence," Montet wrote, saying the count came in every morning with his portfolio under his arm, "but, hardly had he opened it than the princess called for her parrot and her little monkey, who sat familiarly on her shoulders, and she never ceased to talk to them and play with them throughout the conference."[192] The man was so emotionally bereft, he died not long after he left her service.

I believe this episode shows that Neipperg was maintaining a tradition began by Francis and picked up by Napoleon—each of the three men were determined to ensure Marie Louise remained a childish version of herself, and Neipperg's continuation of the pattern was his way of keeping a stranglehold on her, which became official in late 1821. A mysterious note she wrote her friend Victoire in early 1822 hinted that the duchess had decided it was time to reveal she had covertly married Neipperg. "I await with impatience the moment when I can let you read in my heart and confide to you a secret which I hope yours had guessed, but which I will make you swear not to betray to anyone," Marie Louise wrote. "More by word of mouth. Goodbye till luncheon." Cuthell noted, "No actual date or place of this marriage has ever been given. Moreover, in her will, Marie Louise, while giving the date of her subsequent secret marriage to Charles-René de Bombelles, never alludes to any with Neipperg, and in that document merely describes him to his children as 'the general.'"[193] The reason the event could remain so obscure is how simple marriages in Italy were at that time—just a priest in a church, no witnesses required, no records kept. I wondered if the French courtiers ever learned about her marriage to Neipperg and found a few who made it clear they did not approve of her behavior.

After a visit to Parma in 1826, a Comte d'Hérrison left a contemptuous treatise on her insensitivity. During a tour of the palace, he was upset by the out-of-the-way place in which he found the resplendent cradle the people of Paris had given to the King of Rome when he was born. "One goes to see it by an unused staircase to an attic," he wrote. "It is there that one finds the souvenir of the glory of Marie Louise's past power. The rest is forgotten by this woman without any strength of character, without firmness, without principle; this woman, a mere woman, who is still today learning to dance. How many noble characters have died unknown for lack of opportunity to show themselves! But whoever had more favorable occasions than this sovereign? Is it retrogression to the past which haunts her, enveloping her, enfeebling her, to the state in which I saw her this morning?" He said of her attachment to Neipperg, whose health was beginning to fail, "But the love of the Cyclops suffices her! This one feeling dominates her life, which is troubled only by the fear of exciting the latent jealousy of her invalid." [194]

He found it disheartening that she crowned all of her disappointing decisions with the even greater insult to Napoleon's memory of marrying the general. Within a year after d'Hérrison's visit, Neipperg's health worsened to the point that Marie Louise knew she had to plan for a future without him. In December of 1827, she began to raise money to ensure her children with the general would not be penniless when both their parents were dead. The paperwork said her funds were going to be spent on building projects throughout her territories but about one-third of the ten-million francs went toward buying an estate for the two offspring. When Neipperg's protracted illness ended with his death in February of 1829, Marie Louise succumbed to deep grief. She planned a massive marble monument to honor him that would rise above his sepulcher and asked her father if she could have her marriage to him published. Frances's answer was a resounding no because leaving written evidence that a Habsburg princess' reputation had been blemished was unacceptable.

As a concession, Francis made her son William Albert the title, rank, and arms of the Count of Montenuovo. Cunningly, he did so without mentioning the child's last name on the decree. The grief Marie Louise experienced over Neipperg's death; the rheumatism from which she had suffered for years; and the decades of conflicting emotions bought on by her allegiance to her father, which had cast such a pall over her life for so long, had taken their toll and she was being described as looking like a poorly preserved woman of fifty-five when she was only thirty-eight years old.

Without her beloved escort, she shied away from most social engagements except the ones during which she acted in an official capacity as sovereign. One of these was a resplendent evening on May 16, 1829, when the first opera was sung in the Teatro Regio di Parma, known at the time as the Nuovo Teatro Ducal. Not only had her government funded the building, she was invested in how it would be designed, telling the architect Nicola Bettoli to choose a neoclassical style for the interiors in a pale-blue-and-white color scheme. An array of dignitaries joined her on the opening evening to hear Vincenzo Bellini's opera *La Zaira*.

MARIE LOUISE'S life for the next year consisted of periods of depressed hibernation interspersed with appearances as the Duchess of Parma. She had not been to Austria in so long, her father told her it was time for her to pay him a visit in the spring of 1830. Resistant to the idea of going, she kept delaying until fate forced her hand. In early summer, she received the news that her nineteen-year-old son was quite ill. She hurried to Baden where she stayed for several months in a villa near Franz, who had been diagnosed with pulmonary consumption. Cuthell wrote that the mother and son had so little in common, it would have taken more than proximity for them to have formed a true bond. "There was a depth in the soul of Napoleon's son which his mother never plumbed," she explained, "and he had been brought up too remote from her to give her more than mere dutiful affection."[195] By fall, Franz's health had improved so much he was able to return to his military unit and Marie Louise made her way back to Parma.

The winter after her return from Baden, politics once again brought upheaval into the duchess's life. The situation grew so contentious, she realized she had a revolution on her hands. A committee dubbed the "Italian Emancipation" had sent orders to its members in Parma, Modena, and Romagna to rise up on the same night in February of 1831. As she heard the chants in the streets, Marie Louise was so alarmed, she set things in motion to flee. "For the fourth time in her checkered life, she was prepared for flight, and now, not from an enemy, but from her own subjects," Cuthell wrote. "She had no one on whom to lean; Neipperg was no longer there."[196] When the uprising reached a crescendo, she raced out of town toward Piacenza, which was Austrian territory then. The rebellion wasn't quelled until French and Austrian troops reached Italy in March. Once order was restored, Marie Louise returned to her routine of moving her household between her three royal residences.

By the end of 1831, a little more than two years after Neipperg's death, the money she spent on the upkeep of the grand homes; the ball gowns, hats, and accoutrements she ordered from Paris; the institutions she financed; and the costly events she sponsored had depleted her government's finances to the point they were teetering on a precipice. Metternich sent a temporary comptroller to Parma to stabilize the finances and to appoint more capable officials. The minister immediately put Marie Louise's household and offices on a budget that would stop the flow of money going out from eclipsing what was coming in. As he was righting the ship, several life-shattering events took place in 1832. An earthquake struck Parma on March 13th, forcing Marie Louise to hastily retreat with her two younger children to Piacenza, which was outside the quake zone; and Franz died in July at the age of twenty-one. When Franz's lung condition first flared up again, the comptroller wrote Metternich to say he didn't believe Marie Louise should make such an expensive trip, asking his opinion.

THE ART OF CAPITULATION

It was decided she shouldn't go, but by June his condition had worsened and word came from Vienna that her son was dying. She traveled to Austria as quickly as she could and entered Schönbrunn Palace overcome by a sense of dread. She made her way to the imperial family apartments, passing through the gilded and lacquered salon hung with fine tapestries and statuesque portraits of her family members to a suite of three rooms that made up her son's apartment. When she opened the door, she was shocked. In the corner of the bedroom, the young man lay on a plain camp-bed beneath a portrait of his father by François Gérard. It had been two years since Marie Louise had spent time with Franz, then a recovered boy trotting around Baden's wooded hills on horseback. What she saw as she approached his bed was a wasted and gasping human being with sunken eyes and a body burning with fever—she couldn't believe it was her son. For weeks Franz had been asking if she was coming; by the time she stood over him, he was so weak he couldn't raise his arms to embrace her. His diminished state upset her so much, she retreated to an adjoining room so he wouldn't be alarmed by the intensity of her emotions. Francis, who had been informed that Franz was near death's door, decided not to return from Italy.

"Much as he loved his favorite grandson, it was so in keeping with his cold, selfish nature to shun the pain of seeing him die!" Cuthell accused. Marie Louise visited her son nearly every day as he remained bedridden, and on his better days, they talked. During one conversation, he thanked her for sending him the magnificent cradle the French had given him when he was born, which she must have sent to him after d'Hérrison berated her for stashing it in the hallway to the attic. Franz told her he had presented it to the Imperial Treasury Vienna (where it is on display today, as is one of Charlemagne's swords, and the Italian sword and scepter carried by Napoleon). "It is the only monument of my history," he told his mother. "My cradle and my tomb will be very near each other!" Marie Louise was in Vienna for nearly a month before her son's illness took a deadly turn. Not long before he passed, he lamented, "Death! Death! Only death can save me! Let them put the horses to: I must go and meet my father…I must kiss him once again!"[197] The day Franz died, he could no longer speak. When Marie Louise was led into the room, she was trembling so much, she had to cling to a friend's arm for support.

Franz nodded his head slightly to acknowledge she was there as the priest who would administer extreme unction was brought into the room. Everyone knelt while he performed his office and Marie Louise was so overcome, she slumped against a chair as the priest began to quietly pray. "At a few minutes past five a.m., the prince, whose last hour was peaceful and easy, moved his head twice from side to side," Eduard von Wertheimer wrote in his biography of Franz. "Then his breathing ceased and his lips no longer moved."[198] It was July 22, 1832—eleven years, almost to the day, since Franz had been told of his father's death on Saint Helena. When Francis was informed the grandson he had treated so jarringly was gone, he said, "I consider death a happiness for the duke, but I do not know if it will be favorable to public affairs or the reverse. As for me, I shall always regret my grandson."[199] The fact the emperor thought only about politics illustrates the sole consideration that drove his actions regarding Franz, who was entombed in St. Stephen's Cathedral in Vienna with his Habsburg relatives.

Marie Louise wrote to Victoire, "If I had not Albertine and William, who claim my care, I would ask God to take me to Him, there to rejoin the two persons I have lost, and who were dearest to me in this world; but the children who are left make it a duty for me to drag on my sad existence." She was referring to her oldest son and Neipperg, of course, as she had long convinced herself Napoleon never meant anything to her. I didn't believe her feelings could run so deep for a son she had mostly ignored for most of his life, and neither did Méneval. He wrote to his wife from the baths at Auvergne when he heard of Franz's passing, "I believe in his mother's despair, but I do not believe her to be inconsolable. God forgive her! How many sorrows her weaknesses have caused us! I do not know what feelings predominate in me, indignation or grief. My peace is gone for life over it." He also told his wife the doctors had been urging Franz's removal from Vienna for health reasons but the alliance always opposed it. "Metternich dared not disobey, and the emperor, weeping, left his grandson in order not to see him die," he fumed. "God keep us from having the hearts of kings!"[200]

Franz left evidence that he felt just as insulted by his Habsburg family's behavior, particularly Marie Louise's. He wrote to one of his closest friends, "If Josephine had been my mother, my father would not have been buried at Saint Helena, and I should not be at Vienna. My mother is kind but weak; she was not the wife my father deserved."[201] Though his mother's deficiencies had certainly played a significant role in depriving the young man of the life he felt he deserved, his grandfather's selfishness was even more to blame. As Méneval so aptly noted, "The poor child never came to the enjoyment of his estate, for death awaited him at his majority. Thus the Emperor of Austria, although he was very fond of his grandson, gave him nothing."[202] Montesquiou was bereft when she heard of the passing of her former charge. She wrote to Méneval, "I like to perceive, in this premature death, the proof that Providence, in His mercy, has reserved for him an immortal crown, which the powers of earth cannot take from him."[203]

ONCE SHE WAS BACK in Parma, Marie Louise buried the trauma of her oldest son's death by throwing herself into building projects and betrothing her daughter Albertine to Luigi Sanvitale, Conte di Fontanellato, who was one of the duchess's chamberlains and nearly twenty-years older than the seventeen-year-old girl. When Metternich was informed that the temporary comptroller had restored order in the duchy's finances and was leaving his post, he felt it was time to find another 'supervisor' for Marie Louise. Charles-René, comte de Bombelles, a French nobleman and soldier, was tapped for the job. Metternich told him, "The post of comptroller at the court of Parma is vacant by the death of Neipperg. It demands a man who is able to guide the weak character of the Duchess Marie Louise, and of dominating her little court, as well as of governing her little state honestly."[204] Though surprised, Bombelles agreed to take the position, arriving in Parma in August of 1833.

Cuthell described the forty-eight-year-old as dignified, cold, haughty, grave, and reserved; and said he was prudent in business, his manners were well-bred and gentle, and his morals were austere. Marie Louise wrote to Victoire, "Comte Bombelles, whom I feared, delights me; as far as I can judge in such a short time, he combines all one can wish for—firmness and gentleness of manner at the same time; and is such a virtuous man that he is a real find, if only God lets me keep him." Bombelles immediately set about making reforms, both financial and military, to align with his orders from Vienna. After putting in a full day each day—the household staff called him a workaholic—he dined with Marie Louise and accompanied her to the theater or the opera. "Every day, I congratulate myself more and more on the acquisition we have made in M. de Bombelles, who is a real saint, and so

THE ART OF CAPITULATION

agreeable in society," Marie Louise said of him.[205] Six months after his arrival in Parma, she married him, settling into her second morganatic marriage with Bombelles when she was forty-seven. No date was made public so it was up to Marie Louise's will to record it, which said it took place in secret on February 17, 1834.

One of her new husband's nephews, Frédéric-Alfred-Pierre, comte de Falloux, visited them in the spring of 1834 and described Marie Louise. "I do not know if the empress had ever been beautiful," he wrote; "in any case, at the period at which I had the honor to see her, her appearance offered no attraction. She was hollow-chested; her thick lip, of the hereditary type of the Imperial family of Austria, was very pendulous, which made her look older than her age." Falloux accompanied the duchess and his uncle on a drive into the country to give alms to the poor, and he believed her concerns for her subjects were sincere. He said the ducal residence in Parma that I had visited was vast and beautiful, which makes me wish I could have seen more of it than just the gorgeous ballroom. He also noted the absence of Napoleon from the public rooms of the palace where no painting or bust depicting him was in sight—"all breathes profound forgetfulness, or the most courageous resignation."[206] The fact that a portrait of Napoleon was on display in the palace by the time I toured the museum was appropriate since he was the one who ensured Marie Louise ruled in Parma.

The day after I experienced the elegant room in which his solemn presence was so at home, I visited several buildings Marie Louise had erected or preserved, though I didn't know it at the time. One was the Teatro Regio, which was magnificent with its grand concert hall gleaming like a gem. The color palette changed in 1849 when Duke Charles III replaced the blue and white décor Marie Louise had chosen with sumptuous red and gleaming gold hues, but the building's envelope was the same as it had been during her time. Another of the efforts she undertook was the renovation of the Cusani Palace in which she housed the law courts in Parma. By the time I walked through it, the lovely building held a museum called the Casa della Musica. I happened to be in Parma when the city was celebrating Giuseppe Verdi's two-hundredth birthday. Seen as somewhat of a hometown boy because the composer was born in Busseto, around thirty kilometers from Parma, his fame catapulted the town and the theater into the spotlight during the late years of Marie Louise's reign.

The displays in the museum brought the composer's journey to life and his music that wafted through the former palace added to the beauty of the evening. I stepped into a courtyard surrounded by graceful arches in the dim light and marveled at an enormous bronze statue by the Flemish sculptor Theodoor Van der Struck that depicts the struggle between the mythological hero Hercules and the giant Anteo. I remember being awestruck by the writhing muscles as the two combatants clashed, a feeling that returns as I look at the photo I took of the gigantic sculpture. The waring figures inspire even greater admiration now because they mimic the tenor of the last decade Marie Louise would rule. The final five years of the 1830s and the early years of the 1840s were stormy ones that thrummed with uprisings. The hostilities felt by her subjects increased the intensity of the discord that dominated Marie Louise's story for so many decades, which proves how wrong I was when I assumed she had floated happily around the ballroom floor in the gown displayed in the Glauco Lombardi Museum.

By the time she wore it, she was a miserable ruler who would have to endure political unrest until she died. The last round of protests she had to tolerate sprang up during a trip

THE ART OF CAPITULATION

she and Bombelles took to Austria in the summer of 1847 and continued after they returned. The unrest was sparked when the ministers of the regency government her third husband had left in charge followed his orders to squelch any demonstrations that arose while they were gone. When a student protest broke out because the young people were not allowed to gather and celebrate the new pope, Pius IX, the reaction was explosive. Marie Louise didn't want to return to Italy because she saw how readily her subjects had turned against the ministers and she feared for her safety. When she asked Metternich if she had to go back to Parma, he said she owed it to her states to return. A month after she did, she fell ill, the rheumatism she had suffered for many years turning into rheumatic pleurisy and acute pneumonia.

The illness took hold on December 10th, two days before her fifty-sixth birthday, and continued as she began putting her affairs in order, which included a declaration that forgave all of the citizens who had risen up against her government. The illness progressed rapidly and she died on December 17, 1847. After a royal funeral in Parma and a fortnight of lying in state, Marie Louise was escorted back to her home country by a squadron of Austrian hussars and her husband, who had handed over the duchies to the new Bourbon-Parma regime. While some biographers cast Marie Louise in a villainous light because they believe Napoleon and their son deserved better, others defend her. Alphonse Lamartine, a French poet, historian, and statesman, said it was wrong for the people of France to have demanded that Marie Louise feel passion because she only understood duty and respect. He believed her only crime was that she didn't know how to be anyone but herself. "The meretricious world of this court demanded a pretense of conjugal passion from a captive of victory," he explained. "She was too natural to simulate love when she had but obedience, terror, and resignation to offer. History will accuse her, nature will pardon her. She was asked to play a part—the actress failed; the woman remained."[207]

When Lamartine visited Marie Louise in Parma in 1837, he said she was still sheltering herself behind ceremonials, "in retreat and in silence, against the ill-will which arose against her." He said Napoleon had loved her for her pride and superiority; that she "was the blazon of his affiliation to great dynasties."[208] We've traveled far in Marie Louise's story—a journey during which we've witnessed her progression from a teenager who was caught in the crosshairs of power to a dutiful wife and empress to a reluctant duchess. Should we blame her for the downfall of one of the biggest bullies of all time? I don't think so—Napoleon did plenty to undermine his own power, including duping himself into believing he had landed 'the perfect wife,' a match that would inflame the hottest inflection point in his fabled life. Marie Louise proved time and again she was not malicious; her greatest fault was that she was flighty, which could easily be blamed on her circumstances because she was never taught decisiveness. When faced with the affronts she experienced, she gravitated toward acquiescing because resignation was her birthright—to capitulate would be her highest calling throughout the entirety of her privileged life.

7

HOW TO BUILD A BETTER HUSBAND

EDITH WHARTON IN NEW HAVEN

After a day of voyeurism, my back stiff and eyes strained, I made my way out of the Beinecke Library at Yale into a glorious autumn afternoon. The campus was quiet as I walked across Hewitt Quadrangle to Woolsey Hall where Edith Wharton received an honorary degree of Doctor of Letters nearly a century before. I'd been shadowing the famous novelist for hours as I sifted through the objects she had deemed important enough to preserve, which included the newspaper clippings picturing her traversing what was then known as Beinecke Plaza surrounded by rows of men in flowing robes. It was June 20, 1923, and her ensemble was even more voluminous given she was wearing a billowing dress beneath her gown. The sun, which was bright on the summer day she received her award, was arcing its way toward the western horizon to bathe the plaza in a soft light when I stood in the exact spot she had occupied in the grainy black-and-white photo.

The subdued effect matched my mood, as the exhilaration of being handed the first few boxes was past and a poignancy that comes from rummaging through someone else's treasures had taken hold. From then on, Edith's reality set the tone: The larger-than-life author had disappeared, her eminence replaced by a woman made of flesh-and-bone who spoke to me through candid photographs, scribbled confessions, anguished letters, and journal pages filled with self-doubt. Two of the strongest questions that emerged as I handled hundreds of items that day were, "Why did she look so forlorn in her portraits when she was young?" and "Why would her family call this woman, who was so intelligent she would receive a coveted Pulitzer Prize, by the nickname 'Pussy' throughout her life?" Early in my journey through her papers, I assumed Edith's face held a defeated expression because she admitted she had always felt painfully shy and socially awkward.

By the end of the day, I saw that the answers to both of my questions could be found in the behavior Edith's mother Lucretia directed toward her only daughter. Not only did Lucretia come up with the embarrassing endearment (which Edith didn't seem to mind as far as I could tell), the lack of respect her mother showed the young girl contributed to the pain that was evident on her face in so many of her earliest portraits. In Edith's first attempt at autobiography, a manuscript titled "Life and I," she revealed just how much Lucretia was to blame for her daughter's misery. Written in Edith's fluid looping cursive in 1932 when she was seventy, the narrative was a precursor to the memoir Edith would publish as *A Backward Glance* in 1934. The pale green file box holding the fifty-two-page manuscript was the first I'd requested, and it was a thrill to pull it from a beat-up brown envelope on which the title "Life and I" was written in orange pencil. Edith's first happy memory as a small girl, which she described as an "extremely pleasant sensation," was of being kissed on the cheek by her cousin Dan Fearing, who was several years older than Edith, as she walked down Fifth Avenue with her father.[1]

"With equal distinctiveness, I recall the satisfaction I felt in knowing that I had on my best bonnet," she remembered, "a very handsome bonnet made of a bright Tartan velvet with a white satin ground and a full ruffling of blonde lace under the brim." After relating this one gratifying experience, a confessional tone took hold of her story and she was brutally frank about how she perceived herself. "I think my suffering from ugliness developed earlier than my sense of beauty," she explained, "though it would seem that, one being the complement of the other, they must have coincided in my consciousness."[2] This declaration is an example of the tack she took in the earlier attempt at a memoir that did not end up in the published accounts of her life. When she wrote "Life and I," she had not yet fleshed out the family history and genealogy she would present in *A Backward Glance*, and the scene-setting as to where she had traveled with her parents and brothers as a child was only briefly outlined.

She mainly explored an emotional landscape in the private narrative, describing her father George Frederic Jones as tall, splendid, and always kind. She said he lifted her very high in his strong arms and held her safely in the air when she was a tiny girl. In contrast, she presented an aloof portrait of her mother by recounting her beautiful flounced dresses, painted and carved fans in sandalwood boxes, ermine scarves, and "all the other dim impersonal attributes of a mother." Edith said Lucretia never took her education seriously, calling her childhood an intellectual desert that forced the young girl to look for ways to feed her mind in order to counteract the neglect. "This fact did not make me feel any superiority to my playmates," she wrote about her absorption with her father's library, which was one of the tacks she took. "On the contrary, it humiliated me because I was so 'different.'"[3]

Edith said her first attempt at a novel came at the age of eleven, which opened with, "'Oh, how do you do, Mrs. Brown?' said Mrs. Tompkins! If only I had known you were going to call I should have tidied up the drawing room." Edith showed it to her mother, who returned it with the dismissive comment, "Drawing rooms are always tidy," a criticism that Edith said ended her first "creative frenzy."[4] After being rejected, Edith said she consciously turned away from her literary dreams with the new-found belief that someone like her could never write anything worth reading. About halfway through "Life and I," she fast-forwarded to her early twenties and shared a revealing account of Lucretia's disdain during the lead-up to the wedding that would formalize the arranged marriage to Edward Robbins Wharton her mother forced her into. Edith knew Teddy, as he was called, because he was a close friend of one of her brothers and he had visited their Newport, Rhode Island, cottage during summer breaks, though she didn't know him well enough to have formed any sort of bond with him.

Older than Edith by nearly a decade, he was a spoiled thirty-three-year-old who was still living with his parents when Lucretia set her sights on him. The middle-aged man's situation was described by R.W.B. Lewis in his book *Edith Wharton: A Biography*. "Teddy had no money of his own, but his parents gave him an allowance of two-thousand dollars a year, and under the circumstances his needs were few," Lewis wrote. "He had no vocation, nor any intention of seeking one."[5] Teddy considered himself a single man-about-town and had little motivation to make any radical changes to his life, at least early on. Proving how formidable a socialite's mother with Lucretia's fierce determination could be, she eventually achieved her aim and the couple's engagement was announced in March of 1885. The wedding would take place within a month because Edith's mother felt her daughter, at twenty-three years old, was dangerously close to the age at which a woman of Edith's standing was less marriageable and Lucretia couldn't take the chance the match would fall apart.

One of the most revealing anecdotes Edith recorded regarding her mother's lack of respect illustrates how innocent she was at that age, her knowledge of physical intimacy so lacking, her nerves sizzled as she tried to figure out what it meant to sexually consummate a relationship. On page thirty-four of the "Life and I" manuscript, Edith wrote, "A few days before my marriage, I was seized with such a dread of the whole dark mystery, that I summoned up courage to appeal to my mother; & begged her, with a heart beating to suffocation, to tell me 'what being married was like.' Her handsome face at once took on the look of icy disapproval which I most dreaded. 'I never heard such a ridiculous question!' she said impatiently; & I felt at once how vulgar she thought me."[6] Confused to the point of being nauseated, Edith tried to work it out for herself, thinking that pregnancy must result when God witnessed a priest marrying a couple through the roof of a church. In the end, she couldn't let it go, deciding to press her mother once more, hoping for an answer as to what would happen to her once she became a wife.

This time, she was met with a coldness that deepened to disgust and her mother told her she simply couldn't believe Edith was such an idiot she didn't naturally understand. In her own defense, Edith remembered, "The dreadful moment was over and the only result was that I had been convicted of stupidity for not knowing what I had been expressly forbidden to ask about or even to think of!"[7] Lucretia's dismissiveness was so pronounced, Edith was not mentioned by name on the engraved wedding invitations, which read: "Mrs. George Frederic Jones requests the honor of your presence at the marriage of her daughter to Mr. Edward R. Wharton, at Trinity Chapel, on Wednesday April Twenty-ninth at twelve o'clock." The "Mr. and" was missing from the beginning of the sentence because Edith's father had died three years before.

Society buzzed as the invitations landed in New York's grandest drawing rooms because those who knew Edith were surprised she would agree to marry Teddy. I had to wonder why they didn't realize there was no way the dutiful young woman could possibly refuse the wishes of her bulldozer of a mother. Also likely contributing to Edith's docility over marrying someone she didn't love were two previous rejections. During her father's illness, Edith had welcomed the attention of a suitor named Harry Stevens. Their fondness for each other developed in Cannes where the Joneses were spending the winter and spring with the hope the climate would help Edith's father recover his strength. Six months after George died, the engagement was publicly announced but Harry's mother changed her mind about the match, forcing Edith to agree to formally break it off—a humiliating development that left her stunned. Less than a year later in July of 1883, Edith met Walter Van Rensselaer Berry in Bar Harbor, Maine. She thought he might be interested in her because they spent several satisfying days together talking about art and literature, the first experience of an enjoyable intellectual exchange she'd ever had.

In Berry's account of why he didn't follow through, recorded in a letter he wrote to Edith much later in life, he told her he had tossed and turned during a sleepless night after that first afternoon as he wondered whether he should marry her because he felt sure she would accept his proposal. The following day he was astonished he had even considered it, claiming his change of heart was a financial consideration, as he was a law student with just enough money to pay for the canoe rental and his hotel bill. After another day with Edith, Berry felt the moment had passed so he simply left Bar Harbor without mentioning his feelings. He need not have worried about supporting Edith, as she had inherited $600,000 in real-estate holdings when her father died; Berry also knew he would come into a large inheritance of his own at some point.

Rather than fiscal unpreparedness, it would become clear by his flirtations with frivolous women throughout his life that he was destined to be a confirmed bachelor. As the years slid by, he earned a reputation as a 'ladies' man' who enjoyed a series of superficial females, but only in public—a distinctively asexual view of him that explained why he would have shied away from commitment when he and Edith first met. At least with this second blow to her ego no one else knew about her attachment to Berry so Edith was able to keep her mortification to herself. Fourteen years would pass before Berry surfaced in her memoir, though his name is worth noting at this early stage in Edith's story because he shows up often in some very powerful ways.

LESS THAN TWO years after her near-miss with Berry, Edith and Teddy walked down the aisle in New York City on April 29, 1885, and traveled to Newport for their honeymoon at Pencraig Cottage. Edith didn't share any details about her husband or the early years of their marriage in her memoirs so Teddy only comes to life in biographies, which describe him as an extremely good-looking fellow with a calm disposition and as someone who won everyone over with his subservient ways. The title of this essay may have led you to believe my premise highlights this couple and a successful bond they formed. It is ironic that Teddy is the only man mentioned here who does not fit within a brilliant puzzle Edith composed as she intuitively moved toward a higher-quality existence. Teddy looms large in the story simply because he was such an unsatisfactory match—and even an albatross by the time she freed herself from him—his behavior drove her to take steady steps to replace him with more fulfilling companions.

It wasn't just an emotional incompatibility that plagued the couple: He was an outdoorsman at heart with no appetite for mental rigor, and she was an intellectual with an innate passion for reading, writing, and discussing urbane concepts and literature. According to Gloria C. Erlich, who wrote *The Sexual Education of Edith Wharton*, Teddy "felt foolish among her sophisticated friends and generally excluded from the interests that drove her life." Erlich quoted Teddy as saying he was nothing more than a "passenger" in Edith's fast-moving world, and that he seemed "positively frightened" by her literary work, almost convinced "it was a kind of witchcraft."[8] He wasn't completely off-base: Edith described how her creativity had a psychic quality to it when she was a child during an ongoing series of mystical events she called "making up."

She said the episodes had such a powerful pull she was helpless to them and that they required the use of particular books with specific visual characteristics, such as a version of Anthony Trollope's mystery novel *Kept in the Dark* published by Tauchnitz. She called this edition of the book especially inspiring because the pages were covered with very small type. "At any moment the impulse might seize me; and then, if the book was in reach, I had only to walk the floor, turning the pages as I walked, to be swept off full sail on the sea of dreams," she explained, saying the fact that she couldn't read a word added to the completeness of the illusion because the mysterious blank pages allowed her to imagine whatever fancy she chose.[9]

"Parents and nurses, peeping at me through the doors (I always had to be alone to 'make up'), noticed that I often held the book upside down, but that I never failed to turn the pages, and that I turned them at about the right pace for a person reading aloud as passionately and precipitately as was my habit," she wrote. "I had to obey this furious Muse, and there are deplorable tales of my abandoning the 'nice' playmates who had been invited to 'spend the day,' and rushing to my mother with the desperate cry: 'Mamma, you must go and entertain that little girl for me. *I've got to make up.*'"[10] In "Life and I," Edith shared another alchemical aspect to her writing when she admitted she felt a sensuous rapture when the sound of a word melded with its visual distinctiveness.

"They were visible, almost tangible presences, with faces as distinct as those of the persons among whom I lived," she explained. "And, like the Erlkönig's daughters, they sang to me so bewitchingly that they almost lured me from the wholesome noonday air of childhood into some strange supernatural region, where the normal pleasures of my age seemed as insipid as the fruits of the earth to Persephone after she had eaten of the pomegranate seed."[11] Erlkönig is a ballad by Johann Wolfgang von Goethe that depicts the Erl-King beckoning a little boy to the netherworld; and Persephone is the Greek goddess who was forced to return to her husband Hades in hell for several months each year. That Edith had read Goethe by the age of thirteen and knew the Greek myths just as early without having received a smidge of formal schooling presents a forceful contradiction in her story. She would be remarkably well-educated by the time she was in her thirties thanks to her insatiable reading habits and the efforts of a series of men who nurtured her intelligence in vital ways. Edith presents them, one by one, in *A Backward Glance* by explaining how each of them strengthened the mental voracity she had been developing since she was a child.

As she introduced them, a living map of her development emerged, each stop along the way driven by her inclinations toward storytelling. When George encouraged Edith's "making up" during her childhood, he became her first male advocate, a beneficial support Edith recognized when she told a friend just before she died that it was her father who fed her literary dreams when she was little. Soon after he taught her the alphabet, Edith said he seemed astonished when he found her under a table in the library reading a book one day without having learned anything beyond rudimentary ABC's. She said the array of subjects at her disposal in that hallowed room was nearly eight hundred books her father had acquired that amounted to a brilliantly curated collection. As Lucretia watched her daughter digest the contents of one volume after another, she was alarmed that Edith preferred solitude with her favorite stories over playing with other children.

"By the time I was seventeen, though I had not read every book in my father's library, I had looked into all of them," Edith wrote. "Long before the passing of years and a succession of deaths brought them back to me, I could at any moment visualize the books contained in those low oak book cases."[12] Edith's father's last intellectual gifts to her before he died were John Ruskin's *The Stones of Venice* and Walter Pater's *The Renaissance: Studies in Art and Poetry*, which he gave her during the stint in Cannes when he passed away. The first adult male outside her family to further her progress toward being a successful writer was a middle-aged widower named Egerton Winthrop, who had lived in Paris for many years before moving back to New York City soon after Edith and Teddy were married. Winthrop hit upon the idea of teaching Edith how to study when he recognized how intelligent and curious she was.

"It was too late for me to acquire the mental discipline I had missed in the schoolroom, but my new friend directed and systemized my reading, and filled some of the worst gaps in my education," Edith wrote. "Through him I first came to know the great French novelists, and the French historians and literary critics of the day; but his chief gift was to introduce me to the wonder-world of nineteenth-century science." After a childhood during which Edith had been forced to gather scraps of paper torn from parcels delivered to her home to record her poems, this was transformative. In describing the metamorphosis, she said her "vague enthusiasms" had been crystalized, and her "roving curiosities" were finally given nourishment.[13] The experience was so powerful, she looked back over all her years of solitary reading and realized had it not been for her father, she would have been alone in her mental growth. By the time Winthrop was tutoring Edith, she and Teddy were settling into the rhythm of a shared life that included regular jaunts to Italy and other trips abroad.

One striking vacation was a four-month cruise of the Mediterranean aboard a private yacht. Edith left rich accounts of this trip that would be published posthumously in the book *The Cruise of the Vanadis*. The adventurous tone she achieved was likely influenced by the fact that she had gravitated toward the mythic tales scattered among the volumes in her father's library as a child, preferring stories about the Greek gods over fairy tales, which she despised, "as any intelligent child does after a taste of 'real books.'"[14] Her choice of reading material while she was onboard *Vanadis* was one of those "real books," as she had chosen Andrew Lang's translation of *The Odyssey* for the trip. Untamed vistas and experiences flow from the pages of her descriptions, which could just as easily have sprung from the accounts of the mythic wanderer Odysseus. As they left Santorini, Edith wrote, "The red cliff looked less infernal in the early light than at sunset, but the scene was nevertheless a wild and striking one."[15]

After they docked near and set out to explore the Greek town of Corfu, "the scirocco blew with such fury that we plunged and tossed in the open roadstead as if we had been at sea."[16] On their journey to Milos, she said she had awakened early "to find a southeasterly gale blowing and the yacht pitching into a violent head sea. It was useless to struggle against it, so we took refuge in a small harbor called Zemini, on the east side of the Gulf of Messenia. We lay there all day, surrounded by stony hills, which seemed all the more bleak by contrast with the beautiful fertility of the Ionian Islands."[17] As the cruise was winding down in 1893, Edith learned she would inherit $120,000 from Joshua Jones, a cousin of her grandfather whose name she only vaguely remembered hearing. This gave her and Teddy the means to buy their own home when they returned to the U.S., an oceanfront compound in Newport called Land's End.

Edith tapped Ogden Codman, Jr., whom she called "a clever young Boston architect" and addressed by his nickname Coddy, to help her renovate the interiors of the residence. While working together, they realized they shared the same opinions on aesthetics and decided to see if they could gather their ideas into a book,the result of which was published in 1897 as *The Decoration of Houses*. The two novices soon realized they were at a loss as to how to organize the material, and Edith credits Walter Berry for saving the effort from being derailed when he was staying with her and Teddy during the summer she and Codman were struggling to assemble their thoughts. Biographers simply say

Berry was "back on the scene," the thread of their relationship post-Bar Harbor left undocumented. Edith also skipped over this detail in *A Backward Glance*, her thoughts about him focused mainly on his impact on her as an author.

"Walter Berry was born with an exceptionally sensitive literary instinct, but also with a critical sense so far outweighing his creative gift that he had early renounced the idea of writing," Edith explained. "Though he was already a hardworking young lawyer, with a promising future at the bar, the service of letters was still his joy in his moments of leisure."[18] Edith described the timidity she felt once she had summoned the courage to approach him about helping her and Codman with their ideas. "I remember shyly asking him to look at my lumpy pages, and I remember his first shout of laughter (for he never flattered or pretended)," she wrote; "and then his saying good-naturedly, 'Come, let's see what can be done,' and settling down beside me to try to model the lump into a book."[19] Not only did he whip the manuscript into shape, Edith claimed he taught her everything about writing clear, concise English from that time forward.

She said publishing *The Decoration of Houses* amused her but she didn't consider the book's debut to be the beginning of her literary career. "That began with the publishing, in *Scribner's Magazine*, of two short stories," she explained. "The first was called 'Mrs. Manstey's View,' the second 'The Fullness of Life.' Both attracted attention [in 1891 and 1893 respectively], and gave me the pleasant flutter incidental to first seeing one's self in print; but they brought me no nearer to other workers in the same field. I continued to live my old life, for my husband was as fond of society as ever, and I knew no other existence, except in our annual escapes to Italy." The next statement demonstrates how completely her self-worth would be tied to her writing: "I had as yet no real personality of my own, and was not to acquire one till my first volume of short stories was published—and that was not until 1899."[20] With this book, *The Greater Inclination*, she once again credits Berry for helping her produce narratives she felt were eloquent.

"From that day until his death twenty-seven years later, through all his busy professional life, he followed each of my literary steps with the same patient interest," she explained, "and I doubt if a beginner in the art ever had a sterner yet more stimulating guide." Her respect for Berry was profound. "He taught me never to be satisfied with my own work, but never to let my inward conviction as to the rightness of anything I had done be affected by outside opinion," Edith said. "He alone not only encouraged me to write, as others had already done, but had the patience and the intelligence to teach me how. I suppose there is one friend in the life of each of us who seems not a separate person, however dear and beloved, but an expansion, an interpretation, of one's self, the very meaning of one's soul. Such a friend I found in Walter Berry."[21] Once Edith realized her fiction was worthy of being gathered into a book, she knew she would pursue a career as a storyteller, the experience of publishing *The Greater Inclination* so powerful, she said it broke the chains that had held her "so long in a kind of torpor," which included the nearly twelve years since she had been married.

In Winthrop and Berry, she had found "two delightful friends," who had educated her and had widened her interests, though she was still hungry for more. "What I wanted above all was to get to know other writers," she said; "to be welcomed among people who lived for the things I had always secretly lived for."[22] Given she felt she had to hide her passion for writing from her husband, the desire must have been acute. Edith also struggled to come to terms with the rejection she received from the "editorial timidity" of the culture she was born into because it meant she wouldn't find a substantial audience in America during this early stage of her development. She said there was still a quaintness to the stories in books and magazines in the U.S. that amounted to censorship of any tales depicting gender biases, a recurring theme in her work.

Edith also felt rebuffed by her social circle, as those in it found her aspirations to succeed as a novelist unbecoming. Their prejudices were so pronounced, people of her rank deemed the writing of fiction a cross between a 'black art' and manual labor. "My literary success puzzled and embarrassed my old friends far more than it impressed them," she explained, "and in my own family it created a kind of constraint which increased with the years."[23] In light of these American attitudes, Winthrop suggested that Teddy take Edith to London after *The Greater Inclination* debuted there. He had two goals for the few weeks they would spend in the capital: having her meet other successful writers and allowing her to immerse herself in a society in which a woman's career as a writer was not an anathema. In the chapter of her memoir that begins with her introduction to the Edwardian sparkle of the city, Edith is meeting the crème-de-la-crème of the literary set and the social mavens of that time.

The satisfaction from the success of her book and the acceptance she found in England brought her soul to life. "At last I had groped my way through to my vocation, and thereafter I never questioned that story-telling was my job, though I doubted whether I should be able to cross the chasm which separated the *nouvelle* from the novel," she explained. "Meanwhile I felt like some homeless waif who, after trying for years to take out naturalization papers, and being rejected by nearly every country, has finally acquired a nationality. The Land of Letters was henceforth to be my country, and I gloried in the new citizenship."[24] Proving how driven she was, she immediately crossed the abyss she claimed she feared and began to write her first novel, *The Valley of Decision*. As she penned the initial chapters, Berry steered her on a steady course without interfering with her process.

"He looked through what I had written, handed it back, and said simply: 'Don't worry about how you're to go on. Just write down everything you feel like telling,'" she said. "The advice freed me once and for all from the incubus of an artificially pre-designed plan, and sent me rushing ahead with my tale, letting each incident create the next, and keeping in sight only the novelist's essential signpost; the inner significance of the 'case' selected." Once she finished the manuscript, she shared how meticulously Berry studied it before he began "marking down faulty syntax and false metaphors" and "smiling away over-emphasis and unnecessary repetitions." He patiently helped her "through the beginner's verbal perplexities" while "never laying hands on what he considered sacred: the *soul* of the novel, which is (or should be) the writer's own soul."[25] This book, set against a backdrop of political and religious intrigues in eighteenth-century Italy, "established Edith Wharton at a stroke as a major American writer," wrote Lewis in *The Letters of Edith Wharton*, which he edited with his wife Nancy and published three years after his biography debuted.[26] The opening of *The Valley of Decision* illustrates how dynamic Edith's collaboration with Berry was—her creative depth honed by his finesse.

The story launches with this description of a church: "The February day was closing, and a ray of sunshine, slanting through a slit in the chapel wall, brought out the vision of a pale haloed head floating against the dusky background of the chancel like a waterlily on its leaf. The face was that of the saint of Assisi—a sunken ravaged countenance, lit with an ecstasy of suffering that seemed not so much to reflect the anguish of the Christ at whose feet the saint knelt, as the mute pain of all poor down-trodden folk on earth."[27] With the success of this novel and the others that would follow, Edith realized Berry's insight into how her growth as a writer should evolve was so keen, his influence was life-changing. "No words can say, because such things are unsayable, how the influence of his thought, his character, his deepest personality, were interwoven in mine," she wrote. She said he found her when she was hungry and thirsty, and fed her until their last hour together. "With each book he exacted a higher standard in economy of expression, in purity of language, in the avoidance of the hackneyed and the precious," she wrote.[28]

Even after long physical absences, she said there was so much camaraderie that stemmed from their dreaming, thinking, and laughing together that it felt as if they had never been apart. Berry's efforts also paid great dividends financially: The first edition of *The Valley of Decision* flew off the shelves and twenty-five thousand copies sold during the first six months of its second printing. Craving a less-busy life that would foster more creativity, Edith decided she could afford to build a home that would support it, which would become her best-known U.S. residence, and her and Teddy's primary stateside address until 1911. "We sold our Newport house and built one in Lenox, in the hills of western Massachusetts," she wrote, "and at last I escaped from watering-place trivialities to the real country. Now I was to know the joys of six or seven months a year among fields and woods of my own."[29]

Edith described the home that began to rise near the

densely wooded shores of Laurel Lake in 1902 and would be called The Mount after her great-grandfather's estate, as spacious and dignified. The lessening of the soulless social obligations that were demanded of her in New York City and Newport gave her the headspace, and the peace and quiet to develop a rhythm to her writing process that was still very organic at this stage of her evolution. She said it was difficult to explain how the stories she told took shape because the themes seemed to bubble up in a gradual absorption of the myriad details that seeped into her pores by osmosis. "I have often been asked whether the writing of *The Valley of Decision* was preceded by months of hard study," Edith explained. "I had never studied hard in my life, and it was far too late to learn how when I began to write the book." She claimed she hadn't traveled to Italy or read about the country for the purpose of crafting fiction; that her intimacy derived from spending long periods of time there gradually and imperceptibly fermented the tale and compelled her to write it. "Whatever its faults—and they are many—it is saturated with the atmosphere I had so long lived in," she explained.[30]

The molecular infusions that informed the book were absorbed from landscapes, architecture, and antique furniture she had seen. To supplement these, she pulled details from published accounts of the country during the eighteenth-century by memoirists and writers of travel books. Charles Norton, a Harvard professor whom she called a great friend, lent her some of the most important titles. Edith shared how instrumental he was by way of this anecdote, which she called "one of the most graceful *gestes* ever made by a distinguished scholar" to such a neophyte. "I happened to tell him that, though I had been picking up second-hand books on eighteenth-century Italy whenever I could find them (hardly any of the classics of the period being then reprinted), there were a few that I had been unable to buy, and one or two that even the public libraries could not supply," she explained. A few weeks later, a box arrived at The Mount containing the "unattainable treasures" and other books almost as rare. Edith spent an entire summer gleaning details from them, marveling that the treasured titles were left "at the disposal of a young scribbler who was just starting on her first novel."[31]

The success of *The Valley of Decision* earned Edith another project: The editor of *Century* magazine asked her to write a series of essays on Italian villas and their gardens, which would be serialized in the publication and then collected in book form. Eager to begin the project, she boarded a ship from Boston to Rome with Teddy in tow during the winter of 1903. "My long experimenting had resulted in books which brought me more encouragement than I had ever dreamed of obtaining, and were the means of my making some of the happiest friendships of my life," she remembered as she launched herself into the research for the new series of essays. "The reception of my books gave me the self-confidence I had so long lacked, and in the company of people who shared my tastes, and treated me as their equal, I ceased to suffer from the agonizing shyness which used to rob such encounters of all pleasure. It was in this mood that I arrived in Italy."[32]

Edith and Teddy had a most transformative experience during this trip—one so impactful, it would influence their travels for the rest of their lives. George von Lengerke Meyer, the American Ambassador to Italy, took the Whartons from Rome to Caprarola and back, a one-hundred-mile trip, in one day in his car. Given they were accustomed to the hassles that always came with traveling by train, the automobile was a marvel. Edith brushed aside the fact that the dust she'd inhaled brought on a bout of laryngitis because this first taste of motoring had exhilarated her so much, it would be her favorite mode of transportation from this point on. The excitement she and Teddy felt inspired them to buy their own automobile, a Panhard-Levassor, during their trip to Europe the following year. Fortunately the wind screen had been invented by then, which would slightly decrease the particulate the car's occupants inhaled, and Edith found face coverings that would protect her further. After exploring the south of France in the Panhard during the spring of 1904, Edith and Teddy crisscrossed England, driving from London to Rye to visit Henry James.

BY THIS TIME, Edith and James knew each other well, though the moment they met escaped both of them. "As for the date of the meeting which finally drew us together, without hesitations or preliminaries, we could neither of us ever recall when or where that happened," Edith explained. "All we knew was that suddenly it was as if we had always been friends, and were to go on being (as he wrote to me in February 1910) 'more and more never apart.'"[33] James would be instrumental in introducing Edith to more members of her expanding male-companion tribe when he invited her to Howard Sturgis' home, Queen's Acre near Windsor, in late April of 1906. It was a transformative event that she carefully memorialized in her autobiography, introducing each of the young men she would come to know there. Once they were solidly entrenched in her inner circle, the group of Jamesian devotees would be some of her longest-standing friends. The clique of academics that included Sturgis, Gaillard Lapsley, Percy Lubbock, John Hugh Smith, and Robert Norton was collectively known as the Qu'Acre set because they most often gathered at Sturgis's home.

Edith had been introduced to Sturgis in Newport soon after she married Teddy, and she saw him again when Sturgis and James visited The Mount in October 1904. She said of her first encounter with Sturgis: "If ever there was a case of friendship at first sight it was struck between us then and there. Like me, he was a great lover of good talk, and shared my inability to enjoy it except in a small and intimate circle. Continuity in friendship he valued also as much as I did, and from that day until his death, many years later, he and I shared the same small group of intimates."[34] Edith met Lapsley, an American who taught at Trinity College in Cambridge, England, in late August of 1904 while on a motor tour of New England with Berry. James introduced her to the others in 1906 when she arrived at Queen's Acres for an overnight stay. Her entrée to the unconventional world Sturgis created made her the newest member of a band of intellectuals that had been slowly forming.

Lapsley had inducted Lubbock, whom he knew at Cambridge, and Robert Norton, a lifelong friend; John Hugh Smith was lured to Qu'Acre by Lubbock, the two of them friends since their days at Cambridge; and it was Sturgis who connected all of the younger men to James. Edith set the scene when the "inner group," as she called them, took their places in Sturgis' living room—each one gathered around him as he sat by the fire knitting just as the oil lamps were brought in at the end of a foggy autumn afternoon. "In one of the arm chairs by the fire is sunk the long-limbed frame of the young Percy Lubbock, still carrying in his mind the delightful books he has since given us, and perhaps as yet hardly aware that he was ever to put them on paper," she remembered; "in another sits Gaillard Lapsley, down for the weekend from his tutorial duties at Cambridge, while John Hugh Smith faces Percy across the fireside, and Robert

Norton and I share the corners of the wide chintz sofa behind the tea table."[35]

She remembered the most powerful member of the group as he dominated the hearth, and all of them, "Henry James stands, or heavily pads about the room, listening, muttering, groaning disapproval, or chuckling assent to the paradoxes of the other tea-drinkers."[36] From this moment on, as Gloria Erlich put it, these men formed a close circle around Edith, who, as the only female, held a position that "kept her feeling feminine and flirtatiously alive." Erlich described the fusion of masculine energy as "a system of male companionship that functioned almost as a composite husband, although without provision for physical intimacy."[37] Because there were no sexual tensions in these relationships, Edith was able to relax and satisfy her cravings for spending time with highly educated individuals who appreciated the same conversational rigor she valued. When she first joined the cerebral fray in Windsor, she was enjoying great financial gains from the publication of her novel *The House of Mirth*.

Though early reviews were disappointing, and James wasn't as enthusiastic as she would have liked him to be, the book would become a bestseller and Sturgis' reaction to it highlights why. He gushed, "How good! How good! It is to my mind the best thing you have done, so sustained, so closely woven, so inevitable, so living! I am lost in admiration. Except, perhaps, for our beloved Henry, I think you are head and shoulders above any other writer of fiction of the present day in English [...] You will be overwhelmed with congratulations, of course, but I am not going to make any pretty minauderies about your not caring for my humble opinion. On this one subject (and possibly embroidery) I know what I'm talking about."[38] His point in the sentence containing the obsolete French word "minauderies" was that she was not allowed to brush away his praise by declaring it pretentious.

Edith's descriptions of Sturgis are filled with some seriously quirky details: He refused to wire his home for electric lighting—thus the lamps being brought in as the afternoon light dimmed—and he would not hear of having a telephone nor central heating installed. By the time Edith had become a regular visitor to his home, he had published several novels, the last of which received unenthusiastic reviews. James had panned his work, which hurt the younger man so much, he decided he would never publish anything again, and would spend the rest of his life knitting and embroidering. As Edith was describing this eccentric character, a wistful tone crept into her memoir, which makes sense because she was traveling along the spine of her past to extract her memories nearly three decades after the fact, and was writing the narrative after both Sturgis and James were dead, and after Lubbock had turned against her. It must have been poignant to be remembering the earlier times when each of the men were sounding boards who helped her hone her debating skills.

Two of them were responsible for the clear picture we have of her entrée into the brave new conceptual world: Lapsley, who would be Edith's American literary executor, asked Lubbock to record his impressions of her in a collection of essays that were published in the book *Portrait of Edith Wharton* after she died. Lewis said the choice of Lubbock for the project was profoundly puzzling because he and Edith had experienced a falling out in 1933, four years before she passed. The biographer felt Lubbock's anger over the breach in their relationship tainted the narrative with a subtle malice toward her. I was able to forgive Lubbock for his spitefulness because he shed light on Edith's love of bantering as she joined them. "She came, let us put it in a word, for talk—for more talk with more people, and with people as fearless of talk, as familiar with it, as dependent upon it, as herself," he wrote.[39]

Lubbock said Edith had a gift for the most stimulating conversation he had ever heard, attributing her talent for talk to the combination of her feminine consciousness and masculine mind. "More than one of her friends have already noted, without surprise, that she preferred the company of men; and indeed there were some obvious reasons why she should," he added. "She liked to be surrounded by the suit of an attentive court, and she liked to be talked to as a man; and both likings were gratified in a world of men and talk. And there was another reason too, not quite so obvious. The friendships that will go far and last long with a little impersonal dryness in them, the salt of independence, were those in which she was happy, and it was mainly with men that she found them." Lubbock then claimed Edith felt safer with men because personal relationships with women required a closeness she avoided. When he added that Edith "instinctively shrank from intimacy," I could see why Lewis felt Lubbock's sketches of her were tinged with innuendo.[40]

Interestingly enough, I think Edith would have agreed with him—in "Life and I" she was clear that she had always veered toward masculine energy and away from women. "This devastating passion [making up] grew on me to such an extent that my parents became alarmed and called in the aid of toys and playmates to distract me," she wrote. "But the only toys I cared for were animals, and the only playmates little boys. Dolls and little girls, I frankly despised, though I tried to be 'polite' when their company was forced upon me."[41] Since that early time, Edith had been subconsciously refining her choices of the masculine psyches she would draw around her. As she aged, she would limit her male relationships to the men she deemed the most learned and the most satisfying conversationalists. In the chapter of her memoir dedicated to James, she explained that her thrill in lively bantering stemmed from years of intellectual solitude that had made her super sensitive to the joys of intense discussions. "The real marriage of true minds is for any two people to possess a sense of humor or irony pitched in exactly the same key, so that their joint glances at any subject cross like inter-arching search-lights," she said of her experiences with the older author.[42]

Given her closeness with Berry, it surprised me that she claimed James was the most intimate friend she ever had. She said the letters from James, which I feel privileged to have touched, only hinted at his in-person charm. "The talk that, to his closest friends, when his health and the surrounding conditions were favorable, poured out in a series of images so vivid and an appreciation so penetrating, the whole sunned over by irony, sympathy and wide-flashing fun, that those who heard him at his best will probably agree in saying of him what he once said to me of [the French novelist] Paul Bourget: 'He was the first, easily, of all the talkers I ever encountered,'" she explained.[43] Edith said James was at his best when he was with the Qu'Acre set because when all of them were gathered around him "his free and rapid give-and-take of ideas animated his mind, which so easily drooped in dull company."[44]

I saw how respectful Edith and James were in their letters —his written in a chaotic scrawl in a very black ink, hers more refined and delicate. He addressed her as "Dear and admirable confrère [fellow writer]" or "Dearest Edith" and she most often began her letters with "Cher Maître," a French sentiment meaning 'Dear Master.' In one of his chatty moments, James told her, "you will see what I mean—being about the only person who ever does." Though the letters she wrote to James prove she adored him, her feelings about him as an author were not so effusive. Answering a letter from William Crary Brownell, a senior literary consultant with publisher Charles Scribner's Sons who made decisions as to whether to accept her work or not, she pushed back on the idea she was influenced by James' narratives. Brownell had shared with her some reviews for her book *The Descent of Man and Other Stories* in which one of the critics declared she had borrowed characters from James' novels.

She told Brownell she esteemed James as a man but she couldn't bear to read his work so there was no way she could have copied material from his books. Also breaking with Jamesian authority, she tried to convince Sturgis to continue to reach for his own publishing dreams in spite of the older author's feedback. "He was unduly distressed by Henry James's criticism, and it was in vain that I pointed out how foolish it was to be discouraged by the opinion of a novelist who could no longer judge impartially any novel not built according to his own theories," she wrote.[45] She told Sturgis the only reason James was disapproving was because he was blindly invested in his own formulaic way of planning out his fiction, which she felt weakened James' work. That she could be so honest with her "jolliest of comrades," as she called the intelligent beings who gathered at Queen's Acres, reveals how confident she had grown with this tightknit circle.

The forcefulness she was embracing was seeping into her marriage, which increased the tension between her and Teddy, and must have made her entrapment with her husband all the more painful. James was one of her friends who didn't understand Edith's relationship with Teddy, calling it "an almost—or rather utterly—inconceivable thing."[46] As close as she was to James, I couldn't help but wonder if she had ever told him she had been forced into the match and that it had been wearing her down for decades. Judy

Simons presented evidence of the depth of the couple's incompatibility in her book *Diaries and Letters of Literary Women from Fanny Burney to Virginia Woolf*. The author claimed when Teddy was near, his presence stifled Edith to the point she confessed to hearing "the key turn in the prison lock," a clink that brought on emotions she could hardly bear.[47]

Teddy, who was isolated in an emotional jail cell of his own, one that would prove to be mentally debilitating, exposed how mismatched he was when he wrote to Sara (Sally) Norton about his pride in outfitting his wife's car so that she would have every physical comfort. He told Edith's friend it was one of the few things he felt equipped to offer his wife. In the letter, which was filed with Edith's papers, he declared he was "no good on Puss's high plain of thought." Edith never directly disparaged her husband in *A Backward Glance* nor in "Life and I," relating only that over time he became increasingly depressed and ill. But she was honest about what a burden he eventually became in her letters. The year after Teddy had written to Sally Norton, Edith told her friend her husband, who was fifty-eight at the time, had originally been diagnosed with neurasthenia, which includes symptoms like lassitude, fatigue, headache, and irritability brought on by an emotional disturbance. She then said his doctors had recently decided his distress was caused by gout in his head.[48]

By the time Teddy was spiraling down, Edith was determined to spend the society seasons in Paris because she wanted her work to reach a French audience and she knew that being "on the scene" was the fastest way to make that happen. She rented an apartment at 58 rue de Varenne for three years so she could be in the thick of the action. Though her accounts of those early months when she began to make Paris her European home depicted a vibrant existence, her husband was so miserable about being in the French capital, a push/pull developed between them that escalated as Teddy's resistance to living there grew more intense. He resented the fact that Edith chose to spend her time flitting between a number of salons, holding high-minded gatherings in their drawing rooms, and attending plays and operas accompanied by friends with whom he had nothing in common. Also likely contributing to Teddy's aversion to being there was a sudden increase in Edith's coolness toward him after she had become attracted to another man in the fall of 1907, a tryst that began organically as Edith strategized how to achieve higher book sales in France.

THE EXTRAMARITAL FLING didn't become physical until things had grown so strained with Teddy he decided to sail for America in mid-March of 1908 to go to Hot Springs, Arkansas, for treatment. With her husband out of the way, Edith gave full-rein to her romantic notions about William Morton Fullerton, an ex-pat who was one of the Paris-based newspaper reporters for London's *The Times*. Without revealing the true nature of their relationship, she wrote to Sally that she found Fullerton "very intelligent but slightly mysterious."[49] I wondered if Edith was surreptitiously fishing for other tidbits about the reporter since Sally's father Charles, the generous man who had sent Edith books about Italy, had been Fullerton's professor at Harvard. Before landing in Paris, Fullerton had lived in London where he had a protracted dalliance with Margaret Brooke, the Ranee of Sarawak; and had befriended Oscar Wilde and Henry James, the latter a serendipitous connection that made it easier for Edith to draw Fullerton in.

By the time Edith met him, Fullerton had been in Paris

for more than a decade and he had a thorough knowledge of how the press operated there. Their relationship crystalized because she was eager to see her writing publicized in France. Edith's first letter to Fullerton was sent from Paris in the Spring of 1907, a little less than a year before their physical intimacy would blossom. As the French translation of *The House of Mirth* was underway, she asked him for his thoughts about possible media coverage. He successfully advised her over a span of several months during which a spark developed. Once the relationship was consummated, Edith managed their assignations with care, orchestrating their times together in order to minimize any suspicions. She beckoned him to the Louvre, at one o'clock, in the shadow of Jean Goujon's sculpture the *Fountain of Diana*; to the Invalides station at 7 p.m., inside the station so that Cook, her chauffeur, would not see them; and to the Luxembourg Gardens where they would sit for hours in a quiet corner under a tree.

Each of these meetings was spelled out in letters to him, which she would eventually regret having sent. Joining scores of women throughout history who became so distracted by the first throes of passion, Edith wasn't thinking about the fact that her intimate revelations could eventually be discovered. She was so smitten, she admitted she was almost beside herself in the excitement of her love. On several occasions, James was present when Fullerton and Edith were together, and he mentioned the reporter's liaisons with her in a few of his letters filed in his folder at Yale. The fact that she saved these was puzzling to me given she had deemed privacy so important she went to great lengths to obliterate a large cache of correspondence written to and by her. Edith destroyed most of James' letters to her, and in 1915, he burned so many letters to him, including hers, one of Edith's biographers described the event as a "bonfire" in the garden of Lamb House. After Berry's death, Edith collected her letters to him and torched many of them in what Lewis described as "a ritual burning of the lot."[50]

I was most surprised that she felt the need to destroy Berry's correspondence because I would have thought the absence of a romantic attachment and his importance to her writing life would have made the letters to and from him worth saving. Also enlisted to set fire to letters was Elisina Tyler, a very close friend of Edith's, and the executrix of her French will and estate. As Edith lay helpless near the end of her life, she told Tyler to do away with all of Teddy's letters to her, a command she promptly obeyed. Edith took a match to the correspondence Fullerton had sent her and would have made kindling of hers to him if she'd had the chance. As their relationship faltered, she begged him to "cremate" them for her; and when she knew for certain the affair was over, she pressed him time and again to mail them to her apartment in Paris so she could be certain they were eliminated—requests he ignored. My confusion over her contradictory behavior around privacy deepened when I found a love diary she wrote titled "The Life Apart," which I didn't know existed when I went through her papers at Beinecke.

The manuscript, housed in the Lilly Library at the University of Indiana, chronicled the early months of the Fullerton affair, from October 29, 1907, to June 12, 1908. The first three epistolary entries were made by a subdued woman who had never known what it meant to be romantically awakened. By the fourth letter, she turns giddy as a delicious surge of sensuality takes hold. Edith never named the recipient of these outpourings, an element of subterfuge that she would continue in both the published and unpublished versions of her memoirs because she was determined to obliterate Fullerton from her life story by the time she wrote them. These evasions might have held if her correspondence to the journalist hadn't surfaced during the 1980s—the 300 letters now housed in the Harry Ransom Center at The University of Texas at Austin. The reticence Edith maintained puzzled many of her biographers until these letters appeared, their belief before the truth came out that she had written the diary to Berry.

Erlich hinted that Edith could have intentionally manufactured the ruse. "Although she did indeed have a great love for Berry," the author wrote, "she may well have publicized that fact in her memoir *A Backward Glance* as a red herring to throw people off Fullerton's scent."[51] I don't believe Edith was exaggerating her feelings for Berry in order to trick people into thinking he had been her lover, though it is likely she would have been happy for future biographers to be fooled into believing there was no other man she could have glorified in "The Life Apart" than her dear friend. I believe Edith simply told the truth about Berry and left Fullerton out of the picture because she hoped her letters to him would never be found. Why Edith didn't destroy the diary is the most baffling thing about the situation to me, as it exposes how vulnerable she had been and, eventually, how duped she was by a serial cheater. I would pin the survival of "The Life Apart" on Tyler, who had filed the diary away with other items relating to Edith after the author died.

Having the diary archived in a research library ensured that the manuscript would gain notoriety, and Elisina was the only one who could have given it to or told her son Bill where to find it—his role in its survival being he was the one who sold the diary to the Lilly Library. If Edith had wanted it to be included in her papers, I imagine it would have ended up at Yale instead. It was also Elisina who kept another piece of evidence that proves Edith experienced a sexual awakening, though it's not clear whether Edith knew about the proof. Just as revealing as the diary, a letter Fullerton wrote to Elisina said, "Please seize the event, however delicate the problem, to dispel the myth of your heroine's frigidity."[52] This revelation was included with a cache of handwritten notes titled "Les Derniers Mots [The Last Words]" that Elisina recorded with the aim of writing a biography about Edith, though she never organized them into any sort of manuscript. Whether it was Elisina or someone else who saved the diary from being destroyed, the person who made the decision forever transformed Edith from a stiff product of her time seen in the staid images of her throughout her life into a sensuous being.

Edith's declaration of love in "The Life Apart" appears in the fourth letter she wrote, the first entry after her relationship with Fullerton was consummated. "The other night at the theatre, when you came into the box—that little, dim biagnoire (no. 13, I shall always remember!)—I felt for the first time that indescribable current of communication flowing between myself and someone else," she wrote; "felt it, I mean, uninterruptedly, securely, so that it penetrated every sense and every thought...and said to myself: 'This must be what happy women feel.'" She also described a car trip she and Fullerton took when it was snowing, claiming it was then she believed their hearts and minds met. "I felt your dearest side then, the side that is simple and sensitive and true," Edith remembered. "I should like to be to you, friend of my heart, like a touch of wings brushing by you in the darkness, or like the scent of an invisible garden that one passes on an unknown road at night."[53]

Edith wasn't the first to succumb to the combined power of Fullerton's brain and body—Margaret Brooke wrote to him, "Never before have I loved intellectually and with my heart. You are my life companion."[54] Delving into what gave the man who inspired these admissions of passion from two outstanding women such a forceful pull, Marion

Mainwaring approached her book *Mysteries of Paris: The Quest for Morton Fullerton* as a detective would have organized a criminal investigation. Early on, Mainwaring cataloged the number of Fullerton's conquests she was able to uncover—before and after Edith came into his life—which included an array of sexual entanglements with both men and women. One of his most egregious romances was with a girl named Katharine who was raised as his adopted sister when they were growing up. He actually proposed to her and then left her hanging for months on end while she suffered from a keen lovesickness. Fullerton's treatment of Katharine inspired the son of the man she eventually married to call the reporter a con man.

While he held Katharine at bay, Fullerton was romancing Edith, writing her enticing letters that seemed like whispers in her ear. "We are behind the scenes together—*on the hither side*," he told his newest conquest.[55] These were addictive moments of intimacy for such a starved woman who had never before been carnally satisfied. Once awakened, Edith would do everything in her power to keep the dalliance alive but because Fullerton didn't have the bandwidth to satisfy such an emotionally desperate woman, he disappeared for periods of time while Edith remained in an agonized limbo. She must have been so desperate to reel him back in because she knew she would have to return to her former existence, which would sentence her to the loneliness she had endured during the entirety of her marriage. This would likely have weighed on her all the more as she braced herself for her return to Teddy. The night before she sailed for America, Edith gave Fullerton "The Life Apart" diary to read. He returned it to her on the train as they trundled toward their parting the next morning.

Once she had boarded the ship for the transatlantic crossing, she noticed he had scribbled his thoughts in it, which she abruptly removed as the ship moved west. Edith experienced a frenetic creative burst while sailing to America, her writing including a dark short story about adultery titled "The Choice." The entanglement in the tale comes to life when the protagonist Isabelle Stilling is listening as her husband Cobham banters with dinner guests he is escorting to their carriages. Isabelle is alone in the room with her lover Austin Wrayford as the story begins: "By a common impulse Mrs. Stilling and Wrayford had moved together toward the fireplace, which was hidden by a tall screen from the door into the hall. Wrayford leaned his elbow against the mantle-piece, and Mrs. Stilling stood beside him, her clasped hands hanging down before her." The fictional couple planned their next encounter and drifted apart as they heard Isabelle's husband shouting his final farewells.[56]

Their rendezvous later that evening takes place in a boathouse that Cobham had recently built. The pleasant odor of pine that Wrayford usually breathed in as he entered was overpowered by the rancid smell of oil spilling from a can he'd just kicked over. Isabelle comes in and the two lovers sit on a bench to discuss her husband's erratic behavior with money. Wrayford tells her she was mad to make Cobham her trustee because her husband had financially ruined his own mother. Isabelle's gasp was timed perfectly with the sound of the boathouse door opening, her husband's entrance shunting them into chaos as he plunges into the deep water below. As Cobham splashes around in the dredged-out hollow in the lake, Wrayford rushes over and falls into the water. Isabelle, who grabs one of the oars affixed to the wall and submerges it in the lake, saves her husband. Panic ensues as she flings herself down again, "straining over the pit. Not a sound came up from it. 'Austin! Austin! Quick! Another oar!' she shrieked."[57]

Isabelle's husband shouted, "My God! Was it Austin?

What in the hell—another oar? No, no; untie the skiff, I tell you. But it's no use. Nothing's any use. I felt him lose hold as I came up." The narrative closes hours later as Isabelle surfaces from a state of shock to hear her husband say he wished "old Austin" could have known he had been saved.[58] Edith's biographer Hermione Lee sees Cobham as the closest fictional version of Teddy that Edith ever wrote, down to the fact he was known to speculate with Edith's money, which Teddy could access as a trustee of her estate.[59] Given "The Choice" paints her husband in such a disparaging light and echoes her own feelings of loss as Edith is parting from her lover, she must have been bleak even before a depressing reentry with Teddy in the spring of 1908. An excerpt from her next-to-the-last diary entry in "The Life Apart," written just after she'd arrived at The Mount, confirms how painful their reunion was. "I have stood it [the emotional isolation] all these years, and hardly felt it, because I had created a world of my own, in which I lived without heeding what went on outside," Edith wrote. "But since I have known what it was to have someone enter into that world and live there with me, the mortal solitude I came back to has become terrible."[60]

A week later, she wrote in a letter to Fullerton, "I vowed I wouldn't write you again until I had overcome my black mood—& thereupon set to work to overcome it, *in order to write you*. [...] I really am better today, but yesterday, in my despair, I very nearly cabled you the one word: Inconsolable. Luckily, I bethought me in time that you might feel impelled to answer, & as our telegrams are all telephoned from the village—*si figuri!!* [imagine!!]"[61] Two days later, she penned the last entry in "The Life Apart," which began with, "I have not written again in this book because I have written to you instead, my own dear Love, answering the letters you have sent me by every steamer."[62] You can hear the heartbreak as

Edith confesses the atmosphere at The Mount was so depressing she could hardly breathe, and that Fullerton's letter of the day before had left her even more despondent.

"I learned from it that you will certainly not come here till the autumn, & that all your future is in doubt," she wrote. "You don't even know where you will be next winter—at the ends of the Earth, perhaps! Leagues beyond leagues of distance seems to have widened between us since I read that letter—all hope forsook me, & I sent you back a desperate word: 'Don't write to me again! Let me face at once the fact *that it is over*. Without a date to look to, I can't bear to go on, & it will be easier to make the break now, voluntarily, than to see it slowly, agonizingly made by time & circumstance.'" The end of Edith's tortured acknowledgement is a mournful one: "Oh, my adored, my own Love, you who have given me the only moments of real life I have ever known, how am I to face the long hours and days before I learn again the old hard lesson of 'how existence may be cherished, strengthened and fed, without the aid of joy?'"[63]

She told him she knew how to live unsatisfied for many years until she met him but he had kissed away her ability to tolerate tedium. "I have had my hour, and I am grateful for it," she said, "but the human heart is insatiable, and I didn't know, my own I didn't know!"[64] Coming full circle from her admission in the diary that she realized what happy women feel, Edith said she had come to understand what heartbroken women feel. Rather than draw Fullerton closer, Edith's painful admissions sent him fleeing and he fell completely silent for much of the rest of her time at The Mount, which Edith said "entombed" and "suffocated" her as she remained trapped there until early 1909. The reference to asphyxiation is so revealing because Edith was inflicted with serious bouts of asthma, which began early in her marriage and continued throughout her adult life. The tone in the diary signaled that the affair could have been over, but there was more to come, though not until Edith had struggled for months to make sense of Fullerton's inevitable disappearances.

"The affair began again, in Paris, at the start of 1909," Hermione Lee wrote. "But everything was different: she had lost confidence."[65] After the sexual tension resumed, Edith and Fullerton became embroiled in an emotional fencing game that lasted throughout the early months of the year—every time Edith would advance, Fullerton retreated and vice versa. The power struggle didn't end until they spent several days together during the summer of 1909, which culminated in an evening at the Charing Cross Hotel in London. R.W.B. Lewis said the assignation was spelled out in a note Fullerton wrote on a copy of the poem Edith penned to commemorate the passionate encounter. "As he was leaving the suite," the biographer wrote, "Fullerton looked back to see Edith, propped up in bed with a writing board across her knees, scribbling the first words of a poem—typically (and it was a sign of her authenticity as an artist) she began to make a literary transcription of the adventure almost before it was over."[66]

Edith titled the poem "Terminus" because the sensuality contained in it had taken place in a station hotel and because they were there to part as Fullerton sailed for America. The opening lines make it clear she was feeling sexually gratified: "Wonderful were the long secret nights you gave me, my Lover, / Palm to palm, breast to breast in the gloom."[67] During Fullerton's trip to the States, Edith had to bide her time in England for several months in a very anxious mood as her lover evaded questions about his plans. When he finally returned, they spent the night at James' before the three of them embarked on a trip around England in Edith's car. Word was beginning to circulate that Edith was romantically involved with someone. When Sturgis learned of her infatuation, he urged her, "Keep it up—run your race—fly your flight—live your romances—drain the cup of pleasure to the dregs."[68]

It was during this dizzying time filled with romantic highs and dark lows brought on by Fullerton's protracted silences when Teddy reappeared in Paris in the fall of 1909, seriously ill and seething with resentment toward his wife. His absence until then had shown Edith how much she enjoyed her time in the French capital without Teddy's depression weighing her down, which inspired her to look for a permanent home there. She enlisted her brother Harry for help and he found an apartment at 53 rue de Varenne, which was a few doors down on the opposite side of the street from the first flat she had rented. Once Edith moved into it in early 1910, it would be her Parisian home for many years. During one of my sojourns to Paris, I strode along the ribbon of sidewalk running the entire length of the narrow lane with its black iron bollards rising from the ground to protect the buildings hemming the street. It was January 24th, the 153rd anniversary of Edith's birth, and the rain had turned the cobblestones to muted mirrors of damp light as I stood in front of the stately dark-green door she would have entered countless times.

THE WEATHER COULDN'T HAVE BEEN A BETTER fit to capture the mood that would have prevailed when Teddy showed up. Soon after his arrival in January of 1910, he admitted to Edith he had embezzled $50,000 from her trust fund and had used most of the money to buy a property in Boston where he had installed his mistress. He lost the rest of it in risky investments. How apropos this anecdote makes Lee's claim that Teddy had inspired Cobham Stilling's character in "The Choice!" Edith had just turned forty-eight and she was struggling on several fronts: She was overwhelmed with Teddy's histrionics and was enduring one of the most painful phases of her affair with Fullerton. As if this wasn't enough, she had been in the apartment at 53 rue de Varenne for less than a few weeks when the streets in Paris disappeared under a deluge of water pouring into the city from tunnels, sewers, and drains during an event now called the Great Flood.

Though her spot in the Faubourg Saint-Germain neighborhood would remain one of the few patches of dry ground in town, she must have anxiously watched as the waters reached their maximum height, the inundation eerily in sync with the fact she was being emotionally swamped by her sick husband's instability. Months would pass before she was able to resolve this particular stalemate with Teddy, a letter to her friend Bessy Lodge in June illustrating how bad it was. Edith said he was keeping her from furthering the fiction she was determined to finish because she kept putting it aside as she bent over backwards to try and figure out what would help him. For the entire first half of 1910, her sacrifice was a waste because Teddy remained frozen and miserable, vacillating between the ideas of traveling and staying put. Edith finally convinced him to seek help in a sanatorium in Switzerland, though he was there only a week when he began demanding to be released—to no avail.

Without Teddy's tantrums consuming so much energy, things were calmer and Edith was reunited with Berry in July. Newly resigned from his position as one of the Judges of the International Tribunal at Cairo, Berry wanted to live in Paris if he could find interesting work. Before long, he was chosen to be the president of the Parisian chapter of the American Chamber of Commerce and he moved into Edith's guest suite while he searched for an apartment. During this beneficial time, Edith shared a memory as to how her friend was once again involved in her creative process. Each evening, she would read aloud to him her morning's work on her novella *Ethan Frome*, analyzing the piece, page by page, to glean his reactions. With Berry's help she made such steady progress on the story, she was in good spirits and felt her "lost balance" had been restored by the time the year 1911 dawned. When she received the proofs for *Ethan Frome* in April, she said she was in a "state of fatuous satisfaction," a sense of gratification she carried with her when she sailed for The Mount on June 24th.[69] She spent a cheerful week in Lenox with James, Smith, and Lapsley—all of whom were in America for various reasons—and braced herself for her husband's arrival. Teddy had been on a "round-the-world voyage" after leaving the sanatorium in hopes the travel would serve him better than treatment had.

In the end, the excursions were about as useless as the doctors' efforts to improve his health because he was half-heartedly involved in both. He returned home an emotional wreck and began to berate his wife because he believed she was trying to extricate him from her life. The rows grew so stormy, an exasperated Edith wrote Teddy a letter and had it delivered to his room. "As nothing I have done seems to satisfy you for more than a few hours," she wrote, "I now think it is best to accede to your often-repeated suggestions that we should live apart."[70] After several days of bickering, Teddy came to Edith's room on the night of July 22nd and apologized for his conduct. Thinking things were going to calm down, she wrote a letter to Teddy's older brother Billy the next morning so he could serve as a witness to the agreement she and Teddy had reached if she needed an ally. The situation took an about-face before she could mail it so Edith wrote a second letter telling Billy his brother's behavior was seriously erratic.

"When I wrote you the enclosed letter yesterday I thought that Teddy had reached a normal state of mind, & that I had at last succeeded in disposing of the numerous difficulties which he is in the habit of raising whenever I attempt to arrive at some kind of definite plan of life with him," she wrote. She then told her brother-in-law the vehemence in Teddy's tone and the bitterness he lobbed at her, which she called "charges of cruelty, meanness and vindictiveness," had increased so much that brutal scenes were taking place daily. She ended, "I nearly made up my mind to take him at his word & agree to a separation."[71] Edith didn't escape the depressing atmosphere until early September when she sailed for Europe. She left Teddy in charge of the estate with vague plans that they might sell it, though she told Fullerton she had made her husband promise to not finalize anything until she had reached Paris because she wanted to know any conditions before a decision was made.

Teddy did not do as she asked; he sold The Mount while she was at sea. When she reached Paris and found out about her husband's betrayal, her letters to family and friends were furious. She wrote to Fullerton how much it exasperated her that Teddy was so pleased with himself and how he made no mention of the agreement they had reached. Her nerves frayed, she decided to take a spa break on her way to Florence in late September, stopping in Salsomaggiore Terme near Parma, a town known for its warm saline waters. The tenor of her letters reveals a woman who is so frustrated she is far from relaxing into better health, her complaints about the situation she was enduring tantamount. "The present makeshift existence is utterly destructive to any sustained imaginative work, which must be *á l'abri* [outside] of nagging & fault-finding, & of great unexpected shocks, such as I am perpetually getting," she told Fullerton. "I *try* to stiffen myself against this, but I can't. If I didn't feel the irresistible 'call' to write I should give up the last struggle for an individual existence, & turn into a nurse & *dame de compagnie* for Teddy, because after all my experiments & efforts, I have found no solution to the problem between doing this & breaking altogether."[72]

After her time in the spa town, Edith traveled to Villa I Tatti in Florence where she and Berry would be the house guests of Bernard Berenson and his wife Mary. Berenson, a respected scholar who was seen as the greatest living expert on Italian Renaissance painting during his day, would steadily become an important male figure in Edith's life. She had known him socially since 1909 but it was during this trip when their friendship was cemented. Edith, who raved about the library at I Tatti, calling it a "book-worm's haven," would return to the villa many times in the coming years. As she began to fill her life with calmer companions and to satisfy her desire to travel more broadly during 1911 and 1912, Edith began to relegate Teddy's dark behavior to the sidelines of her life and initiated the process of divorcing him.

On March, 23, 1913, Edith wrote to Lapsley that the papers had been filed, "But don't say a word to anyone, as the decree can't be pronounced till the courts sit again next week. I feel as if Pelion & Ossa [two mountains in northern Greece] had been lifted off me, & now at last know how tired I am!"[73] Without a husband endlessly carping at her, Edith began to recover her equilibrium as she visited some of the world's most exotic locales during the last half of 1913 and early 1914. She took an excursion to North Africa during which she stopped in Algeria and Tunisia, which was followed by a three-week stint traveling through Spain with Berry. In a letter from Burgos, on July 26, 1914, Edith wrote to Berenson that the international news in the morning paper there was "pretty black."[74] Edith and Berry departed from Spain soon after and by the time they reached Paris, things were dark indeed. Impending doom was on everyone's mind as it was clear a great war was about to swallow all normalcies of life.

EDITH'S ACTIVITIES during World War I were extensive and, though impressive, not relevant to my theme so I will pick up her story after she had navigated the emotional anxiety by immersing herself in a number of relief efforts—her dogged determination to assist refugees keeping her in Europe during most of the war. Once Armistice Day was declared and it was certain the end of the conflict had come, she found herself longing for a change of scenery. When she wrote about her decision to leave Paris and purchase a home in the nearby suburbs in late 1918, the toll the four years of stress had taken was apparent. "My chief feeling, I confess, was that I was tired—oh, so tired!" she wrote. "I wanted first of all, and beyond all, to get away from Paris, away from streets and houses altogether and for always, into the country, or at least the near-country of a Paris suburb."[75] The villages north of the city had been in the direct line of the German advance so there were many properties that had been abandoned and were for sale. Elisina had been searching for a home she felt would suit Edith, which she found in Saint-Brice-sous-Forêt.

"I saw the house, and fell in love with it in spite of its dirt and squalor," Edith wrote. "At last I was to have a garden again—and a big old kitchen garden as well, planted with ancient pear and apple trees, espaliered and in cordon, and an old pool full of fat old gold-fish; and silence and rest under big trees! It was Saint Martin's summer after the long storm."[76] Edith eagerly launched into turning the residence into a home, deciding she would name the house Le Pavillon

Colombe after a woman who had lived in the villa during the late eighteenth century. The comedic actress who had adopted the stage-name Mademoiselle Colombe must have piqued Edith's sense of whimsy for her to have given the performer such an honor! While Edith's new home was being transformed by the architects and landscape gardeners she hired, she decided to get away to the South of France to rest, inviting her favorite post-war traveling companion and Qu'Acre stalwart Robert Norton to accompany her to Hyères.

As they were picnicking on the beach one day, she noticed a sprawling house that was abandoned. Given it was on the site of a former seventeenth-century convent and was built into the ruined walls of a medieval castle, the fortress-like building intrigued her. In April 1919, Edith took a long lease on the property that looked out over the ocean, and began upgrading the downtrodden building as she planned new gardens to surround it. She named it the Château Sainte Claire and when the renovations were finished, it would be her winter residence from then on. Given how much Edith enjoyed creating luxurious homes, she must have been in heaven—not only did she have a classical villa and garden to plan in Ste. Brice, she had a coastal one on the Mediterranean in Hyères that demanded altogether different plantings than she had ever considered for a garden. Edith had known she wanted to leave Paris since before the war ended, and the satisfaction she felt from having two substantial properties to transform helped her see it was time to leave the apartment behind.

As she prepared to vacate the flat on rue de Varenne, she spent several weeks in the city choosing which pieces of furniture would go to Hyères, which would go to Ste. Brice, and which would be put into storage. While she was sorting out her belongings, Berry told her he was planning to move and he was looking for a new place to live so she transferred the lease to him. Like the director of a symphony, she oversaw the rehabilitation of the two residences while she was creating a crazy number of fictive pieces. There was an added urgency to her output that had never been a necessity until then because her literary earnings had plummeted during the war. It was the first time in her adult life she wasn't able to fully sustain her sumptuous lifestyle with the money she made as a writer. Fortunately, she had savings she could dip into and her next novel would be one of the most financially successful works she ever published. "I found a momentary escape in going back to my childish memories of a long-vanished America, and wrote 'The Age of Innocence,'" she explained. "I showed it chapter by chapter to Walter Berry; and when he finished reading it, he said: 'Yes; it's good. But of course you and I are the only people who will ever read it. We are the last people who can remember New York and Newport as they were then, and nobody else will be interested.'"[77]

Edith, who said she secretly agreed with him, relished the fact that the book proved them both wrong and became one of her bestsellers. In her "Gist of Me" diary, which I found in a folder at Yale, an entry in 1919 revealed how she was trying to decide not only the title of the novel but the name of its main male character as she penned the story. She had originally thought she would call the frustrated man who drove the plot of this drama Langdon instead of Newland. In light of the fact that Newland Archer has become such a famous character thanks to the movie, I'd have to say she made the best choice! Many other details were scratched out or penciled in, the notation that it was finished in 1920 scribbled below the date she began it. *Old New York* was the original title, which she would eventually use for a 1924 collection of novellas. I refer to the notebook as the "Gist of

Me" diary because she had written on the inside cover, "If ever I have a biographer, it is in these notes that he will find the gist of me."

She signed her initials and ended the declaration with the date of 1927, several years after she had begun making entries on the succeeding pages. Considering the fact that she made such a pronouncement, it is interesting that the diary held only intermittent fragments of life, as did other notebooks I found in the library. This is not a surprise given the fullness of her life—there was always a piece of fiction to finish and intellectuals to entertain. When the renovations of Le Pavillon Colombe were completed, she sent a volley of letters to her confidants she had not been able to see often during the war, telling them how her new home would be a wonderful gathering place for them all. "We've got such long arrears to make up for," she wrote to Lapsley, "and we're dancing on such a tight-rope and volcano kind of world that the Happy Few must 'get together' whenever they can—and never let go again."[78]

The group of jolly comrades had grown smaller when James passed in 1916 after what Edith described as a "slow and harrowing" illness preceding the stroke that killed him. It would shrink even more when Sturgis died in early 1920 at the age of sixty-five. As the few remaining members of the Qu'Acres continued to gather around her and new young men came into her life to bring her more great talk, her successes as an author picked up steam. By October, *The Age of Innocence* had been serialized in the monthly *Pictorial Review*, and then appeared in book-form to mostly rave reviews in America. Just before Christmas in 1920, she wrote to Berenson that she was close to finishing the renovations in Hyères, inviting him to come. "Meanwhile the heavenly beauty & the heavenly quiet enfold me, & I feel that this really is *Cielo della Quieta* [a peaceful sky] to which the soul aspires after its stormy voyage," she told him. "Please look toward it steadfastly through the social uproar, & come & bask in it in March."[79] Berenson would show up often from that point forward, as would other members of her inner group during this prolific and glorified time for Edith.

As the 1920s unfolded, she penned six novels and an array of short stories, won her Pulitzer Prize, traveled to Yale to receive her honorary doctorate, and was awarded her Légion d'Honneur. Though this was quite a lot to celebrate, Edith had one of the most significant losses of her life near the end of the fruitful decade. On October 12, 1927, her keen grief is laid bare in an entry in her "Gist of Me" diary when Berry passed away: "The love of all my life died today, & I with him." Berry had recently survived a fairly serious stroke and had instructed his attendant Jules not to tell anyone, not even Edith, if he ever had another one. When he had a more devastating one, it triggered a surreptitious back-and-forth between Jules, Edith, Berry's doctor, and Edith's doctor. The foursome communicated in secret to make it seem they were obeying Berry's wishes while the helpless man lay paralyzed for a week, unable to speak or eat.

On October 9th, noticing Berry's gaze flickering toward the telephone, Jules spoke Edith's name and Berry blinked, which sent Jules rushing to call Edith, who had moved to the Hôtel de Crillon to be closer to Berry in case she could see him. She came at once and would be at his bedside for an hour each morning and afternoon for the next three days. "On the eleventh, she sat by him for long minutes, holding him in her arms and murmuring about old times together," Lewis wrote. "Berry pressed her hand faintly at each memory."[80] When Edith's cherished friend died the next morning before she could arrive, she was inconsolable. Given she was one of the people responsible for dealing with the residuals of his life, she found the continued visits to her old apartment after he passed so painful she could hardly bear them. She wrote to Lapsley the day after Berry died, "All my life goes with him. He knew me all through & [would] see no one else but me."

Three days later she wrote to Smith, "The sense of desolation (though of thankfulness, too, of course) is unspeakably increased by those last days together, when he wanted me so close, & held me so fast, that all the old flame & glory came back, in the cold shadow of death & parting."[81] My mind's eye could picture Berry so succinctly when I read this because I had come across a number of photos of him that were pasted into her albums. In a particularly striking one, he is walking with Berenson through the garden surrounding Le Pavillon Colombe. As was customary of their time, the two men are wearing suits with high stiff collars, ties, vests, and tailored jackets as they stroll along a graveled path. Berenson with his bald pate and full white beard is turned slightly toward Berry, who is equally bald and sporting a white mustache. I studied the intimate moment, forever frozen in black-and-white, and wondered if Edith had taken the photo in order to capture the camaraderie shared by two of her favorite men in the tableau she had created.

The notes and drawings describing and depicting her garden plans included in her papers sprung to life in the image of her two friends. The formality of their attire was so out of place surrounded by the urns of billowing roses; the ivy spreading wildly along the ground, clipped only where the tendrils met the allée; and the pots filled with giant hibiscus. I imagined Edith revisiting this photo as she worked on her memoirs given this bit of musing she recorded in it: "The disappearance of one dear friend after another must always be the chief sadness of a life bound up in a few close personal ties. Such losses seem doubly poignant in the brave new world predicted by Aldous Huxley, and already here in its main elements—a world in which so many sources of peace and joy are already dried up that the few remaining have a more piercing sweetness."[82]

Though she continued to sustain a prolific writing life, Edith never fully recovered from the death of Berry. She told Berenson, "For the first time in my life I feel utterly rudderless."[83] While she worked on her last novel of the 1920s, *Hudson River Bracketed*, a catastrophic winter storm struck the Riviera. Dangerously high winds and extremely low temperatures wrecked the gardens surrounding her Hyères villa and froze the pipes in the house. Bits and pieces of trees and shrubs littered the ground, and the ones that remained intact were covered in ice. Faring even worse was her collection of rare tropical plants, which had been obliterated. This devastation that took place around Edith's sixty-seventh birthday in early 1929 left her in shock and brought on a physical collapse that nearly killed her. It would be months before she would have enough stamina to begin to restore the gardens and to finish *Hudson River Bracketed*.

On October 22, 1929, she reached "the end" on the last of more than five-hundred pages and said she thought it was one of her best novels, though the reviews she received were lukewarm. As the 1930s dawned, the physical tryst with Fullerton had been over for nearly two decades and the number of interactions between them were fewer with each passing year. In a letter to him in response to his revelation that he hadn't read any of her books until *Hudson River Bracketed*, a sparring quality took over her end of the exchange. "Cher ami, A thousand thanks for taking the trouble to tell me so many kind things about 'Hudson River,'" she wrote. "Grateful as I am, it is a shock to find that your avoidance of my presence has for so many years extended to my books! I had flattered myself that though you felt only indifference for the old friend, you still followed her through her books—Why have you robbed me of my few remaining illusions?"[84]

EDITH'S OUTPUT was still strong as she entered her seventies—she was working on *The Gods Arrive*, the sequel to *Hudson River Bracketed*, and was penning the autobiography that would become *A Backward Glance*—but a second bout of concern over money left her feeling more distressed than before because it was coupled with a decline in interest for her work. Coming off the most lucrative decade she'd ever had, the dip in her income resulting from the stock market crash in 1929 was precipitous—with fewer pages to fill, magazine editors began rejecting her stories because they felt her writing was overly formal and dated, and they were being told by readers that the serious subjects in her fiction were no longer popular. Rather than giving up, Edith grew more determined and continued to lob short stories at the less-than-enthusiastic American magazine market. It was during this stressful time when she completed the memoir and began a novel titled *The Buccaneers.*

It may seem amazing to the uninitiated that Edith had so much stamina at her age but the pace she maintained was a natural outgrowth of how strong her writing muscle had grown in the three decades she'd been publishing her books. She described the phenomena herself when she told Elisina during her final days that her mind had always been a "steam engine."[85] The lead up to the 1933 holiday season is an example of Edith's tenacity: She was reading proofs of the memoir; sending off a new collection of short stories; working on the next volume of short stories; maintaining a mountain of correspondence; and welcoming Smith,

Lapsley, Robert Norton, Berenson, and others to gather around her to celebrate. She planned a flurry of trips during the next several years because she believed she had to see the places she had always wanted to see and return to those she had enjoyed before her age prevented her from doing so.

"I am possessed of a strange fever to fill up some of the numerous lacunae in my world map before the curtain falls," she wrote before heading off to Rome, Wales, Scotland, and visiting I Tatti a number of times.[86] After an illness that put her to bed for the entire two weeks she spent in Florence with the Berensons, she returned to Le Pavillon Colombe and settled into a quiet routine for the summer and fall months of 1934. It was during this stretch of stillness in Ste. Brice when she struggled to finish *The Buccaneers*, a novel she would ultimately never finalize. It was clear in this "Gist of Me" diary entry on December 10, 1934, that she was having difficulty finding the story's center: "What is writing a novel like? 1. The beginning: a ride through a spring wood. 2. The middle: the Gobi Desert. 3. The end: a night with a lover." She then declared, "I am now in the Gobi Desert."

The final box I had requested on my last day of riffling through her papers was an oversized carton that included her 1921 Pulitzer Prize for *The Age of Innocence*, and her Légion d'Honneur certificate and the proclamation declaring her honorary doctorate from Yale, both of which she was awarded in 1923. As I held these revered artifacts in my hands, I realized something: No matter what past successes an author has had, even ones of consequence, the struggle to compose the next better thing will always relegate a serious writer to an endless expanse of shimmering sand dunes or some other landscape that is equally barren. The angst Edith expressed as she struggled with *The Buccaneers* was not reflected in the final chapters of *A Backward Glance*, which had just been published in late 1934. A calm, plaintive mood is evident in passages like this one: "The visible world is a daily miracle for those who have eyes and ears; and I still warm my hands thankfully at the old fire, though every year it is fed with the dry wood of more old memories."[87] I couldn't help but wonder who flitted through her mind the most when she was writing such pronouncements.

It was the last move her body would physically make on earth, which she had orchestrated, that I feel answers the question. Three days after she died of a stroke on August 11, 1937, she was lowered into the ground in a plot near the grave of Walter Berry. It wasn't a husband or a lover who would be close at hand for eternity; it was the man she had mourned during the last decade of her life. She recorded her decision to rest near him in a letter to Elisina: "I wish to be buried at the Cimetière des Gonards, at Versailles, & have bought there a double plot, as near as possible to Walter Berry's grave."[88] In the same note, Edith told Elisina she wanted several members of her inner group to surround her at the very end, as she had chosen Smith, Lapsley, and Robert Norton to be three of her pallbearers. These younger men continued to spend time with Edith until she was too sick to see them during her final days.

As her life ebbed slowly away, Edith spoke of Berry the most often, telling Elisina how much he had helped her and how much she missed him. Edith also confessed as much to Berenson, writing in a letter to him, "Since Walter's death I've been incurably lonely *inside*." She said her work brought her solace, "But this long vigil alone with all my past wears the nerves thin."[89] I feel the emphasis on the word "inside" is profound given she had declared earlier in her memoir that Berry was an expansion and an interpretation of her very self, a soulmate quality that they had shared since they met in Bar Harbor, which would have been a wrenching loss. Among the letters of Berry's that Edith kept was the one in which he shared his feelings about their initial meeting and his reasoning for not proposing, which was called "The Canoe Letter" in her papers.

Written in his thick cursive on a piece of stationary from the Knickerbocker Club on February 25, 1923, that he mailed to her in Hyères, it read, "Dearest, The real dream—mine—was in the canoe and in the night, afterwards, for I lay awake wondering how I could have wondered—I, a $less lawyer (not even that, yet) with just about enough cash for the canoe and for Rodick's [hotel] bill—and then, later, in the little cottage at Newport, I wondered why I hadn't—for it would all have been good, and then the slices of years slid by." He closed the letter with, "Well, my dear, I've never 'wondered' about anyone else, and there wouldn't be much of me if you were cut out of it. Forty years of it is yours [you?], dear. W."[90] It is difficult to tell whether the word is "yours" or "you" because this admission trails off in a ball of black ink that could have been an r and an s or just an ink blot.

Though letters from others hold similar endearments—Berenson would begin his by addressing her as "Beloved Edith"—she left clues in her papers that there was a depth in her interactions with Berry that felt more profound. I saw one of them when I lifted a piece of beige paper with ragged edges that looked as if it had been wadded up at one time from a folder marked with Berry's name. The shape and color led me to believe it might have been a manila envelope in its better days. On it, Edith had written in thick blue pencil, "Letters from Walter Berry." Below this, she wrote, "Beginning 1900—& covering years of my earliest publications."

By adding the latter, I think she was explaining to those of us delving into the fragments she allowed to survive that her deepest tie to her friend—beyond any romantic feelings she may have experienced in Bar Harbor—was born and cemented during his involvement in her writing process. Having her work seen and respected was always a subtext in her life no matter which man was flowing into or out of it, and I would go so far as to say that her fiction, which streamed from her "masculine mind," as Lubbock deemed it, was a bona fide member of her collective husband. It was, after all, the most flourishing and ever-present force that drove her choices for the relationships she fused into a more fulfilling life partner—while her creativity always came first, her most ardent literary collaborator was next in line.

8

THE FLOWER OF CHIVALRY

KING CHARLES V IN PARIS

I stopped so abruptly the guy behind me had to swerve to keep from crashing into me. "Mon dieu!" he said under his breath, just loudly enough to be sure I heard him. Had I been in New York instead of Paris, the person who nearly rear-ended me wouldn't have been so polite. This is one of the things I admire about the French: Generally speaking, everyone's manners are so refined, even their epithets are smooth. My near-miss came about because my attention was riveted by a pair of decaying doors set within an arched entryway that no longer belonged to a building. The wreck of a thing stood awkwardly at 6 rue Beautreillis in front of a modern apartment building with a crisp white façade, the contrast making the truncated piece of architecture all the more eccentric in its dilapidation. Studying the scared surface of the bricks, the worn patina of the exposed wood, and the spritzes of graffiti, I grew more enamored as the minutes ticked by because the pediment that rose to a point above the entryway proclaimed it was once attached to the Hôtel de Jean-Louis Raoul, which must have been a commanding property when it was new.

Two centuries later, the sunlight emanating through a crack between the two doors hinted at a secret: Were they pushed open, the battered panels would reveal they had nothing to protect. The mysterious feeling this created made me wonder if the phantom portal could usher me into an earlier time than the one in which it was built. After a bit of digging, I learned it could—without even stepping through it, I time-traveled all the way back to the last half of the fourteenth century when a prince who would become the medieval monarch Charles V built a soaring castle complex on the same spot where Raoul had erected his mansion. I came upon the oddity because I was staying a few blocks away in a loft in Le Marais, a bustling Parisian neighborhood dotted with so many architecturally-significant artifacts, the saddest of which is the battered door. Once I learned the history of the plat of land, I decided to circumnavigate the property and the thirteen-block jaunt through the urban enclave was the counter-opposite experience to what I would have had were I strolling through the bucolic setting when the castle was new.

The future Charles V purchased the land and erected the Hôtel Saint-Pol, as the castle was called, just before he became king in 1364. He had already endured a trying four-year term as regent because his father, King John II, had been imprisoned by King Edward III of England. With John's return, Charles was restored to his former title as dauphin and was free to leave the Palais de la Cité, which was the formal residence of the reinstated king. Charles welcomed this change because living within the inner-city was not a pleasant experience at the time. While he'd filled in for his father, he'd longed for a quieter, less foul-smelling environment, which made the strip of land between the Seine and rue Saint-Antoine a perfect fit for him. By the time the complex was completed, the Hôtel Saint-Pol was a collection

THE FLOWER OF CHIVALRY

of buildings that pointed toward the heavens in a mass of turreted glory, each structure connected to the others by a series of galleries. The grounds of the palace held gardens, orchards, and a zoo that housed boars, lions, and exotic birds. Rising from the tract of land today is a tangle of apartment buildings, none of the edifices old enough to date back to that bygone era—or so I thought! When I stood at a corner that would have been enveloped by the wall encircling the Hôtel Saint-Pol, something compelled me to look up.

What I discovered as I followed a piece of masonry to where its profile met the sky was an anomaly. Embedded in the wall at the end of a building at 32 rue Saint-Paul is a handful of random impressions left by the removal of a piece of architecture that I would later learn had once been an exterior wall of an old church. The fragments from the twelfth century were a pair of indentions that had been window openings, a domed niche with the vestiges of a metal fan lodged in it, and several slices of cornices. These and the toothy edge of uneven stones that jutted out from the side of the façade testify to the fact that a massive building had been lopped off and the openings had been cemented over. The rough scrim that was originally built in 1125 predated the Hôtel Saint-Pol compound by nearly two and a half centuries. Because the appendage oozed the medieval moodiness that would have surrounded Charles when he was building the castle during the Middle Ages, it was a thrilling discovery. The structure that was fused to the scraggy masonry is an apartment building from the late nineteenth-century in the neo-Renaissance style that sprang up all over town beginning in the mid-1800s.

Its attachment to the brute expanse guaranteed the survival of the ancient fortification, a fate the Hôtel Saint-Pol would not share. Like many of the world's sovereigns had and would, Charles V used the built world to prove to his people he was a powerful ruler. The fact that his castle is gone strikes at the heart of something that is such a paradox of history: So many elaborate ancient and medieval buildings (at least elaborate for their time) constructed out of resolute stone no longer remain to serve as the legacy pieces the kings and emperors hoped they would be—they exist now only in footnotes of masonry, in fanciful monumental columns erected to honor where they once stood, or in etchings and paintings that attest to their long-gone glory. The evidence that Charles V's royal residence was statuesque exists in a number of illuminated miniatures in the medieval manuscript *Chroniques*, which was composed by Jean Froissart between 1325 and 1400. The immense work by the 'chronicler of chivalry,' as Froissart has been called, includes a painting that shows the turreted castle rising behind Isabeau of Bavaria as she was ferried into Paris in a covered litter in 1389 to marry Charles V's son, the dauphin and future Charles VI.

In the miniature, the porters carrying her are wearing golden laurel wreaths on their heads, are attired in richly colored robes, and are draped in ermine capes. The fanciful scene depicts trumpeters with their horns pointed skyward, the panels dangling from them in a deep royal blue ornamented with shimmering gold fleurs-de-lis. From the sidewalk in front of the loft, I had the exact view the illuminator had as he captured the merriment, which included a court jester perched atop a rampart, his floppy hat and pointy shoes as whimsical as the fool's scepter he held in his hands. Within the castle's walls in the miniature, a patch of grass spreads out toward the cluster of buildings, calling to mind Christine de Pizan's claim that Charles V enjoyed strolling through the grounds of his extensive compound. As his earliest biographer, she shared anecdotes about his daily life in her memoir of him, *The Book of the Deeds and Good*

Character of King Charles V the Wise, which was published in 1404. In the summertime when he was staying at the Hôtel Saint-Pol, Christine watched as the king meandered through the gardens with the queen and their children, stopping to chat with the women of the court to ask after their families.[1]

Once I found Christine's accounts of the era in which Charles V ruled, she led me through the time-traveling portal that once opened into the Hôtel de Jean-Louis Raoul and introduced me to the dynamics at play during the late fourteenth and early fifteenth centuries. I learned that Christine was an educated woman who created some of the most important historical accounts of her time and that her passion for chronicling her era was one she shared with Charles V. Christine had first-hand knowledge of the monarch because she had known him since she was a child. Her father, Tommaso di Benvenuto da Pizzano (known in France as Thomas de Pizan), moved his family from Italy to Paris in 1368 when Christine was four years old. His position as the king's astrologer put his daughter in the monarch's inner circle and provided her with knowledge of his life that she would avidly record.

CHRISTINE DIDN'T PUBLISH any of her work while Charles V was alive because she was in her teens when he died in 1380 and she wouldn't have anything in print until her poetry was published when she was in her mid-twenties. "Her initial poems earned her significant attention, and over the next twenty-five years she produced a wide range of texts in prose and in verse for a number of patrons in a variety of genres," wrote Margaret C. Schaus in her book *Women and Gender in Medieval Europe*. "During this time she was also involved in the production of manuscripts of her works; her skillful use of the institutions of patronage and book production have led modern scholars to designate her the first professional woman of letters in European history."[2] Christine's drive to create a name for herself was more than a mere desire to be known; the deaths of her father and husband had left her as the only source of financial support for her children and her mother by then. Christine's decision to turn to writing and publishing as a way to make a living was an excellent one given her first-hand accounts of a royal regime and her intellectual advantages. Because she was able to read Latin, which was rare for women of the middle class then, she could study ancient texts.

The knowledge she gleaned from these combined with her observances of Charles V's behavior gave her the expertise to compose several important medieval books, one of which was the biography of the king. Christine referred to "the virtues and deeds of that most exalted prince King Charles the Wise" in one of the early chapters of the memoir. In the section titled "What King Charles Said of the Pleasure of Kingship," she backed up her claim that he was unselfish by recounting a conversation the monarch had with one of his knights. When the chevalier exclaimed to his ruler how wonderful it must be to be a king, Charles V told the soldier it was more of a burden than a glory. When the knight pressed the king by pointing out how well-off monarchs were, Charles V responded that the only pleasure he gleaned from his kingship was the power to do good for others.[3] Echoing Christine's level of respect for the monarch, author František Šmahel pointed out that the medieval definition of the word wise as it relates to Charles V is 'careful' or 'prudent.'[4]

Šmahel's book *The Parisian Summit, 1377-78: Emperor Charles IV and King Charles V of France* is filled with brilliantly researched details about Charles V and his uncle, including

THE FLOWER OF CHIVALRY

the fact that the development of the king's library was one of his most important contributions to the Middle Ages. By the time he died, Charles V had amassed an impressive collection of titles with the help of his librarian Gilles Malet. Christine celebrates the partnership between the king and Malet in the section of her biography titled "How King Charles Loved Books, and the Excellent Translations He Commissioned." She wrote, "Let us now speak further of the wisdom of King Charles, the great love he had for study and learning; the truth of this is shown by his collection of important books and his great library where he had all the most outstanding works compiled by great authors, all very well written and richly decorated." Christine said Charles V once asked Malet how many books he owned; his librarian answered fifty-thousand volumes.[5]

"There is no doubt that Christine was familiar with the translations commissioned by Charles V for his library," explained Charity Cannon Willard, the editor of the English edition of Christine's collected writings. "She mentions them both in her biography of the king and in *The Book of Peace*."[6] The titles financed by Charles V were installed in a tower of the Louvre supervised by Malet, who continued to oversee the collection of books within it until he died in 1411. Willard, who claimed the library had only one equal in Europe at the time—the Visconti Library in Pavia—set the scene for those who visited the section of the Louvre dedicated to the collection. "Above the principal room was another where visitors might come to consult the books," she wrote. "Desks and chairs were provided, as well as iron grilles at the windows to keep birds from flying in."[7] I just love how facts like this rip through the synapses of the mind when they appear: To think that valuable books and illuminated manuscripts were taken into a space with no glass on the windows comes as a shock!

Though the openings left the reading room exposed to the whims of the weather, Šmahel described it as an inviting retreat because the king wanted it to be comfortable for those who were eager to study his cherished books. Šmahel goes into even greater detail in his descriptions of the library, saying when Charles V decided to move the books to the Louvre in 1367, he ordered extensive renovations to be carried out on the three highest floors of the tower in the northwest wing of the palace where the library would be situated. "According to the preserved fragments of the construction receipts, the walls on the first [of the three] floor[s] intended for the library were lined with wood imported from Ireland, and the vaulting was covered with cypress wood to warm the room," Šmahel explained. "Although the solid bookcases as well as swivel easels for the books had been brought along with the benches from the former library, craftsmen refurbished them there."[8]

Šmahel described the grilles as brass bars, which he said were put in place to prevent the falcons and other birds from the neighboring aviary from entering the room. He also noted that thirty candelabra and a silver chandelier provided the readers with enough light to illuminate the pages they examined. When Malet compiled a list of books in 1377, three years before Charles V died, the library had around nine-hundred rare volumes on its shelves, which included thirty-two full Bibles; around sixty books by Greek and Arab physicians; and a number of legal, natural science, and astrological manuscripts. From these and other explorations, the king absorbed the prudent behavior that earned him the designation of 'wise.' Charles V's actions were laser focused on ensuring that wisdom would be his legacy: Not only did he personally select the instructive ancient texts and new cutting-edge books he wished to read, he tapped specific university theologians, jurists, and philosophers to translate

THE FLOWER OF CHIVALRY

them into French, choosing the intellectuals for the quality of their education.

ACCURACY WAS important to the king because he was determined to influence the behavior of his officers who carried out his government's activities by sharing with them the ideals of the 'just' and 'good' decision-making he found in the books he admired. One of the main professors he trusted to translate the works for his collection was Nicole Oresme, head of the College of Navarre when the king chose him to expand his library. Oresme would eventually be appointed to hold a succession of important positions that included royal secretary, chaplain, and counsellor to Charles V. The king entrusted Oresme with the translation of the weightiest of Aristotle's works, the three illuminated books of the Greek philosopher's writings he asked Oresme to translate first—*Nicomachean Ethics*, *Politics*, and *Economics*—were such complex undertakings, sixteen years would pass before they were added to the royal library in 1372. The king selected other scholars to convert important texts into French, hand-picking them for their deep knowledge of the subjects they would tackle.

Once the texts were completed and the miniatures that illuminated them were finished, the manuscripts were copied so they could be shared with others seeking knowledge. Consulting the records of the loans from the library, Šmahel said the books were read by a large number of people. "In its time, it was an entirely exceptional collection for which Charles V reserved special areas in his residences," he explained.[9] One of these was Hôtel Saint-Pol where the king kept a smaller library than the one at the Louvre, a detail Šmahel shared in his book that presents a comprehensive account of Charles V's life from the time he was a boy. Though the author doesn't write about Christine in the context of her interactions with the monarch, he often references her works, alludes to her "expert testimony" regarding so many facets of the king's life, and mentions her "unusual passion for the deeds of Charles V."[10] Šmahel does not take Christine to task for leaving such a flattering picture of the monarch as other authors have. Willard defended Christine against those who said she presented an overly idealized account of the king by pointing out the memoir, which the sovereign's youngest brother Philip II the Bold hired Christine to write, was meant to be a celebration of Charles V's life.

Willard said Christine's contribution to history was to "dramatize his personality, his way of life, and, above all, his intellectual vigor."[11] As Christine looked back on the king's reign twenty-four years after he died at the age of forty-four, she paid careful attention to the "intellectual vigor" by sharing the authors and books he preferred over others—along with Aristotle's writings, his favorites were Saint Augustine's *Soliloquies* and *Epitome of Military Science* by the Roman theoretician Flavius Vegetius. Unlike Christine, Charles V could only read Vegetius once the Roman's book was translated into French. Her ability to read the author's original text made her a highly sought-after author when the royal family wanted to use her writerly gifts for a project in 1410. Having seen how expertly Christine had handled the biography of Charles V, John the Fearless, Duke of Burgundy, asked her to write one of her most ambitious works—a reference manual titled *The Book of Deeds of Arms and of Chivalry*. According to Willard, the duke approached Christine about the project because his son-in-law, Charles V's grandson and the future Charles VII, was not the least interested in warfare and did not

THE FLOWER OF CHIVALRY

show any aptitude for knighthood while he was the dauphin.

As the designation 'Fearless' suggests, John was a brazen military man who felt that such a weakling coming to power on the heels of the insane Charles VI, whose reign was plagued with mental breakdowns, would threaten the survival of the kingdom of France. In an attempt to counteract these challenges, he hired Christine to write the guidebook about warfare and knightly behavior so his son-in-law and other aristocrats could study it. Though she excelled at the task, her role in penning the comprehensive manual was widely disputed at first and many of the editions that would be printed over time did not credit her as the author. To set the record straight, Willard went to great lengths to present evidence of Christine's authorship, saying the medieval writer received a substantial amount of money from the royal treasury in May of 1411, a year after she began working on the project. Willard claimed the book quickly achieved a considerable degree of success, which wouldn't likely have been possible in those chauvinistic times if a female's name had been put forth as the author.

"There was an assumption that a woman would not have been capable of writing such a book," Willard explained.[12] The bias continued after Christine was credited as the author of the manuscript because detractors claimed she "pilfered" the works of Vegetius, which Willard claimed was not true because warfare had changed since the Roman's book had been translated into French numerous times over a century, and had even changed significantly after the prior translation had been published in 1380. Christine did cite Vegetius as a reference quite often in her fifteenth-century edition, but her text would have been out of date from the minute it was published had she merely ripped off the ideas previously put forth without adding her own. Willard illustrated this by pointing out the French were using different types of weapons by the time Christine was writing her narrative, which proved her version of the book was penned during the years she worked on the text.[13]

In her prologue to Part 1, Christine opened the book with this self-effacing announcement: "As boldness is essential for great undertakings, and without it nothing should be risked, I think it is proper in this present work to set forth my unworthiness to treat such an exalted matter. I should not have dared even to think about it, but although boldness is blameworthy when it is foolhardy, I should state that I have not been inspired by arrogance or foolish presumption, but rather by true affection and a genuine desire for the welfare of noble men engaging in the profession of arms." Christine noted how prejudiced the Middle Ages were when she wrote, "As this [writing a book about warfare] is unusual for women, who are generally occupied in weaving, spinning, and household duties, I humbly invoke, in speaking of this very high office and noble chivalry, the wise lady Minerva, born in the land of Greece, whom the ancients esteemed highly for her great wisdom."[14] The mention of the goddess of war, who was actually Athena in the Greek panoply and Minerva in Roman mythology, is also illustrative of how steeped in superstition the era was.

Christine cried out to the deity, "Oh Minerva! Goddess of arms and of chivalry, who, by understanding beyond that of other women, did find and initiate among other noble arts and sciences the custom of forging iron and steel." Christine thanked the goddess for inventing the metal that was hammered into the suits of armor the soldiers wore to protect their bodies from the lead pellets and arrows hurdling toward them in battle. She then implored Minerva, "Lady and high goddess, may it not displease you that I, a simple little woman, should undertake at present time to speak of such an elevated office of arms." Interwoven with the concepts Christine gleaned from the most successful military men of her era and the ideas she found in Vegetius's book, the author sourced material written by Marcus Porcius Cato—a Roman soldier, senator, and historian who penned texts on warfare and chivalry during his lifetime, which spanned from 234 to 149 BC. Also known as Cato the Elder, she called him a valiant warrior whose brilliance in planning battles allowed the Romans to enjoy "many a fair victory."

Christine quoted Cato as saying he felt the writings he composed and bound into a book were more important than anything he had ever accomplished personally because "whatever a man may do will endure only for an age, but what is written lasts for the common profit forever, and from it, innumerable men may derive benefit." Christine added, "Thus it is a matter of no small consequence to compose and create a book."[15] The consequential one she penned is filled with comprehensive details that cover not only arms, armor, and battle tactics; it explains the meanings behind the varied banners and coats of arms on display. By the end of the manual, she had gone so granular, she listed the minutia that should be taken as men marched off to war, including the appropriate ingredients to create fodder for horses and the best materials to take for constructing fortifications. "Likewise, there should be a supply of animal horns to repair the crossbows," she wrote, "and of rawhide to cover the machines and other devices so that they cannot be set on fire."

She cautioned any officer who might be reading the narrative in order to prepare himself for advancement to the rank of general to be certain he had gathered enough soldiers to be victorious. "For, as the proverb says: The wall does not make the castle strong without the defense of good men that make it impregnable," she explained. "Furthermore, it should not be forgotten that on the side that is the weakest should be placed the greatest defense, for that is the place where the attack is usually the strongest."[16] If the battle would take place in the winter, Christine advised that two-hundred cartloads of large logs or thousands of small bundles of wood and sixty loads of coal should be on hand when the advance began. She dug deep into the nitty-gritty of the supplies for food preparation, and the types of and poundage of edible stores needed to feed throngs of soldiers.

ONCE THE WEIGHTY book was completed, Christine continued to be absorbed with concerns about how the leaders of her country were disregarding the well-being of the people of France. She seemed to feel a desperation to help the male aristocracy understand what it meant to be compassionate. In her next work, *The Book of Peace*, she cited the fact that once-powerful civilizations like the Roman Empire had "perished through discord," a fate she feared France was on the brink of facing. Willard said this sentiment was being echoed by many other forward-thinking people at the time.[17] "An interesting aspect of Christine's writings about France is that she shared ideas on the salvation of the country—and the need for a prince sufficiently well-educated to deal effectively with the country's problems—with other intellectuals of the day," she explained.[18] In looking at Christine's oeuvre, the progression from introspective sonnets to allegorical poems and educational treatises to activism is clear, the evolution in sync with the transition of French society from the more orderly rule of Charles V to the chaos created during the next three reigns.

These included stints on the throne for Charles VI and the English King Henry V, whose disputed monarchy that

THE FLOWER OF CHIVALRY

lasted a little more than two years began when the future Charles VII was disinherited by his father in favor of Henry, who was the crazy king's son-in-law. By the time Charles VII could take the throne back for France, the country was steeped in civil war. Given Christine was sixteen when Charles V died, was fifty-eight when Charles VII took command of his realms, and was sixty-seven when she died in 1431, she was trying to make a difference during a period that some historians call an age of unmitigated disaster. This must have fueled her determination as a chronographer to encourage men to act with honor and dignity, and to educate them about the proper behavior in war, the latter including how important it is to protect civilians not involved in a conflict. My mind was blown when I read how strongly she presented the need to spare the lives of innocent bystanders if at all possible because I was finalizing this piece as bombs were obliterating the Gaza strip and Russia was cratering Ukrainian cities in early 2024.

Christine's call to action is still being ignored over six-hundred years after she wrote the manual about how to rightly wage war, concepts that were instilled in her by a king she respected and by the writings of his heroes who had advocated for fairness in battle for many centuries by then. I found very few details about what influenced Charles V to develop a passion for these ancient texts and whether they were included in his childhood studies, but Christine made the point he was still in the impressionable years of his youth when he came into power. This is no exaggeration given he was twelve years old when he was knighted and became the Dauphin of France in 1350, was still a teen when he became regent in 1356, and was twenty-six when he was crowned king in 1364. Christine took every opportunity to record for posterity the attitudes she felt made Charles V a visionary, particularly when she could illustrate his insight about being compassionate.

She believed this quality was innate and that it was deepened in his psyche by the attitudes expressed in works like Saint Augustine's "Just War Theory" and by Aristotle's belief that the preparation for war was an excellent chance to "exercise leadership."[19] It was Christine who called Charles V's rule "the flower of chivalry" because of the masterful way he handled the challenges facing his country when he was charged to lead it. That he would be a kind king was not a given—he had every reason to be a cruel leader because he was repeatedly maligned as he came into power. During the twenty years his regency and kingship spanned, he was battling England as the Hundred Years' War ground on, and spent decades trying to fend off the disloyal Parisian politicians who wanted him dead and wanted the monarchy abolished.

CHARLES, his father, and his male siblings were under so much duress while they were in power, Šmahel said they were being moved around like "figures on a chess board." While his father was imprisoned by the British, Charles was attacked in his chambers at the Palais de la Cité and was then detained while his enemies' goons murdered his royal advisers—an event that haunted him for the rest of his life and would exemplify why a popular catch-phrase during the brutal time was, "An eye for an eye, an intrigue for an intrigue."[20] This would begin to change as Charles gained more control, the wisdom he brought to his regency providing a sense of how fair a king he would be. "He did not want the heads of his subjects," Šmahel noted; "he needed their money and perhaps even their hearts. Instead of frantic executions, he renewed the operation of the regularly established court," which the politicians in Paris had been corrupting during the early years of his regency.[21] This strengthening of legal recourse was even more pronounced once Charles was king.

"The new sovereign on the French throne was not a born warrior," Šmahel explained. "His physical ailments, as well as his spiritual disposition, predestined that he take the Scales of Justice in hand rather than the sword, but it would have been impossible without a well-functioning state administration."[22] Because Charles V's focus was stability, he put together a stronger government than France had seen with many previous kings. What set him apart is that his methodology was advancing a judicial philosophy informed by the knowledge he gleaned from the ancient voices he respected rather than merely instituting practical politics. These ideals radiated through him to his "intellectual club," as his translators were known, because he was the one who chose the historical literature that would be written in French and disseminated. "Charles V did not let things take their own course when there was an opportunity to influence them," Šmahel wrote.[23]

This included plans for visits from European dignitaries like his uncle the Holy Roman Emperor Charles IV, who would travel to Paris for a summit with his nephew in 1377. In preparation for the emperor's stay, Charles V was updating the Louvre and the Hôtel Saint-Pol, both of which would host meetings during the diplomatic conference. The king was also finalizing the books he had been instructing his translators to complete because he hoped to impress his esteemed uncle. This is one of many facts Šmahel unearthed in his deep dive into the summit and the years leading up to it. The book is illustrated with historical statuary, ancient maps, and medieval paintings. Stone faces with blank stares and noses chipped away are juxtaposed against illuminated miniatures of dignitaries wearing colorful cloaks and golden crowns. There is a steady flow of reverent expressions, fingers pointing heavenward, and kneeling bodies that represent the artistic enthusiasm for recording royal and religious events during the Middle Ages.

A number of these featured Christine and the lofty figures prominent in her world. Her last composition, produced in 1429, was a series of sixty-one patriotic lyric verses that celebrated one of these larger-than-life legends. Titled "The Poem of Joan of Arc," Christine placed herself within the beautifully illustrated narrative as a vigilant observer and made it clear how grieved she was that the political climate of the day was not what the respectable people in France deserved, herself included. By the time she wrote the poem, she had left the city to take refuge in a convent in Poissy, a town northwest of Paris, because she had been personally threatened by greedy rulers. She entered the convent in 1418 and remained in self-exile there until she died. The first two verses of her epic poem read:

"I, Christine, who have wept for eleven years in a walled abbey where I have lived ever since Charles (how strange this is!) the King's son—dare I say it?—fled in haste
from Paris, I who have lived enclosed there on account of the treachery, now, for the first time, begin to laugh;
"I begin to laugh heartily for joy at the departure of the
wintry season, during which I was wont to live confined to
a dreary cage. But now I shall change my language from one of tears to one of song, because I have found the good season once again…"[24]

After this declaration, Christine's poem expresses relief that a new day has dawned—a metaphor for the fact that Charles VII had regained the throne for France during his

THE FLOWER OF CHIVALRY

coronation a few weeks before she finished the poem. She shared how the new monarch was attempting to right the country with the help of Joan of Arc. As the unbridled celebration in the tenth and eleventh verses below unfold, Christine declares it was Joan who was inspiring the leaders of France to oppose "all wrong deeds," including a formerly disinterested dauphin-turned-king who now sat on the throne:

"Did anyone, then, see anything quite so extraordinary come to pass (something that is well worth noting and remembering in every region), namely, that France (about whom it was said she had been cast down) should see her fortunes change, by divine command, from evil to such great good,

as the result, indeed, of such a miracle that, if the matter were not so well-known and crystal-clear in every aspect, nobody would ever believe it? It is a fact well worth remembering that God should nevertheless have wished (and this is the truth!) to bestow such great blessings on France, through a young virgin."[25]

She urged her countrymen and women to heed the lessons learned, and ended her poetic soliloquy with this verse:

"This poem was completed by Christine in the above mentioned year, 1429, on the last day of July. But I believe that some people will be displeased by its contents, for a person whose head is bowed and whose eyes are heavy cannot look at the light."[26]

Though she celebrates much in the narrative, Christine makes it clear that France was still at risk, and proof of this was an event that took place nearly two years after she wrote the ballad: Joan was burned at the stake in English-controlled Normandy in May of 1431. The fact that Christine's poems like the one honoring this heroine repeat warnings she had been publishing in works for fifteen years, she must have been extremely frustrated to have watched Charles V's "flower of chivalry" wilt and die as France's social fabric was shred anew. In *The Book of Peace*, she forewarned, "No kingdom divided can stand; nor can cities or households divided against their own good endure."[27] She wasn't the only one voicing concern; Nicole Oresme declared the "will of the people" could have far-reaching repercussions in "a socially tense atmosphere."[28] The eerie echoes in the proclamations by two visionary writers and the measured behavior of their chivalrous king make it impossible to ignore how little we have learned from history, though we've had more than enough time to heed their warnings.

9

THE DIMINISHING VIEW OF MADAME VITRIOL

DJUNA BARNES ON PATCHIN PLACE

Djuna Barnes made a masterful move when she parked herself on Patchin Place for the final four decades of her life. The gated cul-de-sac in Manhattan's Greenwich Village drew me to it on a winter morning when the clouds hung dull and gray over the city. Leaving the hubbub of Sixth Avenue's traffic behind, I ducked into the petite neighborhood through the gate, which provided no protection given it leaned half-broken from the brick column supporting it. Moving along the patchwork of cracked flagstones that ran the length of the alley in front of the dilapidated buildings, I felt a strange sensation of being transported back in time. The quiet enclave tucked into a copse of trees has thumbed its nose at progress since Djuna died inside one of its residences in 1982. Her apartment was just across the little alley from the one in which the poet E.E. Cummings lived until he passed in 1962.

Swiveling as I stood in the middle of the decrepit pastiche, an odd double-standard emerged—on one side at number four, a red plaque marked the building where Cummings lived for four decades, preceding Djuna's arrival by twenty years; on the other side at number five, there was no mention of the fact that she had lived there for the same length of time. Beside the entrance to her stairwell, a brick column slathered in dirty pink paint supported the flue that extended just beyond the roofline of the three-story building. It was ornamented with a busted tile depicting a troubadour that must have been elegant when it was new but was a sad testament to the vestiges of time. It was the perfect symbol for this woman who had gone hungry when she was a young professional and might have been homeless at times as an adult had she not connected with a handful of benefactors who would, often begrudgingly, give her stipends and handouts. A few of these were among the elite in literature and art whom Djuna had come to know during her early years in New York City and nearly two decades in Paris.

Given she was in the thick of it during the 1920s and 1930s, which was a celebrated time of cultural vigor in both of these cities, I felt compelled to ask why her letters and the scant pages she left as she struggled to craft a memoir were filled with bitterness and betrayal; why she grew to be such a terrible grouch; why she was steeped in anger as she fended off visitors; and why she turned surly at any suggestion she should be less morbid. It wasn't long before I found an important early ingredient in the toxic tincture Djuna's psyche would concoct: It began with her philandering father, Henry Aaron Budington, who renamed himself Wald Barnes in order to go by his mother Zadel's maiden name, a tack Djuna would take when she adopted the same last name. Henry moved his mistress Fanny, a friend of his mother's, into their home in 1897 when Djuna was five years old. He believed in polygamy and had a slew of children, five with Djuna's mother Elizabeth and four with Fanny.

Zadel, whom Djuna adored, had been supporting her son's large family by maintaining a career as a journalist.

THE DIMINISHING VIEW OF MADAME VITRIOL

When her assignments dwindled in 1912, Wald kicked his original family out of the house to save money, forcing Djuna, her mother, and her brothers to leave the farm in Huntington on Long Island to fend for themselves in New York City. Djuna, who was twenty, went from being a gal on the farm to her family's breadwinner overnight. Life in New York was extremely hard and Djuna passed many days hungry until she established a reputation as a journalist with her grandmother's help. Early on, she took part-time classes at The Art Students League of New York and Pratt Institute to sharpen her drawing skills. This would be the only formal education she ever received because her father had refused to send her and a number of her siblings to school. In spite of this fact, she would write for the most fashionable magazines and for nearly every English-language newspaper in New York, a resume that doesn't include *The New York Times* because she wasn't up to the paper's standards for spelling. Djuna studied at Pratt for less than a year because she ran out of money for tuition but her short time there would serve her well.

The fact that she had perfected her talent for sketching during her course-work allowed her to illustrate her articles, which is one of the reasons the *Brooklyn Daily Eagle* hired her as a lifestyle reporter after she left Pratt in 1913. Phillip Herring and Osías Stutman, who edited her *Collected Poems With Notes Toward the Memoirs*, shared these details from her life in New York in their introduction to the book. Because it had been drilled into her since childhood that the only life worth living was one of an artist, she concentrated her spare time on creative writing in the hope that she would be noticed. As so many determined writers do, she saw journalism as a conduit for survival, and stories, poems, and plays as her chance at immortality. Falling into the rhythm of a writing life I know so well, she built a flourishing freelance career by using articles from each new publication to land loftier assignments. A large portion of the money she earned during these early working years went to supporting her mother and her younger brothers, and to helping pay for Zadel's hospital bills.

With these financial burdens draining funds away as fast as she could earn them, Djuna was forced to live with the rest of her rejected family in the Bronx. This intensified her grudge against her parents and would become a festering splinter she would never be able to fully extricate, even after she had saved enough cash to move into her own apartment in the Village at the age of twenty-one. Djuna would grow savvier during the nine years she perfected her techniques as a lifestyle reporter in New York City. Christine Stansell, who described Djuna in *American Moderns: Bohemian New York and the Creation of a New Century*, said she swaggered around as a "more-or-less open lesbian-about-town in her job as a roving New York journalist, writing hermetic, involuted essays on Village life."[1] Among Djuna's acquaintances at the time were Edmund Wilson, Edna St. Vincent Millay, Eugene O'Neill, and Peggy Guggenheim. Millay and O'Neill were fellow playwrights in her circle, the trio's works produced by The Provincetown Players, a repertory group founded on Cape Cod in 1915 that moved to Greenwich Village in the fall of 1916.

In a sketch she wrote about the experience of attending the salon held by the art patron Mabel Dodge, Djuna described herself as "naïve and exceedingly timid" as she skirted the fringes of the intellectual world she hoped would eventually welcome her.[2] Her journalistic assignments then included interviewing directors, actors, writers, and artists for features that attracted the attention of two New York editors—Burton Rascoe, an associate editor of *McCall's* magazine, and his boss Harry Payne Burton, who oversaw both *McCall's* and *Cosmopolitan*. They would assign her articles that allowed her to travel abroad for the first time, the early pieces for *McCall's* sending her to France in 1921. "So this is Paris!" she declared as she exited the train station Gare Saint-Lazare and began to learn her way around town.[3] She condescendingly took in the swirling artistic attitude that prevailed as she rubbed elbows with a wide array of writers who would go on to be literary greats, including T.S. Eliot, James Joyce, and Ezra Pound. She also orbited in Gertrude Stein's circle, though everything Djuna wrote about her proved how heartily she disliked Stein.

Soon after she arrived in Paris, Djuna moved from a dingy boarding house to the Hôtel D'Angleterre at 44 rue Jacob, a popular stop for American writers who were looking to get their bearings or just passing through town. She recorded her early recollections of the city in an essay originally published in a literary magazine in 1922 and republished in 1974 in a very slim book titled *Vagaries Malicieux: Two Stories by Djuna Barnes*. In the piece, she wrote about leaning out of her window on the rue Jacob as she thought about churches, which spurred her on a journey. "I put on my cloak and went to Notre Dame in the sad, falling twilight, and wandered under the trees," she wrote; "coming upon an old woman selling oranges, I thought how bitter and quick the odor was, and how charmingly unnecessary it was of them to be like that—and on this unnecessity I came into my own."[4] Djuna said the Parisian cathedral left her largely unmoved and described the church as a lonely creature.

"She is not disturbed by those devotees who fall into two classes; those going toward and those coming from faith—she is in the center condition where there is no going and no coming," she wrote. "Perhaps this is why, for me, there was something more possible in the church of Saint-Germain-des-Prés, the oldest church in Paris. It is a place for those who have 'only a little while to stay'—it too is aloof, but it has the aloofness of a woman loved by one dog and many men. And here one takes one's tears, leaving them unshed, to count the thin candles that rise about the feet of the virgin like flowers on fire."[5] Her description stirs fond memories I have of seeing the church's lit bell-tower, glowing in a warm bisque color against the inky sky, as I would leave Café de Flore or Les Deux Magots at night. She must have seen it much the same as I had because she would have taken similar routes after café hopping in the socially vibrant section of town. As her story continues, she described an encounter she had while making the rounds: "Coming from this church one evening I stopped a moment at the café of the 'Deux Magots' and had a glass of wine, while Joyce, James Joyce, author of the suppressed 'Ulysses,' talked of the Greeks." She described the author as someone who droned on about mythology, and who lived in "a sort of accidental aloofness," the latter an apt description of her own behavior.[6]

DURING HER first few months in Paris, Djuna admitted she was experiencing culture shock and was too giddy to write. She also claimed she heartily disliked the city. In his biography *Djuna: The Life and Work of Djuna Barnes*, Phillip Herring said he believed the latter was a circumstance of sheer will because she was "absolutely determined to be unimpressed, to keep her nose in the air, to see her surroundings only as a source for amusing observations."[7] She eventually succumbed to the city's charm, and Paris would become one of her favorite points on the globe from that time forward. She claimed she grew to appreciate it because the atmosphere was so creatively-charged. "It's awfully hard to work in Paris," she would later tell *The*

Greenwich Villager. "Everyone just sits around and says, 'Gosh, isn't it great to be here!'"[8] Djuna left only a handful of attempts to describe how it really felt to be there, the bare-bones sketches meant for her memoirs amounted to a scant thirty-nine pages of material.

Most of it is highly repetitive and filled with negative descriptions of the literati she scorned with a few positive nods for those she could tolerate sprinkled in. She devoted an entire essay to T.S. Eliot, which was vengeful in spite of the fact that he was an important figure in her professional life by the time she penned it. She said he abused her by praise when he called her "a genius with no talent" and insulted her when he wrote how her verses limped. In another essay, she was out to settle a score with Janet Flanner, the Paris correspondent for *The New Yorker* from 1925 until 1975. Djuna wrote, "The base Janet Flanner said, 'people did not approve' of me and that I was the best writer in Paris in the twenties."[9] This reaction proves how she took umbrage with statements that were simply factual and even those that were complimentary.

Flanner profiled Djuna in her book *Paris Was Yesterday, 1925-1939*, and the assessment included some high praise. "Djuna was the most important woman writer we had in Paris," she wrote. "She was famous among us for her great short story, 'A Night Among the Horses.'"[10] Flanner shared an exchange that explains Djuna's anger toward her and Eliot. Djuna had shown Eliot a play she had written and he told her it contained "some of the most splendid archaic language he had ever had the pleasure of reading but that, frankly, he couldn't make head or tail of its drama." Flanner, who felt much the same, wrote, "She gave it to me to read, and I told her, with equal candor, that it was the most sonorous vocabulary I had ever read but that I did not understand jot or tittle of what it was saying. With withering scorn, she said, 'I never expected to find that you were as stupid as Tom Eliot.' I thanked her for the only compliment she had ever given me."[11]

Even though Djuna's wrath stemmed from personal weakness rather than strength, these anecdotes show how she had a fearless disregard for everyone equally, including those who were destined to become incredibly famous. Djuna wrote about Gertrude Stein, "Some of the Quarter thought her mad, others that she was merely tiresome. Nevertheless, on some few she had a profound influence—Hemingway certainly."[12] Not as dismissive of Joyce's work as she was of the novelist himself, Djuna's response to *Ulysses* was one of her rare positive remembrances. She said when Sylvia Beach, the owner of the Shakespeare and Company bookstore, placed a blue bound copy of the novel in the window of the shop, it was one of the most momentous events she experienced in Paris. She claimed it was so influential on novelists like her, it changed their perspectives overnight and that the book "had more of an effect on the young writers of the postwar period than France itself."[13]

Many of the journalistic pieces Djuna wrote as she settled into life in Paris were interviews that would appear in *McCall's* and in Manhattan newspapers. There's a strength in her voice and a visceral nature to her writing that immediately places the reader in the thick of things. You enter the scene with her in a piece titled "Recruiting for Métachorie: Mme. Valentine de Saint-Point Talks of Her Church of Music," which describes the moment Djuna steps into a dance studio: "Silence—dusk. The sound of tapestries swinging against the darkness; an odor of incense; a sense of rest but lately motion; the moan of water dropping far-away in some lonely chamber. These are the little things that greeted me as I was gently pushed out of a day into the sudden night, the twenty-four-hour atmosphere of Madame

Valentine de Saint-Point, who has come to show us what she means by Métachorie."[14] Djuna was there to see one of Saint-Point's productions of eerie and jarring multimedia dance performances with that strange-sounding name.

Djuna's description of Chanel in an interview she titled "Nothing Amuses Coco Chanel After Midnight" illustrates Djuna's long-winded writing style, which can devolve into a mash-up of errant facts or sensory experiences. The opening of the piece is a run-on sentence that unfolds in waves: "Gabrielle Chanel, the *plus grande couturiére* of Paris with an income of several millions, employing 2,400 persons in her ateliers, practically owner of the rue Cambon where her creations are on display, mistress of several homes in Europe —who refused the hand of the immensely wealthy Duke of Westminster, and who numbers among her friends half the great names of the world, born of humble country folk of the Auvergne, and bowed down to by women who would be well dressed—likes loneliness, fresh air, country life, sport clothes, dogs, fishing, early rising, early retiring, lolling, and hard work, especially hard work."[15] These interviews, which were collected in a book published in 1985, supported her financially as she learned her way around the environs of Paris.

Her first private residence was an apartment she rented at 173 boulevard Saint-Germain with two small rooms and a kitchen. One of the advantages of the address was its proximity to Les Deux Magots; the Café de Flore; and the Brasserie Lipp, known for drawing American expats for late-night mugs of beer, and helpings of sausage and potato salad. Djuna's romantic relationships had been fleeting until the photographer Berenice Abbott introduced her to Thelma Wood in 1921. Wood, who grew up in Saint Louis and was renowned as a hard-drinking partier, was in town studying sculpture. She could easily outpace Djuna in alcohol consumption and was famous for stumbling from café to bistro to bar every night. Djuna fell hard for Wood, who would be a source of great pain for a number of years because Djuna wanted exclusivity and Wood had no taste for monogamy. Djuna claimed she loved Wood because she looked like her grandmother Zadel. Before things grew dicey between them, they were known as lively company in café society, their appearance in a number of memoirs by others depicting them as a happy couple early on.

Wood had ample freedom to cheat on Djuna because the latter's stature as a reporter writing about French culture for an American audience had her sailing between France and the U.S. fairly regularly. By 1922, her cadre of connections had grown to the point she was a cog in Paris' literary wheel. Not only was she hobnobbing with members of the Lost Generation, she frequented a number of salons that introduced her to other writers and a number of patrons. She was also coming into more frequent contact with Paris-based American editors and publishers looking for material from expat writers who had avant-garde points of view. Robert McAlmon was among the professionals who were "always seeking another name and another face." Kay Boyle, one of the new names he published at the time, took McAlmon's shorter memoir *Being Geniuses Together*, expanded it and published it under the same name.

The book was his (and her) autobiographical account of their years in Paris. In one of McAlmon's original chapters in the book, he wrote, "I had known Djuna only slightly in New York because she was a very haughty lady, quick on the uptake, and with a wise-cracking tongue that I was far too discrete to try to rival." He remembered Djuna's "cape-throwing gestures," and expressed surprise that she thought he disliked her and that she said he was a very sarcastic man.[16] "She was wrong about the first idea at least, for Djuna is far too good-looking and fundamentally likeable for anything but fond admiration, if not a great deal more, even when she is rather overdoing the *grande dame* manner and talking soul and ideals," he explained. "In conversation, she is often great with her comedy, but in writing she appears to believe she must inject [into] her work metaphysics, mysticism, and her own strange vision of a 'literary' quality." Djuna's arrogance would be one of the aspects of her personality that biographers, publishers, and fellow writers would mention repeatedly.

McAlmon described an evening in Paris when they were sitting at the Gypsy Bar together and Sinclair Lewis barged in "some three sheets in the wind." Lewis had wanted to be introduced to McAlmon but the publisher said, "Djuna was well up with drink too and was not going to get chummy. I recall that Lewis looked wistful and went away from the table, with Djuna not having introduced him."[17] This was one of many instances in McAlmon's remembrances that describe the expat writers as living in an alcohol haze as they drank the nights away. He described another evening at the Gypsy Bar when he and Joyce were joined by Djuna and Mina Loy a few hours before the owner ran them out at five in the morning in order to close the bar. The two men staggered to a small bistro and decided to try every French drink on the menu. Before long, Joyce was dropping his cigars. "At first I leaned to pick them up and return them to him," McAlmon wrote. "When I could no longer lean without falling on my face, I took to lighting new cigars and handing them to him. He almost immediately dropped them, and I lighted cigar after cigar until they were all gone." They turned to cigarettes and by the time they left at ten in the morning, the floor was littered with barely smoked rolled tobacco.[18]

By this point, McAlmon was publishing Djuna's short

fiction, as was Ford Madox Ford in the *Transatlantic Review* and T.S. Eliot in *The Criterion*. McAlmon included her work in a 1925-anthology titled the *Contact Collection of Contemporary Writers* that also held pieces by Ford, Joyce, Pound, Stein, Hemingway, Loy, Edith Sitwell, and William Carlos Williams. Djuna's "A Little Girl Tells a Story to a Lady" was the first piece in the edition that included this heady list of authors. Proving what a double standard she maintained given her notorious consumption of liquor, she would say McAlmon was a writer with a bright future who had ruined his career and his health by drinking excessively. She said he was one of the saddest people she had ever known and that he "used to cry on every tree in Paris when drunk, and he frequently was."[19] Reading about the crazy deluge of alcohol, I wondered how they were able to produce the steady flow of writing that was being published in the constant stream of magazines and anthologies, and how they were ever sober enough to read their work when the opportunities arose.

One of the most important readings Djuna would give in Paris was at Natalie Barney's salon that Djuna had been attending for several years by then. The literary hostess had tapped Djuna to share her work during a special series she organized in 1927 to introduce French and English-speaking women writers to each other, an effort Barney called the *Académie des Femmes*. Barney had asked Ford to introduce Djuna that afternoon because he had been publishing her work consistently, the result illustrating how caustic Djuna could be if things weren't to her liking. "I had asked him to say a few words about her," Barney explained. "Perhaps he said them, but in a voice so muffled no one heard them." Barney said he blushed when he realized Djuna was offended by his awkwardness. "Djuna Barnes, upright, unblemished, unpolished, grew pale in her corner beneath this insult to her honor," Barney remembered. "I never introduced an author more gauche and more incapable of helping her own cause." [20]

Respect for Djuna's work increased when her first novel *Ryder* was published in 1928. The book, a bawdy mock-Elizabethan chronicle of her family history, was filled with references to her childhood. With the money she made from royalties, she bought an apartment at 9 rue Saint-Romain, and she and Wood moved into it near the end of that year. Djuna had been turning the other cheek to Wood's infidelities for nearly seven years, and this would continue as they settled into the larger home. If only Djuna could have been as brutal when it came to matters of the heart as she was about matters of acquaintance! *Ryder* was listed as one of six best-sellers in the September 8, 1928, issue of *The New York Times Book Review*, and sales were so lively the first printing quickly sold out. By the time her derelict publisher Boni & Liveright could manage a second release, interest had waned and the chance for Djuna to have her first financial boon was dashed. She was furious when they let *Ryder* go out of print and refused to cancel her contract for her next two novels even though they were almost bankrupt.

The affronts caused by her publisher's ineptness combined with the personal insults she felt over Wood's continued betrayals were taking an emotional toll, and Djuna was being described as neurotic as she sat alone in cafés drinking well into the night while Wood roamed Paris looking for conquests. As so often happens, when the personal falters, the career kicks into high gear. Soon after *Ryder* was published, McAlmon paid to have *Ladies Almanack* printed, which would be one of Djuna's most notable books.

She claimed she had written it as a lark to amuse her cadre of gay friends but McAlmon believed it was worthy enough for a larger audience and offered to foot the bill to publish it. The main character, Evangeline Musset, was based on Barney's exploits with the twelve other characters who drive the plot, many of them Barney's lovers at one time. Djuna hand-colored the illustrations in the first fifty copies of the book, which was printed in black and white. When a deal for distribution fell through, a number of the lesbians featured in the book took to the streets of Paris and hawked copies themselves.

"Of all the works Barney inspired, *Ladies Almanack* was the only real masterpiece," biographer Suzanne Rodriguez wrote.[21] Barney loved the book so much, it cemented a lifelong relationship with Djuna, which included financial support in the form of help during emergencies, a monthly stipend in later years, and a small amount of money Barney bequeathed to Djuna when she died in 1972. Because Djuna feared censorship issues due to the racy nature of the material in *Ladies Almanack*, she chose not to list her name as the creator, attributing the effort to "A Lady of Fashion." This mysteriousness made it an underground classic until she had it reprinted under her name in a 1972 release. In the introduction to a 1992 edition of the book, Susan Lanser wrote that forty-four years after it first appeared, the book was finally "recognized as both a brilliant modernist achievement and the boldest of a body of writings produced by and about the lesbian society that flourished in Paris between the turn of the century and the Second World War."[22] With *Ryder* and *Ladies Almanack* appearing in the same year, Djuna was enjoying a modicum of fame, satisfying attention that was overshadowed by her dicey home life.

Wood had been hospitalized with spinal problems and, soon after she was released, she badly burned her arm trying to light the gas oven. "I burst into tears," Djuna told a friend as she related the incident. "She's so utterly unable to look out for herself and moves about her life like a moth."[23] Just after Djuna had settled the medical bills with monies she earned from her hand-colored copies of *Ladies Almanack*, Wood told Djuna she was leaving her for an American-born, French-educated woman named Henriette McCrea-Metcalf. This insult, which everyone in Djuna's circle recognized as profound, pushed Djuna into a devastated mood she hoped she could exorcize by writing the novel *Nightwood*. As she grappled with the storyline that would lay bare her eight-year relationship with Wood, Djuna experienced the mightiest struggle she had ever faced with a piece of fiction. Describing the gnarly endeavor as "a soul talking to itself in the heart of the night," Djuna would be tortured by the plot, with Wood as the main character, for years before she would see it in print.

Soon after she began the gut-wrenching conversation she was having with herself, the stock market crashed and brought the grand creative dramas amusing so many American writers in Paris to a jarring end. While many U.S. citizens promptly returned to the States, Djuna stayed in Europe until the summer of 1930. Almost immediately after she arrived in New York City, she knew she'd made a mistake in returning. In a letter to Mina Loy from the apartment she rented at 62 Washington Square South, she bemoaned the fact that her Paris flat had become a financial burden. "Oh why did I ever buy a home?" she wrote. "Why did I ever meet T. Wood, why did I ever put my face out of my own country?"[24] It would be a year before she could return to Paris, and soon after she arrived, she bumped into fellow expat Wambly Bald in one of the Left Bank cafés they had frequented before the depression changed their lives so drastically. He recorded their reunion in a charming piece he wrote for "La Vie de Boheme," his column in the Paris edition of the *Chicago Tribune*.

He said they were having tea when Djuna declared the Montparnasse they had loved had ceased to exist because there was nothing left but a big crowd. "Don't put it that way," he told her. "I love the Quarter." He said they rested their heads on each other's shoulders and wept for a minute, then swapped anecdotes about the vibe they missed: "'Do you remember—?' she said. 'Yes. And how about—?' That went on for about an hour." When Djuna insisted the magical era was over, he said, "We agreed that it was all over."[25] Though she copped such a negative attitude during this conversation, she wasn't close to being finished with the city, as she would live there part-time for another eight years, leaving for good only when World War II forced her out. Looking back on the years before life was so painfully interrupted, she wrote, "Too little time was given to writing and too much to feeling, as it now stands...did we sense it? We were taking in the last breaths of Rome before the fall, Carthage before the destruction, Pompeii before the ruins. No one in our generation will ever again stage it as it was. Like that now famous madeleine that was dipped in tea, we should bring up its memory with gratitude and love, astonishment and terror."[26]

THE YEARS between Djuna's return to Europe and the beginning of the war bring Peggy Guggenheim into sharper focus in Djuna's life. During the summers of 1932 and 1933, Guggenheim rented Hayford Hall in England, and invited Djuna and Emily Coleman to stay for several months each year. Djuna had met Coleman at Les Deux Magots in 1925 when the latter was the society editor for the Paris edition of the *Chicago Tribune*. The other regular at the English country estate was Guggenheim's lover at the time, John Ferrar Holms. During these reprieves, Djuna was determined to make progress on the novel about her relationship with Wood as her attempts at revenge ground on. In Guggenheim's memoir *Out of This Century*, she dished about how the tight-knit group waged war as ancillary people came and went. "We really had a better time when we were alone with our little foursome, even if we fought and it all got intense," she wrote. "We somehow spurred each other on—we liked to insult each other." Fortunately for Djuna, she was an ace in this department.

Irritated by his arrogance, she pithily called Holms "God come down for the weekend," and said of Coleman's hyper personality, "Emily, you would make marvelous company slightly stunned."[27] Given Coleman was the only one who seldom drank, her edginess sizzled on while everyone else made up for her abstinence—so much alcohol was consumed while the quartet of snarks was in residence, the mansion was dubbed "Hangover Hall." In her book *Now to My Mother: A Very Personal Memoir of Antonia White*, Susan Chitty wrote, "It was custom for everyone to gather after dinner in the great hall, and there, beneath the cathedral window, engage in contests of wit. Djuna, fresh from a day in bed, spun her devastating aphorisms."[28] White was one of the comers-and-goers who observed them when she was staying during the summer of 1933. She said Coleman was more often than not the butt of Djuna's venomous wit, which didn't seem to bother Coleman because she was equally talented at grand put-downs.

In her first diary entry after she arrived in 1933, Coleman wrote, "Djuna talks through her nose like a sea-horn." By the time the first evening had wound down, Coleman was calling Peggy malicious and Djuna stupid. The next night, as they gathered in the living room to have coffee after dinner, everyone but Djuna began chiming in about the books they were reading. "Djuna got up and said she was tired, so to make her stay I said, 'You're a writer, aren't you? Don't you like to talk about books?'" Coleman remembered. "This did not produce the effect I desired, since she believes talking about books to be a pastime of those who do not write."[29] When both Peggy and John agreed with Djuna, Coleman was insulted. After Guggenheim went to bed, Coleman said, "I burst forth on John, saying, 'For two days I have wanted to hit both of them over the head with a cleaver.'"[30] As the tension between the three women continued to simmer, Coleman exploded and pummeled Guggenheim until Holms managed to pull her off his girlfriend, the skirmish leaving Guggenheim with a black eye!

Djuna, who would join everyone for cocktails before dinner "fresh from a day in bed" because she worked on her novel stretched out on the sheets with a writing-board across her knees, managed to escape physical harm but Coleman inflicted an emotional assault that lasted the entire time they were there. "Emily had threatened to burn *Nightwood* if Djuna repeated something Emily had confided to her by mistake," Guggenheim wrote. "As a result, Djuna was afraid to leave the house. She felt it necessary to guard her manuscript."[31] Djuna finished the first draft of the novel during her final stay at Hayford Hall, though a massive amount of editing still had to be done. In spite of their derisive carping at each other, Coleman would eventually put more muscle behind helping Djuna publish the novel than anyone else. The other benefit Djuna would receive from her visits to Hayford Hall during those two summers was financial support from Guggenheim, who agreed to give Djuna a monthly stipend just before their last stay ended.

Even though the money would be crucial to Djuna's survival, the generosity required a tricky negotiation because it was imperative that Djuna not feel the support was a handout—she had such an overbearing sense of pride, she would have been offended if it had been presented that way. Djuna agreed to accept the funds in the end because Guggenheim cunningly claimed it was imperative for the rich to support the arts. This complicated maneuver shines a light on Djuna's overly-sensitive psyche, which Rodriguez called "as complex and winding as a Daedalian labyrinth."[32] When her time in Devon came to an end, Djuna left Hayford Hall for a quick stopover in Paris and sailed for the States in late August of 1933. She was feeling somewhat relieved financially thanks to the money she had secured from Guggenheim and was trying to stay hopeful that her novel would gel. As she began shopping the book to publishers, her lack of formal education reared its ugly head because she found she didn't have the skills to shape her work when requests from publishers asked for a tighter manuscript.

The draft of the novel, said biographer Andrew Field, "shot in and out of the publishers' offices as though it were being ejected from a greased revolving door in an old silent movie."[33] With the manuscript boomeranging back to her, Djuna's brother Saxon, who had been augmenting Guggenheim's stipend, pressured her to move to a cheaper apartment and get a job so she could support herself. When he eventually put his foot down, she took a position with the Works Progress Administration (WPA) that paid her a salary of twenty-two dollars a week. The stress of a meaningless job and the continued rejections of her novel put her in a cagey state of mind that ratchetted up when an American publisher told her the manuscript was witty but over-written. Coleman rescued her, coaching her through nail-biting rounds of revisions and developing a strategy to entice T.S. Eliot, who was an editor at Faber & Faber in London, to publish *Nightwood*. Coleman's plan included enlisting people whom Eliot respected to give her positive feedback so she could pass the comments on to him.

When Djuna found out Coleman was showing her manuscript to so many people, she was upset. Instead of expressing gratitude that Coleman was sending her such detailed letters to keep her abreast of developments, Djuna wrote to her friend, "Darling, you pile up on top of me like a life work! If you had got your hands on Proust he would never have written his great work, he would have written letters of the remembrance of things past."[34] After a back-and-forth that included Eliot being irritated by the book's style and Coleman cutting out pages she knew would annoy him further before sending him the entire typescript, Coleman's tactics worked and he agreed to publish the novel. When Coleman notified her anxious friend that Eliot had accepted *Nightwood*, Djuna set sail for Europe on May 2, 1936. After a few days to straighten out her apartment Paris, which had been trashed by renters, so she could sell it, she headed to London mid-month to negotiate the contract and review the edits being made. Djuna had written one-hundred-and-ninety-thousand words and Coleman had cut it down to sixty-five-thousand before it was sent to Faber & Faber.

Djuna accepted the cuts because she knew *Nightwood* would never make it into print if she didn't. In the rarest of rare moves, she gave Eliot's staff carte blanche to do as they pleased on further edits. When *Nightwood* debuted in Europe on October 15, 1936, Field said of the impact, "The legend of Djuna Barnes was entering a new stage."[35] Biographer Phillip Herring noted, "Word certainly got out that an important novel had been published, for Lady Ottoline Morrell, the Hermione of D.H. Lawrence's *Women in Love*, began sending invitations to Barnes in early November. Barnes was wary of this patron of the arts who had invaded her privacy so far as to ask her if she was a lesbian."³⁶ Djuna declined the invitations and made fun of Morrell's physical appearance when she wrote to friends about how pushy Morrell was—Djuna had met her just after Morrell had had a stroke. With so much attention being lavished on the book by movers-and-shakers like Morrell, the novel's sales picked up steam and Djuna was able to rent a flat in the Chelsea neighborhood of London.

She had hardly moved in when she launched into a dangerous act of self-sabotage—she went on such a devastating drinking binge, she suffered from DTs when she tried to quit. She would awake at night to see strange creatures crawling on her walls, was prone to fainting, and experienced heavy sweats and heart palpitations. She checked herself into a London clinic only to be thrown out the next morning because the staff thought she belonged in an insane asylum. As Djuna the person melted down, the merits of her book were being hotly debated. Dylan Thomas dubbed *Nightwood* one of the three best novels by a woman, which Djuna repeated often in later years. When she bragged about the compliment, she said she heard it with her own ears when she had drinks with Thomas soon after the book debuted. He told her the only writing he liked was Shakespeare, Marlowe, and *Nightwood*. Ezra Pound was on the other side of the fence; he strongly disliked it, which set Djuna off. In her signature cut-them-down-at-the-knees style, she told Coleman, "He writes in the local gazette, and talks like a hick—every time he opens his mouth a stalk of wheat falls out."³⁷ I agree with Pound, who called the novel a "muddle."

I feel Djuna's poetry has more heft; and I think her journalism features, especially her interviews, are less challenging to read. The sentence structure of *Nightwood* bothered me so much, I couldn't get past the first page of run-on descriptions that glommed together without a period in sight! The novel debuted in the U.S. in 1937 with an introduction by Eliot in which I felt he tip-toed. "What I would leave the reader prepared to find is the great achievement of a style, the beauty of phrasing, the brilliance of wit and characterization, and a quality of horror and doom very nearly related to that of Elizabethan tragedy," he wrote.[38] Flanner claimed *Nightwood* was enormously popular with young intellectuals in Europe, but she tempered the accolade by saying it was "a difficult book to describe, since the only proper way of dealing with its strange, nocturnal elements is to have written it in the first place, which surely no one but Miss Barnes could have done."[39] While the novel was being heralded and panned by the literary set, Wood wrote to her former lover that she felt like a truck had run over her when she read it; that she assumed Djuna had set out to ruin her life.

THOUGH DJUNA CRIED over Wood's reaction, she admitted that her former lover was right because writers are prone to mining their lives for material at the expense of everyone else in them. History is littered with such behavior, as it is with authors who used alcohol to dull their frenetic psyches—Guggenheim said Djuna was going through a bottle of whiskey a day at this point and claimed her friends felt she was turning into a nuisance. On May 21, 1938, mired in self-pity, Djuna told Coleman, "I know that my protracted ill health is a bore to everyone." She was prompted to make this declaration because she'd had lunch with Antonia White and the volatile conversation had offended Djuna. "I really get to hate that woman, she is so spotty!" Djuna complained. "One moment something you want in your life and the next someone you would like to see floating in the Arno—she really is a cat. When she said 'What do you really want Djuna?' and I replied 'To die,' she snapped out, with as much venom as would stock the guts of ten adders, 'Then die'! A little unnecessary from a 'friend.'"[40]

Despite her angry push-back, Djuna accepted White's challenge and swallowed a handful of pills. She ultimately failed, and death, a subject that was interwoven into so many of her conversations, eluded her while she languished in London for a little over a year. She finally pulled herself together enough that she could return to Paris in July of 1939. She rented an apartment in the Hôtel Récamier where she had always wanted to live—she admired the property so much, she had chosen it for the setting in which *Nightwood* unfolded. By early September, Guggenheim said Djuna was in a near state of collapse and was exasperating those who were trying to help her because any concern from friends enraged Djuna. When Barney asked the hotel clerk if Djuna drank and, if so, what and how much, Djuna was incensed. She said she didn't need a keeper and that Barney maintained an air of "one perched on God's piss-pot."[41] With her closest friends on the brink of giving up on her, Djuna added some important context to this trying time in her life that tempers the pitifulness they could no longer stomach. She did so in an essay titled "War in Paris (1939)." The backdrop of the piece, which describes how sick Djuna was as World War II loomed, is a chaotic Paris.

"When I went to the American Hospital on the twenty-ninth of August, I had been too ill for too long to care about the news and the newspapers," she wrote; "I had not the faintest idea that all of France was expecting a declaration of war, and I am afraid that at that moment I did not care. I might have guessed it, however, as I got almost no attention at all." She said she was given a sedative, put to bed, and "promptly forgotten." After three days of being largely ignored, she learned they were going to be evacuating the hospital the following day so she returned to the Hôtel Récamier, struggling "through the mists of pneumonia," to find the front door padlocked with all of her belongings inside. "The few people I knew, who had bragged that under no circumstances would they leave Paris in the case of war, had fled in all directions," she remembered; "the one or two acquaintances left were tired of my being ill, my finances were almost nowhere, and I was lying in the dusty, old, small hotel where I had lived when I had first come to Paris some seventeen years before, the Hôtel Académie."[42]

Djuna's frank assessment of her situation takes a poetic turn when she says the Paris she had ridden through as she returned to the boarding house stood before her like a friend who had no memory. You can feel her mourning the city she once knew when she writes, "The childless gardens of the Luxembourg on whose lake tiny boats used to sail, under whose trees Punch hit Judy and children played ball, now left to the silent gray stone Queens, on whose outstretched hands pigeons stood motionless, as they must stand on Nelson's Monument in London." She described the panic she saw, calling the American Embassy "the second weeping wall," and shared how grief-stricken she was. "I thought, man can have everything, but he can keep nothing," she wrote. "When Christ said that man must give up his worldly possessions to follow him, he stated a fact. Man is now yet more desolate, for he must lose his possessions and his life with his convictions shaken."[43]

A cab she was riding in during these haunting days was rammed by another, which left her nose and lip cut and bleeding. She was on her way to the embassy where she had to stand in line for hours to get the papers stamped that would give her permission to stay in France. "When I inquired if the American Civil Relief Committee could use me, I was laughed at," she remembered. "Americans were not wanted in France, and why on earth was I still there after nearly seven weeks [of warnings that all foreigners should leave]? I said it was a very simple matter—I had no money."[44] With Djuna's nerves so frayed she couldn't stop shaking, Guggenheim decided to put an end to her predicament. "On October 24, 1939, I was pushed on a train by Peggy Guggenheim, a pillow thrown at me straight in my face from the platform," Djuna explained. "You could not buy passage on a ship except in dollars, and she had the dollars."[45] By the time Djuna arrived in New York, she had developed bronchitis. She moved into a one-room apartment with her mother but the situation was dreadful.

While Herring wrote that Djuna's distress was intensified because her mom coughed incessantly all night long every night; Ruth Ford, an actress and the sister of one of Djuna's former lovers, Charles Henri Ford, claimed Djuna was anguished because her mother read the Bible aloud into the wee hours of the morning. When Djuna couldn't take it anymore, her brother Charlie agreed to pay for a room at Hotel Earle in the Village for two months. Trying to kickstart some income, she accepted an assignment from *Town & Country* to write an article about Paris but her hands shook so badly, she couldn't type. When her drinking binges picked up in intensity because she felt defeated, her family lost patience and committed her to a sanitorium in March of 1940. This is a betrayal she would avenge in 1958 when she published *The Antiphon*, a verse play that was the next-to-last book she wrote. After leaving the sanitorium, she went to stay with Coleman, who had moved to Arizona, but this didn't last long because Djuna couldn't get along with the man with whom her friend was living.

She returned to the Village and received one of the few

breaks she had had in a while: She landed the rent-stabilized apartment at 5 Patchin Place in September of 1940 for a monthly rent of $49.00. Andrew Field tallied her days there at more than fifteen thousand, and claimed that "thousands of those days went by wordless."[46] The silence was so profound because she had very little will to write, she drank heavily, and she preferred to spend her days alone and mute. She would make up for lost time during the 1970s when her last two secretaries, Chester Page and Hank O'Neal, gave her an audience for an outpouring of conversation that was peppered with gossipy remembrances. They were so fascinated by the stories she told, both men were vigilant about writing down the anecdotes she shared as they clocked an untold number of hours listening to the resuscitated doyenne of dialogue. O'Neal said the best days with her were spontaneous and amusing, and her truest talent was the art of conversation. He deemed her intelligent, perceptive, witty, very quick, and articulate. Page wrote, "Her conversation at its best was like listening to Shakespeare."[47]

The title of secretary for both Page and O'Neal was a misnomer because they were so much more—they aided Djuna in navigating around town as she aged, brought her prescriptions and groceries, and took her to doctors' appointments. As they attempted to organize her papers, both of them urged her to produce a more robust memoir than she had fleshed out but Djuna scoffed at the idea, telling Page she could have made millions writing about all of the expats she had known in Paris during the 1920s and 1930s. "I won't do it," Djuna declared. "They aren't interested in their work. They only want to know dirt—who slept with whom."[48] This stubborn resistance would contribute to her lesser stature in the history of the written word—while the oeuvres of her counterparts like Colette, Gertrude Stein, and Anaïs Nin, each of whom wrote about themselves and their contemporaries, cemented their places in the literary canon, Djuna's writerly legacy is secondary to all that was written about how well-versed she was in the finely-crafted insult. Djuna not only took rudeness to new heights with her verbal jabs at others, she routinely directed her sarcasm toward herself. O'Neal said she once told him, "You may find me witty early in the evening but you'll hang yourself by morning."[49]

Those who remembered Djuna were much nicer about her than she was about them. Natalie Clifford Barney's account of Djuna in her book *Adventures of the Mind* describes her as having "a nose as pointed as an Ever-sharp pencil; a mouth irresistible to laughter, and auburn hair which she stuffs under a hat 'à la Manet,' one of whose most successful sketches she seems to be." She said Djuna was tall and slender, and noted that her clothes broke at a right angle on her sturdy legs. "But let's go back to her brain," she added. "Her thoughts never go all the way to Thought. They are fragments of sensation, broken mirrors of joie de vivre on which one cuts oneself."[50] Biographer Suzanne Rodriguez presented Djuna in Paris as striding "with queenly possession through the cobblestoned streets, a floor-length cape thrown insouciantly over her shoulder."[51] When Mina Loy introduced her daughters to Djuna, they said she had a great sense of style; described her as sure of herself, jaunty, talented, and chic; and said she had an electrifying manner.

Ruth Ford, who said Djuna was "stunning in appearance," also noted her penchant for capes in this description of her: "tall; dashing; with a certain arrogant posture; elegant; short and wavy reddish hair combed back off her face; green-blue eyes (tempting and taunting); and dressed with great style, romantic capes and turbans." Ruth said Djuna's voice, which was softly guttural, drew attention. "She had a quick tongue and could be witty, humorous, confounding, and devastating," she added. "Sure of herself, she was aware of her specialness without a show of ego; eccentric, yes. She was *not* a gypsy. She was an ultra-sophisticate."[52] After Djuna had been living on Patchin Place for nearly thirty years, Page described a similar reaction to her gaze when he met her for the first time in 1970. He said he had been surprised when she invited him for tea given her hostility toward strangers.

"She seemed fascinating, formidable and unapproachable," he explained; "so, it was with feelings of trepidation as well as expectation that I entered picturesque Patchin Place for the first time at three in the afternoon on the twenty-third of May bearing flowers and a tin of Twining's English tea. Directly above the entrance lay the flat of Djuna Barnes, in which so many moments of my life, peaceful, amusing, and turbulent, would be spent over more than a decade. The door opened, and there was the legendary Djuna Barnes, whose wit was the terror and joy of the Paris literati, straight as a spear shaft, eyes the blue of a Tiepolo sky."[53] Page, a young pianist and a friend of the poet Marianne Moore, who had asked him to check in on Djuna, shared his reactions to and conversations with Djuna in his book *Memoirs of a Charmed Life in New York*. During his first visit, he noticed the apartment was in disrepair, though not to the point of being off-putting. "Despite peeling paint, it somehow embodied the atmosphere of another time, the clutter of objects from the past and this tall woman with handsome, luxuriant gray hair and a dark-hued, almost theatrical, voice, the priestess of this sanctum," he wrote. He called his first afternoon with her captivating and somehow alarming because he was extremely on guard.[54]

"Her gaze and penetrating wit, often tinged with the caustic, could be hilarious," he said. "Her mood frequently was bitter. She had been wounded by the world and had, as a consequence, built around herself an almost impenetrable barrier, which few had the audacity to try to cross."[55] Page noticed a number of signs that signaled she was in a fragile physical state. "I sat balancing my teacup and saucer on one knee, listening to her conversation, interrupted several times by attacks of coughing," he explained. "She pointed to a round bedside table that was filled with the clutter of bottles of medicines in varying sizes and explained that she had only recently returned from having had stomach surgery." She shared with Page that she was often dizzy and had been told twice that she had only six months to live. Signaling the rage she felt toward her family, she added how this news had prompted her brother to ask her if she'd written her obituary. Djuna told Page it was "a terrible thing to have said." She admitted to the young pianist that he was the first stranger she had invited to visit her in two decades, which is interesting given it had been exactly twenty years since Djuna had stopped drinking in 1950.[56]

PAGE SAID she unnerved him because she was so hypervigilant. "'Don't sit on the edge of your chair like that,' she admonished. 'You look nervous.' And I was," he remembered. In spite of the fact that they had just met and that Djuna was so prone to secrecy, she shared many details of her life with Page that day, including the fact that the name Djuna was invented by her father. He was inspired by a character in Eugène Sue's book *The Wandering Jew*. She told Page her namesake in the story was an Indian prince. Page was curious as to whether she had come to know Colette because he noticed Djuna had fashioned a blue paper shade around her bedside lamp, as her French counterpart had famously done. When he asked, Djuna simply answered, "Yes." Not willing to leave it at that, he pressed, "What was she like?"

She said, "A cat."[57] Djuna also told him how nice E.E. Cummings had been to her. If she was ill, he would take her chicken soup and would call up to her second-floor window every few weeks to see if she was still alive because she was such a recluse.

Djuna said Cummings had rescued her when she fell and broke her shoulder, climbing up the fire escape to get to her after he heard her calling for help because she couldn't get up to unlock the door. To his surprise, Page was invited back. After he had visited a few times, Djuna began to trust him enough to let him take her shopping and run errands for her. He asked a friend to help him paint her apartment, which hadn't had a fresh coat in decades. He called it a trying experience given "the stress of having a very critical Djuna Barnes commenting on our every brush stroke."[58] When he was in public with her, Page saw how people treated her with nervous deference because she had such a formidable air. He introduced Djuna to his employer Louise Crane of the Crane & Co. paper family. At Page's suggestion, Crane made her car available so that Djuna's outings would be easier on her physically.

Crane also gave Djuna a monthly stipend for a while, though she was not a fan—she was so offended by Djuna's corrosive attitudes, she gave her the nickname "Madame Vitriol." There couldn't have been a better label for the bitter woman who called Edmund Wilson "a louse" and asked Edna St. Vincent Millay why she "put on all those British airs," calling her "stuck up on herself." These slights spilled out during the afternoons Page spent with her as Djuna dipped the witch's brew of negativity she had expertly stirred for decades out of the caldron. She said she couldn't imagine anyone falling for Alice Toklas as Stein had because she "had a big lump in the middle of her forehead, hence the bangs."[59] Djuna also complained that Anaïs Nin kept using her name in her books, saying she resented the fact that someone whose work she did not admire would dare to do so.

Page was bowled over by the rapidity with which spiteful comments, pompous remarks, and namedropping flowed. Djuna told him that during a bad illness when she thought she was dying, she sold a signed unnumbered press copy of *Ulysses*, which Joyce had given her, to Harvard's Houghton Library for a hundred dollars. "We all became something, though at the time only Joyce had any pretense as to importance," she told the young man.[60] Djuna also recalled a dinner given by the English political advocate Harriet Weaver during which Djuna blurted out that Joyce drank alcohol. Djuna told Page, "Ezra [Pound] stepped on my foot under the table. 'Don't ever say that in front of Miss Weaver,' he said. 'She is helping support Joyce and can't endure anyone who drinks.'" Djuna said she retorted, "I thought everybody knew Joyce was a drunk."[61]

Page put up with Djuna's put-downs and temper tantrums for nearly a decade before deciding he'd had enough. When Djuna began to get under his skin, he knew it was time to let go because he wanted to stay friends with her. Hank O'Neal, who stepped into the role in 1978, described her papers as he began assisting her, which seemed to reflect a chaos as frantic as her mental state. "There are hundreds of poems lying scattered all about, dozens of versions of the same poem, long poems, short poems, complete and incomplete drafts all mixed together—some are edited, others are not," he wrote. "Boxes and piles and piles of unorganized papers. Perhaps I can make sense out of some of it so she can at least try to finish a portion of her work." As he sifted through the quagmire, he would find lines in published poems that Djuna had pulled to use as openings for new ones twenty years later. One poem they were eventually able to refine had five-hundred drafts with varying titles.[62]

With the intent of bringing a renewed audience to her work, O'Neal encouraged her to take calls from people who could give her publicity but she stubbornly refused. "The less she appeared in public, and the many years between publications, only made the mystery of Barnes deepen," he explained. "As years passed the legend grew, and more literary critics and others with specific causes began to take increased notice of her. The more the critics and literary figures wrote, and the more various groups or publications pleaded for a comment from her, the more resolute she became in ignoring everyone."[63] Explaining herself, Djuna said she "felt like a whore" when she answered questions about her life.[64] Mary Dearborn, Guggenheim's biographer, said that over the years Djuna became increasingly angry with Guggenheim because the art heiress kept sending admirers, fans, and potential biographers her way.

Dearborn quoted these exchanges in letters that passed between them: Guggenheim berated, "I think it is a great pity that you don't want anyone to write about you. Don't you want to be immortal? How can you be so private? It's all too bad." Djuna scoffed in return, "Being immortal? Being biographed? — so? Do you really think immortality is a matter of talking to unknown, unrelished persons?"[65] As the months ticked by, O'Neal presented a woman filled with scorn. When a hefty biography of Samuel Beckett was published, Djuna was angry about the way she was described. She said it was inaccurate that the writer had portrayed her as "a lifelong friend," claiming she hardly knew the man.[66] While "lifelong" was incorrect, her assertion that she didn't know Beckett well was a lie. They became friends in 1938 when Djuna stayed at Yew Tree Cottage, a Cotswolds home Guggenheim bought when she opened her London gallery.

Beckett was Guggenheim's lover at the time and was also staying there while Djuna visited. After that initial introduction, Beckett and Djuna wrote to each other fairly regularly. O'Neal said Beckett's letters were the most valuable when the second half of Djuna's papers were sold. "When I found the folder of letters from him, she said they had not only corresponded, he had given her some money from his *Waiting for Godot* royalties in the 1950s," he added.[67] Once O'Neal found evidence they had indeed been friends, and illustrating how contradictory Djuna could be, she told him she had been desperate and was grateful that Beckett was willing to give her the money. The title of O'Neal's book—*Life is painful, nasty and short...in my case it has only been painful and nasty*—was meant as an insult to Djuna but it was also seriously apropos by the time he met her because she had grown so helpless, she used this as an excuse to rage at everyone.

Djuna said she didn't feel she had the power to change her circumstances and this made her furious. Page called her behavior "uncomprehendingly difficult," but said he felt it was unconscious on Djuna's part.[68] Margaret Anderson, the founder, editor, and publisher of *The Little Review*, agreed, famously saying that Djuna was "not on speaking terms with her own psyche."[69] Djuna was also prone to deluding herself about finances, lamenting to O'Neal that she was poverty-stricken in spite of the fact that he found she had around one-hundred-and-eighty-thousand dollars in four different savings accounts when he put her finances in order. Another point of persecution that would grow in ferocity was the fact that her literary legacy was so slight. Neither Page nor O'Neal said whether she knew the situation was of her own making due to the fact that she was determined to protect her privacy.

Three statements she made prove she was caught in the classic conundrum of trying to have it both ways. The first, she told to Page: "Oh, why do people get famous? Isn't it disgusting! Don't dream of it! Don't go through all this mess. People think it's so easy. It's dreadful. The whole thing is terrible. Have nothing to do with it! Stop immediately—if you have any thought of such a thing."[70] The second she wrote in a letter to Natalie Barney in 1963: "There is not a person in the literary world who has not heard of, read and some stolen from *Nightwood*. The paradox is that in spite of all the critical work flooding the press since 1936, not more than three or four have mentioned my name. I am the most famous unknown of the century! I can't account for it, unless it is that my talent is my character, my character my talent, and both an estrangement."[71] The third, she shared with O'Neal, who said she was upset by the young writers approaching her on the streets of the Village because she wanted to be left alone.

THE BUDDING authors who accosted Djuna would likely have been shocked to know that for decades she had written very little new material. She spent much of her time culling snippets from a small brown notebook that included entries from the 1920s. She had always intended to present a cohesive mosaic of her memories but only managed to leave the sparsest accounts of her life. As her health and eyesight failed her, the pull to share her recollections aloud grew more magnetic than the act of facing the typewriter. She was in tremendous pain by the time O'Neal was helping her—he listed her ailments as a pinched nerve in her spine, a weak heart, crippling arthritis, emphysema, and oncoming blindness from cataracts, which contributed the most to the disorganization of her papers. Everything Djuna had written was out of print and she wanted to remedy this but she didn't have the energy to edit even the most trivial verses or prose.

O'Neal blamed her irritability, confusion, and irrational behavior on the cocktail of drugs she was taking, particularly Darvon, a painkiller she wouldn't give up, though he claimed it gave her little relief. As illness dogged her, she had a premonition that death was at hand, which added greater urgency to the act of putting her papers in order. She feared if all of the rough drafts and wayward scraps of poems remained, they would be published as representing the quality of her work. "She is terrified (not a sufficiently strong word) of this happening," O'Neal wrote, "but she can't gather the courage to throw anything away and is unable to see well enough, despite all the new glasses, to get anything in proper order."[72] O'Neal advised her to select the best drafts of each poem and throw the others away but the idea made her feel bereft because she couldn't maintain her concentration. She told him one day, "I don't know if I should try and finish my poetry, burn all my papers, or lie in bed and scream!"[73] He said the more she panicked, the harder it was for him to keep her focused on the work, a quest he was so determined to achieve because he felt it would be wonderful if an elderly Djuna Barnes issued a book of serious poems.

Soon after he began organizing the material, O'Neal realized the sadness he was seeing in person was nothing new, as common themes were emerging in her work, including death, grief, unrequited love, an overwhelming sense of doom, and a pessimistic view of humanity. "While she was exceptionally clever and revealed a keen mind in conversation, she was narrow in her outlook and was one of the most morbid writers I had ever met," he wrote. "Almost everything in her life was out of control. She'd rage at the injustice of it all because she didn't want to face the reasons why such things were happening to 'poor Miss Barnes.'"[74] A few months after O'Neal had become her assistant, Page visited Djuna during the Christmas holidays in 1978. "I rang her bell, received an answering buzz, walked up the dingy flight of stairs, and read the tiny typed sign, 'Do Not Disturb,'" he remembered. "The door opened and there was Djuna, hardly changed."[75] Once they were settled, Djuna told him Berenice Abbott, who had introduced her to Wood, was the one who had connected her with O'Neal.

As Djuna began relating the tug-of-war she was having with O'Neal, Page was relieved he was no longer the one having to endure the volatile scenes after years of trying to help her. O'Neal turned out to be a sterner force than Page had been—when Djuna was awarded a fifteen-thousand-dollar grant from the National Endowment for the Arts to complete a book of poems called *Creatures in an Alphabet*, he stayed on her until she completed it. This was quite a feat since she had been piddling with the incredibly slim volume of short verses since the 1960s. It would be her last book and would not be published until after her death. According to O'Neal, the quality of the book would have infuriated Djuna and she would have been saddened by the two-inch notice of it in *The New York Times*, which called it a "slight work."[76] As she struggled, a keen sadness crept into the story—when he was leaving her apartment one bleak winter afternoon, O'Neal said she looked at her desk and said, "This table is all that has kept me alive, and they want to take it from me."[77]

She was alluding to the library staff from the University of Maryland, who had recently come into her apartment, piled the first round of her books and papers she was selling to them into boxes, and hauled them off. She had chosen the college herself but she wasn't prepared for the horror she felt when the librarian's aids were so perfunctory as they gathered the treasured possessions she had guarded for so long. Her stamina was so diminished by the time they finalized *Creatures in an Alphabet*, she admitted she had to let go of the last thing that really mattered to her. "I can't write anymore," she told O'Neal. "The spark is gone."[78] This would turn out to be the case for the remaining three years of her life. "My grand plan for a small book [of serious poems] was ultimately a failure," O'Neal lamented. Ditto with his effort to bring new people into her life who might have written about her work. Because she felt most people were "vile, insufferable charlatans, or stupid," she preferred to remain the mysterious cult figure she had created, which was much easier to do if she avoided everyone.[79] In following Page and O'Neal through all the goading and spitefulness they had endured, it occurred to me that Djuna must have clung to the past because her present was so unsatisfying and the future terrified her.

"If she couldn't be marvelous she didn't want to be anything at all, except perhaps left alone," O'Neal explained.[80] To comfort herself, she had turned her tiny apartment in Patchin Place into a time machine peopled by the notorious beings who had become her intimates so many years before when life held some promise and she could still see the letters that embedded themselves in the paper when her long fingers plunked the typewriter keys. The capsule she inhabited was about to grow silent once again—as she told Page, Djuna "excommunicated" O'Neal in 1981, three years after he began managing her affairs and two years before she died.[81] Page hinted that the reason Djuna got rid of O'Neal was because he was dishonest, though he didn't go into any details, likely for fear of being accused of libel. Djuna lived to see her ninetieth birthday, and Page called on her the afternoon of June 12, 1982, with her favorite yellow roses and brought ice cream to go with the sponge cake her devoted housekeeper Jussi had made her. Page said Djuna was able to eat only a tiny piece. When he returned six days later, he said she looked dreadful.

"I sat by the bed, holding her hand. She held mine tightly," he remembered. "Her eyes had an awful, glazed look, her cheeks sunken. When I left around 4:30, I kissed her goodbye and told her, 'I'll see you tomorrow.' She turned her head in my direction, gave a wan smile and said, 'It was darling of you to come.' And it was a real goodbye."[82] Five months after she died, Page carried out Djuna's wishes that her ashes be scattered near where her life began. "On the 28th of November, 1982, a small group of us met at Storm King Mountain above Cornwall-on-Hudson, where Djuna was born," he explained.[83] Once Jussi had scattered Djuna's ashes, Page placed a yellow rose at the base of each of a number of dogwood trees that grew on the knoll, and the little party said their final farewells to Madame Vitriol. I was relieved when this once-brazen woman who was in such tremendous pain let go of her stormy quarrel with life. Oddly enough, I was also glad I had taken the labyrinthian journey with her as I followed her striding purposefully up and down the long avenues of New York City and into those Parisian streets teeming with an energy that was so different from any time before or since.

Djuna was right when she said she and her compatriots were taking in the last breaths of Rome before the fall, Carthage before the destruction, and Pompeii before the ruins. She also nailed it when she said they would never be able to recreate the atmosphere exactly as it was before a war changed the world's gestalt forever. With her voice silenced, the essays in "Notes Toward the Memoirs" are all that's left of her view of life in Paris during such a lauded time. In one, she wrote, "[Marsden] Hartley sat all day long at La Rotonde for fear that he might miss something. Every American does exactly the same thing; they sit for hours as if nailed to their seats waiting on the most famous corner in the world, where the Montparnasse runs into the Raspail, for here the world did pass for ten to fourteen years, and if one sat long enough everyone went by."[84]

In "A Way of Life," she wrote, "The plump, prolonged ecstatic steps of the Wall Street broker's wife dancing with the South American gigolo, who looked over her head into a future that he hoped would be golden; the roulette; the bazaar; the Monte Carlo pavilions; the sea fronts of the south; the promenade at the Battle of Flowers—all of this came back and sat at the Café du Dôme, La Rotonde, and Le Sélect. That magnet, the Latin Quarter, may have seemed to hold its pins in its teeth forever, pins that had been drawn from every spot on the globe, and now that the magnet is broken, the pins should not forget. The terrifying part of it is that it is done. Not what we did, but that it is over."[85] Given Djuna had a front-row-seat, she would have known just what a significant loss this was.

10

THE DRAWING-ROOM DIPLOMAT
CONSUELO VANDERBILT IN NEWPORT

Taking in the interiors of Marble House—the Newport, Rhode Island, mansion that William Kissam Vanderbilt funded as a fortieth-birthday present for his wife Alva—was like eating a box of bonbons for breakfast. Even without the ostentatious furnishings, the Rococo and Gothic decorative shell, which was built between 1888 and 1892, would have been cloying. The gilded gaudiness of the main living spaces continued as I made my way to the second floor until I reached a surprisingly somber room where the finery abruptly came to an end and was replaced with dark-wood furniture carved with chunky medieval motifs. Only the fabrics and wallcoverings held any hint of elegance, the bed and the walls sheathed in red satin heavily embroidered with gold. Just after the thought popped into my mind that it must have been the bedroom of one of their sons, I found that my assumption was wrong.

On a table was a photo of a young woman in a luxuriant gown trimmed in ermine, a coronet atop her mass of dark curls. The placard placed near it proclaimed the depressing room was the domain of the Vanderbilt's oldest child and their only daughter Consuelo. The expression that clouded her face was the saddest I'd ever seen mar the features of such a beauty. I couldn't wait to return home and find out more about this creature whose name I'd never heard before. My search led me to an array of sources, one of whom was Michael C. Kathrens. In his book on Newport villas, he declared the English Tudor-style room with its dark wainscoting and heavy canopied four-poster bed was hardly appropriate for a teenage girl. He believed it represented the mother's ambitions because Alva had surrounded Consuelo with furnishings suitable for the English peeress she was determined her daughter would become.[1]

Ironically, the pale blue bedroom that the two sons shared was more feminine than the mausoleum in which Alva had entombed Consuelo. Furthering the shrine-like quality of the girl's room over a century after she left it was a vanity on which a gold-framed mirror and a set of hairbrushes were perfectly arranged, bristles up, next to a lace-covered pin cushion that matched the dressing table's flouncing skirt. In her memoir *The Glitter and the Gold: The American Duchess—in Her Own Words,* Consuelo's description of her gloomy prison was frank. "Upstairs my own room was austere," she explained. "It was paneled in a dark Renaissance boiserie. There were six windows, but at best one could only glimpse the sky through their high and narrow casements. An unadorned stone mantel opposite my bed greeted my waking eyes."[2] She remembered the small desk by the window on which ornate candlesticks and a miniature clock were still sitting when I visited, along with pens and several small journals. They were just as she described them—in such perfect order she wouldn't have dared touch them.

"My mother had chosen every piece of furniture and had placed every ornament according to her taste, and had

THE DRAWING-ROOM DIPLOMAT

forbidden the intrusion of my personal possessions," she remembered. Consuelo was so disregarded, she felt like her mother saw her as nothing more than an unfinished piece of art, "a work-in-progress that might eventually become as revered as St. Ursula depicted by Carpaccio." Remembering the extent of Alva's control, she added, "I reflected that it was her wish to produce me as a finished specimen framed in a perfect setting, and that my person was dedicated to whatever final disposal she had in mind."[3] As I plumbed her story, I flinched at the cruelty she was forced to endure, the final disposal Alva had in mind was to see her daughter take the title of duchess. The determined woman's campaign would have put a military man to shame. Though Consuelo did not realize it at the time, her mother had already chosen her prey—the 9th Duke of Marlborough. When Alva heard the Brit, whose name was Charles Spencer-Churchill, was looking for a wealthy wife, she enlisted a powerful ally to bring her daughter to the attention of the duke.

Alva's accomplice was Lady Paget, whom Consuelo remembers meeting. "Once greetings had been exchanged, I realized with a sense of acute discomfort that I was being critically appraised by a pair of hard green eyes," she wrote.[4] Paget did agree to support Alva's efforts but the statement she made in front of Consuelo was biting. "'If I am to bring her out,' she told my mother, 'she must be able to compete at least as far as clothes are concerned with far better-looking girls,'" Consuelo remembered. "It was useless to demur that I was only seventeen. Tulle gave way to satin, the baby décolletage to a more generous display of neck and arms, naïveté to sophistication." Consuelo met the duke during a dinner party at Paget's home. "My hostess had placed the Duke on her right and put me next to him—a rather unnecessary public avowal of her intentions," she explained. "He seemed to me very young, although six years my senior, and I thought him good-looking and intelligent."[5]

After several more face-to-face gatherings, including one at the duke's ancestral home of Blenheim Palace, Alva's dreams were realized. Visiting the Marble House in September of 1895, Sunny, as his friends called the duke, proposed to Consuelo. The eighteen-year-old debutant braved her fate, even while she was grieving over a young man whom Alva forbid her to ever see again. Because Consuelo had agreed to marry him behind Alva's back, her mother threatened to shoot the interloper if Consuelo ever laid eyes on him again! I laughed when I read this because I had so admired the painting on the ceiling of Alva's bedroom at Marble House. It depicted Athena, the goddess of war, a deity who must have been her exclusive muse![6] Consuelo's memory of the moment she became engaged had dark undertones. "It was in the comparative quiet of an evening at home that Marlborough proposed to me in the Gothic Room, whose atmosphere was so propitious to sacrifice," she explained. "There was no need for sentiment. I was content with his pious hope that he would make me a good husband and ran up to my mother with word of our engagement."[7]

THE WEDDING DATE was set for November 6th and the money began flowing from U.S. banks into Great Britain at once. The *New York World* published this list of her physical attributes and the financial details once the news broke that Consuelo was engaged: "Chin: pointed, indicating vivacity… Eyebrows: delicately arched…Length of hand: six inches… Waist measure: Twenty inches…Marriage settlement: $10,000,000." The paper wasn't aware that W.K., as Consuelo's father was known, had given her and her new husband £500,000 to buy a house on Curzon Street in London and that her father had, as Dana Cooper noted in her book *Informal Ambassadors*, "conferred on his new son-in-law some $2.5 million in fifty-thousand shares of railroad stock, with a guaranteed annual payment of four percent." The tally of the monies Sunny received was approximately $15 million USD, which would be more than $532 million in US currency in 2023.[8]

Consuelo was disturbed by the negotiations and by her mother's continued control, though she wouldn't have dared to complain, even when Alva didn't allow her daughter to choose her own bridesmaids because she wanted the group to achieve a balanced aesthetic in weight and height. This meant there were several girls Consuelo barely knew walking down the aisle before her. "The arrival of my wedding dress brought the realization that my mother had ordered it while we were still in Paris, so sure had she been of the success of her plans," Consuelo said. "I spent the morning of my wedding day in tears and alone; no one came near me. A footman had been posted at the door of my apartment and not even my governess was admitted." The bride dressed for her wedding like an automaton, then was finally allowed out of the dark and dreary bedroom to walk toward her sacrificial moment. "I felt numb as I went down to meet my father and the bridesmaids who were waiting for me," she remembered. "My mother had decreed that my father should accompany me to the church to give me away. After that he was to disappear."[9]

He was persona non grata because Alva had divorced him. "My mother had forbidden me to receive any gifts from my Vanderbilt relatives and I felt hurt and pained when I was made to return them without excuse or thanks," Consuelo said. "My grandmother was the only Vanderbilt whom I was allowed to visit and the only one invited to my wedding, but she naturally refused to come to a ceremony from which her entire family was to be excluded." Consuelo described very little about the wedding, only saying, "The usual hymns glorifying perfect love were sung, and while I glanced at my husband shyly I saw that his eyes were fixed in space."[10] She titled the chapter about her union "A Marriage of Convenience," describing in it her husband's arrogant behavior after they boarded a train bound for Idle Hour, her father's estate in Oakdale, Long Island, where they would start their honeymoon.

"Marlborough whiles away the journey reading congratulatory telegrams, handing them on to me with the proper gestures of deference or indifference the senders evoked," she wrote. "Unfortunately, there was no silver platter on which to present Her Majesty Queen Victoria's missive, but it was read with due respect, and a sense of her intimidating presence crept even into that distant railway car." It was then she realized the aristocracy in the foreign country that would now be hers was governed by silent rituals she knew nothing about. "To me, seated beside the man who would now rule my life, absorbed as he was in contemplation of the future at a moment when the present should mean so much, the outlook was somber," she so aptly decreed.[11] Blenheim Palace was undergoing such a massive renovation with Consuelo's family's money that the couple traveled around the world for months on a protracted honeymoon. She described the places they went—a veritable grand tour—and noted how her husband spent his time with art dealers and went on a spree of "ransacking the antique shops" of Rome. She wrote, "I was not allowed to accompany him because he claimed that my appearance in furs and furbelows caused prices to rocket."[12]

Consuelo used words like 'formidable' to describe the family she had married into, particularly her mother-in-law.

"I can remember still my surprise when one member after another of that well-bred company remarked to me that I was the first American she had condescended to receive!" she explained. "Could they imagine they were paying me a compliment?" Consuelo called the snobbishness "an enthroned fetish which spreads its tentacles into every stratum of British national life."[13] She set the scene once they finally arrived in London: "I gazed anxiously at the station platform where a small group of people were waiting to welcome us. I felt the scrutiny of many eyes and hoped my hat was becoming and that my furs were fine enough to win their approval. The sight of these strangers, Marlborough's family, brought the loneliness of my position sharply into focus."[14] You've likely guessed by now that she had exchanged one bondage for another, her newest chains including not only her new husband and his overbearing family but the social strictures demanded of Britain's upper classes.

The day after her arrival, her husband's mother—the Dowager Duchess Albertha Spencer-Churchill—consented to the audience Consuelo had been told she should value so highly. "After an embarrassing inspection of my person, she expressed great interest in our plans," she remembered. "Then fixing her cold grey eyes upon me she said, 'Your first duty is to have a child and it must be a son, because it would be intolerable to have that little upstart Winston become Duke. Are you in a family way?' Feeling utterly crushed by my negligence in not having insured Winston's eclipse and depressed by the responsibilities she had heaped upon me, I was glad to take my leave."[15] The upstart the dowager duchess referenced was Winston Churchill, Marlborough's first cousin. Winston was the son of another American-born, British-wed woman named Jennie Jerome, who became Lady Randolph Churchill when she married Winston's father.

Because Marlborough had no brothers, if he died without an heir, Winston would be handed the title of duke because Winston's late father was the youngest son of the 7th Duke of Marlborough. "Both sides of the family were evidently equally concerned with the immediate necessity of an heir to the dukedom, and were infecting me with their anxiety," Consuelo wrote. Once she had endured this intimidating inspection and had, for the moment, passed muster, the couple traveled to Woodstock where Blenheim is located. She was surprised when she was heartily celebrated by the townspeople, the staff of the palace, and local tenant farmers. "As I stood on the steps listening to the various speeches, I realized that my life would be very strenuous if I was to live up to all that was expected of me," Consuelo explained. "My arms were full of bouquets, the fur coat felt heavier and heavier, the big hat was being blown about by the winds, and I suddenly felt distraught, with a wild desire to be alone."[16] But the solitude she craved would not be granted as long as she was at Blenheim. As she began to grow accustomed to the way of life there, she realized the staff lived under deplorable conditions—no running water in the tower where the housemaids slept, for instance.

She wanted to help them by having plumbing installed but was told it was how the housemaids had lived for nearly two centuries so she would do nothing of the sort. She also lamented how unlivable the palace was, noting it was planned to impress rather than to please. "Blenheim was perhaps not designed as a home," she explained. "We slept in small rooms with high ceilings; we dined in dark rooms with high ceilings; we dressed in closets without ventilation; we sat in long galleries or painted saloons. Had they been finely proportioned or beautifully decorated I would not so greatly have minded sacrificing comfort to elegance." Early on, her happiest times were daily inspections with the estate agent,

THE DRAWING-ROOM DIPLOMAT

who was an accomplished horseman. "We used to gallop across the countryside to our outlying farms, where I met Marlborough's tenants," she said. "They were fine men, good farmers, and loyal friends, and some had lived on the estate for over fifty years."[17]

A THEME that would color many years of her life surfaced as she began to realize she truly cared about the disadvantaged. "It was the custom at Blenheim to place a basket of tins on the side table in the dining-room and here the butler left the remains of our luncheon," she wrote. "It was my duty to cram this food into the tins, which we then carried down to the poorest in the various villages where Marlborough owned property. With a complete lack of fastidiousness, it had been the habit to mix meat and vegetables and sweets in a horrible jumble in the same tin." In spite of the fact that she was considered impertinent for not conforming to precedent, she sorted the food into separate containers and was pleased at how delighted the recipients were.[18] She described their first months at Blenheim as busy but uneventful, noting that Marlborough spent a good deal of time away in London and that he summoned her to town when her first London season as a duchess began. She described glittering balls and concerts, and a trip to Buckingham Palace for a 'Drawing Room'—an afternoon in-person with the Prince and Princess of Wales in an intimate state room.

The younger royals were standing in for Queen Victoria because she no longer attended such ceremonies. Consuelo described the fervor when the princess, the future Queen Alexandra when the prince was coronated as Edward VII, entered. "I can still feel the little thrill of excitement the roll of drums and the National Anthem gave me as the royal procession entered the ballroom," she remembered. The event foreshadowed an invitation to meet Queen Victoria at Windsor Castle, which included some seriously ironic moments. "Having heard so much about the queen's terrifying personality, it was with some trepidation that I awaited her appearance before dinner," Consuelo explained. "When eventually she came in, a little figure in somber black, I discovered to my dismay that I almost had to kneel to touch her outstretched hand with my lips. My balance was precariously held as I curtsied low to receive her kiss upon my forehead, and a diamond crescent in my hair caused me anxiety lest I scratch out a royal eye."[19]

After dinner, each person had a moment with the queen. "I found it embarrassing to stand in front of her while everyone listened to her kind inquiries about my reactions to my adopted country, which I answered as best I could," Consuelo remembered. "I was, moreover, haunted by the fear that I might not notice the little nod with which it was her habit to end an audience, having heard of an unfortunate person who, not knowing the protocol, had remained glued to the spot until ignominiously removed by a lord-in-waiting." The social calendar continued with a hunting trip to Sandringham at the invitation of the Prince and Princess of Wales followed by the royal couple's five-day visit to Blenheim during which numerous activities were planned. Happy to have made it through the grueling week of the Wales' visit with only the final dinner remaining, Consuelo marveled that she had pulled everything off.[20]

"As I went on a last round of inspection before dinner I thought the state rooms, which we had redecorated in Louis XIV boiseries of white and gold, were a splendid setting for such a festive scene, and the long suite of reception rooms filled with orchids and malmaisons looked to me truly palatial," she explained. "Later, as the royal procession wound its way through the throng of guests, the prince stopping here and there for a word of greeting, I realized that the Crown stood for a tradition that England would not easily give up." Soon after their week of hosting, they attended Queen Victoria's Diamond Jubilee on June 22, 1897, that ended with a fancy-dress ball at Devonshire House, which lasted into the early hours of the morning. "The sun was rising as I walked through Green Park to Spencer House, where we then lived," a heavily-pregnant Consuelo wrote. "On the grass lay the dregs of humanity. Human beings too dispirited or sunk to find work or favor, they sprawled in sodden stupor, pitiful representatives of the submerged tenth. In my billowing period dress, I must have seemed to them a vision of wealth and youth, and I thought soberly that they must hate me."[21]

It is interesting to see these words flow into her narrative given how helping the dregs, as she called them, would eventually fuel her greatest life purposes. But one particular duty had to be fulfilled before she could immerse herself in philanthropy—that of having a son. She achieved this on September 18, 1897, and the Prince of Wales offered to be godfather to Albert Edward William John Marlborough, who would be called Blandford because this was his title. Consuelo shared how much happiness her baby brought her, saying he "lightened the gloom that overhung our palatial home."[22] In her book *Consuelo & Alva Vanderbilt*, Amanda Mackenzie Stuart wrote, "The weeks and months after the birth of Blandford in 1897 were the high-water mark of the Marlborough marriage. Sunny had now assured both the future of the Marlborough dynasty and put in hand a new Golden Age for Blenheim. He had brought home a beautiful duchess who had charmed society and was idolized by the people of Woodstock and the Blenheim estate."[23] The bleak winter that followed found Consuelo pregnant with her second child, Ivor, who was born the following autumn. Just after the birth, her mother-in-law haughtily declared, "You are a little brick! American women seem to have boys more easily than we do!"[24]

Consuelo's success at birthing an heir and a spare—a phrase she coined—freed her from having to worry about struggling through any other pregnancies, which was convenient considering the cracks in her marriage were growing into chasms. There were a number of reasons she and her husband were not getting along: They disagreed greatly over how the Blenheim estates should be run, particularly where the human rights of its people were concerned; they were on opposite sides during many conversations about politics; and their views on philanthropy couldn't have been farther apart. Whereas she felt buoyed by the audience's response during a speech she gave to a group of blind men in Birmingham, England, her talk aimed at encouraging them to improve their lives by gaining a technical education; Marlborough always had to brace himself for any exposure to the "lower orders," as he called the downtrodden. Stuart said that Consuelo's tentative step into public life was one of several strategies by which she distracted herself from the unhappiness of her marriage.[25]

Marlborough was not only engaged in his own activities to create emotional distance between them, he expanded the physical divide by signing on to serve in the Boer War, leaving for South Africa on January 20, 1900. During the five months he was away, the only visitor of note to sign the guest book at Blenheim was the French painter Paul Helleu, whose daughter claimed he and Consuelo likely had an affair sometime after his arrival on May 11, 1900, which she said lasted into 1901. Stuart believed her, offering as evidence Helleu's pastels, dry-point etchings, and drawings of Consuelo that he produced at Blenheim and in Paris. The author said, "Some of these are delightfully tender and intimate, particularly a drawing of Consuelo dozing on a sofa at Blenheim, a dog asleep on her lap." The biographer also noted that when Consuelo went to Paris in June of 1900, the backdrops in the drawings that were completed in the French capital match photographs of Helleu's studio. Consuelo brushed aside her relationship with Helleu in her memoir, though this hasn't kept biographers from speculating there was likely physical intimacy between them.[26]

Stuart noted, "He offered her companionship when she needed it as well as limitless admiration of Consuelo's blossoming beauty."[27] The duchess's confidence was also growing, thanks in no small part to Winston, who was by then rushing headlong into his brilliant political career. "Whether it was his American blood or his boyish enthusiasm and spontaneity, qualities sadly lacking in my husband, I delighted in his companionship," she remembered. "His conversation was invariably stimulating, and his views on life were not drawn and quartered, as were Marlborough's, by a sense of self-importance." She credited their discussions about politics for the sense of civic responsibility she was developing. "I began to look beyond the traditional but superficial public duties expected of me," she explained. "Opening bazaars and giving away prizes with a few appropriate words could be successfully done by a moron—indeed, I realized that my dress and appearance were more important than any words I could utter. So perhaps it was not surprising that I became inspired to turn to more serious efforts."[28]

As she slowly moved toward these earnest endeavors, the superficiality of their public life was wearing on her. "Looking back on the last years of the Victorian era, I see a pageant of festive scenes. But pomp and ceremony were becoming tedious to one who, as my husband complained, had not a trace of snobbishness," Consuelo explained. "The realities of life seemed far removed from the palatial splendor in which we moved and it was becoming excessively boring to walk on an endlessly spread red carpet." She described a dressing down from the Prince of Wales when she attended a soiree with a diamond crescent in hair rather than a tiara. "Such an incident illustrates the over-importance attached to the fastidious observance of ritual," she declared.[29] The public appearances demanded by her rank were some of the most important historical events as England transitioned from Victoria's reign to the Edwardian Era. When Consuelo and Sunny were entering St. George's Chapel in Windsor Castle for the queen's state funeral in January of 1901, she said her husband paid her a rare compliment. "If I die, I see you will not remain a widow long," he told her.[30]

This might have bode well for the couple had things not grown so dicey by this point in time. Not only did Marlborough believe his wife had had the affair with Helleu, he blamed her that he was passed over when the position of Lord Lieutenant of Ireland was given to someone else because she had let it be known she preferred to remain in England. As the rifts between them piled on, he began to strengthen a relationship with another woman who would have a great deal to do with the undoing of their marriage. In her memoir, Consuelo remembered meeting her competition just after she gave birth to Blandford. "During my convalescence Marlborough had met a young woman named Gladys Deacon, who had come to London on a visit from Paris, where she lived with her mother and sisters," Consuelo wrote. "Gladys Deacon was a beautiful girl endowed with a brilliant intellect. Possessed of exceptional powers of conversation, she could enlarge on any subject in an interesting and amusing manner. I was soon subjugated by the charm of her companionship and we began a friendship which only ended years later."[31]

I found no proof that Marlborough began a romantic relationship with Deacon soon after that initial meeting in 1897, but Hugo Vickers wrote in his biography *The Sphinx: The Life of Gladys Deacon—Duchess of Marlborough*, that Sunny left Blenheim soon after Deacon arrived because he was so bowled over by her he doubted his self-control, which would eventually crater. The duke wrote the first of many letters to Deacon as soon as he arrived in Harrogate where he went to enjoy spa treatments. His intentions are cloaked but fairly obvious when he quotes this sentiment by François de La Rochefoucauld: "Absence diminishes mediocre passions and enflames the big ones, as the wind extinguishes candles but lights fires." He then told Deacon he cherished "the fond illusion that the candle has not been blown out" and "lingered on the possibility of its burning." Vickers noted there's proof that Deacon and Sunny were physically intimate by August of 1901 when Deacon had become a regular visitor at Blenheim.[32]

Vickers said Sunny was absolutely smitten with her. "Her arrival relieved the tedium of the Marlborough's doomed marriage," Vickers explained, "which the duke described as a 'false and sordid story.'"[33] Stuart elaborated on Sunny's enchantment with Deacon: "By 10 August 1901, the unhappy duke of Marlborough was helpless in the face of her beauty, intelligence, intensity, and capricious charm." Consuelo was equally enamored with Deacon, a closeness that solidified during a trip the two women took to Germany. "Consuelo had never experienced this kind of friendship, and by the time their short holiday ended, and Gladys returned home to Paris, she was almost as entranced by Gladys as her husband had been earlier," Stuart wrote, noting that they exchanged locks of hair and were referring to each other with silly endearments by then. Once Deacon was back in Paris, a shadowy triangle was unfolding—both Consuelo and her husband were writing Deacon effusive letters.[34]

Vickers said when Deacon returned to Blenheim, Consuelo adored talking to her about art and literature late into the night. He went so far as to say that Deacon inspired love in both the husband and the wife, a feat he said she had achieved with other couples.[35] Consuelo was unaware that when Deacon heard about her engagement to Sunny, she had lamented the marriage because Deacon had fancied herself in the role of the Duchess of Marlborough. She would eventually achieve this but it would be nearly a decade before Consuelo was released from the burden of hiding her discontent over her husband's unfaithfulness and the endless string of grand events she was forced to endure. One of the most magnificent was the coronation in which the Prince of Wales was crowned Edward VII on August 9, 1902. Alexandra had asked Consuelo to be one of the four duchesses who were her canopy bearers during the ceremony, and this is the moment when I was able to connect the dots to the photo I had seen of Consuelo in her bedroom: It was taken at some point during the ceremony to commemorate her participation.

No wonder her face was a mask of despair! Not only was her husband having an affair, hers with the French painter had ended over the fact she resented Helleu for indiscriminately selling etchings of her without her permission. She was also exhausted from having to pretend everything was fine each time she appeared with her husband in public, the coronation included. Consuelo was twenty-five years old at the time and had been married for almost seven years. In the photo, she was dressed to the nines in red velvet robes trimmed in miniver, and dripping with pearls and diamonds, the wealth of the incredibly attractive woman such a contrast to the hopelessness marking her face. The image depicted a perfect arm charm to accompany a duke whose political career was taking off—not only had he just been made a Knight of the Garter, he was the newly-appointed Under-Secretary for the Colonies. He and Consuelo took grand trips to India and Russia as their marriage faltered, and the lauded names of the people who floated into and out of Blenheim was a who's who of Edwardian England.

As Marlborough's star rose, he hired John Singer Sargent to paint their family portrait at Blenheim in 1905. Consuelo was very fond of the artist and her expression in the painting is not as beleaguered as it is in the black-and-white photograph. Though she still seemed somber, she also appeared to be somewhat bemused. As I studied her demeanor in the painting, I grew convinced it had been choreographed to reflect her station in life at the time. Within a year after she struck that pose, things would be drastically different. She titled the next chapter in her memoir "Deed of Separation," which opened with her comment that the eleven years she and Sunny had been married had not brought them closer together so they would be living apart from then on. "The nervous tension that tends to grow between people of different temperaments condemned to live together had reached its highest pitch," she explained.[36]

NOT WANTING to have to navigate the stigma that divorce would have brought them, they decided she would move out of Blenheim in 1906 and make her home Sunderland House in London, which had been built with the money her father had given her husband. The home was no palace but it was substantial—it had a ballroom with décor modeled after the La Galerie des Glaces at Versailles that was so long, two orchestras—one at each end—were required to fill the room with music during parties. Consuelo felt fully supported in living apart from her husband, even by many of Marlborough's family members. "My mother-in-law and many of my English family and friends gathered round me," she wrote, "and I was deeply touched by the innumerable letters I received, even from people unknown to me, expressing hopes for my future happiness."[37] She surprised me when she revealed she had made amends with her mother, who came to stay with her at Sunderland House, saying that Alva's sympathy was precious to her. It is at this point in her life when she proved she would not be typecast as a 'poor little rich girl.' She dove into philanthropy like a woman obsessed, learning from other more experienced females how to create successful campaigns and manage committees.

Like the other American-born aristocrats, she had an ace up her sleeve—she had a massive and influential list of contacts who were eager to help her raise large sums of money for her charities on both sides of the Atlantic. She was particularly interested in working to help the poor, whom Dana Cooper said "absolutely adored her compassionate methods of soft power." Winston's mother became a close friend as they plunged into philanthropic activities as members of a group called the American Amazons, which Lady Churchill had founded. "Consuelo began to hone her ability to negotiate her British and American identities," Cooper explained. "Over the next several years, she discovered that she could manipulate her national identity depending on the circumstance."[38] Championing the poor began to shift toward a focus on women and children. Eventually, she became involved in the suffragette's movement, influenced by Alva who was advancing the cause in America.

Cooper said that while some may dismiss Consuelo's efforts as little more than "emotional therapy for an unhappy aristocrat" or an attempt to reinstate her social position after a much-discussed marital breakdown, her involvement in charitable works went far beyond writing a check or lending her name to an institution. "Consuelo's philanthropic works were not an attempt to reestablish her membership in London society," the author added; "she genuinely cared about changing the lives of women, children, and the poor."[39] The list of Consuelo's accomplishments is long and she proved to be forward-thinking in her philosophy. "In a statement that eerily foreshadowed Secretary of State Hillary Clinton's demand a century later to see 'women's rights as human rights once and for all,'" Cooper explained, "Consuelo announced, 'This is the age of feminism…[but] not so much feminism as humanism.'"[40]

Consuelo and the other American Amazons spearheaded relief efforts when World War I broke out. After the conflict ended, Consuelo ran for and gained a seat on the London County Council in March 1919, the first woman to be elected to serve. During the portions of her book recounting the years after her separation, she revealed little about any contact with Marlborough, concentrating instead on how much she enjoyed championing her own interests. But her husband was not finished diminishing her life. He roars forth in the memoir again when he pressures her to allow him to end their marriage so he could make an honest woman out of Deacon, who had been his mistress for years. "In 1920, the duke and duchess began a series of legal battles that revealed Britain's depth of social ostracism for divorcees," Cooper explained. "Their official divorce forever placed Consuelo and Sunny outside social circles in England and ended Consuelo's political career."[41]

As Consuelo put it, "The long vista of lonely years behind me prodded the courage I needed to face the publicity of an English divorce court. But when I consulted my lawyer, he informed me that a legal separation freed a husband from the obligations contracted by marriage and that to secure a divorce I should first have to live under the same roof with Marlborough again." She described the humiliating process that lay before her: the husband was required to leave his wife and inform her in writing that he refused to return to her; she then had to appear in court and ask the judge for an injunction granting her "a restitution of conjugal rights"; on the judge's pronouncement, the husband would be ordered to comply; on his refusal to do so, the woman could bring action for divorce, provided she had the evidence required to secure it. "These were the steps I took to obtain my divorce in the year 1920," she explained, "having first, in order to comply with existing regulations, spent some days at Crowhurst with Marlborough." This home in Surrey, which she owned, was chosen as a sort of middle-ground for their supposed reunion.[42]

THE TREATMENT she endured because of such chauvinistic laws was a last straw and she decided she'd had enough of Great Britain's formalities. With the divorce behind her and grieving the loss of her father, who died the same year, she made the decision to leave England for France. "I spent a few weeks in London to pack my belongings, to arrange the sale of Sunderland House, to transfer a house I had leased in Portman Square to my married son, to give up Crowhurst, and to wind up the many activities that had become dear to me," she remembered. "Leaving my work was a wrench and saying farewell to my fellow workers saddened me."[43] She settled in a lovely house her father had given her in Paris where she was joined by her mother and her aunt Jenny Tiffany. Consuelo was finally able to move toward a happiness she couldn't have dreamed of as an English duchess. She began a relationship with a Frenchman who had noticed her during her teen years when she made her debut in Paris. "Curiously enough, my second husband, Jacques Balsan, who was present [in Paris], told his mother the following day, 'I met at the ball last night the girl I would like to marry,'" Consuelo said. "It was twenty-seven years later that his wish came true."[44]

They married on July 4, 1921, in a civil ceremony in a chapel in London at nine in the morning. "This unusual hour had been chosen to avoid the glare of publicity which had been focused on the marriage of Marlborough and Gladys Deacon earlier that spring in Paris," she remembered. "In shedding the luster of the coronet, it was my hope to avoid publicity. If not quite successful in that respect, in every other, life with Jacques Balsan has brought me the profound happiness that companionship with one who is equally loved and honored means." Unfortunately, she was not fully free of Marlborough's manipulations: Five years after Consuelo married Jacques, the duke demanded she agree to an annulment. "The shadow of my first marriage was once again to fall across my life when some years later Marlborough, having joined the Roman Catholic Church and wishing to regularize in that Church his civil marriage to Gladys Deacon, asked me to take steps to have our marriage annulled," she explained.[45] This meant that Alva would have to admit she had forced her daughter to marry the duke.

"It pained me to approach my mother for her consent, but on learning that the proceedings were entirely private we agreed to take the necessary steps," Consuelo noted. "The evidence once collected, I appeared with other witnesses before an English tribunal of Catholic priests versed in canonical law. My former governess, Miss Harper, gave valuable testimony, since she had personally witnessed the coercion to which I had been subjected." Before the annulment was fully granted, Marlborough caused a splash of publicity by going to Rome to seek an audience with the Pope, the move exposing Alva's complicity. "News of the annulment then got about and promptly unloosed a blast of Protestant wrath aimed at the Rota for annulling an Episcopal marriage," Consuelo said. "Alas, gone were our privacy and peace of mind as once again the press exposed my story. My mother, with her usual courage, remained undaunted, but I suffered to see her in so unfavorable a light, knowing that she had hoped to ensure my happiness with the marriage she had forced upon me."[46]

In the end, the annulment, which was finalized in 1926, benefitted Consuelo. The Balsans, who were devout Catholics, had never fully recognized her marriage to their son. "After the annulment was granted, I was married to Jacques in a Catholic ceremony and joined the family circle," she explained.[47] Consuelo said that during these happy years of her life, she was often asked if she ever regretted giving up the title of duchess. She said she never had because she was much better suited to a life of philanthropic and political endeavors that helped struggling people better their lives than she was to vapid ceremonial roles. With her personal life in the best place it had ever been, the tone of her memoir turns chatty and cheerful. In the chapters devoted to the initial years of their marriage, she shared how she and Jacques loved renovating houses and how they transformed a number of residences from Paris to the Riviera.

The memoir is filled with details of their decorating, their lavish entertaining, and the important visitors they hosted in Paris and in the south of France. These included diplomats, politicians, and personalities as diverse as Charlie Chaplin and Edith Wharton. "Luncheons centered round a literary or political personality became our specialty," she remembered. "Our cosmopolitan parties were gay and the house with its objects of art provoked interesting discussions, for nearly everyone in France 'collects' or has a hobby."[48] The Balsans' names were also included on some of the most coveted guest lists. She recounted one glittering evening at the home of the Duchesse de Doudeauville on the rue de Varenne, a mansion that is now the Italian Embassy in Paris. It had been spared from looting during the revolution and was filled with exquisite furnishings unlike many *hôtels particulier* that had been burned or emptied of their contents. Doudeauville had requested that everyone come in period dress popular during the reign of Louise XV.

"I copied mine from a Nattier portrait—a white taffeta dress with a pink sash slung across one shoulder and in my powdered hair a tuft of roses," she remembered. "When I entered the ballroom a spontaneous burst of applause greeted my appearance, a compliment which for me enhanced an already enchanted evening." The list of high-ranking members of French society the couple counted as their intimates was impressive, but her desire to do good that had risen to the forefront in her past was niggling at her. "Throughout all these years, I was blissfully happy in my life with Jacques and with our wide circle of friends," she explained; "but I missed the work I was accustomed to in England. I was therefore glad when in 1926 a group of social workers asked me to help them to build and equip a hospital for the professional classes."[49] She didn't hesitate to join them in their fundraising efforts and was pleased when other groups began reaching out to her after she made such a positive impact. As her desire to serve spread, she was about to be grounded in a community where she would do an immense amount of good.

After having spent the warmer months in the Riviera for years, Consuelo and Jacques decided they wanted a summer home that was in the country but closer to town so they could draw their Parisian clique to them more often. They found Saint Georges-Motel, a château on the border of Normandy near the Dreux forest, where they would spend summers until they left France. She described the parties on the lawn and the champagne brunches that drew their friends from town. Her next philanthropic effort organically took shape as she and Jacques grew more familiar with the local inhabitants. "During the summer holidays we opened a recreation school for the village children, for I was dismayed to find how little French children played," Consuelo wrote. "There was a stream where they swam and a playground for games, and the girls were taught how to sew, while the boys engaged in carpentry. At the end of the holidays, the children put on an entertainment in our honor, and a grand finale with 'The Star-Spangled Banner' sung in English."[50] The combined efforts she directed during her years in France earned her the coveted Légion d'Honneur in 1931.

As Consuelo moved through details like these, Alva entered the picture a number of times, her presence the most pronounced as Consuelo and Jacques settled in Normandy. "Our happy life at Saint Georges-Motel had inspired my mother to acquire a château near-by," Consuelo explained. "Not far from Fontainebleau, it was built of stone and was of the Renaissance period. Once settled, she proceeded to let her fancy roam, creating improvements so steadily that in spite of failing health, her last years were happily employed." Consuelo remembered an afternoon when she and Jacques were walking through Alva's gardens with her, the determination in her mother's character ever-present. Alva pointed to the river and said it was not wide enough. "When next we came, an army of workmen would have enlarged it," Consuelo explained. "A great forecourt separated the village from the house. It was sanded instead of paved. 'This is all wrong, it should be paved,' my mother commented severely; the year of her death, old paving stones brought from Versailles covered the court." It was 1933, and Consuelo described Alva's funeral at St. Thomas Church in New York City as "triumphantly symbolic with suffrage societies flying their banners as they came up the aisle wave upon wave."[51]

She said a hymn that Alva had composed was sung and, "It was only fitting that such a tribute should be paid to the courage she had shown in braving popular prejudice by securing better conditions for women the world over."[52] Just as Consuelo let bygones be bygones with her mother, she would loyally return to Blenheim, the scene of so much heartbreak and loneliness, for family milestones once her son had become duke. "How rewarding are my memories of Blenheim in my son's time when his life, with Mary and his children, was all that I wished mine could have been," she wrote. Given the poignancy of this statement, my rancor toward Alva grew, and I struggled more than ever with how to forgive the heavy-handed woman, holding out even after her daughter had done so. It was thanks to Stuart, who did not see Alva's machinations as completely negative, that I was finally able to admit I could cut Alva a little slack.

"It had been one of the ironies of her story that, after she left the Duke, the position of Duchess of Marlborough helped Consuelo to evolve an independent life, which in turn brought self-respect, confidence, autonomy and freedom, and quasi-professional roles far beyond anything that Alva had envisaged when she first arranged the marriage," Stuart wrote.[53] Given Consuelo had Alva's blood running through her veins, it makes sense that she would have turned out to be a resilient woman in spite of the fact that it was highly unlikely she could have ever had a successful marriage with a money-grabbing duke. Blenheim certainly benefitted from her sacrifice, a grandness that I saw mirrored in Marble House when I walked up that commanding staircase. I had no idea when I stepped into her bedroom that I would find within those monumental interiors the story of such a nurturing individual who would dedicate herself to the downtrodden so much so that she would be renowned as an "informal ambassador" and a "drawing-room diplomat" in the highest of societies in Europe.[54]

Though these terms may sound demeaning today, at the turn of the century they were powerful positions for the few American-born, British-wed women who cracked the gilt ceiling to hold. What I respect so much about them is that they didn't do so for the sake of dominance, but for the benefit of humanity. By the time Consuelo and Jacques fled Europe for America in order to escape the Germans who were about to invade France at the beginning of World War II, she had made remarkable contributions to the charities she assisted. Forced once again to leave behind efforts she had so diligently built, Consuelo and Jacques boarded a plane in Lisbon after a harrowing trip from Normandy to Portugal. They did so just as Hitler's troops would have made their leaving impossible. She described her relief once they were airborne: "As we moved through the waters and rose to our flight, I looked at the sky above and the slowly fading coast beneath and felt I had embarked on a celestial passage to a promised land."[55] It is with this sentence that she ended her story, and I was disappointed that she decided not to share anything about her life after she returned stateside because I would have loved to know whether she returned to Marble House; whether she walked up that sweeping staircase and entered the bedroom where she had been so unhappy. I would like to think she would have smiled at the framed photograph of herself, which Alva must have placed on the dresser at some point to represent all that she had achieved for her daughter.

I believe Consuelo would have been pleased because she could by then declare she was "a finished specimen framed in a perfect setting" because she was no longer imprisoned in that room or in the marriage she was enduring when the snapshot was taken. It would have been such a victory for her to close the door for the last time knowing she had achieved her own success in spite of the fact that her reality had been so denied when she was growing up that she wouldn't have dared touch any of the elegant accoutrements in that room. Once her marriage to the duke fell apart, Consuelo could easily have lived a superficial life as an extremely wealthy woman. The fact that she chose to concentrate a tremendous amount of energy over the years doing good for those less fortunate, she charted a path from self-denial to soft power and managed to find some happiness along the way. What more can any woman of any era ask for?

11

NO ONE GETS OFF SCOT-FREE
THE FITZGERALDS IN MONTGOMERY

I was face-to-face with the king and queen of the Jazz Age. Not literally, of course, F. Scott and Zelda were long gone by the time I was visiting The Fitzgerald Museum in Montgomery, which is housed in the only residence in the Alabama town they briefly called home. The museum is a veritable time capsule filled with artifacts from the Roaring Twenties when wild girls shrieked and flapped, and polished young men pulled gleaming flasks out of breast pockets and cigarettes out of engraved cases. On the walls, framed letters penned by Scott and Zelda, some sent from the home and others mailed from exotic locales as they galivanted around the globe, bear witness to their handwriting—his dynamic and heavy-handed, hers more ethereal. Portraits of Zelda hold penetrating stares, sweet glances, and dark expressions of sadness. She met me in all directions, her demeanor changing as she aged. Photographs of Scott spanned the decades—from the dashing young man with a devil-may-care attitude to a still handsome profile by the time he had become a bona-fide literary figure.

On display are the books he wrote intermingled with

neatly arranged memorabilia, each item cataloged by year: a Chesterfield tin, his cigarette of choice, which would be half empty by the time he finished a day's writing; their tennis rackets flanking a charcoal portrait of Scott sitting on the fireplace mantle; an Underwood Typewriter No. 5 Standard, Scott's preference when he wasn't writing longhand, across the room. Two photographs of Zelda in ballet costumes bookmark her passion for dance—the first when she was nineteen, a haunting photograph of her in costume surrounded by a riot of flowers in her role as Folly in the *Les Mysterieuses* Ball; the second when she was pert and pretty at thirty-one in the front room of the house, an image that also illustrates the dust jacket of the first edition of her autobiographical novel *Save Me the Waltz*. The home was remarkably calm, the atmosphere a far cry from how it would have been when they were in residence considering how much rancor they felt for each other by the time they lived in it.

The quietude could only exist because their spirits were muted—the figures the camera captured serving as voiceless stand-ins in black and white, and many shades of gray. Built in 1909, the house at 919 Felder Avenue on the edge of the historic Old Cloverdale neighborhood was the scene of the Fitzgerald's doomed attempt at a home life from the fall of 1931 through early 1932. It was a pivotal time in their relationship, as Zelda had only recently been released from treatment for schizophrenia at a sanitarium in Switzerland. The reason for their short-lived stay was her relapse and hospitalization in Maryland. I stood for a long time in front of a photo of them captured by paparazzi while they attended a performance at the Music Box Theatre in Baltimore in October in 1932. The expressions of the still attractive couple bore witness to the fact they were experiencing significant strain. Approaching a glass case holding souvenirs from their trips to the Côte d'Azur, I thanked a visionary couple, Julian and Leslie McPhillips, who saved the home from demolition in 1986 when developers wanted to tear it down to build townhomes.

Julian, a Princeton graduate just as Scott was, set the wheels in motion to save and restore the then-dilapidated Craftsman-style house. His effort means it now resembles the home Scott and Zelda inhabited and preserves a brief but important chapter in the Fitzgeraldian saga. The items in the museum's collection celebrate the style of the era they embodied, their participation inspiring actress Lillian Gish to say, "They didn't make the twenties; they were the twenties."[1] Why Montgomery? It was Zelda's hometown and the scene of her most audacious childhood exploits. A rambunctious southern belle, Zelda flaunted convention from an early age, her shamelessness notable because her father was the well-respected Alabama Supreme Court Judge Anthony Sayre. She lived on Pleasant Avenue when she was growing up, the family home chosen by her father because it was close to the trolley line—he was so nearsighted, he had never learned to drive.

Cloverdale was just being built when she was old enough to scamper around town, and one of the early edifices constructed in the lush area was the Montgomery Country Club where she would swim as a girl and dance as a teenager. I was able to plumb Zelda's life for tidbits like these because Sara Mayfield, who was five years younger than Zelda and a devoted friend of hers when they were growing up, put them in writing. Mayfield said Zelda was the typical baby of the family, forgiven more often than her brother and three older sisters because her mother Minnie was partial to her. Prone to hyperbole, Zelda claimed her mom had breast-fed her until she was old enough to bite a chicken bone in half! "Whether from a lack of discipline in her early years, a biological mutation, or the unconscious influence of her name, taken from that of a gypsy queen her mother had run across in a novel, from the beginning Zelda was like a wild grapevine grafted onto the traditional stock in a Confederate vineyard," Mayfield wrote in her biography of Scott and Zelda *Exiles from Paradise*.[2]

She said the grapes had a "rare, intoxicating flavor" of their own and described how deep rebellion was embedded in Zelda's makeup by sharing Minnie's set of "no ladies" rules, which were: No lady was to sit with her limbs crossed (the word "legs" prohibited here for being too unladylike), to allow her upper torso to touch the back of a chair, to leave the house without a clean linen handkerchief tucked into her purse, to appear in public unless the last button on her gloves was fastened, or to let her bare feet touch a bare floor. "Miss Minnie tried dutifully to instill these rules of conduct in her daughters," Mayfield explained. "Zelda's sisters, who were more conventional than she was, endeavored to follow their mother's precepts, but Zelda saw more humor than value in such old-fashioned notions and not only laughed at them but also deliberately defied them." Zelda's only rival in daredevilry growing up was Dutch, better known today as Tallulah Bankhead.[3]

The two romped through town with the same tomboy bravado, though Mayfield said Zelda could also be decidedly feminine when she chose to be, her somewhat magical personality filled with "charm and sweetness as spontaneous as the sparkle of champagne."[4] The critic and editor Edmund Wilson, who met Scott when they were both at Princeton and would become one of his closest friends and his literary executor, wrote that the fairies must have been tipsy at the christening of Zelda because they heedlessly squandered on her "choice gifts" with a minimum of stabilizing qualities.[5] Zelda fascinated other children because she invented games for them to play and told enthralling stories, which turned boring days in one of America's southern towns into dramatic ones. Mayfield depicted Zelda as both generous and fearless as she remembered what could have been a dangerous, if not deadly, day.

Zelda would take off down the hill from the top of Sayre Street on roller skates and careen along, always gracefully sweeping around just in time to avoid the cobblestones at the bottom. One day, ignoring her nurse's warning, Mayfield launched herself down the hill on borrowed skates and quickly realized she was out of control. "Zelda overtook me, going at breakneck speed," she explained. "Some fifty feet short of disaster, she put her arm around me and swung me out of danger. 'Listen,' she said, 'you'll break your neck. Wait until a dray comes along to pull us back up the hill; then you can go down holding on to me until you learn to make the turn.'"[6] This moment cemented Mayfield's status as a Zelda acolyte for the rest of her life. Mayfield's father James, also a supreme court judge, frequently played chess with Anthony Sayre in the evenings. Zelda was fascinated by the strategy behind their moves but she couldn't resist snark when it came to her dad, whose middle name was Dickinson.

She called him "Old Dick" behind his back, the insult her form of rebellion against his antiquated views about how she should behave. James described Judge Sayre as one of the most honorable men of his time, saying he had the most brilliant mind he had ever known and that Sayre had an encyclopedic store of general knowledge. His opinions were rarely overruled, and his decisions were cited in textbooks from Harvard to the University of Alabama. Mayfield believed that Zelda's father's position could have contributed to his daughter's ability to forge her own personality during a time when decorum was everything to everyone else because no one dared correct Judge Sayre's wild daughter. In the end this level of independence would come with a price.

"She had inherited blue blood, a brilliant mind, and, if not riches, at least social and economic security," Mayfield explained, "but she never acquired the defense mechanisms necessary to protect herself from the people she charmed—and whose pursuit of her hastened her downfall."

This presents an eerie foreshadowing of life during her marriage to F. Scott Fitzgerald, the young man who would step into her world in July of 1918 when she was about to celebrate her eighteenth birthday. He was one of many soldiers stationed in Montgomery during World War I who would find themselves jockeying for position as they went in hot pursuit of her. A steady succession of cars and motorbikes pulled up to the curb in front of the Sayre residence and honked their horns, the young men hoping to avoid a face-to-face with her father, who was infuriated by their casual attitudes because he said no gentleman should ever call for a lady in such a manner. This was one of many outmoded beliefs Zelda would ignore as she flitted from party to party and flirted with every guy whose looks she liked. Teens in Montgomery had the soldiers to thank for the lively atmosphere that took hold in their hometown during the early twentieth century because they brought Dixieland jazz to the ballroom, which trickled down to college campuses and frat houses before long.

Zelda, whose favorite dances were the Shimmy, the Charleston, and the Black Bottom, raised her hemlines to the knee, bobbed her hair, smoked, tippled, and kissed her suitors when they brought her home. She also rode behind her admirers from the varied military bases with her arms encircling their waists as they zipped along on their motorcycles, behavior that appalled Judge Sayre. When he witnessed one of her goodbye kisses, he ordered her to come into the house and said, "I won't have you carrying on in such a fashion, you little hussy."[7] She blew him off by saying that's what hussies did! She later defended her behavior in "Eulogy on the Flapper," an article she wrote for the June 1922 issue of *Metropolitan Magazine* in which she said, "She flirted because it was fun to flirt and wore a one-piece bathing suit because she had a good figure; she covered her face with powder and paint because she didn't need it and she refused to be bored chiefly because she wasn't boring. She was conscious that the things she did were the things she had always wanted to do."[8]

Mayfield debunked the lies that some of Scott's biographers have told about Zelda. Whereas they claimed she was not above taking swigs of corn liquor when the bottle was passed around by the soldiers she dated, Mayfield said she had champagne tastes, and was far more likely to have sent one of them to fetch her a split of Pommery or a Sazerac cocktail. Zelda was also accused of being fast and loose, which Mayfield said was flatly untrue because she didn't have to stoop to that level. Being a reigning beauty, she could tease on her own terms without having to take it all the way. "Flirtation was an old Southern custom, 'going the limit' was not," Mayfield explained. "Zelda was far too popular to have to 'put out' for her beaux and far too shrewd in the tactics and strategy of popularity to grant her favors to one suitor and thereby alienate a regiment of them."[9] Mayfield did admit that Zelda was partly responsible for her reputation because she couldn't help but tell elaborate stories about her escapades in order to build an aura of excitement around her that made admirers determined to be in her orbit.

While Scott would claim Zelda was a heartless charmer during fits of jealousy, her friend declared, "she was simply an unusually attractive young girl, having a good time with her crowd—and usually in a crowd."[10] Until the military men showed up, Zelda's suitors were wellborn and wealthy, one of them describing her as one of the south's truly fine examples of feminine brains, beauty, and charm. Another claimed she was always the most popular girl at any dance and it was far from fun to be her partner because two or three steps was the extent of dancing before another chap cut in on him. It was the long lines of these eager young men that Scott noticed when he spotted her for the first time on a sultry evening in July. Zelda's tan had turned her skin to the color of a ripe peach and she boldly took stock of him with her smoky gray eyes, which inspired him to say she reminded him of "a Viking Madonna." He was just as striking in his Brooks Brothers uniform, his profile the epitome of the fresh-scrubbed faces emblazoned on the Arrow-collar advertisements of the day.

In *Save Me the Waltz*, Zelda described his blonde hair, parted in the middle and slicked down as was the style for men about town, as, "green gold under the moon."[11] By this time, Scott had gone beyond simply dreaming of becoming a published writer. He had spent his off hours at Camp Sheridan working on a draft of a manuscript with the working title "The Romantic Egoist," which he had mailed to editor Maxwell Perkins at Charles Scribner's Sons a few weeks before he spotted his future wife. The publisher's response was that they had reviewed it with a "very unusual degree of interest" because it displayed so much originality but they wouldn't be able to publish it because the story didn't seem to work up to any conclusion. Perkins told Scott this was especially true with the hero's career and his character, which weren't fleshed out well enough to justify the ending. He said if Scott would consider a revision, they would welcome a chance to take another look.[12]

Scott's reworking of the manuscript would not be sent to

Perkins until over a year later—a span of time that encompassed his first dance with Zelda in 1918 and the subsequent disappointments he experienced trying to court her. Zelda was not immune to Scott's charms—she just wasn't ready to settle down. Proof that she found him attractive is her description of how fleet-footed he was as they moved across the dance floor. "There seemed to be some heavenly support beneath his shoulder blades that lifted his feet from the ground in ecstatic suspension, as if he secretly enjoyed the ability to fly but was walking as a compromise to convention," she wrote.[13] Mayfield met Scott about a month later when Zelda was showing him the star on the steps of Montgomery's capitol building where Jefferson Davis had taken the oath of office as the president of the Confederate States of America.

Mayfield was amused that the infantry lieutenant had spurs on his cavalry boots, which she noted illustrated his aspirations to present himself to the southern belles as a more intriguing fellow than if he'd worn the usual leather leggings strapped around the calves of the other soldiers. Hoping to take the one Alabama beauty who had caught his eye off the market, Scott asked Zelda to marry him before he left with his regiment for Camp Mills on Long Island. Though she said yes, her Yankee suitor took a backseat in her thoughts as she became one of the most popular eighteen-year-old debutants in the region. She went to dances at the University of Alabama, the University of Georgia, Auburn University, and Sewanee: The University of the South. At Auburn, she was so popular her admirers founded Zeta Sigma, a fraternity that limited its members to those who pledged devotion to Zelda and provided proof they had had at least one date with her. Her military suitors were just as avid. To salute her, aviators from Taylor Field would buzz her house, flying dangerously low. When one of them died after his plane went down during a barrel-role, their commanding officer forbade any further aerial acrobatics. Not to be outdone, a squad of infantrymen from Camp Sheridan executed a drill in front of her house to impress her.

This behavior surprised Scott when he returned to Camp Sheridan for the last time. Initially, he was proud that her popularity had grown, but when she broke a date with him to attend the governor's inaugural ball with one of her local guys and went to a dance with Auburn's famous quarterback, he denounced her as a tease. When the relationship with the football player grew more serious, Scott exploded, only to quickly realize he had gone too far. When he tried to kiss her to make up for his outburst, she broke off the engagement. This blowup took place soon after Scott's discharge from the Army on February 14, 1919, and he left Montgomery for New York in a dark mood. "Zelda was cagy about throwing in her lot with me before I was a money-maker, and I think by temperament she was the most reckless of all," he wrote. "She was young, and in a period where any exploiter or middle-man seemed a better risk than a worker in the arts."[14] Scott penned persistent letters to Zelda, saying he hoped she would soon be with him in New York and declared how optimistic he felt about their future together.

His positivity was surprising given he was clawing his way through a string of disappointing jobs—first as a newspaper reporter, then as a writer of slogans for street-car advertisements. The pay was so low for both, he was living in a horrible apartment house that he described as situated in the middle of nowhere. He was actually just off Broadway in Morningside Heights several blocks west of Columbia University. While he was having a very slow start as a "worker in the arts," something surprising was fermenting in Zelda's mind. During a date with one of her local suitors, she

NO ONE GETS OFF SCOT-FREE

confided she didn't think she was in love with Scott but she felt it was her mission in life to help him realize his potential as a writer. "This is a more likely explanation of Zelda's marriage to Scott than those given by some of his biographers who claim that she was madly in love with him and insinuated that he had seduced her before her marriage to him," Mayfield wrote. She said she knew the latter wasn't true because Scott was angry that Zelda continued to hold him, in his own words, "firmly at bay."[15]

AS SCOTT STRUGGLED to figure out how to build a career, Zelda's social calendar was overflowing with parties and dates with other men. She saw this as a duty of sorts because she was a young, desirable southern belle who felt she had one shot at stacking her deck with potential husbands. She must have seen Scott as an ace up her sleeve because while all of her dance cards were full, she wrote extravagant expressions of love to him, which claimed she didn't like having to wait for him to make his fortune so she could marry him. Scott was clueless that she was merely keeping him in play—taking the declarations she made at face value, he sent Zelda an engagement ring. She responded with a rapturous letter after blithely tossing the ring into her "trophy box." She was having way too much fun as one of the most sought-after girls in the tri-state region of Alabama, Georgia, and Tennessee to be swayed by his advances. When I read that she sent Scott a photo of herself with an inscription meant for a well-known Atlanta golfer, I wondered if she was flighty or passive aggressive. In the picture, she was wearing the golfer's fraternity pin and the note to him that she placed in the envelope was tender in its tone.

This led Scott to notice how her letters to him had cooled

and I questioned why he was putting up with the on-again/off-again nature of the situation he was navigating. I found a clue in his autobiographical novel that was initially titled *The Romantic Egoist* and would eventually be published as *This Side of Paradise*. "I was by no means the 'Captain of my Fate,'" he admitted. "I had a curious cross-section of weakness running through my character. I was liable to be swept off my poise into a timid stupidity." He confessed to being a slave to his own moods: "At the least crisis, I knew I had no real courage, perseverance, or self-respect."[16] His confidence was taking daily hits when the stories he sent to magazines came back about as fast as he sent them out. The rejections were so numerous, he created a decorative frieze of them in his room, pinning them to the walls after retrieving them from the mailbox.

When a particularly disappointing one was fished from the post without a letter from Montgomery, he went on a bender with some pals from his college years and tried to jump out of an upper-story window at the Princeton Club, his friends pulling him back into the room just in time. His short-story losing streak ended in June 1919 when the editor H.L. Mencken accepted "Babes in the Woods" for *The Smart Set*, a placement that netted Scott thirty dollars. He bought a magenta feather fan for Zelda, a white pair of slacks for himself, and hopped on a train bound for Montgomery. Instead of caving to his pleas that she must pledge herself to him, Zelda broke off the engagement yet again and gave him the ring back. A despondent Scott returned to New York and landed another placement with Mencken but knew the meager money wasn't enough to support himself, much less a wife. He decided to move back in with his parents in St. Paul, Minnesota, so he could revise the novel he sent to Perkins the year before.

He went into seclusion, slaving away at the book and

having his mother deliver his meals to his attic room while he worked up to fifteen hours a day. He pinned outlines of chapters to the curtains, revising old sections and adding new ones. He wrote to Perkins in July 1919, "After four months attempt[ing] to write commercial copy by day and painful half-hearted imitations of popular literature by night, I decided that it was one thing or another. So I gave up getting married and went home."[17] He said he had finished a revised draft of the novel that held a mix of new ideas and bits of the storyline in the previous manuscript, the combination of which had significantly changed it. I was floored to learn that some of the material he used to create the updated narrative included love letters other men had written to Zelda and excerpts from her diary, which he had read while he was courting her. Sara Haardt, another of Zelda's childhood friends, wrote about the Fitzgerald's relationship in her book *The Constant Circle: H.L. Mencken and His Friends*.

Describing the Fitzgeralds' union as doomed, she declared, "Every time Scott writes a book, he performs a literary vivisection on poor Zelda."[18] The first of these dissections was about to appear in print—his sequestered servitude paid off and Scribner's accepted the novel he'd rewritten with the new title *This Side of Paradise*. He immediately wrote to Zelda and asked if he could see her. She agreed to let him make his case and he headed south. Convinced he was on his way to fame and fortune, he pressed her to renew their engagement and she said yes as long as the wedding wouldn't take place before the following January. Her parents tried to dissuade her for a number of reasons that included his lack of stability but they eventually gave in. Her mother wrote to Scott saying they would give their blessing because, "Zelda has had several admirers, but you seem to be the only one to make anything like a permanent impression." The fact that Scott was a Catholic and Zelda was an

Episcopalian had been on their list of concerns but Minnie smoothed it over by declaring, "A good Catholic is as good as any other good man and that is good enough. It will take more than the Pope to make Zelda good; you will have to call on God Almighty direct."[19]

When their engagement was announced in the *Montgomery Advertiser* in March of 1920, it sent a shockwave through the deep south because Zelda hadn't bothered to inform her other suitors she was about to be unavailable. Her close friends were also floored, as they never imagined she would actually marry Scott, even with his literary star on the rise. *This Side of Paradise* and "Head and Shoulders," a story which appeared in *The Saturday Evening Post*, debuted in tandem, and the movie rights for the novel sold to Metro Pictures for $2,500 soon after. Though this doesn't seem like a windfall in 2024, the sum had the purchasing power of around $40,000 today, which made Scott so giddy at the change in his prospects, he summoned Zelda and began making plans for their wedding. When she arrived in New York City shortly before the fateful date, he sent her to Fifth Avenue with one of his former girlfriends to buy what he felt was a suitable wardrobe for a glamorous woman of the world. On April 3, 1920, the ceremony took place in the rectory of Saint Patrick's Cathedral.

It was over by the time Zelda's sister Clotilde and her husband, who lived several hours north of New York City, could arrive. As soon as the Fitzgeralds said their vows, the two of them cut and run, abandoning her other sister Marjorie and her husband, who had traveled north with the soon-to-be bride. It is fortunate that Zelda's parents had decided not to attend because the absence of music, flowers, a photographer, and a cake to cut would have upset her mother. The newlyweds launched straight into party-mode, the celebrating so intense, the management at the Biltmore

NO ONE GETS OFF SCOT-FREE

Hotel asked them to leave before their honeymoon was over. The last straw for the manager was when Scott left the spigots open during a long, hot bath and flooded the rooms below. As if their honeymoon had set the tone for the early years of their marriage, the Fitzgeralds were insatiable revelers, spurring each other on during follies, plays, and wild private parties. When it became clear the socializing was keeping him from writing, Scott attempted to create an environment in which he could work by renting a secluded gray-shingled cottage with its own beach and garden in Westport, Connecticut.

As they attempted to settle into the home, a theme that would continue throughout the rest of their relationship emerged: Scott would have trouble writing given the many distractions brought about by life with a feisty girl; and Zelda would do everything in her power to keep him from working because she was bored when he was distracted. In theory, the cottage was an idyllic setting for Scott to flourish as an author but the couple found suburbia tedious, which resulted in a fair amount of shuttling to and from New York City to break the monotony. When they managed to stay put in their beachside home, life was far from settled enough to foster a productive writing ritual because their pals from the city flocked to the beach for overnights and weekends. Scott's inability to produce during this early phase of their marriage presented the first of many pressure-filled times he would experience after taking money from publications. With each non-working day that passed, his anxiety increased—his worry at this moment in time was over a $7,000 advance from *Metropolitan Magazine* for the serial publication of his next novel that would eventually become *The Beautiful and the Damned*.

Though Zelda had a great deal to do with his stalled writing assignments, his behavior during this episode in Westport that took place during the only visit Zelda's parents paid them, shows how he was equally culpable. When the Judge and Minnie arrived, two of Scott's friends were passed out in hammocks on the lawn. As everyone was gathered around the dining room table for a family dinner, the men awoke and turned the room into a cabaret. When Zelda came downstairs the next morning, she discovered Scott had eventually joined his drunken pals. The kitchen was in shambles and ashtrays were overflowing, which made the house smell like a pool hall. When she tried to wrest the bottle of gin from Scott's hands, he pushed her aside and she took a swinging door full in the face. She tried and failed to cover her bloody nose and black eye with heavy makeup so her parents wouldn't notice. As they descended the stairs, it was obvious they did, her battered gaze met with chilly disapproval from both of the Sayres as they came face-to-face.

Appalled at what was going on, they ended the visit earlier than expected and Zelda was so upset, Scott whisked her off to Manhattan so the celebrity set into which they were becoming more entrenched every day could take her mind off her parents' disapproval. Actress Lillian Gish said of the Fitzgeralds, "They were both so beautiful, so blonde, so clean and clear. Zelda could do outlandish things—say anything. It was never offensive when Zelda did it, as you felt she couldn't help it, and was not doing it for effect."[20] This included flirting with Scott's friends and rivals, which tested her husband to his depths. The combination of her youth, beauty, and wit was like a man-magnet, and Scott frittered writing time away when she was out because he worried she was making new conquests. Alex McKaig, a friend of Scott's from Princeton, declared Zelda one of the most brilliant and beautiful young women he had ever known.

McKaig said her mind was undisciplined but her intuition was marvelous and he worried about how absorbed Scott was as he cannibalized Zelda's personality for his fiction because he saw Zelda as the stronger of the two, which McKaig believed put Scott in danger of losing his ability to create female characters that weren't inspired by his wife. Scott confessed to his friend that there was something of Zelda in all of his female characters; that he had used her ideas for his stories "The Ice Palace" and "The Jelly Bean," and for the novel he was writing at the time. Lawton Campbell, a young businessman who had grown up in Montgomery and had also gone to Princeton with Scott, was working in New York when the Fitzgeralds were on the scene. He also noted the importance of Zelda's influence on Scott's work. "I have always thought that Zelda did more for Scott than Scott did for Zelda," he explained. "I have seen him many times write down the things she said on scraps of paper or the backs of envelopes. *The Beautiful and the Damned* was pure Zelda."[21]

Before long, it was glaringly obvious that a quiet country retreat wasn't going to be more conducive to writing than the bustling city of New York so Scott propelled them back into the action. They rented an apartment near the Plaza Hotel, which quickly became party-central. Campbell, who arrived to take the couple to lunch one day, said their apartment looked like a cyclone had hit it and they were so trashed, they were just getting out of bed. During the winter months to come, the couple were slaves to their popularity, their list of conquests reading like a who's who of public personalities—Dorothy Parker, Charles MacArthur, Helen Hayes, Lillian Hellman, and Gish among them. The revelry reached such heights, the cash it took to maintain it exceeded advances and royalties. Perkins blamed Zelda because he said she wanted everything she saw. Mayfield pointed out that

Zelda didn't have a clue about finances: She had never had a bank account and she had never been taught to manage money when she was growing up. When Zelda took a friend to lunch at the Plaza one day, she pulled out a wad of cash the size of a baseball when she went to pay the bill.

When her friend asked what on earth she was doing carrying around so much money, she answered, "Scott gave it to me as I went out the door, so what else could I do with it but bring it along."[22] Stressed to the max that he was stalled on the novel, Scott pulled together a book of short stories that had been published in magazines titled *Flappers and Philosophers*. Mencken lambasted it while other critics deemed it entertaining. In spite of inconsistent reviews for numerous published works in 1920, Scott was making enough money to have a good life, though what he and Zelda considered good would have been out of reach if they had lived within their means. A copy of page fifty-two from his ledger, framed in the museum in Montgomery, listed his earnings as $18,850 that year, which would value a little over $300,000 today. By this time, no amount was ever enough, and the extravagance with which they lived meant his bank account was overdrawn at the end of the year and he was in serious debt with his publisher.

In a desperate move, he offered Scribner's his next ten books as security on a $1,600 loan, the manuscripts still a pipe dream given he'd already been paid for *The Beautiful and the Damned*, which he had to finish. As the calendar flipped to 1921, he was finally able to complete a draft of the novel in spite of the raucousness of their day-to-day existence. The pressure valve released, he and Zelda decided to plan a trip to Europe because she was three months pregnant and they wanted to have an adventure while she could still travel. They sailed on the RMS *Aquitania* on May 3rd, and quickly set the theme for the entire trip: disappointment. When Scott scrutinized the names on the passenger list, he decided the few celebrities he spotted there were beneath his interest. "In London, Tallulah, who was then the toast of the town, introduced the Fitzgeralds to the Marchioness of Milford Haven," Mayfield wrote; "but that, Scott said indignantly, was as near to royalty as they came."

Zelda described Buckingham Palace as a "Town Hall with redskins walking around it"—her snarky way of identifying the Queen's Foot Guards in their lush red jackets and tall black fur hats.[23] The couple had dustups with the management at the Hotel Cecil where they stayed while in the British capital, and with the staff at the elegant Hôtel St. James Albany in Paris where they went next. Zelda complained that the elevator of the latter was too slow when she was ready to leave their suite so she would lash the lift to the gate on her floor with her belt. Before long, she and Scott were asked to leave. They decided to travel to Italy where they intended to spend an entire year, but they swiftly returned to London because they met no interesting people, were unimpressed while sightseeing, couldn't take the heat, and had both been invaded by intestinal parasites. Scott wrote to Wilson from the Hotel Cecil where they'd scrambled.

"God damn the continent of Europe. It is of merely antiquarian interest." He said France made him sick: "It's silly pose as the thing the world has to save. I think it's a shame that England + America didn't let Germany conquer Europe. It's the only thing that would have saved the fleet of tottering old wrecks." He then admitted he had a philistine, antisocialistic, provincial, and racially snobbish point of view, all of which pepper his correspondence with bigotry and unseemly asides. Eager to see the British coastline disappearing in the distance, they sailed for the U.S. in early July. When they disembarked in New York, Scott told reporters they'd had a rotten time. Smarting from having drained away cash on such an unsatisfying trip, he wrote to Wilson that he was going down to Montgomery, or "The Sahara of Bozart," as he called it, for life.[24] Zelda was keen on having her baby in Alabama and she wanted them to look for a house to see if settling in her hometown would be a good fit. Though Scott was open to this as they traveled south, several factors quickly changed his mind: They were blasted by a hellish heatwave as soon as they stepped off the train at Montgomery's Union Station, and they arrived at Zelda's parents' house where they would be staying to find that Judge Sayre wouldn't allow alcohol in the house because he presided over trials dealing with breaches in prohibition laws.

Scott found speakeasies where he could imbibe but Zelda was too far along in her pregnancy to join in—she sat around and sulked during her husband's boozy evenings. Mayfield shared an anecdote about Scott and Zelda during this trip to Montgomery that amplified how he couldn't have possibly fit in if they had decided to permanently settle there. The couple went to Mayfield's house for afternoon tea one day, presided over Sara's mother, Susie. When Scott spotted a portrait of one of the family's ancestors that had a rip in it, he asked why she didn't have it fixed. Susie answered, "Because it was made by a Yankee bayonet." Scott responded, "You sound like Zelda's mother; you people down here cherish your scars, don't you." With a smile, Susie countered in French: "I suppose so; like the Bourbons, we haven't learned anything nor forgotten anything."[25]

As they sipped tea, Zelda told Mayfield that Scott's attitude about Alabama had changed since they had stepped off the train so she didn't see them settling there. His excuse was the disruption in his party-life because prohibition was so much stricter in the south, and his inability to work caused by the heat and humidity, which was torturous given Zelda's parents' house had no air conditioning. By the time he'd put in a few hours at the writing table, Scott's shirt was so wet, it clung to his back, which was stinging with heat rash. After less than a month in Zelda's hometown, the couple left for St. Paul where he had rented a house on White Bear Lake. Once again, he would find that a quiet life that fostered the creative was impossible, as his status as the hometown literary hero brought fans pouring through the front door.

Frustrated that he couldn't work, he rented an office and hunkered down to revise *The Beautiful and the Damned* to satisfy his publisher's feedback. A bored Zelda complained about her "lone wolf poignancy," which she blamed on isolation and homesickness as she sat, heavily pregnant, alone in the house for hours on end. On October 26, 1921, her complaints ended with the birth of their daughter. As soon as Frances Scott Key Fitzgerald, whom they would call Scottie, was born, Scott stepped into Zelda's room with a notebook and recorded his wife's first words as she surfaced from the fog of anesthesia: "Goofo [her nickname for him], I'm drunk. Mark Twain. Isn't she smart—she had the hiccups. I hope it's beautiful and a fool—a beautiful little fool." During the winter that followed, Scott was churning out short stories, working on a play, and polishing the final edits for *The Beautiful and the Damned*. "Zelda not only helped him greatly with the proofs but also suggested another ending for the novel," Mayfield wrote. "More than one critic was to say that Anthony and Gloria bore a striking resemblance to Scott and Zelda."[26] The novel was published by Scribner's on March 4, 1922.

IN A REVIEW of the book Zelda wrote for the *New York Tribune*, which appeared on April 2nd, she breezily suggested, "It is a wonderful book to have around in case of an emergency. No one should ever set out in pursuit of unholy excitement without a special vest pocket edition dangling from a string around the neck." After telling the newspaper's readers a list of things she'd like to buy if the book sold well, she wrote, "It seems to me that on one page I recognized a portion of an old diary of mine which mysteriously disappeared shortly after my marriage, and also scraps of letters which, though considerably edited, sound to me vaguely familiar. In fact, Mr. Fitzgerald—I believe that is how he spells his name—seems to believe that plagiarism begins at home."[27] Critics' opinions about the novel were mixed and sales fell far short of Scott's expectations, which pushed him into a desperate mood. He went on lockdown to see if he could finish the play he was writing. In a letter to author James Branch Cabell, Mencken wrote that Scott's effort had a good chance of succeeding, "But it seems to me that his wife thinks too much about money. His danger lies in trying to get it too rapidly."[28]

Zelda was pouty in St. Paul because she had little in common with Scott's friends and she detested the winter weather, which not only subjected the town to intermittent deep freezes that year, it unleased a black-dust blizzard that blanketed Minnesota with dirty snow blowing in from North Dakota. As the frigid temperatures began to ease in early 1923, Scott finished the play and they set out for New York City where he had lined up a reading. Though his advances on royalties then already tallied $5,600, he and Zelda left Scottie in St. Paul with a nurse, and headed straight for the Plaza Hotel, disregarding the fact that the cost of the rooms far exceeded their budget. Known by now as "the Fabulous Fitzgeralds," Scott's fame as an author was cemented with his second novel; Zelda's reputation as a beauty and a wit was renowned; and they were such hard-partiers, they were sunk in a hazy drunkenness from the time they arrived until they left Manhattan.

When the reading revealed that the play needed significant revision, they returned to White Bear Lake and moved into the yacht club for the summer. Scott asked Perkins for another advance of $1,000, telling him the play would make him rich and he'd never have to bother the editor for money again. Scott worked like mad to improve the theatrical piece with the reading notes in hand, and it was refined enough that he and Zelda returned to the Plaza in the fall of 1923. Mayfield, who was stopping over in New York after a trip to Europe, had tea with Zelda in The Palm Court. "After the summer at White Bear Lake, she looked fit, tanned, and rested," her friend noted. "She and Scott were 'theoretically on the water wagon,' she announced, so she ordered tea for herself and hot chocolate for me."[29] Scott eventually joined them, excited that he'd found a producer for his play after a number of bigwigs had turned him down. Its debut was scheduled for a tryout in Atlantic City that November, and Scott wanted to stay in the area so he could be around for rehearsals. He rented a mansion in Great Neck on Long Island and bought a used Rolls-Royce while Zelda went to St. Paul to fetch Scottie.

Mencken told Mayfield and Haardt that the residence was so ostentatious, it was "a Babbitt's palazzo," a reference to Sinclair Lewis' satirical novel about the social pressures members of the middle-class face when trying to impress their peers. He asked Zelda's two friends if they had known her in Montgomery. When they said yes, he declared, "What a girl! Cleverer than Scott, if the truth were known." Mencken then called Scott an odd fellow, erratic and undisciplined, though a good writer. When Haardt replied he certainly was as long as Zelda supplied the copy, Mencken responded, "Joe Hergesheimer told me that when Zelda's baby was born, Scott stood by, pencil in hand, taking notes."[30] Scott's play, titled "The Vegetable," opened on November 20, 1923, at the Apollo Theater in Atlantic City with a gala evening. It was such a dud the audience began leaving after the second act. Scott was ready to ditch it then and there, but the producers wanted to give it a week, at the end of which it folded. Zelda told a friend "the show flopped as flat as one of Aunt Jemima's famous pancakes."[31]

While she lamented that she'd bought a pricy dress for the gala that she couldn't return, Scott wrote to Perkins that he was $5,000 in debt and needed $650 so desperately, he'd have to sell the furniture. When the media conglomerate Hearst canceled its bid for a collection of Scott's short stories, he took his pencils, paper, and typewriter to a room over the mansion's garage and began churning out fictive pieces. He would work all night each night and was in the habit of completing a finished draft between dinner and breakfast. The effort earned him $17,000, a sum he believed would liberate him to start on the next novel. This might have worked out if the partying set hadn't discovered that the Fitzgeralds' digs in Great Neck were even more exciting than their Manhattan hotel suite. Zelda called the evenings that followed so alcoholic and chaotic they had never been equaled except in Rome and Nineveh. Drunken trips to the city with visiting friends sometimes culminated with Zelda crashing the car into ponds and fire hydrants because she felt the mishaps added excitement to the evenings.

Family and old friends from the south were appalled, including Zelda's sister Rosalind, who berated her for the lifestyle they maintained. Scott was as prone to shocking behavior as his wife. Gardeners had to remove him and Ring Lardner, a sports columnist and fiction writer, from publisher Nelson Doubleday's lawn when novelist Joseph Conrad visited because they whirled around in a Bacchic dance that would have gone on for hours and disturbed the neighbors. After one of his outbursts during which he yanked the tablecloth out from under the dishes and sent everything flying to the floor, Scott threatened to kill Zelda and author Anita Loos with a candlestick. With this level of drunkenness and recklessness consuming their days and nights, he was stalled as he tried to come up with a plot that would sustain a novel. In a letter to Perkins, he blamed his inability to work on three things: laziness; sharing his ideas with Zelda for advice; and word consciousness, which he dubbed self-doubt. He also busted himself on his irresponsible behavior: "If I'd spent this time [the last two years] reading or traveling or doing anything—even staying healthy—it'd be different but I spent it uselessly, neither in study nor in contemplation but only in drinking and raising hell generally."[32]

He asked Perkins to be patient about the next book because Scott was serious about trying to rid himself of the bad habits he had developed. The novel he was grappling with at the time would become *The Great Gatsby*, a narrative set in a swanky Long Island mansion that would fictionalize their wild behavior in Great Neck. Illustrating what a supportive dialogue Perkins maintained with the authors he published, he responded, "I understand exactly what you have to do and I know that all these superficial matters of exploitation and so on are not of the slightest consequence alongside of the importance of your doing your very best work. So as far as we are concerned, you are to go ahead at just your own pace." He added that his view of the future held "very great optimism and confidence."[33] For decades, Perkins would be extremely generous in helping Scott financially but it was never enough to support the Fitzgeralds' spendthrift lifestyle. The loan Scott had received as 1923 drew to a close drained away like a receding tide, which forced him to reassess how he and Zelda were living.

SCOTT DECIDED to see if the French Riviera would be a better spot to land because he had heard it was cheaper to live there than in the Northeastern U.S. They sailed for Europe on May 3, 1924, stopping in Paris before they made their way to the South of France. During their pause in the capital, Scott met Ernest Hemingway at the Dingo American Bar and Restaurant in Montparnasse. A number of chapters in Hemingway's 1964 memoir of his time in Paris, *A Moveable Feast*, are dedicated to the Fitzgeralds, the sketches of them insulting and unflattering for the most part, particularly the things he wrote about Zelda. Scott would be crucial to Hemingway's success because the younger writer went to great lengths to champion the slightly-older and very ungrateful Hemingway. In Scott's first letter to Perkins about his new acquaintance, he told the editor he believed the then untested writer was headed for a brilliant future. It was Scott's insistence that Perkins take Hemingway on that landed the Lost Generation-great his early publishing successes.

Also during this stint in Paris, American socialite Esther Murphy introduced the Fitzgeralds to her wealthy and well-connected brother Gerald, who was a painter, and his wife Sara. The two couples clicked right away, and the Murphys made Scott and Zelda's transition to the Riviera an easy one because they were very familiar with the seaside towns in the South of France. During the initial stay, Scott and Zelda encamped at the Grand Hôtel du Cap in Antibes, which was near Villa America, a home the Murphys had purchased and were renovating. Deciding they liked the area enough to stay for a while, the Fitzgeralds rented Villa Marie in Saint Raphaël, about an hour's drive from where the Murphys were staying. Scott and Zelda dined with their new-found friends most evenings and went to the beach with them on weekends. Though the Murphys were fond of both of the Fitzgeralds, they were particularly enamored with Zelda, who reveled in the balmy weather in the South of France.

She swam and sunned on the balconies of the Moorish villa for hours watching Scottie play. As his wife and daughter enjoyed the hot days out of doors, Scott was finally able to work steadily on the narrative that would become *The Great Gatsby*. Calvin Tomkins wrote in his biography of the Murphys, *Living Well is the Best Revenge*, "Looking back on their friendship in later years, both Murphys stressed their feeling for Zelda, whose strange, willful beauty somehow eluded all the photographs that were taken of her. 'Her beauty was all in her eyes,' Gerald said of her. 'She had a way of looking directly at you, an unflinching gaze like an Indian's. And then she moved so beautifully, with her rangy figure, and she had a great sense of her own appearance and what was right for her—dresses that were full and graceful, and bright colors."[34] Despite the camaraderie the foursome felt, the Fitzgeralds' idyllic stay at the hem of the Mediterranean was about to go off the rails.

According to an entry in his ledger on July 13, 1924, Scott said he believed Zelda was having an affair with a French naval aviator named Edouard Jozan, which he called "The Big Crisis." Mayfield claimed it was a mere flirtation on both their parts, but Zelda's own account of the relationship in *Save Me the Waltz* was either an attempt to paint herself in a more adventurous light or the truth that physical intimacy took place. Zelda recaptured the magic she had felt in this excerpt: "He drew his body against her till she felt the blades of his bones carving her own. He was bronze and smelled of the sand and sun; she felt him naked underneath the starched linen." She said the lover obliterated all thoughts of her husband and that "kissing the white-linen stranger was like embracing a lost religious rite."[35] Years later, Scott would write in a letter to one of Zelda's doctors that her affair with Jozan, and his dalliance with Lois Moran, which was "a sort of revenge," forever shifted their relationship because the episodes "shook something out" of them.[36]

The Murphys recognized that Scott and Zelda's marriage was strained, and they surmised it was because some type of gauntlet had been thrown down about her seeing the other man, a particular clue being Zelda tried to overdose before the summer was over. "One night, after everyone had gone to bed, the Murphys were awakened by Scott, who stood outside their door with a candle in his violently trembling hand," Tomkins explained. "'Zelda's sick,' he said; he added in a tense voice, as they hurried down the hall, 'I don't think she did it on purpose.' She had swallowed a large, though not fatal, quantity of sleeping pills, and they had to spend the rest of the night walking her up and down to keep her awake."[37] An entry in a diary Scott kept, eventually published as *The Notebooks of F. Scott Fitzgerald*, proved how profoundly the Jozan incident had affected him: "By September 1924, I knew something had happened that could never be repaired."[38] Feeling restless, the forever-changed couple decided to spend several months in Italy. Zelda was suffering from one of many bouts of gastritis she would have over the years and Scott was fretting over how his publishers were going to feel about his latest draft of *The Great Gatsby*.

When Perkins wrote him that he thought the Gatsby character was somewhat vague, Scott countered that Zelda had created a series of pencil sketches of the protagonist to help him envision his physicality and that they were so remarkable, he felt he knew the character better than he did his own child.[39] His publisher held his ground, which sent Scott into an exhaustive period of rewriting that resulted in a protagonist with clearer characteristics, the revisions finished in January 1925. With a favorable response from Perkins, the Fitzgeralds left Rome for Capri and Zelda met a clique of Parisian artists encamped there who inspired her to take painting lessons. She was particularly taken by Romaine Brooks, an American painter who was famous for her portraits of the brazen cult of lesbians surrounding the avant-garde Parisian salonnière Natalie Barney. Within five weeks Zelda had learned color theory and began her first of many periods of painting that would continue throughout her life. While she kicked her creative energy into high gear, Scott was feeling extremely insecure about how *The Great Gatsby* would be received when it appeared in bookstores in the spring.

He drank to calm his nerves as the weeks ticked by but this did little to eliminate his anxiety. He wrote to Perkins on April 10th, the day of the novel's debut, "The book comes out today and I am overcome with fears and forebodings."[40] Perkins wired him on April 18th, "Sales situation doubtful. Excellent reviews." The Fitzgeralds were leaving Italy so they could be in Paris to experience the swirl of energy that always accompanied a new novel, and Scott wrote to Perkins from Marseille that the telegram had depressed him. "I hope I'll find better news in Paris," he added. Other reviews that weren't so positive trickled in and Scott was reeling, noting in a fretful letter to his publisher on May 1st that the $1,000 Perkins was sending him was so appreciated but it meant that he owed Scribner's $7,200. "Thank you for all your advertising, and all the advances and all your good will," Scott told Perkins. "When I get ahead again on trash, I'll begin the new novel."[41] The garbage Scott referenced were the short stories he had to keep churning out in order to make a living.

The same day he sent Perkins the letter, he signed an eight-month lease on an apartment in Paris on rue de Tilsitt. His spirits were lifted by Wilson, who said, "Your book came yesterday and I read it last night. It is undoubtedly in some ways the best thing you have done—the best planned, the best sustained, the best written. In fact, it amounts to a complete new departure in your work."[42] And Mencken, whom he also respected, was mostly positive. "I think it is incomparably the best piece of work you have done," he wrote. "Evidences of careful workmanship are on every page. The thing is well managed, and has a fine surface. My one complaint is that the basic story is somewhat trivial—that it reduces itself, in the end, to a sort of anecdote. But God will forgive you for that." Mencken then told Scott he intended to write a review for the *Chicago Tribune*.[43] Perkins called all but two reviews he had seen "absolutely stupid and lousy." Angrily, he added, "Someday they'll eat grass, by God!"[44]

Scott wasn't fully appeased until he read that T.S. Eliot declared the book the first step that American fiction had taken since Henry James. When the dramatic rights sold in June of 1925, Scott was supremely relieved that he could breathe easier financially. This allowed him to slow down on the number of stories he had been pumping out, and Zelda began filling in the gaps. She added short fiction to her repertoire that still included a steady pulse of painting. A point of contention that would swell during the remaining years of their marriage arose when her short story "Our Own Movie Queen," to which Scott had only contributed a climactic ending during a revision, was published in the *Chicago Sunday Tribune* with her husband's name in the byline because his agent said the newspapers and magazines paid more money for the ones with his name on them.[45]

Zelda felt slighted by the deception and by the fact that her husband's fame was making it harder for her to build her own renown.

Gatsby was opening important doors for the couple, but many of the avant-garde Parisian literary circles into which they were welcomed left Zelda feeling unimpressed. Hemingway introduced them to Gertrude Stein at her request, a meeting that would find Zelda and Scott at odds over the eccentric woman's domain. "Although she was accustomed to being the center of attention in any gathering of men at which she was present, Zelda in Paris had been among the wives who were left to talk to [Stein's partner] Alice B. Toklas while Miss Stein held forth to their husbands on art and letters," Mayfield wrote. "To Zelda, Miss Stein did not appear to be an oracle but a stout, dumpy old woman with her hair cut short and brushed forward like a French barber's." Zelda told Mayfield Stein's conversation was "sententious gibberish."[46] It was inevitable that the two strong-willed women would be less compatible than oil and water.

"As part of her Southern heritage, Zelda was endowed with a pride that would not let her truckle to the great and near-great as Scott did—a trait that sometimes offended those who felt entitled to respect," Mayfield noted. "It was the kind of *hubris* that invites *nemesis*, and it was probably a tragic flaw in Zelda's character. Certainly, it was the one that did much to alienate Scott."[47] Given there was one salon that Zelda did enjoy—and it, too, had a woman at its helm—Zelda's problem with Stein was not that she was a female; it was that she saw Stein as a stuffy broad who presided over the men who flocked to her in a staid way. It was the lively camaraderie that Natalie Barney maintained in her salon, to which Romaine Brooks had introduced Zelda after their initial meeting in Capri, that fascinated Zelda. She enjoyed the witty repartee, which was the counter opposite to the pedantic conversations at Stein's. Zelda was painting steadily and she found the group who flowed into Barney's apartment stimulating. Buoyed by the fact that they took her art seriously, she began to work on a self-portrait in watercolor and gouache, and completed other paintings while in Paris that year.

AMONG THE DEVOTEES who regularly attended Barney's salon was Esther Murphy, whose relationships with the women in the clique caused her brother Gerald to distance himself from his sister.[48] Scott was equally uncomfortable with his wife's association with them, his angst over it so galling he would eventually insinuate she was a lesbian before she would question it herself. Annoyed with Scott, Zelda turned the tables on him by saying she had heard a rumor that he was having a homosexual relationship with Hemingway. The writer and publisher Robert McAlmon had told Hemingway that Scott was gay, but did not suggest the two were having sex; Zelda decided she'd inflate the rumor when she shared it with her husband. Scott wrote to Perkins, "God knows he [McAlmon] shows more creative imagination in his malice than in his work."[49] It was during these trying times for the Fitzgeralds when Hemingway first experienced the couple he would depict in his harsh portraits. One of the episodes he later exploited took place during an afternoon when Hemingway said he and his girlfriend Pauline Pfeiffer had visited the couple on rue de Tilsitt.

He called the apartment "gloomy and airless," and said the only thing in it that resembled the couple were Scott's novels bound in light blue leather with the titles in gold. Scott showed Hemingway his ledger that noted advances and royalties for books, stories, and films, which he had cataloged "as carefully as the log of a ship." Hemingway said Zelda had a bad hangover and was quarrelsome with Scott because she wanted him to party while he wanted to work. "Zelda was treating him as though he were a kill-joy or a spoilsport," Hemingway remembered, adding that the foursome struggled through an almost inedible lunch. He said Zelda had hawk's eyes, and a deep-south accent and manners. "Watching her face you could see her mind leave the table and go to the night's party and return with her eyes blank as a cat's and then pleased, and the pleasure would show along the thin line of her lips and then be gone," he wrote. "Scott was being the good cheerful host and Zelda looked at him and she smiled happily with her eyes and her mouth too as he drank the wine. I learned to know that smile very well. It meant she knew Scott would not be able to write."[50]

Hemingway said she was extremely jealous of Scott's work and, as he grew to know them better, her sabotage became a regular pattern. The grudge-bearing title of Chapter 18 in *A Moveable Feast* in which he presented Zelda as a predator is "Hawks Do Not Share." Hemingway claimed every time Scott would sit down to write, his wife's interference revved up. "Zelda would begin complaining about how bored she was and get him off on another drunken party," Hemingway alleged. "They would quarrel and then make up and he would sweat out the alcohol on long walks with me, and make up his mind that this time he would really work, and would start off well. Then it would start all over again." He said Scott was very much in love with Zelda and that her husband was extremely jealous of her. "He told me many times on our walks of how she had fallen in love with a French navy pilot," Hemingway said, noting that each time Scott repeated it, the nuances changed.[51]

When I read this, I thought about how he must have been going through the same mental process as when he edited different versions of real-life events for a story or a novel, a habit that was so engrained, it must have happened on instinct. Hemingway ended the chapter by hinting at Zelda's impending mental difficulties, saying her hawk's eyes were clear and calm as she leaned forward to tell him her "great secret," which was, "Ernest, don't you think Al Jolson is greater than Jesus?"[52] He said Pauline was the only one who thought anything of the comment, adding, "It was only Zelda's secret that she shared with me, as a hawk might share something with a man. But hawks do not share. Scott did not write anything anymore that was good until after he knew that she was insane."[53] Sally Cline, who wrote a brilliant biography about Zelda, found evidence that the lunch Hemingway chronicled actually took place in the apartment Hemingway shared with his then-wife Hadley. He must have decided to change the story's locale so he could disparage the Fitzgeralds with greater intensity by belittling their home life.

There is also proof in Hemingway's letters to Scott that he was initially charmed by Zelda so this animosity would not have been felt so early in their relationship. By the time Hemingway wrote the memoir—about three decades after the lunch he described had taken place—a long war between him and Zelda had been waged, the vestiges of it lingering only in his mind, as both Fitzgeralds had been dead for at least a decade by the time he penned his remembrances of them. Zelda had a deep dislike for Hemingway because she was threatened by his influence over her husband and she felt his treatment of his first wife Hadley, who was actually present at the fateful lunch, was despicable because he ditched her after he began the affair with Pauline in early 1926. The liaison blossomed as the lovers joined the Murphys and the Fitzgeralds on the Riviera for a short stay. For the two months the Fitzgeralds resided in Juan-les-Pins, they rented a damp villa they complained about to their friends. In spite of its mildewed atmosphere, Zelda was painting and writing up a storm, though Sara Murphy said she still didn't seem happy. Her descriptions of Zelda's fervency bring a manic woman whose drive was psychically unhealthy into focus.

As spring turned to summer, Zelda's notoriety for shocking behavior took a dangerous turn as she began to be an incredible risk-taker. Biographers believed Zelda grew so reckless because she was desperate to be noticed. In her book about the Murphys, *Everybody Was So Young*, Amanda Vaill illustrated several incidents that were noteworthy for Zelda's intensity as she acted out. "Suddenly there was a pervasive feeling of malaise in the air," Vaill wrote. "Scott Fitzgerald, it was clear, was drinking more than ever; and although Zelda was in better physical health since an appendectomy in June, her behavior was exceedingly peculiar. Late one evening when the Murphys had joined the Fitzgeralds at the casino in Juan-les-Pins, all four of them were sitting at their table when Zelda suddenly got up and, lifting the skirt of her evening dress above her waist, began, slowly, hypnotically, like a dervish, to dance. 'She was dancing for herself,' Gerald remembered, 'she didn't look left or right, or catch anyone's eyes. She looked at no one, not once, not even at Scott. I saw a mass of lace ruffles as she whirled—I'll never forget it. We were frozen.'"[54]

An even scarier episode played out in the picturesque medieval village Saint Paul de Vence, which sits atop a steep hillside. Gerald and Sara were dining with the Fitzgeralds on a stone terrace overlooking the Loup valley with a view of Antibes in the distance. The modern dancer/choreographer Isadora Duncan was seated at a neighboring table with three of her admirers. "Although she was hugely fat and middle-aged and henna-haired, she still had enough of her old star power that Fitzgerald—when Gerald and Sara told him who she was—went to sit at her feet," Vaill wrote. "Duncan was entranced by this blonde, boyish acolyte and began running her hands through his hair and calling him her 'centurion.' That was when Zelda, without warning, stood up on her chair and leaped over the table—and over Gerald, who was seated with his back to the view—into the darkness beyond the parapet."[55]

The diners were immobilized with fear that she was dead but moments later Zelda reappeared. Given she had landed on a stone staircase that ambled down the cliff from the terrace, it was remarkable that the extent of her injuries amounted to bloody knees. As I read about these scenes, I thought how reminiscent they were of that invincible girl careening along on her roller skates at break-neck speed, the devil-may-care attitude of childhood turning into a dangerous defect in adulthood. While Zelda alarmed everyone with her crazy cries for help, Scott irritated his friends to the point they were talking amongst themselves about how they might rein him in. He had developed a habit of being overly-personal—asking friends inappropriate questions, following strangers around as he inquired about their lives, and barraging those he knew with absurd accusations.

Fortunately for the expats along the Riviera, they caught a break from the caustic behavior just as they decided it had become too much—Hollywood lured Scott and Zelda back to the U.S. in early 1927 when Scott was hired to collaborate on a flapper comedy for the silent film star Constance Talmadge. The screenplay, titled "Lipstick," was rejected, which meant Scott had earned a $3,500 advance but would not receive the $12,000 pay-out he would have been awarded had it been accepted. Given the expenses of living in tinseltown, the advance was gone before they limped east after less than three months in California. During the short stay there, a trying string of arguments took place because Scott had been fascinated with the budding actress Lois Moran, who would eventually be the lover he chose to revenge Zelda's tryst with Jozan. The fights over his crush were so antagonistic because Scott made the mistake of telling Zelda he respected Moran more than he did her because the actress did something with herself that required effort and talent, whereas he felt his wife never had. This made Zelda furious.

As they took up residence in Ellerslie, a sprawling mansion in Edgemoor, Delaware, on the banks of the Delaware River, Zelda subconsciously set out to prove to her husband she was just as talented and capable as Moran, which led to some seriously maniacal behavior as she began painting and writing at a fever pitch. The stories she penned were selling to magazines, though her literary output was not being properly credited. With one piece after the other, Scott claimed the editors insisted his name, placed before hers, had to be in the byline because they could earn more. Scott told his wife the extra funds were critical in helping them afford the rent for Ellerslie, which was $150 a month. Though this sounds paltry now, it wasn't in that day and age, and the money he was making, even with her magazine pieces, was falling short yet again. Scott was asking his literary agent Harold Ober for advances of $500 and $800 for short stories on a weekly basis, which he would never write. As money fears consumed him, Scott began to have nervous attacks, which he recorded in his ledger as "Stoppies."[56]

Zelda added ballet to her list of obsessions, booking lessons for herself and Scottie in Philadelphia with Catherine Littlefield, who had been a student of Madame Lubov

Egorova, a former principal for the Ballets Russes. Just as she had with painting, she developed a mania for dance, purchasing a large ornate mirror that she had hung in their front room and had a ballet barre installed in front of it. As if she had plunged down a new rabbit hole, Zelda practiced constantly, including during meals and when guests were visiting. She was dancing to "The March of the Toy Soldiers" from Tchaikovsky's *The Nutcracker*, which she played repeatedly. With his nerves frayed by the repetitive tune wafting through the house, I bet Scott was regretting being the catalyst for her intensity, a role he admitted years later in a letter to one of his wife's doctors when he said her inferiority complex was his fault: "Years ago I reproached her for doing nothing and she never got over it."[57]

Each of them seemed absolutely incapable of supporting the other, and Scott would begin a campaign to undermine Zelda's desire to become known as a dancer because he believed her dedication to ballet was a rebellion against him. As Zelda's self-discipline went into hyper-drive, Scott's slowed to a crawl and he referred to 1928 as the year he began relying on alcohol to stimulate his writing. A desire to spend time in Europe nudged him out of his writer's block and he began a successful series of short stories that financed their return to Paris where they would reunite with the Murphys. By this time Gerald and Sara owned two apartments in the city, and they offered to loan the Fitzgeralds the one that overlooked the Luxembourg Gardens. Zelda had been so keen to return to the French capital because she wanted to study ballet under Egorova. Because she was twenty-eight, Scott thought Zelda's desire to be a professional dancer was ridiculous.

"There are limits to what a woman Zelda's age can do," he said.[58] As he watched his wife pour her energy into dance, he drained bottles of alcohol, belligerent with her and anyone else who made the mistake of trying to convince him to lighten up. In Chapter 19 of *A Moveable Feast*, "A Matter of Measurements," Hemingway presented a picture of Scott during this time as a man whose self-confidence was just as damaged as his wife's self-esteem was. Hemingway said Scott summoned him to Michaud's for lunch one day because he had something important to run by him. "I knew that he was writing something good and that he was having great trouble with it for many reasons but that was not what he wanted to talk about," Hemingway remembered. He said Scott waited until the end of the meal to bring up his concerns. "Zelda said that the way I was built I could never make any woman happy and that was what upset her originally," Scott confessed. "She said it was a matter of measurements. I have never felt the same since she said that and I have to know truly."[59]

Hemingway summoned him to the water closet to take a peek at Scott's penis. When they were back at the table, he said, "You're perfectly fine." He then stated the obvious, explaining how when a man looks down, he sees himself foreshortened. He suggested that Scott go to the Louvre and look at the statues, then go home and look at himself in the mirror in profile. Scott countered that the statues weren't likely accurate. Hemingway said they were lifelike enough that most men would be happy to favor them. "But why would she say it?" Scott asked. "To put you out of business," Hemingway answered. "That's the oldest way of putting people out of business in the world." Hemingway asked Scott if he believed him and Scott admitted that he still didn't know. Hemingway insisted they go to the museum together. "We went over to the Louvre and he looked at the statues but still he was doubtful about himself," Hemingway remembered. He then told Scott, "It is not basically a question of the size in repose. It is the size that it becomes. It is also a question of angle."[60]

Hemingway gave Scott a few more tips on technique and then told him to forget Zelda because she was crazy. Scott then admitted he was asking because there was "a girl" he had met who was being nice to him. "Just have confidence and do what the girl wants," Hemingway said. "Zelda just wants to destroy you."[61] I wasn't surprised she was sewing these seeds of doubt and doing all she could to humiliate him by pointing out his sexual inadequacy because she was so enraged at him over his dismissiveness. She was also confused about her own sexuality, as she had begun to wonder if her attraction to her ballet teacher meant she was gay. The sexually confused, feuding couple returned to Ellerslie in September 1928 in a shambles. "Zelda mixed her paints thicker and thicker, and danced on carpet, wearing it thinner and thinner, as if she could paint over or stamp out her turbulent thoughts," Cline wrote.[62] As she strove to banish her demons, Zelda learned that the Hemingways (by then Ernest had married Pauline) would visit and she dreaded coming face-to-face with the man she loathed. Scott couldn't wait to see his friend, who gave him the excuse to engage in adolescent behavior.

Their vulgarity as they swapped manly jokes grated on Zelda's nerves, and she watched in silent fury as her husband's antics grew increasingly absurd. This ridiculousness peaked when Hemingway and Pauline joined the Fitzgeralds and the painter Henry Strater for a Princeton-Yale football game one afternoon. Afterwards, they took the train from Princeton to Philadelphia where they would meet Scott's French chauffeur, who had been shipped to the States with their Buick, and drive back to Ellerslie. During the train ride, Hemingway cited a string of embarrassing episodes during which he and Strater had to follow Scott through the cars to keep him from getting into fights. "We had no choice but to try to take care of him and as he realized that he was being taken out of trouble as soon as he started it he began to expand his operations alternating indiscrete questions with excessive courtliness while one of us gently moved him along and the other apologized," Hemingway remembered.[63]

Scott approached a medical student who was reading a textbook, which he took from the student while saying in an overly suave tone, "Do you mind, Sir?" He glanced at the book and returned it to the young man with a bow. Then, "in a voice pitched for all that part of the car," Scott yelled, "Ernest I have found a clap doctor!" The student ignored the outburst but Scott kept after him to the point that it was humiliating for the other two men to watch.[64] Scott's relationship with Hemingway would cause some of the most contentious fights between him and Zelda during the next several years. Though Scott would eventually feel that Hemingway had deliberately tried to break up his marriage, he was not yet suspicious. Scott's attachment to the other writer at this point was so strong because he felt seen and heard by Hemingway. The spell wouldn't break until he realized his friend was far outpacing him when it came to fictive quality and quantity. By early 1929, letters between Hemingway and Perkins present a lively give-and-take about Hemingway's work ethic as they discussed his next novel, *A Farewell to Arms*.

WHILE PERKINS WAS GIVING Hemingway professional advice as to whether to serialize or not, Scott was apologizing to the publisher that he was going to be late on another project. "I'm sneaking away like a thief without leaving the chapters," he confessed; "there is a week's work to straighten out + in the confusion of my influenza + leaving, I haven't been able to do it. I'll do it on the boat + send it from Genoa."[65] The Fitzgeralds had decided to return to Paris that March so Zelda could resume lessons with Egorova, and Scott was referencing their stopover in Genoa. Zelda dove back into ballet with as much fanaticism as she had before. When the Murphys went to watch her dance in Egorova's studio, Gerald described the experience as particularly awkward. "There was something dreadfully grotesque in her intensity—one could see the muscles stretch and pull; her legs looked muscular and ugly," he remembered. "It was really terrible. One held one's breath until it was over. Thank God, she couldn't see what she looked like."[66] Mayfield, who was in Paris as her friend's zeal propelled her along, presents a much less brawny view of Zelda, whom she bumped into at the café Les Deux Magots.

"The first person I saw was Zelda, sitting at a table in the corner, looking like a Fra Angelico angel on the morning after the night before," Mayfield remembered. She motioned for Zelda to join her at another table, not wanting to end up penned in by Scott and the stragglers who had gathered there after an all-night party. "You have to drink yourself blotto to keep from being bored to death," Zelda told Mayfield, who said she was "thin as a rail" and had triangular hollows beneath her eyes. She asked Zelda if she was eating enough. "I eat everything in sight," she answered. "But I work it off at the studio, straining and stretching and ending in nothing." The look in Zelda's eyes, which Zelda herself had once described as "a soul lost in the mist on a moor," set Mayfield's teeth on edge. Zelda said, "Look at my stomach; it's so flat it'll come out at the back. And then I'll have to begin life all over again, hind-part before. I wish I could. Really, I do. I'd try so hard. Scott and I had it all—youth, love, money—and look how we've ended up, sitting around cafés, drinking and talking and quarreling with each other."[67]

When Scott lurched over and fell into a chair beside Mayfield, she felt despair. "It is not a pleasant experience to see people you are fond of wreck their lives when there is nothing you can do about it but sit on your hands and bite your tongue," Mayfield wrote.[68] That Zelda was sabotaging her life was not an exaggeration—in spite of her devotion to dance, she shocked many of those who knew her by turning down an opportunity to join the San Carlo Ballet Company in Naples. Her fear of going alone; of leaving Scottie, who was eight; and of making Scott more furious than he was, were greater considerations than her ambitions. The result of her own self-abdication was brutal—she turned scornful towards herself and returned to her dangerous brand of acting out. When she and Scott were driving along a winding road a month after she declined the offer to join the dance company, she grabbed the steering wheel and attempted to force the car over the cliff—coming close to killing them both.

Her literary output at this time was vigorous, but it wasn't healthy because the pace was fueled by desperation tinged with anger. Not only was Scott sharing bylines on her stories to which he had contributed nothing, Zelda's name was left off of one particularly skillful narrative that Ober said was so good it would have been recognized as his fiction no matter whose name was one it. While she was being treated with such a lack of respect, friends like Haardt were being honored by their partners. Mencken, who would soon be Haardt's husband, never claimed ownership of her writing and tirelessly worked to support it. Cline presented proof that Zelda felt resentful and frustrated that she was being treated the opposite. "The original manuscripts of all six stories [published during this period] show her vigorous black handwriting scrawling out Scott's name on every by-line," Cline wrote. "Words like 'No!' and 'Me' are inserted where appropriate."[69]

Brilliantly summing up how hypocritical Scott could be, Cline pointed out that he generously praised the work of other writers, and not just pieces by chums like Hemingway, but by Zelda's friends as well, Haardt included. When it came to his wife, he deigned to acknowledge her as she struggled to build a separate identity, one she was determined to solidify so she could disprove his low estimation of her as he continued to measure her against Moran. As they approached Zelda's first mental breakdown, the Fitzgeralds' relationship was spiraling into something otherworldly, a breach that the Murphys watched with concern. Sara shared a story about going to a luncheon with Zelda during which a number of people came up and introduced themselves. As they did so, Zelda took their hands, smiling, and mumbled under her breath, "I hope you die in a marble ring." Sara recalled, "She was so charming and polite as she said it. Of course no one suspected that she was saying anything but the usual pleasantries; I heard her because I was standing right next to her."[70]

Approaching the Fitzgeralds' apartment building one day, where they were fetching Zelda to take her to an art exhibition, the Murphys saw Scott and the poet John Peale Bishop on the sidewalk trying to calm Zelda down. Zelda insisted the two men had been talking about her during lunch. "Gerald was stunned," Vaill wrote. He was so puzzled, he turned to his wife and asked, "'How *could* they have been talking about her without her knowledge? I mean, she was sitting right there with them!'"[71] Two months later, when walking through a flower market with Scott, Zelda told him the blossoms were talking to her. Soon after, she burst into the flat where Scott was drinking with the playwright

Michael Arlen and was so upset, Arlen suggested she try going to a clinic. She must have been at wits end because she agreed it was time to do just that. When she arrived at the Malmaison Clinic on the outskirts of Paris on April 23, 1930, the doctors reported an anxiety-ridden young woman obsessed with a professional dancing career, one who was harboring fears she was a homosexual in love with her ballet teacher and other women.

After only ten days she left the clinic against her doctor's wishes and returned to ballet. The topsy-turvy turns these about-faces signify hastened her meld-down because she was forced to admit sheer will was not going to be enough to hold her psyche together. Within a few weeks she was hallucinating and she would try to kill herself to silence the voices she was hearing in her head. When Scott's reaction was to keep watch over her so she couldn't attempt suicide again, she said he was behaving like a prison guard. Though Zelda had struggled with digestive issues for years, Scott's next move was strange. He took her to the Valmont Clinic in Glion, near Montreux, Switzerland—an odd choice because the program specialized in gastrointestinal ailments, not mental issues. The doctors at Valmont sedated her heavily and reported there was nothing to diagnose in terms of a brain disorder. "Nobody in either Malmaison or Valmont picked up on the effects that the consistent denial of her ambitions and exploitation of her talents might have had on her psyche," Cline wrote. "Uncovering and re-interpreting them would be left for the battery of psychiatrists who followed."[72]

One of those who didn't understand the real issues at the time was Dr. Oscar Forel, whom the physicians at Valmont called in as a consultant two weeks after Zelda arrived. He was on staff at Les Rives des Prangins, a clinic near Nyon, Switzerland, which specialized in psychiatric disorders. Forel agreed to take Zelda to Prangins but only if she went of her own free will and if she would temporarily separate from Scott. "Presumably, Zelda at first agreed to enter Prangins," wrote Mayfield, "but after a violent scene with Scott in Lausanne, in which she charged that he had abused, humiliated, and broken her, she changed her mind."[73] Feeling he needed back up, Scott reached out to Rosalind's husband, Newman Smith, who agreed to come. Because the Smiths were living in Brussels, Belgium, he was able to arrive quickly, reaching the clinic the next day to help persuade Zelda to put herself under Forel's care. Zelda's description of traveling to the hospital dripped with despair.

"Our ride…was very sad," she said; "we did not have each other or anything else and it half-killed me to give up all the work I had done." She admitted she had come to the end of her physical resources and that she felt so forsaken she had thought about destroying her photo of Egorova, her tutus, her ballet slippers, and her pointe shoes.[74] In her first letter to Scott from the expensive asylum, which resembled a country club on the shores of Lake Geneva, she asked him to come and see her so he could see she was making progress. When the letter turned bitter and blaming, it was clear she wasn't thinking straight. If she had really wanted him to visit, she wouldn't have insulted him by saying she wanted him to witness how the treatments were counteracting the abuse he flung at her in Lausanne. She then wrote, "At any rate one thing has been achieved: I am thoroughly humiliated and broken if that was what you wanted."[75]

Scott would eventually mine her heartbreaking letters—this one and more like it—for his next novel *Tender Is the Night*, which had never been focused on mental illness until his wife's breakdown. The idea for the narrative was likely cementing in his mind as he was shuttling back and forth between Nyon and Paris where he had left Scottie. Though his biographers give him credit as an attentive husband and father for staying nearby, I suspect he wanted to be close so he could better flesh out the character he was creating that would expose Zelda's mental fragility. "Though Scott would make many grave errors during the next ten years over decisions regarding Zelda's hospitalization and treatment, and would put control of Zelda consistently ahead of understanding or releasing her, he never shirked his financial obligations to her and to Scottie," Cline wrote.[76] It was clear from his letters that the fiscal demands he had always struggled to meet increased dramatically once he began footing the bills for his wife's psychiatric care.

Scott told Harold Ober in November, "I haven't written so long to you because I've been swamped with worries + anxieties here. Zelda has been in a hell of a mess, still in the sanitarium—she came within an ace of losing her mind + isn't out of the woods yet." He added, "I figure I've written about 40,000 words to Forel (the psychiatrist) on the subject of Zelda trying to get to the root of things + keeping worried families tranquil in their old age + trying to be a nice thoughtful female mother to Scotty [sic]." After discussing a few business issues, he ended the letter, "Thought very little of Swanson offer. Haven't touched novel for four months, save for one week."[77] After writing to Zelda's parents about her situation, he penned a very long letter to Forel laying out how he saw his wife's path to illness by the year and, as he approached present-time, by the month. As Mayfield would claim, Scott was completely controlling the narrative because most of the reports from the clinics in France and Switzerland were Scott's side of the story. Zelda's letters to him were pitiful. "Every day more of me dies with this bitter and incessant beating I'm taking," she lamented.[78]

Whereas Dr. Forel recorded his impressions of Zelda as "gay, playful, optimistic, artistic, and independently minded," the main feeling she experienced internally was terror. Cline did not agree with Forel's eventual diagnosis of schizophrenia for a number of reasons. First of all, he had never experienced anyone with such a quirky personality and quaint manners that sprang from the deep American south. Secondly, the doctors spoke no English, and Zelda's French, which had a thick southern drawl, was peppered with non sequiturs and extravagant hyperbole.[79] I would add that there's no way a Swiss doctor could have known the emotions he ascribed to her were drummed into her as a southern female, as women then were taught to respond pleasantly to anyone in authority regardless of the situation, particularly when their true feelings were pain, fear, or suffering. Forel was so concerned over the depths of Zelda's despair about the interruption in her dancing career, he asked Scott if he would write to her former teacher and have her tell her pupil it was okay to take a pause in training. Scott took a different tack, sending Egorova a letter that asked if she felt Zelda could achieve the level of a first-rate dancer.

Egorova answered that Zelda had begun too late to become a prima ballerina, but she was good enough to become an accomplished dancer capable of appearing in important roles for companies like New York's Massine Ballet Company. Forel felt it wasn't a good idea to show Egorova's reply to Zelda given the way it was worded so Scott saved the teacher's response for when he needed a weapon of humiliation to tamp Zelda down. Letters zinged between the Fitzgeralds like sallies—hers accusing him of failing to give her guidance before her illness; his defending himself, then storing her jabs away to use as fodder for his next female protagonist. Though this battle makes him seem like an unfeeling monster, I sensed his attitude must have been fueled by humiliation because he was getting gut-punched by guilt and shame as her sessions uncovered aspects of their marriage he had hoped would stay buried. Assigning fault for their failing relationship became the name of the game for both of them.

Zelda sent him a letter that read, "Please don't write to me about blame. I am tired of rummaging my head to understand a situation that would be difficult enough if I were completely lucid. I cannot arbitrarily accept blame now when I know that in the past I felt none. Anyway, blame doesn't matter."[80] This was a bit disingenuous on her part given she was constantly accusing Scott of ruining her life as they berated each other like spoiled children. Sensing they were in the perfect below-the-belt moment, Scott told her about Egorova's letter and Zelda asked him to send it to her. He did and she was devastated when she read it, as her hopes were forever dashed that she could be a top-notch ballerina. A fascinating plot twist developed at this point: By destroying Zelda's fantasy that she could be a ballet star, Scott birthed a fierce competitor. Fiction rose to the top of Zelda's ambitions, replacing dance as her call-to-arms. Within a month, she had completed three stories, which Scott sent to *Scribner's Magazine*, whose editors rejected them.

Though the pieces of fiction no longer exist, Scott's critiques of them, which survived in his correspondence with Perkins, claimed there was a beauty and richness to them because they were written in the midst of her nervous breakdown. He said the stories had a "strange haunting, evocative quality that was absolutely new."[81] Perkins agreed but felt they were for a select audience so he regretted having to say no. He said if she could write enough that a book could be released, some small magazines would possibly be interested in excerpting and publicizing the work. Scott mentioned the idea to Zelda but she said she didn't feel up to it, which inspired her husband to write to Perkins that she was "still sick as hell." He went on to say how expensive her treatment was because the psychiatrist was devoting most of his time to her. "I was so upset in June when hopes for her recovery were black that I could practically do no work and got behind," he added, asking for another advance.[82]

Wilson, who had been through electric shock treatments and hydrotherapy during a hospitalization for a nervous breakdown the year before, wrote an empathetic letter to his long-time pal that contained this advice, "I have just heard from Max Perkins about Zelda's illness. From what he has written me, I can't tell precisely what has happened, but I know from my own experience that these breakdowns where people seem to go off their heads aren't necessarily serious, and as people in that condition are extremely sensitive to suggestion, I thought it might be worthwhile to write her—use your own discretion about giving her the letter." He told Scott not to let the neurologists depress him, adding, "If Zelda is in Switzerland, I shouldn't hesitate to go to [Carl] Jung at Zurich about her. He got Stan Dell out of a sad condition a year or two ago, and everybody who had anything to do with him seems to swear by him."[83]

Jung was not in Zelda's future as she wavered between bouts of recuperation and deepening illness. At a very dark moment, Forel asked her to write a summary of how she felt about herself and her family. The seven pages scrawled with her quirky French gave the doctor insight into aspects of Zelda for the first time, her memory of her mother particularly moody. "I can always see her sitting down in the opalescent sunlight of a warm morning, a black servant combing her long gray hair," Zelda wrote before admitting she drew a blank on her father in terms of his appearance, writing only that he was "a man without fear—intellectual, silent, serious."

Zelda told the doctor her parents had had no influence on her and that her relationships with her siblings were vague. She also claimed her marriage was one of the greatest emotional events in her life because it had shunted her into another world, "one for which I was not qualified or prepared, because of my inadequate education."[84]

She also mentioned her "love affair" with the French aviator in a bitter tone. Zelda poured out her frustration and regret at having to leave dance and her ballet teacher, whom she claimed she loved "more than anything else in the world." She then contradicted herself by saying she didn't know what it meant to really love, and said she blamed Scott for forcing her into Valmont, "and now I am here, with you, in a situation where I cannot be anybody, full of vertigo, with an increasing noise in my ears, feeling the vibrations of everyone I meet. Broken down." She ended the soliloquy with, "I must add another thing: this story is the fault of nobody but me. I believed I was a Salamander—and it seems that I am nothing but an impediment." In her book *Zelda: A Biography*, Nancy Milford believed Zelda referenced the amphibian because the mythical salamander had become a talisman for her after she came across fables that claimed it could withstand the most intense flames without being harmed. Milford felt Zelda's declaration meant she had come to realize she was not the invincible being she had previously believed she was.[85]

Fire was an interesting reference given Zelda had developed a serious case of eczema and the treatments were as caustic as the disease. She begged her doctors to stop them, as she was spending weeks in her room feeling charred under bandages. Contradicting her claim that blame did not matter, she wrote in a letter to Scott that Forel had asked her to inquire as to whether he was still drinking because the doctor strongly believed her husband's alcohol intake was a major contributor to her illness, and that he was actually treating two people because Forel knew Scott had to be sober if she was going to be able to live with him after her release. Scott refused to accept the doctor's point of view, responding with a slew of justifications in his letters to Forel. Zelda was contemplating divorce but she never moved on it because she believed that if she didn't stay with Scott, the doctors would never let her out of the "nut farm." Accepting that she would have to remain dependent upon him, the tone in her letters softened and she showed greater affection for him when they were together.

She was effusive when she wrote to him, "Goofy, my darling, hasn't it been a lovely day? I woke up this morning and the sun was lying like a birth-day parcel on my table so I opened it and so many happy things went fluttering into the air."[86] Scott admitted to being relieved that she was no longer harboring violent feelings toward him but he was still smarting that she had insulted him just before her letters turned sweeter. Her put-down was pointed when she told him all he had to offer were his good looks and that there were so many others with the same, citing the head waiter at the Ritz and her hairdresser in Paris! Mayfield said Scott had gradually begun to recognize that his conduct was partially responsible for his wife's behavior; that he tried to make up for the suffering he had caused her by sending her books and flowers, and by treating her to lunch in Geneva or taking her to Lausanne for a weekend.[87]

As the conflicts between them quieted, Forel felt Zelda was calm enough to put her under hypnosis, which gave her almost immediate relief from the eczema she'd been enduring. When she was deep in the trance, she recognized connections between the rash and her marital problems—the realization freeing her of the searing pain, though little else had changed. Persistent still were infatuations with other women, a deep depression, and bouts of uncontrollable masturbation, which the doctors felt warranted a straitjacket so she couldn't touch herself. When Scott revealed to Rosalind that her sister had a "lesbian complex," Rosalind was horrified and decided to steer clear of the subject, limiting her letters to sharing tips about treating eczema instead. Illustrating how funny Zelda was, she told her sister that her skin was better, though it certainly would not have been soothed by the Cuticura soap Rosalind had suggested. Zelda wrote, "The Brussels fire brigade might have skirted the edges."[88] Insulin shock treatment was added to Zelda's treatment protocol, which didn't stabilize her mentally, so Forel brought in Dr. Paul Eugen Bleuler for a second opinion about his patient.

Bleuler was a big gun because he was the one who had given schizophrenia its name. Bleuler agreed with Forel's diagnosis but he contradicted the other doctor's belief that Scott's behavior and their marital problems were contributing to Zelda's illness. Following Bleuler's directives, Forel became stricter with her, forbidding dancing and saying her choices for activities were limited to weaving, carpentry, and greenhouse work. It was also decided she would have limited visits from Scott and she would not be able to see Scottie for several months. "Forel's reeducation program would, they hoped, check Zelda's 'incipient egomania,'" Cline wrote. "Bleuler saw her as a woman competing publicly with her more famous husband in an inappropriate manner. That Zelda was also charged with ineptitude at housework, cooking and servant management was another example of pronounced gender implications in the way the label schizophrenia was constructed in the Thirties." Cline noted that the hospitals in which Zelda had been placed aimed at "changing 'inappropriate' feminine behavior into something nearer the conventional wifely model of the era."[89]

She added, "Like other women of her time including Vivien Haigh-Wood (wife of T.S. Eliot), Jane Bowles, Sylvia Plath, and her [Zelda's] friend Sara Mayfield, Zelda's failure to live up to a traditional feminine role was to some extent buried within a diagnosis of mental disorder." Cline is referencing the fact that Mayfield's story has a similar tragic element to it because her brother committed her to Bryce State Hospital in Tuscaloosa in October 1949 against her will. Mayfield left a treasure-trove of papers that are housed in the University of Alabama's W.S. Hoole Special Collections Library that include an exposé on the conditions at the hospital and reports of the mistreatment patients had to endure. Cline proposed that women from that time, particularly those who were artists married to artists and were unwilling or unable to conform, could find themselves subjected to "cures" in mental asylums for long periods of time, which were seen as ways to contain them.[90]

In a letter to one of Zelda's doctors, Scott exposed his participation in this form of discrimination by accusing her of shunning the "wifely model." He said her attempts at self-expression brought about "extreme neglect of home, child, and husband."[91] As the clinic amped up a stifling rigidity, Zelda's pleas to Scott were heartrending—she said she was being butchered and begged him to rescue her from the "great imbecile" Bleuler. When he refused, she reached out to Rosalind's husband, saying if he didn't come for her, she would write to her father. Smith didn't come and Zelda never made good on her threat, admitting she was so frightened she was afraid to think. Though Mayfield could be extremely harsh about Scott, she pointed out that he wasn't numb to Zelda's situation because her accusations brought him shame and her agony tortured him. Instead of asking Forel to free her, he poured these feelings into the short story "Babylon Revisited" with Charlie Wales—a rich, guilt-ridden American businessman who was also an alcoholic—as the main character.

Mayfield claimed the story was written in reaction to Scott's visit to Zelda's family in order to explain to them what had happened to his wife. He did so in January 1931 after attending his father's funeral in St. Paul. Zelda's family were indignant with him, both for sending Zelda to Prangins and for leaving Scottie alone with her nurse in Paris. His defense was that Zelda had improved in the sanitarium, that he hadn't wanted to take Scottie out of school, and that he went to Paris to see her regularly. While Scott was away in America, Zelda improved so much she was snow skiing and translating Arthur Rimbaud's *Une Saison en Enfer* into English. Day-trips to Lausanne or Geneva were arranged during which she was only accompanied by another patient. "I went to Geneva all by myself with a fellow maniac," she quipped.[92] When she asked if she was well enough to leave, she was told she would be at Prangins for at least six more months.

Cline noted that not one of the doctors equated her improvement with her husband's absence. When he returned to Europe, Scott began churning out stories in order to afford the medical bills. According to Mayfield, he earned $40,000 in 1931, the most he'd ever made in a single year, but he was still floundering on the novel he hoped to produce. Each time he thought about settling down to work on it, something got in the way—in this moment, it was Bleuler's opinion that Scott should see his wife with greater frequency and should bring Scottie more often. They planned a two-week family vacation that was a surprisingly happy time so they followed the getaway with a visit to the Murphys at Ramgut, a hunting lodge the couple had rented in the Austrian Alps. After these successful jaunts, Zelda was released from Prangins after having spent more than a year in the facility.

Her diagnosis was summarized as stemming from a reaction to her feelings of inferiority, primarily towards her husband, and the inappropriate ambitions she held, which were seen as self-deceptions that caused difficulties in her marriage. Her prognosis was favorable as long as all conflicts could be avoided, a notion I found to be incredibly short-sighted.[93] When Zelda left the clinic in the fall of 1931, the Fitzgeralds made their way to Montgomery and moved into the home that now houses the museum. Though Scott was unaware of his wife's ambitions at the time, she was just as determined to work on an autobiographical novel as he was —while he was stalled on *Tender Is the Night*, she began to flesh out *Save Me the Waltz*, which meant she was moving more concretely into Scott's professional territory. It was a tense time because Zelda's family and friends felt she needed to make a final break with Scott. Even her father, who was normally staunchly against such moves, urged her to divorce him.

She decided not to take their advice because she and Scottie were financially dependent upon him. Not long after they landed in the Alabama capital, Scott was saved from her family's anger and the boredom of Montgomery by Hollywood, as MGM had offered him $1,200 a week for six weeks to rewrite the screenplay *Red-Headed Woman*, which would star Jean Harlow. Before leaving, Scott had the audacity to kneel beside the bed where Zelda's gravely ill father lay and ask the judge to say he believed in his ability to be a good husband. His father-in-law wearily replied, "I think you'll always pay your bills, Scott."[94] The day of Scott's departure, Zelda picked a fight with him because she knew he would be surrounded by elegant women while he was away. He promised to be home by Christmas and left—likely thrilled to put some distance between himself and Montgomery. In her first letter to him, Zelda wrote, "It's unbearable to think that I was mean to you."[95] Her reports from home during his absence exude a calm, loving tone. A few days after she wrote the apologetic letter, she told him the house was pleasant and she had everything in the world she needed but him.

She said, "Scottie is engrossed in protecting herself against being disillusioned about Santa Claus and is as pretty as a moon-beam. She dresses herself by my fire and it's a joy to watch her long sweet delicate body and the cool of her pale hair quenching the light from the flames." She said she was feeling down so "it is just as well that you are out of this homely lyric."[96] Scott was humming a depressing tune of his own because he was struggling to write the intelligent-sounding dialogue producers demanded. As he lurched along, Zelda wrote to him, "I realize more completely than ever how much I live in you and how sweet and good and kind you are to such a dependent appendage." There was a perplexing mix of lethargy and productivity in Zelda's life during Scott's absence, which likely had something to do with the fragile mental state her melt-down and hospitalization had brought on—while her letters had a murmuring tone, her literary output had a frenetic feel to it.

She read one of Scott's stories every night, hoping to learn new ways to construct her own fiction; was honing seven new stories; had begun a children's play; and was working on her novel. Mayfield, who claimed one thousand words poured out of her for each gallon of coffee she drank, believed Zelda was so determined to write because she thought she could lessen her dependence upon her husband by producing saleable prose.[97] She penned more than thirty letters to Scott during the two months he was away, telling him in several that she hoped some day she could write like him. This lack of confidence permeated every communique she sent her husband during this stint in Montgomery, particularly those in which she dissed her own work. "I am sending my story to Ober—as it now seems satisfactory to me, but nobody will buy it," she told him.[98] The piece was "A Couple of Nuts," which she had been revising at the agent's request.

There is a caustic feel to the opening of the story that seems to reflect her mix of malaise and animosity at the time: "The summer of 1924 shriveled the trees in the Champs-Elysées to a misty blue till they swayed before your eyes as if they were about to go down under the gasoline fumes. Before July was out, dead leaves floated over the square of St-Sulpice like paper ashes from a bonfire. The nights lifted themselves exhausted from the pavements [...]"[99] *Scribner's Magazine* accepted the story and one other, which was published as "Miss Ella," the tale about an old maid in the south as seen through the eyes of her younger self. Zelda was disappointed about the fact that almost four times the number of stories were rejected and told Scott that her writing was "no good." In another letter she called herself "Scott's stupid wife." While her self-confidence wavered, she found joy in her relationship with her daughter. She told Scott, "You will be absolutely ravished by her riding trousers and yellow skirt and Scottie rearing back in her saddle like a messenger of victory. Each time she goes she conquers herself and the pony, the sky, the fields, and the little black boy who follows on a fast-shaven mule." Zelda said she wished she could be fine and sweet like Scott and Scottie, and that she hoped he was not working himself to death. She ended with, "Darling—How much I love you."[100]

NO ONE GETS OFF SCOT-FREE

SCOTT RETURNED for Christmas as promised but Zelda was in for a disappointing holiday. In spite of the fact that the house was decorated with holly and mistletoe, and prettily wrapped presents were slid beneath the lighted tree, the atmosphere was far from cheerful. Disillusioned by the fact that his script had been rejected, her husband came home in a rotten mood. At least the effort had earned him a nice chunk of change, which he felt would buy him some time to work on the novel he'd been plotting for years. His desire for a stable working environment evaporated soon after he returned when he learned his wife was writing her own novel, which ushered in one of the couple's most combative times of power struggling. "He feared that she would inevitably draw upon the material of their joint experiences, which he intended to use in his own book," Mayfield wrote. "Zelda felt stifled by his new attempt to repress her talents." [101] While he was demanding his wife not mine their lives, Cline noted how he "utilized every scrap of what he had learned about Zelda's mental breakdowns, remorselessly pilfering her letters, her fears, her punishments. Her madness became his new material."[102]

The biographer saw Scott's tactics as reprehensible because he was disregarding Zelda's mental fragility and ignoring the psychological consequences his actions could bring. Early on, Zelda refused to give in to his demands that she stop writing, feverishly putting words on paper as she squinted through the cigarette smoke swirling around her face. She angrily accused Scott of causing her eyestrain, and the fights picked up in intensity. Scott was so frustrated, he was considering institutionalizing her again. To see if he could preempt another hospitalization, he hit upon the idea of a Florida getaway but the trip turned out to be a disaster.

Both Cline and Mayfield speculate that Zelda's impending breakdown could have resulted from the fact that she realized how closely he was basing the character of Nicole Diver in *Tender is the Night* on her. Zelda would have known Scott was revealing aspects of her mental issues that she would have preferred remain unknown because it was his habit to read material aloud to her for feedback.

Cline so fittingly wrote, "It was one thing to have your husband turn you into a flapper, quite another to have him display your mental illness as the *raison d'être* of his main female character."[103] Proof that some destabilizing conflict took place was the fact that Zelda's eczema flared up again. As soon as they returned from Florida, Scott hurried her into another clinic. As they drove away from Felder Avenue, heading for the Montgomery train station in February 1932, Zelda left the house for the last time, her destination The Henry Phipps Clinic in Baltimore. Scott had decided to stay on in Montgomery until Scottie could finish the fifth grade, anguishing over the hospital bills that would force him to concentrate on short stories and delaying his novel further. Before long, Zelda was flourishing at Phipps. Art therapy helped her immensely, and though she told Scott about her painting, she did not mention she was continuing to work on the novel she was determined to publish. He would find out about it from Mildred Squires, a young medical resident treating Zelda, who wrote that his wife was "writing at an enviable speed" as she created a narrative that was "vivid and charming."

Squires reported to Scott in early March that Zelda's anxiety had decreased and her second chapter was completed. The intern then said she predicted the book would be a success. Zelda finally revealed to Scott that she was still working on the manuscript, telling him, "I am proud of my novel, but I can hardly restrain myself enough to get it written. You will like it—it is distinctly Ècole Fitzgerald, though more ecstatic than yours."[104] Zelda finished *Save Me the Waltz* during her first institutionalization at Phipps and dedicated it to Squires. Instead of sending the manuscript to Scott as she had promised to do, she switched the address on the envelope when it was being mailed from the hospital and sent it to Perkins. The note she included said, "Scott, being absorbed in his own [novel], has not seen it, so I am completely in the dark as to its possible merits, but naturally, terribly anxious that you should like it...As soon as I hear that you have safely received the copy, I want to mail the MS to Scott, so could you wire?"[105] The anxiety of holding onto the manuscript got the best of her so she sent it to Scott before she heard back from Perkins.

Her husband's anger was volcanic. He wrote to Squires that Zelda had produced an imitation of his own unfinished novel, the very book he so desperately needed to complete but could not because he was taking work that would pay for her treatment. He said he was certain she was trying to destroy him. Zelda had made some provocative moves that she must have known would set him off—naming an unattractive character Amory Blaine, the same as the Princeton-undergraduate protagonist in *This Side of Paradise*, for instance. Scott said he was tired of rationalizing the irrational as he watched her build a "dubitable career" with morsels of living matter chipped out of his mind, his belly, his nervous system, and his loins.[106] How rich his responses were! She was merely adopting the moves he'd made before and during their marriage by being a consummate poacher. As she used his tactics against him, she was simply showing him what a humiliating system he had created, which he now hated because he was the one being cannibalized.

He must have also been irked that he had been outsmarted. She wrote him a letter defending her decisions, which read, "Dr. Squires tells me you are hurt that I did not send my book to you before I mailed it to Max. Purposely I didn't—knowing that you were working on your own and honestly feeling that I had no right to interrupt you to ask for a perious [sic] opinion." Scott scribbled marginalia beside this paragraph noting she had meant perilous. He also wrote that her excuses were evasions. The last paragraph, beside which Scott put a checkmark, reads, "Goofo, please love me—life is very confusing—but I love you."[107] In the next letter, she asked him, "Shall I wire Max to send it back?" She needn't have bothered because Scott had already sent a wire to Perkins from Montgomery that said Perkins should not even consider Zelda's book until he received a revised version, telling him a letter would follow. Nine days later, he wrote that if Perkins liked it and wanted to publish it to remember the middle section had to be radically rewritten.

He also said the title and the name of Amory Blaine had to be changed: Because no copies of the original manuscript exist, it's not clear what disturbed him about the title. "Arriving in Baltimore Thursday to confer with Zelda," he added. "Will immediately decide on new title and name changes. Revising should take a fortnight." Several weeks later, he wrote to Perkins, "Zelda's novel is now good, improved in every way. It is new. She had largely eliminated the speakeasy-nights-and-our-trip-to-Paris atmosphere. You'll like it. It should reach you in ten days. I am too close to it to judge it but it may be even better than I think." Scott then told Perkins, "<u>But</u> I must urge you two things. (1.) If you like it please <u>don't</u> wire her congratulations, and please keep whatever praise you may see fit to give <u>on the staid side</u>—I mean, <u>as you naturally would</u>, rather than yield to a tendency one has with invalids to be extra nice to cheer them up. This seems a nuance but it is rather important at present to the doctors that Zelda does not feel that the

NO ONE GETS OFF SCOT-FREE

acceptance (always granted you like it) means immediate fame and money."[108]

His second thing: "Don't discuss contract with her until I have talked to you."[109] Though Zelda agreed to most of her chauvinistic husband's alterations on her manuscript, she was furious. She was overheard saying to herself that she had always done whatever she wanted to do, whenever she could possibly manage it; and that her book was none of her husband's goddamned business. When Scott asked for further changes, the letter she wrote was a strong push-back. "I would like you to thoroughly understand that my revision will be made on an aesthetic basis: that the other material which I will elect is nevertheless legitimate stuff which has cost me a pretty emotional penny to amass," she declared.[110] The odds were stacked against her, not only in terms of keeping her version of the novel intact, but regarding the book's success. No one even bothered to correct the grammatical errors. Evidently, Scott's only edits were focused on taking sections out that he felt could damage his own public image or would spoil his novel's chances. Perkins allowed the book to be published in its flawed state, which was a disservice to Zelda.

When she was told she would be a published novelist if she agreed to the edits, she wrote to Perkins that she authorized him to print the book and that she was overjoyed. The feud between the Fitzgeralds during this fraught time had largely been a hand-written one; they were about to be face-to-face combatants again. On April 15, 1932, Scott and Scottie left the Montgomery residence behind and moved to Baltimore to be near Zelda, whom he began visiting daily. They were fighting like mad, and doctors were finding it difficult to communicate with Zelda, who was refusing to give up her writing because she didn't believe it was causing her the mental strain her husband claimed it was. Once he had found a home to rent in a Baltimore suburb, Scott set up a schedule for them that had Zelda visiting Scottie every morning and returning to Phipps in the afternoons. She began to see that her daughter was growing away from her, which saddened her. She told Dr. Thomas Rennie, who was on her treatment team, "I can't help her at all. I'm like a stranger in the house."[111]

SCOTT SOON DISCOVERED that Zelda was planning to begin a new novel about insanity and his blowback was fierce. He told Squires that she absolutely must not "write any more personal stuff while she is under treatment" and "she mustn't start another personal piece of work—she spoke today of a novel on our personal quarrel & her insanity." He threatened, "Should she begin such a work at present I would withdraw my backing from her immediately because the sands are running out again on my powers of indurance [sic]."[112] Zelda caved to the pressure and let the subject go for a while but she was seething. With so much vitriol being directed at her, I was surprised she was deemed well enough to leave Phipps in June 1932. The condition of her release was that she and Scott would attend regular outpatient sessions at the clinic. They were to participate in couple's therapy because the doctors did not see her as cured. This illustrates the labyrinth she was endlessly wandering through: She couldn't possibly be well until they understood her instability was caused by trauma resulting from their overt attempts to deny her the right she had to explore her own creative process.

The fact that she was trading a team of controlling doctors, who had at least encouraged her creative ambitions, for her husband's iron fist only increased the unlikelihood of full recovery. As a distraction, Scott set up a painting studio in their new home, which worked for a while as she concentrated on creating a series of wildly morphing compositions featuring ballet dancers. Scott wrote to Dr. Rennie that the "situation has reduced itself in my mind to a rather clear-cut struggle of egos between Zelda and myself."[113] Mayfield and Haardt experienced the Fitzgeralds' stand-off first-hand when the friends visited the couple soon after Zelda was released. Mayfield said they were not prepared for what had become of the "Princeton Adonis and the most beautiful girl in Alabama." She said Scott's muscles had gone soft, that he had become quite stocky, and had a strutting walk. Zelda was alarmingly changed with a gray pallor to her skin that was marked by eczema, an eye that twitched, and a twisted mouth. The conversations were so strained, Zelda launched into a rambling monologue about painting to fill the halting silences.

"To see Scott and Zelda now and to remember them in their early days together in Montgomery was like reading a palimpsest on which a stark Greek tragedy had been written over the faint traces of a romantic comedy," Mayfield wrote. "And it was not the way to spend a pleasant afternoon." As Zelda was telling her friends about an exhibition she was going to have in New York City, Scott summoned Haardt into his study to show her the *Tender Is the Night* manuscript. "Like most egotists, Scott was basically insecure," Mayfield remembered. "As if to reassure himself, he said, 'It *is* good, isn't it, Zelda?' Her reply was a peal of irrelevant, mirthless laughter. For a moment, I thought Scott was going to slap her. Their eyes met and locked in a conflict that had rent them both and reduced them to the tarnished specters of the golden boy and girl of the Jazz Age. Anger flashed in the dead silence between and then paled into inward desolation and despair that was no longer a mere dark night of the soul with some promised morning, however far away, but a sickness unto death."[114] Scott insulted his wife by blurting out she was mad in front of her and her two friends.

When they looked shocked, he added hastily, "Schizophrenia, the doctors say." In Zelda's defense, Mayfield said, "Whatever Scott, the doctors, or anyone else might call Zelda's illness, the simple truth in human terms is that removed from the warmth and security of a familiar environment, plunged into a maelstrom of conflicting emotions, and faced with more professional, financial, and mental problems than she—or anyone else of her background and temperament—could cope with, she broke down. During the times when the pressures relaxed and when there was even relative harmony between her and Scott, she rebounded quickly and appeared to be her old self again."[115] *Save Me the Waltz* debuted in October 1932 with a litany of challenges—it was given little publicity, was printed on cheap paper, and had a tiny print run of three thousand copies. Dorothea Brande reviewed the excerpted novel for the November 1932 issue of *The Bookman*, which she began, "There is every chance that fifty readers will take up Zelda Fitzgerald's first novel, *Save Me the Waltz* (*Scribner's*. $2.00), and drop it again within the first chapter to every one reader who will persist to the end."[116]

She then pointed out how inappropriate it was that the publishers had not given the book "the elementary services of a literate proofreader," hadn't seen fit to "curb the almost ludicrous lushness of writing," and hadn't corrected "the number of absurd errors in the book" that were beyond counting. Brande added, "If one can persist past the mistakes and the verbiage one comes on an earnest, honest, good little story of a girl trying desperately to make a character for herself which will carry her through life." Brande's one compliment was, "There is a warm, intelligent, undisciplined mind behind *Save Me the Waltz*. Mrs. Fitzgerald should have had what help she needed to save her book from the danger of becoming a laughing-stock."[117] Only one review pleased Zelda; the subhead read "Mrs. Fitzgerald's First Novel Places Her On Scott's Level." It was one of the publications that chose to ignore the grammatical and linguistic disasters. Financially, it was a bust; it sold fewer than fourteen hundred copies and the check Zelda received for it totaled $120.73. Perkins told her he should have warned her that the royalties would be slim because of the increase in costs from so many changes during the proofing phase—the alterations to satisfy Scott. The financial failure and negative reviews drove Zelda into isolation.

She locked herself in her room and, bent on revenge, began the novel she'd wanted to write about her own asylum experiences. Scott complained to her doctors that she was breaking her promise not to write any more life-revealing narratives until he could finish his novel. This presented the couple in stark relief: He imbibed instead of writing; she wrote at a furious pace to try and stay sane, hiding the manuscript at the end of each day to protect it. By the time full-on autumn arrived and the trees were radiating brilliant colors, Zelda spent the majority of her time in her studio—writing, dancing, and painting—while Scott rasped his way through revisions. Because he had decided *Tender is the Night* had to be his magnum opus, the pressure hamstrung him. His secretary at the time, Isabel Owens, said she typed the full manuscript three times that year and sections of it many more times.

Owens told Milford, "Zelda's memory was good and he would go up to her room and ask advice about things they had done together, conversations they had...He couldn't write about anything he didn't know. Some of those stories were terrible that he turned out during that time—we all knew it. He was convinced he was dead and buried."[118] As he struggled along, he wrote an article for *The Saturday Evening Post* titled "One Hundred False Starts" in which he admitted that he still had a feeling of utter helplessness when he sat down and faced a block of legal-sized paper with a sharpened pencil. Owens also confirmed what I'd suspected: Scott's determination to "protect" Zelda from visitors was a projection—the protection she needed was from Scott, his boozing, his maniacal desire to control her, and his desire that no one witness his oppressive behavior.

IN A LETTER to Dr. Adolf Meyer, one of Zelda's physicians at Phipps, he admitted that Zelda "would have been a genius" if they had never met. Then Scott contradicted himself by saying she had "frail equipment of a sick mind and a berserk determination." He was angry that Meyer was more liberal than the doctors in Europe and that the physician felt Scott needed as much psychological help as Zelda did. The psychiatrist wrote as much in a letter and told Scott he needed to stop drinking if he and Zelda were to have a stable life. Scott denied that he was the problem, warning the doctor that Zelda was a consummate actress and was fooling him. He then shared a strange analogy to push back on the idea that his drinking was problematical, writing to the doctor, "When you qualify or disqualify my judgment on the case, or put it on a level very little above her, on the grounds that I have frequently abused liquor I can only think of Lincoln's remark about a greater man and heavier drinker than I have ever been—that he wished he knew what sort of liquor Grant drank so he could send a barrel to all his other generals."[119]

To preempt any thoughts the doctor might have that Scott was being childish, he wrote he was merely "an overextended, imaginative, functioning man using alcohol as a stimulus." Calling Zelda "a schitzophrene," he declared he was beginning to feel he was degrading himself by stooping so low as to "collaborate in this cure."[120] Scott's rage toward Zelda's novel was also on full view in these letters. He told her doctors it was plagiaristic and unwise in every way, and that it should never have been written because he had "a certain public weight." He claimed he had back-up because he had spoken to his cronies, who were other first-rank writers like him, and they told him they would have felt the same if they had learned their amateur wives were secretly trying to cash in on their lust for "self-expression" by publishing a book about their private lives, particularly if the neophytes were doing so with material the professionals were exploring at the time. Scott then said he was not to be confused with "the local Hunt-Club-Alcoholic" and he would give up liquor under only one of these two conditions: if Zelda healed and became a helpmate or if they divorced regardless whether she recovered or not.[121]

A discussion between Scott and Dr. Rennie, which was recorded by a stenographer and ran on for one hundred and fourteen pages, reveals how much Scott was in denial. While he disparaged Zelda as the sick one, he showed his own mental instability, berating Zelda in her presence by calling her a third-rate writer and a third-rate ballet dancer. As the session wore on, he completely lost it and stopped even trying to curb his hostility or his arrogance. He claimed Zelda picked up the crumbs he dropped at the dinner table and stuck them in books. Unfortunately, the doctor sided with Scott that Zelda should stop producing novels and that she should have everything she wrote go through Scott's hands. Rennie asked her how she rated her work against Scott's. "I do not rate myself as anything compared to him, Dr. Rennie, but I certainly want to write." During this knock-down-drag-out, the physician said that whether she published would be up to Scott. Zelda then argued that she'd never get anything in print if that was the case. They wore her down and she finally suggested that her disagreements with her husband be put on hold until Scott's novel was finished.[122]

"That means a complete abnegation of yourself until this paramount thing is over," Rennie said. "You are willing to do that?" When she answered yes, the doctor suggested she stick with writing the play she had been working on until *Tender Is the Night* was published. Scott countered that she would do no such thing. "It has got to be unconditional surrender on her part," her husband demanded. "Otherwise, I would rather go to law, because I don't trust her…it is necessary for her to give up the idea of writing anything." He ended his bluster by saying it was the only way he could ever organize his life again. *What a weakling!* I thought as I made my way through this recounting of the session. Scott then pushed the doctor even further by adding that Zelda should have no independence of life or mind whatsoever. When she countered that she had the right to regain control of her activities when his novel was finally published, Scott shut her down yet again. Cline noted that Zelda's biggest challenge was she had accepted the notion that Scott was the professional genius and she was merely a gifted amateur.[123] While Scott was pretending to be a mental stalwart as he interacted with Zelda's doctors, a surprising source claims emotional instability was a thread that was woven into his psyche.

Chapter 17 in *A Moveable Feast*, which is a profile of Scott, presents him at his most phobic. In it, Hemingway recounts a trip he took with Scott as they traveled from Lyon to Paris. According to Hemingway, whom it is important to remember he lied in other chapters in the book, Scott was supposed to be taking the lead in their travel plans but he had repeatedly bungled every aspect of the excursion. The

NO ONE GETS OFF SCOT-FREE

first evening they were underway, Scott convinced himself he was going to die of "congestion of the lungs" before the sun came up the next morning. When the pair checked into a hotel, Hemingway tried to prove to Scott that he was fine by checking the hypochondriacal writer's pulse and feeling his forehead, which Hemingway said was cool. "You haven't any temperature," he told Scott. "How the hell are you going to have congestion of the lungs without a temperature?" Scott shot back, "Don't swear at me." By this time, "Scott was lying in bed to conserve his strength for his battle against the disease," Hemingway wrote, saying he "looked like a little dead crusader" and that the situation was turning into a "silly comedy."[124]

Scott demanded a thermometer be found so Hemingway could prove to him he didn't have a fever. When Hemingway came back from inquiring if there was one in the hotel, he said, "Scott was still lying as though on his tomb, sculpted as a monument to himself, his eyes closed and breathing with exemplary dignity." After the bellman delivered two whisky sours, a handful of aspirin, and a bathtub thermometer, Hemingway placed the instrument under Scott's armpit and reported that his temperature was normal. Scott demanded Hemingway put it under his own armpit to prove the thermometer's accuracy. Hemingway did and read the same result. "How do you feel?" Scott asked. "Splendid," Hemingway answered. After his bluff was called, Scott said, "We can be happy it cleared up so quickly, I've always had great recuperative power."[125] Given the neurosis this episode exposes, if it's true, Scott was damn lucky he was the man in the relationship or he would have been the scapegoat locked away in some mental institution.

"I will probably be carried off eventually by four strong guards shrieking manically that after all I was right and she was wrong, while Zelda is followed home by an adoring crowd in an automobile banked with flowers, and offered a vaudeville contract," Scott wrote to Dr. Meyer.[126] *Couples counseling sure looks different today than it did then*, I thought when I read this summation of how bruised his ego had become. During these turbulent months, Scott met with a lawyer as he considered a divorce but decided against it because Maryland state laws made it difficult to achieve the conditions he would want in a settlement. Still reeling from the stricture she felt over the limitations her husband forced upon her, Zelda would soon be shaken to her core when the depression, anxiety, and suicidal behavior that was glaringly present in her family tree reared its head again. Her favorite brother Anthony, called Tony, was hospitalized and ended his life by flinging himself out the window of the institution in which he'd been placed. His doctor wrote to Scott that he had been diagnosed with "neuro-psychosis—possibly familial."

In her biography *Zelda Sayre Fitzgerald: An American Woman's Life*, Linda Wagner-Martin claimed that Zelda's mother Minnie may have sabotaged her daughter's diagnoses early on by writing to the doctors at Valmont that there had never been any mental instability in the Sayre family, which wasn't true. "Both the Judge and their oldest child, Marjorie, had had nervous spells if not actual breakdowns, and Minnie's mother and sister both died of suicides," Wagner-Martin wrote. "Zelda had told Scott that Minnie had recently written her that she knew what the trouble was, so her mother's reticence manifested itself only officially."[127] Zelda wasn't told that Tony had committed suicide: Her family said he was suffering from acute malaria that he contracted on the job as a civil engineer while surveying a swamp in Mobile, and that in his delirium he had rushed out of bed thinking he was playing football and accidentally fell through an open window.

NO ONE GETS OFF SCOT-FREE

The tale, which illustrated that a talent for intriguing storytelling was also alive in the Sayre DNA, was a contrivance anyone who grew up in the south during that era knows very well. Ensuring that no shame was leveled at the family name made it necessary to lie about a tragedy and to deny that anything resembling mental illness existed in a bloodline. Though the psychiatrists at Valmont may not have known about this susceptibility to instability, Scott wrote to Dr. Meyer that there was a predisposition of mental troubles in the Sayre family history so by the time Zelda was being treated at Phipps, her doctors would have known. Devastated over her brother's death, Zelda immersed herself in art—the only thing she cared about that she could still do because painting didn't threaten her husband's ego. Contrite that Zelda was overwhelmed with grief, Scott returned to a loop he cycled through each time a storm subsided and he got his way.

To appease his guilt over suppressing his wife yet again, he tried to make amends by giving her a treat. This time the reward was a trip to Bermuda where they both had always wanted to go. Hypocritically, he encouraged her to write a magazine article about the experience—the non-fiction safe enough territory and the income helpful. In the piece, which appeared in *Esquire* and was titled "Show Mr. and Mrs. F. to Number—," Zelda wrote, "The Elbow Beach Hotel was full of honeymooners, who scintillated so persistently in each other's eyes that we cynically moved. The Hotel St. George was nice. Bougainvillea cascaded down the tree trunks and long stairs passed by deep mysteries taking place behind native windows. Cats slept along the balustrade and lovely children grew. We rode bicycles along the windswept causeways and stared in a dreamy daze at such phenomena as roosters scratching amidst the sweet alyssum." She ended the piece with, "We had traveled a lot, we thought. Maybe this would be the last trip for a long while. We thought Bermuda was a nice place to be the last one of so many years of traveling."[128]

AFTER THIS IDYLLIC PRELUDE, the Fitzgeralds returned home to smaller quarters in Baltimore because Scott was hemorrhaging money. He was in the final stages of correcting the galleys for *Tender is the Night* and the first two serialized installments were published in *Scribner's Magazine*. When Zelda read the pieces that publicly exposed her, she collapsed. On February 12, 1934, she was hospitalized at Phipps again, her third breakdown well underway. She was put on suicide watch and lost more than a dozen pounds, which made her look malnourished. She silently took the sedatives she was given and didn't protest the complete bedrest she was prescribed. Scott wrote of Zelda's relapse, "I left my capacity for hoping on the little roads that led to Zelda's sanitariums."[129] Though the situation must have been seriously demoralizing, Scott's statement was pretty self-righteous given he drew his diagnoses in *Tender* from reports that came out of these institutions.

Had Zelda not been hospitalized, he may never have found the center for the novel, the subject for which had changed a handful of times over nearly a decade as he watched his wife's every move to glean further inspiration. Milford didn't mince words about the dire effects Scott's behavior had on his wife. "He mercilessly exposed Zelda in his characterization of Nicole Diver," she pointed out. "He drew upon Zelda's most terrible and private letters to him, written in the anguish of the early months of her illness in Switzerland, snipped and pieced them together in Book II with very little regard for Zelda's reaction or for the precarious balance of her sanity." Zelda said about the novel, "What made me mad was that he made the girl so awful and kept on reiterating how she had ruined his life and I couldn't help identifying myself with her because she had so many of my experiences."[130]

As he read the serialized chapters, Hemingway said in a letter to Perkins that he felt the narrative had all the brilliance and most of the defects Scott always had. "In spite of marvelous places there is something wrong with it and, as a writer, this is what I believe is wrong," he wrote. "He starts with two people Gerald and Sara Murphy. He has the accent of their voices, their home, their looks marvelously. But he knows nothing about them." Hemingway claimed where Scott's knowledge was lacking was in their emotional makeup, which left him no choice but to create romantic figures instead of human beings. Hemingway added that Scott was so shallow, he had merely taken a series of incidents from his life and used them arbitrarily. He then told Perkins he believed Scott had destroyed himself and Zelda, and that Zelda had set out to destroy Scott—the two of them caught up in an immature "whining for lost youth deathdance."[131] Though Hemingway felt the intermittent scenes that carried the book along partially succeeded, they did so in spite of all the "worn Christmas-tree ornaments" that were sprinkled into Scott's idea of literature. He then ended the letter with, "Don't show any of this above to Scott or tell him I said anything. I'll write him but have been too busy so far."[132]

His critiques illustrate how much he had developed as a writer since the trek from Lyon with Scott, whom Hemingway saw as more accomplished at the time because he had yet to write a novel and didn't know if he'd ever be able to craft such a long narrative. While he felt many of Scott's pieces of fiction were silly, badly written, and collegiate, Hemingway did admire one particular novel. "If he could write a book as fine as *The Great Gatsby* I was sure that he could write an even better one," he claimed.[133] When Hemingway first read *Gatsby*, he had not yet met Zelda; once he had known her for a handful of years, he wrote to Perkins, "Poor old Scott—He should have swapped Zelda when she was at her craziest but still saleable back 5 or 6 years ago before she was diagnosed as nutty—He is the great tragedy of talent in our bloody generation."[134] The serialized excerpts from *Tender is the Night* in the magazine shocked and offended the Murphys because, as Hemingway had pointed out, Scott had mined their lives for his characters, entwining aspects of their relationship with his and Zelda's marriage.

Sara said the things Scott shared in the book revealed truths about her and her husband that she could barely admit, and that the exposure frightened her. It would be quite some time before she could be civil to Scott again. She scolded him in a letter in which she wrote a "consideration for other people's feelings, opinions or even time is *Completely* left out of your makeup. You don't even know what Zelda or Scottie are like—in spite of your love for them. It seemed to us the other night (Gerald too)—that all you thought and felt about them was in terms of yourself— the same holds good of your feelings for your friends…"[135] Scott's defense was that he wasn't trying to expose Sara; he merely wanted to illustrate the effect she had on men. He ran on and on in a difficult-to-follow drift of thoughts about her and Gerald, then admitted when he read over the letter, he felt it conveyed no particular point but he was sending it anyway. He closed it with, "Like Cole [Porter's] eloquent little song [*You're The Top*], 'I think it'll tell you how *great* you are.'"[136]

Vaill said Sara was so outraged and shaken by the bits of the book that had already been published in the magazine and even more incensed when she read the full novel. Time did not ease her agitation, as "more than twenty-five years later she couldn't speak of it without indignation."[137] Sara's angry reaction, which was highly appropriate, juxtaposed against Zelda's collapse highlights the difference in the realities of these two women. While Sara had the luxury of being angry because she knew she would be supported by a husband who respected her, Zelda was under Scott's thumb and knew she had to sublimate herself to him, which forced her to bury her anger in illness. By the time the full novel had been serialized, Zelda she had improved to the point that she could have been released from Phipps but Scott said no. He was feverishly working on the final corrections for the galleys for the full release of *Tender Is the Night* and he didn't want a sick wife at home carping about her ills or his book. He decided to make a move that would solve two dilemmas.

Zelda was complaining that she couldn't be in New York City for the opening of her one-woman art exhibition that would take place in April because Scott didn't want to take the time to escort her there. By moving his wife to Craig House, an expensive sanitarium in Beacon, New York, located a few hours north of the city by train, he could avoid having Zelda at home and make it possible for her to attend. She was promised that if she stayed steady, she would be allowed to go to the opening. The emphasis on patient freedoms at Craig House was good for Zelda, and she did make enough progress that she could travel to Manhattan accompanied by her nurse for the show's opening in April 1934. Scott attended the event, and he and Zelda were at the opposite ends of the emotional spectrum: She was cheerful and vivacious, and he was morose and edgy, rasped raw by financial strain. He was paying $750 a month for the services his wife received in New York, and he was $12,000 in debt by then.

Once again, he was putting all of his hopes on a novel that had just debuted but the first reviews were insulting. The April 14, 1934, issue of *The New Yorker* contained critiques of the book and of Zelda's show. The latter was dubbed a collection of "paintings by the almost mythical Zelda Sayre Fitzgerald; with whatever emotional overtones or associations may remain from the so-called Jazz Age." About *Tender Is the Night*, which had appeared on bookstore shelves two days before, the magazine's critic, Clifton Fadiman, wrote, "In Mr. Fitzgerald's case, money is the root of all novels." He said the book went to seed in the latter part to become merely an anatomy of more disintegration.[138] Mayfield put it rather succinctly when she said the novel's "chief flaw was it was written with one eye on the Book-of-the-Month Club and the other on the divorce court."[139] When Hemingway read the full novel, he told Perkins he found the characters in it to be beautifully faked case histories rather than people.

After nine years of working on the book, Scott was drained of his self-confidence because he saw it as a failure and the thirteen thousand copies that had sold were far below his expectations. Because Zelda knew how the financial strain would grow even worse given the book's low sales, she was begging him to move her to a state hospital that wouldn't cost as much as Craig House but he said no. She was also insisting that she be able to begin the novel she had hoped to write because his book was in print, to which his answer was also no. With the no's piling up, and her concerns over money, Scott's drinking, her separation from Scottie, and her own illness, Zelda fell into a downward spiral in May. She returned to Baltimore from Craig House by ambulance in a catatonic state. Scott placed her in The Sheppard and Enoch Pratt Hospital in Towson, Maryland, which was far cheaper than the Beacon sanitarium or Phipps Clinic. Zelda must have been clueless about what it would mean for him to have her moved to a cheaper facility when she urged him to save money. Once she surfaced, she was horrified by the barred windows, locked doors, and dismal rooms, calling it a sinister-looking place. She was also in shock over her treatment—she was physically searched in a degrading way; her money, make-up, and cigarettes were confiscated; her clothes were taken from her; and she was often doused with disinfectant.

Locked in a stark ward with no possibility of communicating with family or friends, she was feeling hopeless. "This time there was no doubt about it," Mayfield wrote; "she had broken down—or, perhaps, more accurately, after four years between the upper and the nether millstones, she had been ground down by Scott and the doctors."[140] Zelda loathed the physician assigned to her case, William Elgin, because, like the doctors who had previously treated her, he sided with her husband and was harsh with her, which caused her to decline further. With his creativity sapped, Scott wasn't faring much better. In an attempt to maintain his own sanity, he began deluding himself into thinking he'd married Zelda reluctantly and had immediately regretted it, his knee-jerk an attempt to distance himself from her emotionally. During this months-long hospitalization, Scott visited Zelda only nine times and he was up to his old tricks. He absconded more of her work—rewriting a number of her articles, which he sold to *Esquire*—and then left for an extended bender in New York City.

ONCE SHE WAS lucid enough to think, Zelda wrote to him, "You have been so good to me—and all I can say is that there was always that deeper current running through my heart: my life—you." She went into a long memory about when they first began dating in Montgomery, then said, "It is a shame that we should have met in harshness and coldness where there was once so much tenderness and so many dreams." She said she wanted him to be happy and that if there was any justice in the world, he would be.[141] Sadly, he was moving farther away from contentment rather than toward it: He was drunk most of the time and was having trivial affairs that he flaunted inappropriately in front of their friends. By the spring of 1935, he was quite unwell—the threat of cirrhosis of the liver shocked him into sobriety, but doctors had also found a serious cavity in one lung caused by some mild tubercular lesions from decades before. He had also turned forty and was clearly having a mid-life crisis. To escape the cold Baltimore winter, Scott went to Hendersonville, North Carolina, where he felt he would have no distractions and could write.

He sent Zelda a letter from there asking her what she needed. She replied, "I don't need anything at all except hope, which I can't find by looking either backwards or forwards, so I suppose the thing is to shut my eyes."[142] By now, she was suicidal and wouldn't come out of the protracted period of wanting to do self-harm until the fall. The day after visiting her in September, Scott wrote to Laura Guthrie, whom he had hired as his typist in North Carolina, "First Zelda—she was fine, almost herself, has only one nurse now + has no more intention of doing away with herself. It was wonderful to sit with her head on my shoulder for hours and feel as I always have, even now, closer to her than to any other human being. This is not a denial of other emotions—oh, you understand."[143] When he left Baltimore, he moved into the Grove Park Inn in Asheville where he had an affair with a rich Texan named Beatrice Dance. She fell for him and when she pushed for more of a commitment, he said he wouldn't leave Zelda. Dance was hospitalized for distress, which pushed Scott off the wagon.

Soon, he had to check himself into a clinic because his tuberculosis had flared to the point he was a complete wreck. Cline interviewed a young writer named Tony Buttitta, who was also the owner of the Intimate Bookshop in Asheville at the time. He told her Scott would come into the store and start sobbing, crying out, "We meant so much to each other in our early life. But Zelda wanted to be a star. She didn't feel what I did was important to her." Buttitta remarked that it was Scott who wanted to be the star and he wanted Zelda in the audience. He said Scott would moan, "I feel responsible because now she's gone batty."[144] This was one of the rare honest statements to come out of his mouth, one it appears he could only share with a stranger he likely thought he would never see again. Proving how restless his spirit was at this point, he flung himself like a boomerang between North Carolina and Maryland, leaving Scottie in Baltimore with Owens during his absences. Extremely depressed and deeply in debt, he penned a series of mediocre stories, only two of which sold.

Determined to shake off the losing streak, he rented a room at the Skylands Hotel in Hendersonville and wrote "The Crack Up," "Pasting It Together," and "Handle with Care," which he called a "trilogy of depression" about a writer who was completely blocked. While Scott deemed the essays explorations of awareness, Perkins felt they were steeped in self-pity and would further damage Scott's diminishing reputation. Mayfield had an insightful take on Scott's state of mind at this point. She believed he was haunted by the idea that his success as a writer could be traced back to the time when Zelda had shown him the diary and the letters he used to create the narrative in what would eventually become *This Side of Paradise*. "In some strange way," she explained, "his talent for fiction was bound up with his love for her. By his treatment of her and his merciless psychological dissections of her, on which his novels and many of his stories were based, he had not only killed the thing he loved but he had also dried up the wellsprings of his literary success."[145]

In "Pasting It Together," he declared his and Zelda's relationship had been "one of those tragic loves doomed for lack of money," and proved he had never forgiven his wife for breaking off their engagement sixteen years earlier. "A man does not recover from such jolts—he becomes a different person and, eventually, the new person finds new things to care about," he said. Describing his side of the story after she dumped him the second time, he added, "During a long summer of despair I wrote a novel instead of letters, so it came out all right, but it came out all right for a different person. The man with the jingle of money in his pocket who married the girl a year later would always cherish an abiding distrust, an animosity, toward the leisure class—not the conviction of a revolutionist but the smoldering hatred of a peasant."[146] What did the peasant do next? He tried yet again to borrow from her life because he was so desperate for money. He began negotiating with Samuel Goldwyn to write a movie about a ballet dancer. He considered himself an expert on the subject because he had watched Zelda try to forge a career as a ballerina.

He wrote to his literary agent, Harold Ober, that *Save Me the Waltz*, which he had enclosed with the letter, gave him the insight he needed to produce such a script. When Ober was negotiating, the essays Scott had written during his stint at the Skylands Hotel came out in print. As Perkins had feared, the tone of the pieces shut the door on Scott's chances with the producers because they saw his mental state as so unstable they wouldn't take the risk of hiring him.

Meanwhile Zelda was declining fast in the Maryland sanitarium. Rosalind visited her in April of 1936 and was stunned by how much weight she had lost. The doctors told Rosalind that Scott interfered with her care to the point they could do nothing for her sister, which compelled her to fight for Zelda, insisting that she be moved to the Highland Hospital in Asheville, which she had heard had an innovative approach to treating psychiatric issues.

Scott, who agreed to the plan, wrote to Sara Murphy, "I am moving Zelda to a sanitarium in Asheville—she is no better, though the suicidal cloud has lifted." He added, "In an odd way, perhaps incredible to you, she was always my child (it was not reciprocal as it often is in marriages), my child in a sense that Scotty [sic] isn't, because I've brought Scotty [sic] up hard as nails (Perhaps that's fatuous, but I _think_ I have.)" Near the end of the letter, he claimed, "Outside of the realm of what you called Zelda's 'terribly dangerous secret thoughts,' I was her great reality, often the only liaison agent who could make the world tangible to her."[147] His hubris was on full display here as he bragged about his role in Zelda's life given the state she was in. His letter also proved what a skewed view he had of his involvement in his wife's illness: Not only had he tried to smother her during those early days when he couldn't concentrate because he was afraid she was making other conquests, he had taken continuous steps to make her a helpless version of herself in order to reduce her stature in their relationship to that of a dependent.

As Scott elevated himself in his fantasies, Zelda was about to have her first instance of good luck in a long time—the move to Highland Hospital was extremely positive for her. The pleasant, homelike atmosphere, and the fact that Dr. and

Mrs. Robert Carroll, who ran the sanitarium, recognized her charm and intelligence did wonders for her. "Zelda bloomed again," Rosalind said, "and on several visits to me in New York during that period [she] was almost like her old self, beautiful once more, still interested in music, the theater, and art, but toned down to an almost normal rhythm. Any thought of gay life was now far behind her, but she still retained a zest for living that was characteristic of her."[148] In a letter to Perkins in September, Scott wrote that he had been within a mile and a half of his wife all summer and had seen her about a half dozen times. Mayfield numbered his visits at five and noted that they were disastrous because his behavior toward Zelda was ludicrous as they bickered like adolescents.

Scott's unsteadiness as he over-imbibed led to several serious injuries—he dislocated his shoulder attempting a swan dive in the pool at the Grove Park Inn, and fell in the bathroom of his suite, laying there for a long time as he called for help in the off-chance someone was walking past the door. After a painful bout of arthritis that followed, he went to bed for ten weeks and drank himself into a stupor. He was only able to pull himself out of it because he caught a financial break when he received a $20,000 inheritance from his mother when she died, which he used to pay off his bills and to take a pause for several months to "rest in a big way." He told Perkins, "I have to admit to myself that I haven't the vitality I had five years ago."[149] Dr. Carroll urged Scott to leave North Carolina, calling him an "emotional disorganizer," and Scott agreed to return to Baltimore. With her husband out of the way, Zelda calmed down and Carroll began controversial treatments that included injecting placental blood and horse blood into her cerebrospinal fluid, which caused meningitis and violent physical reactions but increased lucidity.[150]

She was also receiving electro-shock and insulin shock, both of which by then had been found to cause memory loss. It's a wonder anyone ever survived these inhumane treatments mentally intact, but Zelda did, and she would continue to improve to the point she was well enough to visit Scott and Scottie by the spring of 1938. She was there when MGM producer Hunt Stromberg hired Scott to be a screenwriter for the film *The Women*, which would star Norman Shearer, Joan Crawford, Paulette Goddard, and Rosalind Russell. Before he left for the west coast, Scott took Zelda and Scottie to Montgomery for a short stay. Mayfield, who bumped into Zelda during the visit, said she looked pretty in a sleeveless white sharkskin dress and spectator pumps, that her tan was becoming, and that she looked far healthier and happier than she had when Mayfield saw her in Baltimore. Upon his arrival in L.A., Scott began the rounds, namedropping in letters to Zelda the panoply of stars with whom he was rubbing elbows.

He arranged for Scottie to visit him for a month and she had a blast, dining with Crawford and Shearer, and meeting Fred Astaire, her favorite star. Mayfield had been hired to direct a play for a summer theater troupe in Los Angeles. When she arrived soon after Scott, she spotted him as he escorted a blonde, who could have been mistaken as a young Zelda from a distance, into a party. He told Mayfield he was "sitting on top of the world," which she thought was nonsense.[151] She then bumped into him at the MGM commissary during lunch one day and listened to his descriptions of his fabulous life until she couldn't take it anymore. Mayfield interrupted Scott by asking him about Zelda, which threw him; before long, he was heading for the door. Mayfield was lunching with actress Margaret Sullavan that day. After Scott left, Sullavan told Mayfield he was "shacking up" with the blonde, whose name was Sheilah

Graham and who had replaced Zelda as his new sparring partner. Mayfield said Scott referred to Graham as "his paramour" and described the twenty-eight-year-old British woman who was working as a gossip columnist at the time as radiant.

"With Zelda safely locked away in Highland Hospital and Scottie at the Ethel Walker School, where she was preparing to take her entrance examinations for Vassar, he was free to do as he pleased in Hollywood," Mayfield wrote, saying Graham was a stabilizing influence on Scott until he ran into trouble with a particular script a powerful producer rejected.[152] He began sneaking alcohol into the apartment against Graham's wishes and would take swigs when he went to the bathroom where he had stashed the liquor. "Sheilah kept him away from parties and tried to help him regain his self-control," Mayfield noted. "But while he was working on *Infidelity*, a picture for Joan Crawford, his actions became so erratic that his friends were alarmed."[153] As Scott's downward spiral picked up speed, his contract with MGM was not renewed in January 1939 and he began freelancing for various studios beginning in March.

By contrast, Zelda was reaching new creative heights at Highland Hospital because its founders took her art seriously. The Carrolls arranged trips that enabled Zelda to expand her knowledge, taking her to Sarasota so she could participate in life drawing classes and learn costume design at the Ringling College of Art and Design during a three-week stay. They had also arranged a trip to Cuba but Scott didn't give them his permission in time. Zelda suggested the two of them go on their own and he agreed. When he arrived in North Carolina in April, he was drunk and exhausted after a fight with Graham because he was going to spend time with his wife. When the Fitzgeralds arrived at Club Kawama in Varadero, Scott drank heavily and got into a serious fistfight during which he was injured. Zelda had to get them both back to the states and admit him to a hospital, which she managed with the help of her sister Clotilde and Clotilde's husband. It was the last time Zelda and Scott would see each other in person.

In a letter to his wife on May 6, 1939, Scott wrote, "Excuse this being typewritten, but I am supposed to lie in bed for a week or so and look at the ceiling." The bedrest had been ordered because his tuberculosis had flared up again. "You were a peach throughout the whole trip and there isn't a minute of it when I don't think of you with all the old tenderness and with a consideration that I never understood that you had before," he told her. "You are the finest, loveliest, tenderest, most beautiful person I have ever known, but even that is an understatement because the length that you went to there at the end would have tried anybody beyond endurance." He ended by sending her his "dearest love."[154] This was a preferred sentiment for him, as he signed his letters to Scottie with "Dearest Love, Daddy," and called her pet names like Scottina and Pie. She had been accepted at Vassar and was in college by the time the Cuban debacle took place. Hearing about how resilient her mother had been in handling the situation there, Scottie sided with her maternal grandmother and aunts, who had begun a campaign to have Zelda released into their care because they believed she would be better off living with Minnie. Scott wouldn't have it and he pressured Dr. Carroll to agree that Zelda should stay put.

Carroll caved and wrote to Minnie that, though Zelda's behavior seemed normal, her psyche was shattered; that she was basically damaged goods. Illustrating Scott's disingenuousness after his praise-filled letter thanking Zelda for rescuing him in Cuba, he had a staffer at the hospital inform Scottie that her mother could hold up for short periods but she would never be able to operate in the world without guidance.[155] In a predictable twist, Scott would soon be treating his daughter to the same controlling tactics he maintained over Zelda as the young woman embarked on her own writing career. When Scottie published her first article in *Mademoiselle* in July 1939, Scott pitched a temper tantrum because she had written about the Fitzgeralds' lives. He told Ober, who had agreed to be Scottie's literary agent, that he wanted to see everything she would publish before it appeared in the future. Scottie had also written a biography about her parents that Scott forbid her to publish.

When she landed a job with *Harper's Bazaar*, he told her he was pleased to see a picture of her in the magazine but he objected to her calling herself Frances Scott Fitzgerald because it pushed him into the background given she was the fresh new Fitzgerald face—he then said she made him feel like a has-been. "It calls attention to my being of my generation, which is not too good since I hope to have a big book out in a year," he said.[156] Though she agreed to stay away from material that would expose her father's private life, Scottie didn't tone her career down to soothe Scott's ego. She also joined ranks with her Sayre relatives in demanding Zelda be released, as they would soon find the evidence they needed to prove her mother was ready to be freed from the cage in which Scott had been keeping her. As Christmas 1939 drew near, she was well enough to travel to Montgomery on her own and she was stable the entire time she was there. When she returned to Asheville in January, she begged Scott to sign a release. He ignored her, but he couldn't ignore Dr. Carroll, who finally wrote to him in early March that he felt Zelda was ready to go home. Scott said he was surprised and claimed to be delighted.

NO ONE GETS OFF SCOT-FREE

When Zelda boarded a bus for Montgomery on April 15, 1940, it was the first time Scott didn't show up in person during one of her departures from a clinic to take her safely to where she was traveling. His presence was replaced by a perfunctory letter that told her she must be frugal because he was in dire straits financially. "The main thing is not to run up bills or wire for extra funds," he warned. "There simply aren't any and as you can imagine I am deeply in debt to the government and everyone else." He told her he would send her an address when he had one; that she should send all correspondence to his new agent until then.[157] Zelda arrived in Montgomery to find it blossoming. Purple and white wisteria climbed the giant trees along the oak-vaulted streets, roses bloomed against the walls and columns of the antebellum homes, and the fields were blanketed with pink primroses. She worked in her mother's garden, built a patio where she could paint, and rented a bicycle on which she rode around town.

While she took positive steps toward a normal life, Scott's was disintegrating as he was bedridden with greater frequency. Graham left a record of his final meltdown in a memoir titled *The Beloved Infidel* that chronicles the same disfunction that took place in Scott and Zelda's marriage. Once passion faded, Scott waffled between ambivalence and cruelty. Polarized between love and hate, he lashed out the only way he knew how—with his pen. As he had in the past, he treated Graham like a specimen to be dissected, analyzed, and observed for his next novel. Fortunately, Graham's capacity for enduring such hyper-examination was strong enough to keep her from going off the deep end, and she adroitly, though unknowingly, took the pressure off Zelda. Having escaped her husband's vampire-like behavior, she was quietly settling into her new reality. Mayfield found her to be subdued and a little sad.

"After all, it was a devastating experience to have to come back to her hometown, where she had been a belle in her youth, as a semi-invalid, many of whose friends had been alienated by her book and alarmed by the stories Scott had spread to justify himself," she explained. Zelda's financial support from her husband was $30 a week and she took his warning about money to heart—she rarely went to the hairdresser; only occasionally went to the movie; didn't drink; smoked about a half-dozen cigarettes a day; limited herself to one Victrola album a month, which cost her $5; spent about the same amount on paints; and went to bed at nine o'clock in order to save on the electricity bill, which she was helping to pay.[158] She was painting prolifically and was writing again. Though it wouldn't be widely known until she had been dead for sixty-five years, a short story Zelda penned not long before she met Scott was included in a literary journal published by Sidney Lanier High School in 1918, which proves she hadn't written her first piece to compete with her husband.

The story titled "The Iceberg" was found just before it was reprinted in the December 20, 2013, issue of *The New Yorker*. When Zelda's granddaughter Eleanor Lanahan read the story, she asked, "Who knew Zelda wrote stories before Scott entered her life? Who knew she'd give a working girl the happiest of destinies?" She called the piece "a charming morality tale of sorts" and pointed out that it was fascinating because it illuminated the expectations of southern women during the early 1900's. *The New Yorker* called its tone lighthearted, winking, and ironic. Editors also noted how it alluded to some of the tensions in Zelda's life that swayed between independence and entanglements with men.[159] The mightiest of the latter was about to end. In November 1940, Scott was standing in line in a drugstore waiting to buy a pack of cigarettes when he nearly fainted so doctors sentenced him to bedrest. He had stopped drinking and was desperately trying to finish the first draft of *The Last Tycoon*, the story based upon his liaison with Graham, so he could send it to Perkins by the middle of January. By the evening of December 20th, Scott had finished the first part of chapter six, and he and Graham went to see a movie.

As he stood up to leave the theater, he told her he felt awful and grasped the back of his seat to steady himself. She took him home and put him to bed. After a night's sleep, he said he was feeling better. By that afternoon he would be dead, succumbing to a fatal heart attack. He was forty-four years old. At the news of Scott's death, Zelda was overcome by shock and grief but she held herself together and was pleased that Scottie traveled to Montgomery to be with her. Suddenly, one of the most intense themes running through her life story—the control her husband had been driven to maintain—evaporated. "Few women have ever been placed in such a painful position as that in which Scott placed Zelda," Mayfield concluded. "She bore it so loyally, with such proud dignity and Spartan fortitude that it should have won her more respect and admiration than she has received from the critics. Almost without exception, they represent Zelda in her last years as an eccentric recluse, leading an aimless, vegetative life. But their reports do not tally with those of her family and friends."[160]

A letter Zelda wrote to the Murphys after Scott died shows how strong her devotion was, even after everything her husband had put her through. "Those tragically ecstatic years when the pockets of the world were filled with pleasant surprises and people still thought of life in terms of their right to a good time are now about to wane," she told them. "That he won't be there to arrange nice things and tell us what to do is grievous to envisage."[161] When Mayfield saw Zelda for the last time, it had been five years since Scott's death and she was still wearing black. Mayfield was not the only one to prove Zelda had not frittered her last years away: Cline conducted exhaustive research that resulted in the same conclusions. The level of inquiry the author launched into is reflected in the subtitle of her book: "The Tragic, Meticulously Researched Biography of the Jazz Age's High Priestess." This hints at the voluminous evidence Cline collected to refute the lies about Zelda in so many books written about Scott.

Whereas many writers merely repeated claims they found in earlier biographies, Cline dug deeper, combing through myriad files and notebooks that included treatment records; and recording conversations with Rosalind that convinced her Zelda was not damaged goods when she was first hospitalized and her years after Scott's death were not wasted ones. The biographer found that Zelda was not institutionalized nearly as often nor for as long as had been claimed in books about Scott, and she felt it was important to set the record straight that Zelda had not been an invalid, frail, or creatively unproductive during her final years. Zelda's output proves this: She not only created an array of paintings, she made beautiful historical paper dolls that were exhibited in Montgomery with her other works. She also maintained a lively writing life. One of Zelda's projects that she never finished was a novel she titled *Caesar's Things*, which she began during her final years in Montgomery. Cline noticed themes running through it that included the silencing of her fiction and "the attempted murder of her literary creativity." She said Zelda was making a similar move as Scott made when he wrote "the trilogy of depression" because she was attempting to "burn away traumas and start anew." Cline saw the progression of Zelda's manuscript as a journey from sanity through madness to rehabilitation.[162]

Though Zelda developed a religious fervor during this

time in her life that I found excessive, Cline shared the view of Kirk Curnutt, a scholar of modern American literature, who said it was not a sign of madness; it was her way of assuaging decades of psychological instability. Other actions Zelda took prove she was stronger than Scott believed, as she had learned the warning signs that signaled she was about to have an episode before she broke down and took measures to stabilize herself. When she recognized she needed steadying, she traveled to Highland Hospital for treatment during sessions that were weeks-long, not months-long, as had been written. Cline found evidence of these short stays when she tracked the different addresses from which Zelda mailed her letters. During the winter of 1948, Zelda felt the need to return to the institution for one of those recuperations, her actions just before she left home convincing Mayfield she had had a premonition. When she was walking to the car after saying goodbye to her mother, her sister Marjorie, and a friend—all of whom had gathered on the porch—she ran back to Minnie and threw her arms around her, declaring, "Mama, don't worry, I'm not afraid to die."[163]

On the night of March 10th, a fire broke out in one of the kitchens at the sanitarium. It spread rapidly and patients were trapped in their rooms behind locked doors and barred windows. A quagmire of twisted metal and smoldering embers were all that remained the next day. Nine women were lost in the fire. Among these was Zelda Fitzgerald, whose remains were identified by their location, her dental records, and a charred slipper beneath the ashes that would have been her body. When I read this, I couldn't believe the irony that for so many of the years Zelda had maintained a fearlessness of spirit, it had been the mythic salamander from which she had drawn her strength. How sad that the flames came for her in the end. The dark culminations of both of the Fitzgeralds' lives lent the visuals in the Montgomery home they once inhabited a haunting quality. Scott's handwritten letters to Perkins and Wilson, a page from his ledger listing the women he'd loved, reviews of his books, and photos of Scott and Zelda with Scottie coalesced into a cache of souvenirs that could have represented the life of any couple at that moment in time.

But these chronicled a legendary couple who danced and drank and duked it out during a rambunctious time in history, and who both met tragic ends. Scott's words from his essay "Echoes of the Jazz Age" wafted through my mind as I stopped in front of a Victrola sitting on a table in the center of the living room where they had once gathered as a family. "Sometimes, though there is a ghostly rumble among the drums, an asthmatic whisper in the trombones swings me back into the early twenties," he wrote. He said it all seemed "rosy and romantic to us who were young then, because we will never feel quite so intensely about our surroundings anymore.[164] I could see Zelda, floating down the stairway in a filmy pastel dress during Scottie's birthday party on October 26, 1932, looking like a glamorous woman even though she was not being treated as such. Several friends from her childhood who visited the Fitzgeralds during their Montgomery era told Mayfield that Scott's attitude toward his wife was akin to "an anxious parent toward a sick child."[165]

As I stepped onto the front porch on my way out of the museum, I wondered if Zelda had taken the time during her last years in Montgomery to ride past the house on her rented bicycle to see how much the magnolia tree had grown since she had struggled to find equilibrium in the home. Did she stand, one foot on the pavement, the other on a pedal as she gripped the handlebars while memories of Scottie riding her pony across the lawn that fanned out around the tree wafted through her mind? Scottie was a young woman by the time she attended her mother's graveside service in St. Paul, Minnesota. Two days after Zelda's casket was lowered into the ground next to Scott's, she wrote to Minnie, "Seeing them buried there together gave the tragedy of their lives a sort of classic unity" and that it was reassuring "to think of their two high-flying and generous spirits being at peace together at last."[166]

Scottie then told her grandmother she had simply put out of her mind all of their troubles and sorrows in order to think of them as they were when they were young. About these troubles, Scott had written, "Perhaps fifty percent of our friends and relatives would tell you in all honest conviction that my drinking drove Zelda insane—the other half would assure you that her insanity drove me to drink. Neither judgment would mean anything: The former class would be composed of those who had seen me unpleasantly drunk and the latter of those who had seen Zelda unpleasantly psychotic."[167] He said both of these groups would likely unanimously say that each of them would have been better off if they had been rid of the other. After making this stormy journey with this couple, I had to agree, and I felt that one of the most tragic flaws in the relationship was that Scott had been clueless about how life would play out with a spoiled, high-strung wife.

The intoxicating cocktail of Zelda's personality that included irreverent debutant, gypsy queen, and Viking Madonna rolled into one, couldn't be completely snuffed out by mental institutions, dire treatments, and a husband's stifling jealousy, though they did so much damage trying. "Psychiatry is worse than witchcraft," Zelda once said, and she would definitely have known.[168] I walked to my car parked in the shadow of the magnolia feeling admiration for the battle she fought inside the home that looked so tranquil in the bright light of a summer afternoon. Given Scott told

Wilson just before introducing him to Zelda, "I wouldn't mind if she died, but I couldn't stand to have her marry somebody else," he already saw her as his property before he "owned" her. This means it was inevitable that what began as a pair of broken engagements would end in all-out war, and after the last battles were fought, no one escaped scot-free.

NOTES

1. WORTHY OF APPLAUSE

1. Morgan, Sydney. *Lady Morgan's Memoirs: Autobiography, Diaries and Correspondence*, ed. William Hepworth Dixon Editor. Charleston, South Carolina: BiblioLife, LLC, 2009, p. 361.
2. Stern, Kenneth. *Giuditta Pasta: A Life on the Lyric Stage*. Palm Springs, CA: Operaphile Press, 2011, p. 23n.
3. Pleasants, Henry. *The Great Singers: From the Dawn of Opera to Caruso, Callas, and Pavarotti*. New York: Simon & Schuster, Inc., 1966, p. 14.
4. Ibid., p. 139.
5. *The Examiner*, 19 January 1817.
6. Morgan, p. 361.
7. Stern, p. 43.
8. Stendhal. *Memoirs of an Egotist*. London: Hesperus Press Limited, 2003, pp. 70-73.
9. Ibid., pp. 69-70.
10. Stern, p. 86.
11. Stendhal, *Egotist*, p. 43.
12. Stendhal. *Memoirs of Rossini*. London: T. Hookham, 1824, p. 262.
13. Stern, pp. 165-166.
14. Ibid., p. 256.
15. Ibid., pp. 270-271.
16. Weinstock, Herbert. *Vicenzo Bellini: His Life and His Operas*. New York: Alfred A. Knopf, 1971, pp. 71-72.
17. Ibid., p. 97.
18. Glinka, Mikhail Ivanovich. *Memoirs*, trans. Richard B. Mudge. Norman: Univerisity of Oklahoma Press, 1963, p. 61.
19. Ibid., p. 61.
20. Weinstock, pp. 97-98.
21. Ibid., pp. 39-40.
22. Ibid., p. 101.
23. Ibid., pp. 104-105.
24. Ibid., pp. 105-107.
25. Ibid., pp. 118-121.
26. Ibid., p. 127-128.
27. Ibid., pp. 129-130.
28. Ibid., pp. 130-131.
29. Ibid., pp. 148-149.

30. Ibid., p. 150.
31. Ibid., pp. 196-197.
32. Stern, p. 490.
33. Ibid., p. 405.
34. Ibid., p. 431.
35. Kemble, Adelaide Sartoris. *Past Hours*. London: Richard Bentley and Son, 1880, pp. 208-209.
36. Ibid., pp. 209-212.
37. Ibid., p. 213.
38. Ibid., pp. 215-216.

2. A FORCE OF NATURE

1. Colette. *Letters from Colette*, trans. Robert Phelps. New York: Farrar, Straus and Giroux, 1980, p 92.
2. Goudeket, Maurice. *Close to Colette*. New York: Farrar, Straus and Cudahay, 1957, p. 5.
3. Ibid., p. 8.
4. Ibid., pp. 10-11.
5. Ibid., pp. 11-12.
6. Ibid., pp. 14-16.
7. Ibid., p. 17.
8. Ibid., pp. 123-124.
9. Colette, *Letters*, p. 160.
10. Goudeket, pp. 18-19.
11. Ibid., p. 19.
12. Ibid., p. 39.
13. Ibid., pp. 40-41.
14. Ibid.
15. Ibid., pp. 41-42.
16. Ibid., p. 45.
17. Colette. *The Evening Star*, trans. David le Vay, Trans. London: Peter Owen, 1973, p. 102.
18. Colette, *Letters*, p. 87.
19. Goudeket, pp. 62-63.
20. Ibid., pp. 62-63.
21. Ibid., p. 102.
22. Ibid.
23. Ibid., p. 103.
24. Barney, Natalie Clifford. *A Perilous Advantage: The Best of Natalie Clifford Barney*, trans. Anne Livia. Hereford, AZ: New Victoria Publishers, 1992, Loc. 3021.
25. Goudeket, p. 210.
26. Colette, *The Evening Star*, p. 143.

27. Ibid., p. 143-144.
28. Ibid., p. 33.
29. Ibid., p. 129.
30. Ibid., p. 17.
31. Colette. *The Blue Lantern*, trans. Roger Senhouse. New York: Farrar, Straus and Giroux, 1963, pp. 6-7.
32. Ibid., p. 7.
33. Ibid., p. 58.
34. Ibid.
35. Goudeket, p. 125.
36. Colette, *The Blue Lantern*, p. 161.
37. Goudeket, p. 217.
38. Ibid., p. 225-26.
39. Ibid., p. 77.
40. Colette, *Letters*, p. 200.
41. Goudeket, p. 233.
42. Ibid., p. 239.
43. Ibid., pp. 242-244.
44. Ibid., pp. 244-245.

3. WHERE SERENDIPITY WAS BORN

1. Walpole, Horace. *Description of the Villa of Mr. Horace Walpole, Youngest Son of Sir Robert Walpole Earl of Orford, at Strawberry-Hill near Twickenham, Middlesex, with an inventory of the Furniture, Pictures, Curiosities, etc.* London: Pallas Athene, 2015, p. 439.
2. Walpole, Horace. *Horace Walpole: Selected Letters*, ed. Stephen Clarke. New York: Alfred A. Knopf, 2017, p. 161.
3. Ibid.
4. Ibid., p. x.
5. Ibid., p. 161.
6. Hawkins, Laetitia. *Anecdotes, Biographical Sketches, and Memoirs.* London: F.C. and J. Rivington, 1822, pp. 105-106.
7. Ibid., p. 106.
8. Ibid., p. 87.
9. Clark, Kenneth. *The Gothic Revival: An Essay in the History of Taste.* New York: Harper & Row, 1962, pp. 64-65.
10. Ibid., p. 60.
11. Iddon, John. *Strawberry Hill & Horace Walpole.* London: Scala Publishers, Ltd., 2011, p. 6.
12. Clark, p. 59.
13. Walpole, Horace. *The Letters of Horace Walpole Fourth Earl of Orford*, ed. Peter Cunningham. Edinburgh: John Grant, 1906, pp. xxiii-xix.
14. Ibid., p. lix.

NOTES

15. Lewis, Wilmarth Sheldon. *Collector's Progress*. New Haven: Yale University Press, 1951, p. xv.
16. Eighteenth-Century Studies, Vol. 34, No. 2, Antiquarians, Connoisseurs, and Collectors (Winter, 2001), pp. 227-249 (24 pages) https://www.jstor.org/stable/30053967
17. Lewis, *Collector's Progress*, pp. xix-3.
18. Ibid., pp. 12-14.
19. Ibid., pp. 18-21.
20. Ibid.
21. Ibid., pp. 26-27.
22. Ibid.
23. Ibid., pp.40-43.
24. Craveri, Benedetta, *Madame du Deffand and Her World*. London: Peter Halban Publishers, Ltd., 2002, p. 599.
25. Ibid., pp. 265-266.
26. Ibid., pp. 266-267.
27. Strachey, Lytton. *Biographical Essays*. New York: Harcourt Brace Jovanovich, 1111, p. 192.
28. Craveri, p. 267.
29. Ibid., pp. 267-268.
30. Ibid., p. 269.
31. Lewis, *Collector's Progress*, p. 41.
32. Smith, Warren Hunting. "Cipher and Code in Horace Walpole's Correspondence." The Yale University Library Gazette, vol. 25, no. 3, 1951, pp. 117–19. JSTOR, http://www.jstor.org/stable/40857499.
33. Craveri, pp. 269-277.
34. Ibid., p. 271.
35. Lewis, Wilmarth S. *Rescuing Horace Walpole*. New Haven: Yale University Press, 1978, p. 6.
36. Lewis, *Collector's Progress*, p. 71.
37. Ibid., pp. 31-32.
38. Lewis, *Rescuing Horace Walpole*, p. 10.
39. Lewis, *Collector's Progress*, p. 46.
40. Ibid., p. 168.
41. Ibid., p. 159.
42. Ibid., pp. 159-160.
43. Lewis, *Rescuing Horace Walpole*, p. 17.
44. Ibid.
45. Ibid., pp. 17-18.
46. Ibid., pp. 18-22.
47. Ibid., p. 22.
48. Ibid., p. 1.
49. Walpole, Horace. "Short Notes on the life of Horatio Walpole, youngest son of Sir Robert Walpole, Earl of Orford, and of Catherine

Shorter, his first wife." https://babel.hathitrust.org/cgi/pt?id=uva.x030526869&view=1up&seq=77, p. lxxxi.
50. Craveri, pp. 260-261.
51. Ibid., pp. 261-262.
52. Walpole, "Short Notes", p. lxxx.
53. Lewis, *Collector's Progress*, pp. 165-166.
54. Ibid., pp. 166-167.
55. Ibid., pp. 39-40.
56. Ibid., pp.40-43.
57. Ibid., p. 90.
58. Ibid.
59. Ibid., pp. 110-111.
60. Ibid., p. 152.
61. Ibid.
62. Ibid., p. 102.
63. Clark, p. 57.
64. Ibid., pp. 57-61.
65. Walpole, *Selected Letters*, p. 366.
66. Lewis, *Collector's Progress*, p. 105

4. A RIVER OF ANGST

1. Goethe, Johann Wolfgang von. *Autobiography: Truth and Fiction Relating to My Life*. Philadelphia and Chicago: J.H. Moore and Company, 1901, p. 35.
2. Ibid., pp. 27-28.
3. Ibid., pp. 31-32.
4. Ibid., p. 39.
5. Ibid.
6. Ibid., p. 30.
7. Ibid., p. 253.
8. Ibid., pp. 259-60.
9. Ibid., p. 271.
10. Ibid.
11. Ibid., pp. 271-272.
12. Ibid.
13. Ibid., p. 272.
14. Harry Slochower (1970). *Mythopoesis: Mythic Patterns in the Literary Classics*. Wayne State University Press. p. 182.
15. Chisholm, Hugh, ed. (1911). "Charles Augustus". Encyclopædia Britannica. Vol. 5 (11th ed.). Cambridge University Press. pp. 939–940.
16. Goethe, Johann Wolfgang von. *Italian Journey*. London: Penguin Books, 1962, p. 74.
17. Ibid.

18. Zilcosky, John. "Learning How to Get Lost: Goethe in Italy." *Eighteenth-Century Studies*, vol. 50, no. 4, 2017, pp. 417–35. JSTOR, http://www.jstor.org/stable/44631619.
19. Goethe, Johann Wolfgang von. *West–eastern Divan. West–oestlicher Divan, Rendered Into English by J. Whaley*, trans. Edward Dowden. Augsburg, Germany: Jazzybee Verlag, 2020, p. 120.
20. Goethe, Johann Wolfgang von. *Selected Poetry*, trans. David Luke. New York: Penguin Classics, 2005, p. 400.
21. Ibid., p. 119.

5. THE HOUSE WHERE THE MIND RULED

1. Souhami, Diana. *Wild Girls: Paris, Sappho, and Art: The Lives and Loves of Natalie Barney and Romaine Brooks*. New York: St. Martin's Press, 2005, p. 52.
2. Ibid., p. 53.
3. Barney, Natalie Clifford. *A Perilous Advantage: The Best of Natalie Clifford Barney*, trans. Anne Livia. Hereford, AZ: New Victoria Publishers, 1992, Loc. 2842-2853.
4. Barney, Natalie Clifford. *Adventures of the Mind*. New York: New York University Press, 1992, p. 2.
5. Ibid., Loc. 2162.
6. Hall, Radclyffe. *The Well of Loneliness*. London: Wordsworth Classics, 2005, Loc. 222.
7. Ibid.
8. Pougy, Liane de. *My Blue Notebooks: The Intimate Journal of Paris's Most Beautiful and Notorious Courtesan*. New York: Jeremy P. Tarcher/Putnam, 1979, p. 108.
9. Ibid., p. 140.
10. Ibid., p 175.
11. Ford, Ford Madox. *It Was the Nightingale*. Philadelphia: J.B. Lippincott, 1933, p. 184.
12. Barney, *A Perilous Advantage*, Loc. 3154.
13. Wickes, George. *The Amazon of Letters: The Life and Loves of Natalie Barney*. New York: G.P. Putnam's Sons, 1976, pp. 260-261.
14. Rodriguez, Suzanne. *Wild Heart: A Life; Natalie Clifford Barney's Journey from Victorian America to the Literary Salons of Paris*. New York: Harper Collins, 2002, p. 199.
15. Barney, *A Perilous Advantage*. Loc. 3132.
16. Ibid., Loc. 3175-3185.
17. Ibid., Loc. 3189.
18. Ibid., Loc. 3332.
19. Ibid., Loc. 3601.
20. Barney, *Adventures of the Mind*, p. 31.

NOTES

21. Wickes, p. 183.
22. Ibid., p. 202.
23. Barney, *A Perilous Advantage*, Loc. 2183.
24. Ibid., Loc. 2185.
25. Barney, *Adventures of the Mind*, p. 137.
26. Ibid., p. 133.
27. Allan, p. 70.
28. Ibid., p. 171.
29. Page, Chester. *Memoirs of a Charmed Life in New York*. New York: iUniverse, 2007, p. 148.
30. Benstock, Shari. *Women of the Left Bank: Paris, 1900-1940*. Austin: University of Texas Press, 2010, Loc. 295.
31. Barney, *A Perilous Advantage*, Loc. 2197, 1615.
32. Ibid., Loc. 1673.
33. Ibid., Loc. 242-253.
34. Ibid., Loc. 1964-1975.
35. Ibid., Loc. 1985-1995.
36. Ibid., Loc. 2064-2075.
37. Wickes, p. 253.
38. Rodriguez, p. 301.
39. Wickes, pp. 241-242.
40. Ibid., pp. 242-243.
41. Ibid., pp. 251-252.
42. Barney, *A Perilous Advantage*, Loc. 2162.
43. Wickes, p. 253.
44. Barney, *A Perilous Advantage*, Loc. 202.
45. Ibid., Loc. 213.
46. Rodriguez, p. 361.
47. BBC 2 archives: https://www.youtube.com/watch?v=ihzoLrUkNoc.
48. Souhami: p. 31.
49. Rodriguez: pp. 240-241.
50. Benstock, Loc. 233.
51. Ibid., Loc. 369.
52. Wickes, p. 212.
53. Rodriguez, p. 367.
54. Wickes, p. 232.
55. Ibid., p. 205.
56. Ibid., p. 209.
57. Ibid., p. 235.
58. Benstock, Loc. 1092.
59. Barney, *A Perilous Advantage*, Loc. 1941-2151.
60. Ibid., Loc. 2162.
61. Ibid., Loc. 1963-1973.

6. THE ART OF CAPITULATION

1. Méneval, Claude François. *Memoirs of Napoleon Bonaparte: The Court of the First Empire*, Vol. II. New York: P.F. Collier & Son Publishers, 1910, p. 611.
2. Saint-Amand, Leon Imbert de. *The Happy Days of the Empress Marie Louise*. Free Kindle version. Loc. 50. [English version published by Charles Scribner's Sons in 1890.]
3. Ibid., Loc. 36.
4. Cuthell, Edith E. *An Imperial Victim: Marie Louise Archduchess of Austria, Empress of the French, Duchess of Parma*, Vol. 1. New York: Brentano's, 1912, pp. 67-68.
5. Ibid., p. 69.
6. Ibid., pp. 69-70.
7. Ibid., pp. 73-74.
8. Ibid., p. 74.
9. Ibid., pp. 81-82.
10. Saint-Amand, Loc. 1271.
11. Ibid., Loc. 1312.
12. Ibid., Loc.1331.
13. Bausset-Roquefort, Baron Louis-François-Joseph de. *Private Memoirs of the Court of Napoleon*. Auckland: Pickle Partners Publishing, 2011, Loc. 3583-3593.
14. Ibid., Loc. 3593-3602.
15. Saint-Amand, Loc. 1375.
16. Ibid., Loc. 1375-1390.
17. Durand, Madame la Générale. *Napoleon and Marie-Louise: 1810-1814*. London: Sampson, Low, Marston, Searle & Rivington, 1886, p. 10.
18. Ibid., p. 11.
19. Ibid., p. 13.
20. Méneval, Vol 2, p. 652.
21. Durand, p. 14.
22. Saint-Amand, Loc. 50.
23. Rovigo, Duke of. *Memoirs*, Vol. 2/Part 2. London: Henry Colburn, 1828, p. 194.
24. Durand, p. 15; Méneval, Vol. 2, pp. 646-647.
25. Durand, pp. 15-16.
26. Ibid.
27. D'Abrantès, Laure Junot. *At the Court of Napoleon: Memoirs of the Duchesse d'Abrantès*. New York: Doubleday, 1989, p. 352.
28. Ibid., pp. 352-354.
29. Ibid., p. 355.
30. Durand, pp. 23-24.
31. Méneval, Vol. 2, p. 749.

NOTES

32. Méneval, Claude François. *Memoirs to Serve for the History of Napoleon I*, Vol. 3, London: Hutchinson & Co., 1895, pp, 18-19.
33. https://www.napoleon.org/en/history-of-the-two-empires/articles/how-history-is-written-marechal-lannes-last-words-to-napoleon/
34. Durand, p. 44.
35. Durand, p. 49; Méneval, Vol. 2, p. 729.
36. Durand, pp. 49-50; Méneval, Vol. 2, p. 730.
37. Durand, pp. 47-50.
38. Méneval, Vol. 2, p. 728.
39. Durand, pp. 47-51.
40. Méneval, Vol. 2, p. 727.
41. Ibid.
42. Durand, pp. 70-71.
43. Ibid.
44. D'Abrantès, p. 16; p. 365.
45. Ibid., pp. 360-361.
46. Méneval, Vol 2, p. 751.
47. Ibid., pp. 752-753.
48. D'Abrantès, p. 357.
49. Ibid.
50. Durand, p. 77.
51. Durand, pp. 83-84; Meneval, Vol 2, p. 796; Rovigo, Vol3/part 1, pp.144-149.
52. D'Abrantès, pp. 22-23.
53. Durand, pp. 90-91.
54. Durand, p. 91; Meneval, Vol 3, p. 19; Rovigo, Vol. 2/part 2, pp. 258-259.
55. Durand, p. 95; Meneval, Vol 3, p. 20.
56. Durand, p. 97; Méneval, Vol 2, p. 824.
57. Méneval, Vol. 2, p. 824.
58. Méneval, Vol 2, pp. 824-825.
59. Cases, Emmanuel de Las. *Memoirs of the Life, Exile, and Conversations of the Emperor Napoleon by the Count de Las Cases*, Vol. 2. London: Henry Colburn, March 1836, p.p. 5.
60. Durand, p. 102; Méneval, Vol 3, pp. 30-31.
61. Méneval Vol 2, p. 828; Vol 3, pp. 24,25.
62. Cuthell, Vol 1, p. 192.
63. Méneval, Vol 3, pp. 52-53.
64. Ibid., pp. 58-59.
65. D'Abrantès, p. 372.
66. Cuthell, Vol 1, p. 197.
67. Durand, p. 107; Méneval, Vol. 3, p. 86.
68. Méneval, Vol. 3, pp. 48, 67.
69. Ibid., pp. 71-72.

NOTES

70. D'Abrantès, p. 372.
71. Rovigo, Vol. 3/Part 2, p. 41.
72. Durand, pp. 110-111.
73. Cuthell, Vol 1, p. 208.
74. Méneval, Vol. 3, p. 12.
75. D'Abrantès, p. 373.
76. Durand, p. 113.
77. D'Abrantès, p. 373.
78. Durand, p. 114.
79. Rovigo, Vol 3/part 2, p. 63.
80. Bourrienne, Louis Antoine Fauvelet de. *Memoirs of Napoleon Bonaparte Complete*. New York: Charles Scribner's Sons, 1891, pp. 298-299. + Cuthell, Vol 1, p. 295.
81. Méneval, Vol 3, pp. 110-111.
82. Cuthell, Vol 1, p. 220.
83. Ibid., pp. 230-231.
84. Méneval, Vol 3, p. 112.
85. Cuthell, Vol 1, pp. 231-232.
86. Rovigo, Vol 3/part 2, pp. 71-72.
87. Méneval, Vol 3, p. 119.
88. Bourrienne, pp. 298-299; Las Cases, Vol 2, p. 67.
89. Bourrienne, p. 299.
90. Rovigo, Vol 3/part 2, pp. 100-101.
91. Méneval, Vol 3, pp. 131-135.
92. Durand, pp. 121-122.
93. Cuthell, Vol 1, p. 255.
94. Rovigo, Vol 3/part 2, p. 151.
95. Bourrienne, pp. 305-306.
96. Ibid., pp. 306-309.
97. Durand, pp. 123-124.
98. Bourrienne, pp. 305-306.
99. Durand, p. 125.
100. Méneval, Vol 3, p. 168.
101. Saint-Amand, Loc. 109-119; Méneval, Vol 3, p. 195.
102. Méneval, Vol 3, p. 200.
103. Durand, pp. 127-128; Méneval, Vol 3, p. 193.
104. Cuthell, Vol 1, p. 267.
105. Ibid., pp. 271-272.
106. Rovigo, Vol 4/part1, pp. 129-130.
107. Cuthell, Vol 1, pp. 272-274.
108. Ibid.
109. Ibid.
110. Cuthell, Vol 1, p. 280.
111. Méneval, Vol 3, p. 201.
112. Durand, p. 130.

NOTES

113. Bourrienne, p. 310.
114. Durand, p. 134.
115. Bourrienne, pp. 313-314.
116. Durand, p. 138.
117. Ibid., pp. 138-139
118. Cuthell, Vol 1, p. 291.
119. Ibid., pp. 291-292.
120. Rovigo, Vol 4/part 1, p. 111.
121. Méneval, Vol 3, pp. 225-226.
122. Rovigo, Duke. of [Anne Jean Marie René Savary]. *Memoirs*, Vol. 3/Part 1. London: Henry Colburn, 1828, p. 118. Bourrienne, p. 327.
123. Rovigo, Vol 3/part 1, pp. 118-120; Bourrienne, p. 327.
124. Rovigo, Vol 3/part 1, pp. 118-120.
125. Méneval, Vol 3, pp. 228-232.
126. Méneval, Vol 3, p. 257; Bourrienne, p. 336.
127. Méneval, Vol 3, p. 236.
128. Rovigo, Vol 3/part 1, p. 127.
129. Ibid., pp. 129-131.
130. Ibid., pp. 132-133.
131. Rovigo, Vol 4, part 1, p. 69.
132. Ibid., Vol 3/part 1, p. 147.
133. Bourrienne, p. 328.
134. Méneval, Vol 3, pp. 243-254.
135. Cuthell, Vol 1, pp. 320-324.
136. Ibid., p. 337.
137. Méneval, Vol 3, pp. 273-274.
138. Cuthell, Vol 1, p. 354.
139. Méneval, Vol 3, pp. 292-293.
140. Ibid.
141. Ibid., p. 302.
142. Cuthell, Vol 1, pp. 397-398.
143. Méneval, Vol 3, p. 301.
144. Cuthell, Vol 1, p. 400.
145. Ibid., pp. 379-380.
146. Ibid., p. 260.
147. Méneval, Vol 3, pp. 311-316; Bourrienne, p. 339.
148. Méneval, Vol 3, p. 312.
149. Ibid., pp. 336-339.
150. Ibid., p. 350.
151. Bourrienne, p. 342.
152. Méneval, Vol 3, p. 352-355.
153. Cuthell, Edith E. *An Imperial Victim: Marie Louise Archduchess of Austria, Empress of the French, Duchess of Parma*, Vol. 2. New York: Brentano's, 1912, p. 56.
154. Méneval, Vol 3, pp. 358-359.

NOTES

155. Ibid., pp. 366-367.
156. Méneval, Vol 3, pp. 363-368; Las Cases, Vol. 1, p. 48.
157. Bourrienne, pp. 342.
158. Ibid., p. 342-344.
159. Ibid., p. 355.
160. Ibid.
161. Méneval, Vol 3, p. 392.
162. Ibid., pp. 437-438.
163. Ibid., p. 440-441.
164. Ibid., p. 443.
165. Ibid.
166. Bourrienne, p. 348.
167. Ibid., pp. 348-349.
168. Ibid., p. 349-350.
169. Ibid.
170. Ibid., pp. 351-364.
171. Kauffmann, Jean-Paul. *The Black Room at Longwood: Napoleon's Exile on Saint Helena*, trans. Patricia Clancy. New York: Four Walls Eight Windows, 1999, pp. xvi-xviii.
172. Ibid.
173. Méneval, Vol 3, pp. 474-480.
174. Wertheimer, Edward de. *The Duke of Reichstadt (Napoleon II): A Biography Complied from New Sources of Information*. New York: John Lane Company, 1906, p. 212.
175. Cuthell, Vol. 2, p. 93.
176. Ibid., p. 133.
177. Ibid., pp. 156-159.
178. Méneval, p. 438.
179. Saint-Amand, Loc. 257.
180. Cuthell, Vol. 2, pp. 22-23.
181. Bourrienne, p. 369.
182. Ibid.
183. Las Cases, Vol 3, p. 245.
184. Cuthell, Vol 2, p. 185.
185. Bourrienne, p. 371.
186. Las Cases, Vol 3, pp. 186-187.
187. Cuthell, Vol 2, pp. 188-189
188. Ibid., pp. 189-195.
189. Ibid., p. 200.
190. Bourrienne, p. 371.
191. Las Cases, pp. 248-250.
192. Montet, Alexandrine Prévost de la Boutetière de Saint-Mars Du. *Souvenirs de la Baronne du Montet, 1785-1866*. Paris: Librairie Plon, 1904, p. 299.
193. Cuthell, Vol 2, p. 128; p. 217.

194. Ibid., p. 250.
195. Ibid., p. 276.
196. Ibid., p. 268; pp. 281-282.
197. Ibid., pp. 310-311.
198. Wertheimer, pp. 420-421.
199. Cuthell, Vol 2, pp. 311-314.
200. Ibid., pp. 314-316.
201. Markham, Felix. *Napoleon*. New York: Signet Classics, 1963, p. 261.
202. Méneval, Vol 2, p. 439.
203. Cuthell, Vol 2, p. 316.
204. Ibid., p. 321.
205. Ibid., p. 322.
206. Ibid., p. 346.
207. Ibid., p. 282.
208. Ibid., p. 253.

7. HOW TO BUILD A BETTER HUSBAND

1. Wharton, Edith. "Life and I" manuscript, 1932. The Wharton Collection, Beinecke Rare Book and Manuscript Library, Yale University, pp. 1-4.
2. Ibid.
3. Wharton, Edith. *Novellas and Other Writings*. New York: Library Classics of the United States, 1990, p. 804.
4. Ibid., p. 839.
5. Lewis, R.W.B. *Edith Wharton: A Biography*. New York: Fromm International Publishing Corporation, 1985, p. 50.
6. Wharton, "Life & I," pp. 34-35.
7. Ibid.
8. Erlich, Gloria C. *The Sexual Education of Edith Wharton*. Berkeley: University of California Press, 1922, p. 117.
9. Wharton, *Novellas*, p. 810.
10. Ibid.
11. Wharton, "Life & I," pp. 10.
12. Wharton, *Novellas*, pp. 833-838.
13. Ibid., pp. 856-857.
14. Ibid., p. 1077.
15. Wharton, Edith. *The Cruise of the Vanadis*. New York: Rizzoli, 2004, p. 111.
16. Ibid., p. 87.
17. Ibid., p. 99.
18. Wharton, *Novellas*, p. 865.
19. Ibid.
20. Ibid., p. 868.

NOTES

21. Ibid., pp. 868-870.
22. Ibid., p. 875.
23. Ibid., p. 889.
24. Ibid., p. 873.
25. Ibid., 870.
26. Wharton, Edith. *The Letters of Edith Wharton*, eds. R.W.B. and Nancy Lewis. New York: Collier Books, 1988, p. 53.
27. Wharton, Edith. *The Valley of Decision*. A Public Doman Book, Kindle, p. 4.
28. Wharton, *Novellas*, pp. 870-873.
29. Ibid., pp. 876-879.
30. Ibid., pp. 881-882.
31. Ibid.
32. Ibid., pp. 881-885.
33. Ibid., p. 913.
34. Ibid., p. 954.
35. Ibid., p. 958.
36. Ibid.
37. Erlich, pp. 117-118.
38. Lewis, pp. 152-53.
39. Lubbock, Percy. *Portrait of Edith Wharton*. London: Jonathan Cape, 1947, p.53.
40. Ibid., pp. 54-58.
41. Wharton, *Novellas*, p. 1076.
42. Ibid., p. 914.
43. Ibid., p. 918.
44. Ibid., p. 930.
45. Ibid., p. 960.
46. Lewis, p. 52.
47. Simons, Judy. *Diaries and Letters of Literary Women from Fanny Burney to Virginia Woolf*. Iowa City: Univ. of Iowa Press, 1990, p. 144.
48. Wharton, *Letters*, p. 136.
49. Ibid., p. 113.
50. Lewis, p. 478
51. Erlich, p. 87.
52. Lewis, p. 222.
53. Price, Kenneth M., and Phyllis McBride. "'The Life Apart': Text and Contexts of Edith Wharton's Love Diary." American Literature, vol. 66, no. 4, 1994, p. 672-673. JSTOR, JSTOR, www.jstor.org/stable/2927693.
54. Mainwaring, Marion. *Mysteries of Paris: The Quest for Morton Fullerton*. Hanover: University Press of New England, 2001, p. 45.
55. Simons, p. 139; Lee, p. 315; Lewis, p. 222.
56. Wharton, Edith. *The Choice*. New York: Charles Scribner's Sons, 1916, p. 5.

57. Ibid., pp. 23-24.
58. Ibid.
59. Lee, Hermione. *Edith Wharton*. New York: Vintage Books, 2008, p. 350.
60. Price, p. 682.
61. Wharton, *Letters*, p. 150.
62. Price, pp. 682-683.
63. Ibid.
64. Ibid.
65. Lee, p. 332.
66. Lewis, p. 259.
67. Ibid.
68. Ibid., p. 262.
69. Ibid., pp. 296-297.
70. Wharton, *Letters*, p. 250-51.
71. Ibid., pp. 247-248.
72. Ibid., pp. 255-261.
73. Ibid., p. 289.
74. Ibid., pp. 325-26.
75. Wharton, *Novellas*, pp. 1049-1050.
76. Ibid., pp. 1050-1056.
77. Ibid., pp. 1056-1057.
78. Lewis, p. 425.
79. Wharton, *Letters*, p. 434.
80. Lee, p. 656.
81. Wharton, *Letters*, p. 504.
82. Wharton, *Novellas*, pp. 1060-61.
83. Lee, p. 656.
84. Wharton, *Letters*, p. 530.
85. Lee, p. 748.
86. Lewis, p. 515.
87. Wharton, *Novellas*, p. 1064.
88. Wharton, *Letters*, pp. 594-595.
89. Lewis, p. 514.
90. WB to EW, Edith Wharton Collection. Yale Collection of American Literature, Beinecke Rare Book and Manuscript Library, Yale University.

8. THE FLOWER OF CHIVALRY

1. Pizan, Christine de. *The Writings of Christine de Pizan*, ed. Charity Cannon Willard. New York: Persea Books, 1994, p. 238.
2. Schaus, Margaret C. *Women and Gender in Medieval Europe: An Encyclopedia*. Oxfordshire: Routledge, 2007, p. 133.
3. Pizan, *Writings*, pp. 234-242.

NOTES

4. Šmahel, František. *The Parisian Summit, 1377-78: Emperor Charles IV and King Charles V of France*. Prague: Karolinum Press, 2014, p. 89.
5. Pizan, *Writings*, pp. 240-241.
6. Ibid, p. 250.
7. Ibid, p. 247n.
8. Šmahel, p. 119.
9. Ibid., p. 118.
10. Ibid., p. 353.
11. Pizan, *Writings*, p. 232.
12. Ibid., pp. 256-257.
13. Ibid., p. 255.
14. Pizan, Christine de. *The Book of Deeds of Arms and of Chivalry*, ed. Charity Cannon Willard. University Park, PA: The Pennsylvania State University Press,1999, pp. 11-13.
15. Ibid., pp. 13-14.
16. Ibid., pp. 109-110.
17. Pizan, *Writings*, p. 310.
18. Ibid., p. 259.
19. Husby, Tristan K. "Justice and the Justification of War in Ancient Greece: Four Authors" (2009) *Classics Honors Papers*, 1.
20. Šmahel, pp. 89-92.
21. Ibid., p. 94.
22. Ibid., p. 108.
23. Ibid., pp. 120-123.
24. https://www.jeanne-darc.info/contemporary-chronicles-other-testimonies/christine-de-pizan-le-ditie-de-jehanne-darc/
25. Ibid.
26. Ibid.
27. Pizan, *Writings*, p 310.
28. Šmahel, p. 118.

9. THE DIMINISHING VIEW OF MADAME VITRIOL

1. Stansell, Christine. *American Moderns: Bohemian New York and the Creation of a New Century*. Princeton: Princeton University Press, 2000, p. 153.
2. Field, Andrew. *Djuna: The Life and Times of Djuna Barnes*. New York: G.P. Putnam's Sons, 1983, p. 13.
3. Barnes, Djuna. *Vagaries Malicieux*. New York: Frank Hallman, 1974, p. 10.
4. Ibid., p. 11.
5. Ibid.
6. Ibid., pp. 11-12.

NOTES

7. Herring, Phillip. *Djuna: The Life and Work of Djuna Barnes*. New York: Penguin Group, 1985, p. 132.
8. Field, p. 116.
9. Barnes, Djuna. *Collected Poems With Notes Toward the Memoirs*. Eds. Herring, Phillip, and Stutman, Osías. Madison: The University of Wisconsin Pres, 2005, p. 231.
10. Flanner, Janet. *Paris Was Yesterday:1925-1939*. New York, Harcourt Brace Jovanovich Publishers, 1988, p. xvii.
11. Ibid., pp. xvii-xviii.
12. Barnes, *Collected*, p 235.
13. Ibid., p. 244.
14. Barnes, Djuna. *Interviews*, ed. Alyce Berry. Washington, D.C.: Sun & Moon Press, 1985, p. 224.
15. Ibid., pp. 378-379
16. McAlmon, Robert. *Being Geniuses Together*. San Francisco: North Point Press, 1984, p. 31.
17. Ibid., pp. 31-33.
18. Ibid., pp. 117-118.
19. Herring, p. 136.
20. Barney, Natalie Clifford. *Adventures of the Mind*, trans. John Spaulding Gatton. New York: New York University Press, 1992, pp. 165-166.
21. Rodriguez, Suzanne. *Wild Heart: A Life; Natalie Clifford Barney's Journey from Victorian America to the Literary Salons of Paris*. New York: Harper Collins, 2002, p. 285.
22. Barnes, Djuna. *Ladies Almanack*. New York: New York University Press, 1992, Loc. 107.
23. Souhami, Diana. *Wild Girls: Paris, Sappho, and Art: The Lives and Loves of Natalie Barney and Romaine Brooks*. New York: St. Martin's Press, 2005. p. 167.
24. Herring, p. 147.
25. Bald, Wambly. *On the Left Bank: 1929-1933*, ed. Benjamin Franklin V. Athens: Ohio University Press, 1987, pp. 74-75.
26. Barnes, *Collected*, p. 245.
27. Guggenheim, Peggy. *Out of This Century*. London: Carlton Publishing Group, 1979, pp. 113-116.
28. Chitty, Susan. *Now to My Mother: A very personal memoir of Antonia White*. London: Weidenfeld and Nicholson, 1985, p. 62.
29. Coleman, Emily. *Rough Draft: The Modernist Diaries of Emily Holmes Coleman*, ed. Elizabeth Podnieks. Newark: University of Delaware Press, 2012, pp. 93-97.
30. Ibid., p. 97.
31. Guggenheim, p. 116.
32. Rodriguez, p. 284
33. Field, p. 207.
34. Herring, p. 225.

NOTES

35. Field, p. 211.
36. Herring, p. 232.
37. Ibid., p. 235.
38. Barnes, Djuna. *Nightwood*. New York: New Directions, 2006, loc. 172.
39. Flanner, p. xvii.
40. Herring., p. 240.
41. Ibid., pp. 246-247.
42. Barnes, *Collected*, pp. 264-265.
43. Ibid., pp. 264-266.
44. Ibid., pp. 266-268.
45. Herring, p. 247.
46. Field, p. 236.
47. Page, Chester. *Memoirs of a Charmed Life in New York*. New York: iUniverse, 2007, p.3.
48. Ibid., p. 125.
49. O'Neal, Hank. *Life is painful, nasty and short...in my case it has only been painful and nasty.* New York: Paragon House, 1990, p. 84.
50. Barney, p. 169.
51. Rodriguez, p. 281.
52. Broe, Mary Lynn. *Silence and Power: A Reevaluation of Djuna Barnes*. Carbondale, IL: Southern Illinois University Press, 1991, p. 340.
53. Page, p. 110.
54. Ibid., 109-111.
55. Ibid., 110-111.
56. Ibid., pp. 111-112.
57. Ibid., pp. 113-115.
58. Ibid., p. 118.
59. Ibid., pp. 122-125.
60. Ibid., p. 114.
61. Ibid., p. 135.
62. O'Neal, p. 48.
63. Ibid., p. xv.
64. Page, p 142.
65. Dearborn, Mary. *Peggy Guggenheim: Mistress of Modernism*. London: Virago Press, 2004, pp. 366-367.
66. Page, p. 141.
67. O'Neal, p. 140.
68. Page, p. 131.
69. Rodriguez, p. 284.
70. Page, p. 118.
71. Benstock, Shari. *Women of the Left Bank Paris, 1900-1940*. Austin: University of Texas Press, 1986, p. 234.
72. O'Neal, p. 60.
73. Ibid., p. 83.
74. Ibid., pp. 84-87.

75. Page, pp. 123-124.
76. O'Neal, p. 91.
77. Ibid., p. 60.
78. Ibid., p. 95.
79. Ibid., pp. 116-117.
80. Ibid., p. 124.
81. Page, p. 149.
82. Ibid., p. 160.
83. Ibid., p. 164.
84. Barnes, *Collected*, p. 252.
85. Ibid., p. 247.

10. THE DRAWING-ROOM DIPLOMAT

1. Kathrens, Michael C. *Newport Villas: The Revival Styles, 1885-1935.* New York: W.W. Norton & Company, 2009, p. 87.
2. Balsan, Consuelo Vanderbilt. *The Glitter and the Gold: The American Duchess in Her Own Words.* New York: St. Martin's Press, 1952, p. 21.
3. Ibid., p. 21.
4. Ibid., p. 32.
5. Ibid.
6. Kathrens, p. 87.
7. Balsan, pp. 42-43.
8. Cooper, Dana. *Informal Ambassadors: American Women, Transatlantic Marriages, and Anglo-American Relations, 1865-1945.* Kent, Ohio: Kent State University Press, 2014, pp. 129-130.
9. Balsan, pp. 44-45.
10. Ibid., pp. 45-46.
11. Ibid., pp. 47-48.
12. Ibid., p. 55.
13. Ibid., pp. 47-48.
14. Ibid., pp. 57-58.
15. Ibid., p. 60.
16. Ibid., pp. 61-64.
17. Ibid., pp. 66-71.
18. Ibid., pp. 72-73.
19. Ibid., pp. 80-91.
20. Ibid., p. 92.
21. Ibid., pp. 100-102.
22. Ibid., pp. 102-105.
23. Stuart, Amanda Mackenzie. *Consuelo & Alva Vanderbilt: The Story of a Mother and a Daughter in the Gilded Age.* New York: Harper Collins, 2012, p. 223.
24. Balsan, p. 105.

NOTES

25. Stuart, p. 244.
26. Ibid., pp. 244-248.
27. Ibid., p. 248.
28. Balsan, pp. 110-112.
29. Ibid., p. 128.
30. Ibid., p. 114.
31. Ibid., p. 105.
32. Vickers, Hugo. *The Sphinx: The Life of Gladys Deacon—Duchess of Marlborough*. London: Hodder & Sloughton, Ltd., 2020, pp. 86-87
33. Ibid., p. 87.
34. Stuart, pp. 252-255.
35. Vickers, pp. 86-87.
36. Balsan, p. 158.
37. Ibid., pp. 158-159.
38. Cooper, p. 135.
39. Ibid., pp. 138-139.
40. Ibid., pp. 141-142.
41. Ibid., p. 148.
42. Balsan, pp. 198-199.
43. Ibid., p. 202.
44. Ibid., p. 29.
45. Ibid., pp. 199-202.
46. Ibid., p. 205.
47. Ibid., p. 206.
48. Ibid., p. 208.
49. ibid, pp. 210-212.
50. Ibid., pp. 240-241.
51. Ibid., pp. 243-245.
52. Ibid., p. 245.
53. Stuart, p. 389.
54. Cooper, p. 125.
55. Balsan, pp. 276-278.

11. NO ONE GETS OFF SCOT-FREE

1. Mayfield, Sara. *Exiles from Paradise: Zelda and Scott Fitzgerald*. New York: Dell Publishing Co, Inc., 1971, pp. 84-85.
2. Ibid., p. 11.
3. Ibid., pp. 11-12.
4. Ibid., p. 12.
5. Wilson, Edmund. *The Bit Between My Teeth: A Literary Chronicle of 1950-1965*. New York: Farrar, Straus, Giroux, 1965, Loc. 300.
6. Mayfield, *Exiles*, p. 13.
7. Ibid., p. 21.

NOTES

8. Fitzgerald, Zelda; Matthew J. Bruccoli (ed.). *The Collected Writings of Zelda Fitzgerald*. New York: Scribner, 1997, p. 429.
9. Mayfield, *Exiles*, pp. 22-23.
10. Ibid., p. 23.
11. Fitzgerald, Zelda. *Save Me the Waltz*. Bath: Handheld Press Ltd., 2019, Loc. 1047.
12. Perkins, Maxwell E. *The Sons of Maxwell Perkins: Letters of F. Scott Fitzgerald, Ernest Hemingway, Thomas Wolfe, and Their Editor*, eds. Matthew Joseph Bruccoli and Judith Baughman. Columbia: University of South Carolina Press, 2004, p. 2.
13. ZSF, *Waltz*, Loc. 1047. [ZSF is an abbreviation for Zelda Sayre Fitzgerald.]
14. Fitzgerald, F. Scott; Bruccoli, Matthew (ed.). *The Notebooks of F. Scott Fitzgerald*. New York: Harcourt Brace Jovanovich, 1945, p. 79.
15. Mayfield, *Exiles*, p. 47.
16. Fitzgerald, F. Scott. *The Works of F. Scott Fitzgerald: 21 Novels and Short Stories*. Garden City: Halcyon Classics Series, 2009, Loc. 197.
17. Perkins, p. 3.
18. Mayfield, Sara. *The Constant Circle: H.L. Mencken and His Friends*. New York: Delacorte Press, 1968, p. 73.
19. Mayfield, *Exiles*, pp. 52-53.
20. Ibid., pp. 59-60.
21. Ibid., pp. 61-62.
22. Ibid., p. 65.
23. Ibid., p. 67.
24. Fitzgerald, F. Scott. *F. Scott Fitzgerald: A Life in Letters*, ed. Matthew J. Bruccoli. New York: Charles Scribner's Sons, 1995, pp. 46-47.
25. Mayfield, *Exiles*, pp. 70-71.
26. Ibid., pp. 74-75.
27. ZSF, *Collected*, p. 427.
28. Mayfield, *Constant Circle*, pp. 43-44.
29. Mayfield, *Exiles*, p. 81.
30. Mayfield, *Constant Circle*, pp. 5-6.
31. Mayfield, *Exiles*, p. 87.
32. Perkins, pp. 20-21.
33. Ibid., pp. 21-22.
34. Tomkins, Calvin. *Living Well Is the Best Revenge*. New York: The Viking Press, 1962, p. 102.
35. ZSF, *Waltz*, Loc. 2167.
36. FSF, *Letters*, p. 211. [FSF is the abbreviation for F. Scott Fitzgerald.]
37. Vaill, Amanda. *Everybody Was So Young: Gerald and Sara Murphy—A Lost Generation Love Story*. New York: Houghton Mifflin Company, 1998, p. 147. Tomkins, p. 42.
38. FSF, *Notebooks*, p. 113.
39. Perkins, p. 33.

NOTES

40. Ibid., pp. 40-47.
41. Ibid.
42. Wilson, Edmund. *Letters on Literature and Politics 1912-1972.* New York: Farrar, Straus and Giroux, 1957, p. 121.
43. Fitzgerald, F. Scott. *The Correspondence of F. Scott Fitzgerald*, eds. Margaret M. Duggan, Matthew Joseph Bruccoli, and Susan Walker. New York: Random House, 2008, p. 158.
44. Perkins, pp. 49-50.
45. Milford, Nancy. *Zelda: A Biography.* New York: Harper Perennial; Modern Classics, 2013, p.101.
46. Mayfield, *Exiles*, pp. 219-220.
47. Ibid., p. 220.
48. Cline, Sally. *Zelda Fitzgerald.* New York: Arcade Publishing, 2002, 2012, p. 177. Vaill, p. 157.
49. FSF, *Letters*, p. 171.
50. Hemingway, Ernest. *A Moveable Feast.* New York: Scribner, 1964, pp. 153-154.
51. Ibid., pp. 154-155.
52. Ibid., p. 155.
53. Ibid., pp. 160.
54. Vaill, pp. 181-182; Tomkins, p. 103; Milford, p. 120.
55. Vaill, p. 182; Tomkins, p. 109; Milford, p. 117.
56. Cline, pp. 209-211.
57. FSF, *Letters*, p. 230.
58. Tomkins, p. 111.
59. Hemingway, pp. 161-162.
60. Ibid., p. 162.
61. Ibid., pp. 162-163.
62. Cline, p. 224.
63. Hemingway, pp. 209-210.
64. Ibid., p. 210.
65. Perkins, p. 94.
66. Tomkins, p. 103.
67. Mayfield, *Exiles*, 138-140.
68. Ibid., p. 140.
69. Cline, pp. 240-241.
70. Tomkins, p. 103.
71. Vaill, p. 219.
72. Cline, p. 261.
73. Mayfield, *Exiles*, pp. 152-153; Cline, p. 262; Milford, p. 160.
74. Cline, pp. 262-263; Milford, p.160.
75. Cline, pp. 263-264; Milford, p. 168.
76. Cline, pp. 263-264.
77. FSF, *Letters*, pp. 200-207.
78. Cline, p. 266; Milford, p. 176.

NOTES

79. Cline, pp. 268-267.
80. ZSF, *Collected*, pp. 484-485.
81. Fitzgerald, Scott. *Dear Scott/Dear Max: The Fitzgerald-Perkins Correspondence*, eds. John Kuehl and Jackson Bryer. New York: Charles Scribner's Sons, 1971, pp. 166-168.
82. FSF, *Letters*, pp. 186-187.
83. Wilson, *Letters*, pp. 201-202.
84. Milford, pp. 173-174.
85. Ibid., pp. 174-175.
86. ZSF, *Collected*, pp. 493-494.
87. Mayfield, *Exiles*, p. 163.
88. Cline, pp. 285-286.
89. Ibid., pp. 287-288.
90. Ibid., p. 288; p. 445. You can read more about Sara's institutionalization at The Straightest Story Project https://thestraighteststoryproject.wordpress.com/.
91. FSF, *Letters*, p. 230.
92. Mayfield, *Exiles*, pp. 160-161; Cline, pp. 291-292.
93. Cline, p. 293; Milford, p. 191.
94. Mayfield, *Exiles*, pp. 173-74; Cline, pp. 295-296.
95. Cline, p. 296.
96. ZSF, *Collected*, pp. 498-499.
97. Mayfield, *Exiles*, pp. 175-76; Cline, pp. 296-97.
98. ZSF, *Collected*, p. 499.
99. Ibid., p. 393.
100. Ibid., pp. 499-500.
101. Mayfield, *Exiles*, p. 180.
102. Cline, p. 303.
103. Mayfield, *Exiles*, pp. 181-182; Milford, pp. 208-209.
104. Fitzgerald, Scott and Zelda. *Dear Scott, Dearest Zelda: The Love Letters of F. Scott and Zelda Fitzgerald*. New York: Scribner, 2019, p. 155.
105. Ibid., p. 145.
106. FSF, *Letters*, p. 210.
107. ZSF, *Collected*, pp. 503-505.
108. Perkins, pp. 143-144.
109. Ibid., pp. 151-152.
110. ZSF, *Collected*, p. 505.
111. Milford, p. 265.
112. FSF, *Letters*, pp. 210-213.
113. Ibid., p. 219.
114. Mayfield, *Exiles*, pp. 194-196.
115. Ibid., pp. 196-197.
116. "The Bookman," Volume LXXV, April-December, 1932. New York: Bookman Publishing Company, p. 735.
117. Ibid.

NOTES

118. PDF titled "One Hundred False Starts" from http://fitzgerald.narod.ru/crackup/058e-falsest.html.
119. FSF, *Letters*, pp. 230-231.
120. Ibid., p. 231.
121. Ibid., pp. 232-233.
122. Cline, pp. 328-330.
123. Ibid., pp. 330-33.
124. Hemingway, pp. 138-142.
125. Ibid., pp. 142-146.
126. FSF, *Letters*, p. 228.
127. Linda Wagner-Martin. *Zelda Sayre Fitzgerald: An American Woman's Life*. London: Lume Books, 2018, p. 136.
128. ZSF, *Collected*, p. 465.
129. FSF, *Notebooks*, p. 205.
130. Milford, pp. 284-86.
131. Perkins, pp. 176-177.
132. Ibid., pp. 177-178.
133. Hemingway, p. 151.
134. Perkins, p. 155.
135. Vaill, pp. 245-246.
136. FSF, *Letters*, p. 289.
137. Vaill, pp. 244-245.
138. Mayfield, *Constant*, pp. 205-206.
139. Mayfield, *Exiles*, p. 211.
140. Mayfield, *Exiles*, pp. 214-215; Cline, p. 350.
141. ZSF, *Collected*, p. 515.
142. Cline, p. 355.
143. FSF, *Letters*, p. 290.
144. Cline, pp. 356-357.
145. Mayfield, *Exiles*, pp. 230-231.
146. Fitzgerald, F. Scott. *The Crack Up*, ed. Edmund Wilson. New York: New Directions Publishing, 1945, Loc. 1013.
147. FSF, *Letters*, p. 298.
148. Mayfield, *Exiles*, pp. 231-223.
149. Perkins, p. 213.
150. Mayfield, *Exiles*, p. 233.
151. Ibid., pp. 247-248.
152. Ibid., pp. 249-251.
153. Milford, p. 333; Mayfield, *Exiles*, pp. 252-254.
154. FSF, *Letters*, p. 391.
155. Cline, pp. 369-371; Milford, p. 329.
156. Mayfield, *Exiles*, pp. 273-275.
157. FSF, *Letters*, p. 441; Milford, p. 337.
158. Mayfield, *Exiles*, p. 275; Milford, p. 341.

NOTES

159. PDF titled "The Iceberg" downloaded from https://www.newyorker.com/books/page-turner/the-iceberg-a-story-by-zelda-fitzgerald.
160. Mayfield, *Exiles*, p. 281.
161. Vaill, p. 306.
162. Cline, pp. 390-391.
163. Cline, p. 400; Milford, 382; Mayfield, *Exiles*, p. 285.
164. FSF, *Crack-Up*, loc. 229-239.
165. Mayfield, *Exiles*, pp. 171-172.
166. Cline, p. 403.
167. FSF, *Letters*, p. 211.
168. Mayfield, *Exiles*, p. 215.

ABOUT SAXON HENRY

Saxon Henry has been a journalist for over two decades and a content strategist for fifteen years. She is an indie author who publishes her own work through the imprint Sharktooth Press, and a collaborative author who helps clients realize their own books through major publishers around the globe, such as *Collaborations: A Houston Penthouse for 212box* that Australian publishing house Images released in late 2023. Journalistically, Henry's byline has appeared in a wide variety of national shelter and travel publications, as well as in *The New York Times* and *The Wall Street Journal*. Henry's books include *Stranded on the Road to Promise*, *Anywhere But Here*, *Four Florida Moderns*, *The Modern Salonnière*, and, with this publication, *Lives Illuminated*. This sixth book intermingles experiences she has had during years of traveling while reading, each adventure woven into the essays between the covers of this book.

𝕏 ◉

www.ingramcontent.com/pod-product-compliance
Lightning Source LLC
Chambersburg PA
CBHW060545080526
44585CB00013B/452